A Dream in the World

MW00835027

How can science and religion co-exist in the modern discipline of psychotherapy?

A Dream in the World explores the possibility of genuine religious experience during the process of depth psychotherapy. At the heart of this book is a series of archetypal dreams presented by the author's patient during an analytic process. These dreams heralded an unanticipated break-through encounter with the divine – an "experience of soul" – that reoriented and energized life and became what the author calls a "dream-in-the-world."

To explore the phenomenology of this religious experience, the author compares her patient's religious encounter with mystical experience in general and with the visions and poetry of Hadewijch of Brabant, a thirteenth-century woman mystic, whose ecstatic experience of the divine closely parallels the patient's material.

A Dream in the World details a classical Jungian psychotherapeutic process through analysis of a modern woman's dreams. It searches out relationships between religious encounter and psychotherapy, and psyche and soul, and it demonstrates the gradual unfolding and maturation of what C. G. Jung called a "religious instinct" in the human psyche.

Robin van Löben Sels is a Jungian analyst in private practice in Manhattan and Katonah, New York, and Ridgefield, Connecticut.

A Dream in the World

Poetics of Soul in Two Women, Modern and Medieval

Robin van Löben Sels

To Nancy, with thanks and best wishes, Robin

Brunner-Routledge
Taylor & Francis Group

HOVE AND NEW YORK

First published 2003 by Brunner-Routledge
27 Church Road, Hove, East Sussex BN3 2FA

Simultaneously published in the USA and Canada
by Brunner-Routledge
29 West 35th Street, New York, NY 10001

Brunner-Routledge is an imprint of the Taylor & Francis Group

Copyright © 2003 by Robin van Löben Sels

Typeset in Times by Mayhew Typesetting, Rhayader, Powys
Paperback cover design by Terry Foley, Anú Design
Printed and bound in Great Britain by MPG Books Ltd, Bodmin,
Cornwall

This publication has been produced with paper manufactured to strict
environmental standards and with pulp derived from sustainable
forests.

British Library Cataloguing in Publication Data
A catalogue record for this book is available from the British Library

Library of Congress Cataloging-in-Publication Data
Van Löben Sels, Robin E., 1938–
    A dream in the world : poetics of soul in two women, modern and
medieval / Robin E. van Löben Sels.
        p. cm.
Includes bibliographical references and index.
    ISBN 1-58391-918-X (alk. paper) – ISBN 1-58391-919-8 (pbk. : alk.
paper)
1. Dream interpretation–Case studies. 2. Jungian psychology–Case
studies. 3. Dreams–Religious aspects–Christianity–Case studies. 4.
Jungian psychology–Religious aspects–Christianity–Case studies. 5.
Dreams–Therapeutic use–Case studies. 6. Hadewijch, 13th cent. I.
Title.

    BF175.7.D74V36 2003
    154.6'3–dc21

                                                        2003007326

ISBN 1-58391-918-X (hbk)
ISBN 1-58391-919-8 (pbk)

For Don, editor extraordinaire,
husband and beloved life partner

Contents

Acknowledgments

To Mairi and other patients who honored me with their openness

To Edward Edinger, of the tortoise and the eagle, and to Joseph Ruff, teacher, dream-catcher and extraordinary spirit

To Ann Ulanov, for her patient encouragement in and out of academe

To Ewart Cousins, Renate Craine, Walter Odajnyk, Shelley Griffee, Lynn Osgood and Eva Pattis, appreciative readers all, and to Patricia Finley-Taylor, for her thoughtful reading and years of gracious friendship

To Lorraine Keating, Susanne Sholz and Martha Newell, for ready camaraderie, supportive warmth and generous laughter

Introduction

The focus of the following reflections is a remarkable series of dreams that led to a breakthrough of numinous[1] material in which the religious experience of a modern woman in psychotherapy shattered her previous sense of identity, and left her radically transformed, and – in a fundamental way – healed. During this process my patient Mairi[2] taught me that in some cases of depth psychotherapy, religious experience may take priority over psychological experience, and that when this happens, religious language may be more appropriate than psychological language for describing what happens within the therapeutic situation.

Mairi's transformative experience was akin to what many religious people recognize as salvation or redemption, and it embraced a dimension of otherness that she had not experienced before. At the moment of breakthrough, Mairi felt met by an Other – the Holy Spirit as Feminine Presence (her words). This experience followed a great deal of personal suffering and personal development both within and outside of the psychotherapeutic process, but when finally it occurred, Mairi felt a great sense of wonder and relief.

The experience of her whole body being lit up from within and the profound sense of Presence that greeted Mairi moved her deeply and required that she stretch her usual modes of apprehension in the direction of a religious sensibility. Mairi felt as if she had been inwardly baptized[3] and given a second chance in life – a second chance to live as a fully embodied person "ensouled" as never before, and a second chance to love the everyday life she had. This did not end her suffering, but it infused her life with a new meaning in relation to a larger Reality in which she felt included. As a result, Mairi felt "real" for the first time. Later she came to call this whole experience an "experience of soul" – not *the* soul, Mairi informed me, but *soul* – as if to emphasize that soul was not a metaphysical entity but a state of Being. Eventually Mairi's life gravitated around and was illuminated by this experience, and it was a touchstone in our work together. It became what I call her "dream-in-the-world."

Transformative experiences such as Mairi's belong to the epiphanic oral and written traditions of all the great religions.[4] The fact that the human body is frequently recognized as the locus for this kind of profound religious awakening is something that mystics of all religions have described for centuries and that a particular mystic from the thirteenth century, Hadewijch of Brabant,[5] writes about with special vividness. Hadewijch was a leader in a small community of laywomen known as Beguines who lived their vision of religious life outside the Church. Like Mairi, Hadewijch also encountered God in passionate relationship and embodied imagery. God appeared to Hadewijch as a feminine Presence that she called *Minne*, or Lady Love. Hadewijch's writings declare her as a foremost representative of the *minnemystiek* (love mysticism) that sprang up in the Low Countries of Europe during the second half of the twelfth century, particularly in the area that corresponds to present-day Belgium. Her experiences took place over many years, and she left us a remarkable record of "showings" or visions (van Baest 1998), letters, and two forms of poetry, all of which she used in her teachings.

Unlike my patient Mairi, Hadewijch was completely embedded in the collective assumptions of medieval Christianity. Yet her experience of the divine shows marked similarities to Mairi's. By comparing both the content and form of these two women's religious experience I hope to explore some of the ways in which a transformative encounter with otherness can transcend time and place, occurring even in the mundane arena of ongoing psychotherapy, albeit in universal language. While my focus here remains on religious experience *within* psychotherapy, Hadewijch provides an important counterpoint as she vividly describes religious experience *outside* psychotherapy, indeed, seven hundred years before psychotherapy was conceived of. Jung once remarked that religion is where the psyche "was" before modern psychology made it the subject of investigation. In the pages to follow I hope that the meaning of Jung's statement will come to light.

Essentially depth psychology is a study of the unconscious sources of our conscious experience, including experience that our traditions describe as ineffable, "higher," transcendent, or spiritual. Traditional western (Abrahamic) religion (the world in which Hadewijch lived) usually identifies the object of such experience as God and places God in a celestial realm superior to or "above" the realm of human suffering, imperfection, and mortality. The Swiss psychoanalyst C. G. Jung was unique among depth psychologists in understanding that such religious imagery was a meaningful projection of deep instinctual and structural patterns in the human psyche. But even more important – and beyond a theory of projection – was Jung's insight that such imagery constituted humankind's best (and universal) picture of *actual encounters* with numinous dimensions of human life. More important still was Jung's conviction that such encounters provide the *satisfaction of an instinct* for wholeness and meaning – a "religious instinct" – inhabiting the depths of the body and filling us with longing for meaning and a wholeness that lies beyond the ego.

If we overlay the medieval image of spiritual height with our contemporary template of psychological depth, the possibility of touching upon individual religious experience within a psychotherapeutic setting today resonates with the universality of Hadewijch's mystical message in the thirteenth century. When she started therapy, Mairi knew nothing about a "religious instinct" or her unconscious longing for transcendent wholeness, whereas Hadewijch tells us that she had been filled with an almost unbearable love of God from the time she was ten years old. Mairi had to immerse herself in the unconscious and its archetypal dreams in order to gain access to levels of imaginal experience that came to Hadewijch naturally and spontaneously through her surrounding culture, saturated with religious ideas. And while Hadewijch freely and unthinkingly used a surrounding Christian cosmology to sustain herself through her immersions in immediate experiences of the numinous, Mairi worried that maybe she was having a nervous breakdown and felt that she had only the scaffolding of her therapist's mind and heart to sustain her through her "spiritual emergency" (Grof and Grof 1989).[6]

Yet there were common themes in the two women's experience. Both were filled with a sense of feminine presence – for Hadewijch, her sense of the soul's union with God as *Minne* or Lady Love; for Mairi, the Holy Spirit as Feminine Presence. For both women the notion of the soul, or soul was central, and the soul's union with God was experienced in passionately erotic images and embodied union. Both Hadewijch and Mairi came to realize that the ecstasies of immediate unity-with and immersion-in the divine were not ends in themselves but only the beginnings of what would evolve for each into a paradoxically joyful yet suffering relationship to the divine. Hadewijch was clear that the "sweetnesses" and "indulgences" of her ecstatic visions were ultimately signs of immaturity that she had to outgrow, suffering her love for a God that could be absent because wholly "other." Mairi came out the other side of her unity experience with a renewed sense of mission and dedication to service to others through her yoga teaching and a renewed sense of loving her ordinary life in all its particularity. Both women discovered that they had to outgrow the very thing that helped them "grow up," Hadewijch in pursuit of "full grownup-ness" and Mairi rededicated to achieving "fully human consciousness." In this way, Hadewijch lived out a complex and difficult destiny, and Mairi carried forward her individual "dream-in-the-world."

Dream-in-the-world

By dream-in-the-world, I mean the awakening within a person of a consciousness-altering "realization" which comes into presence first through the body, then in thought as a major "idea." The person who experiences such an awakening and whose mind is inflamed by its associated idea remains aware that although this idea is present in consciousness, nevertheless it is rooted in and ringed about with powerful unconscious components. The idea comes "trailing clouds of glory," so to speak.

To call such a realization a dream-in-the-world is to recognize that it has one foot beyond the ego's frame of reference. While a dream-in-the-world is always experienced in the moment, it is also bigger than the moment, as if rooted beyond one's personal understanding of the frame of time and space. This "larger" reality to which a dream-in-the-world gives access is what, in traditional religious cultures, would have been called the sacred or the divine. In our secular, materialistic world, this numinous, immaterial reality has retreated, and is not available as it once was through religious ritual and/or a surrounding religious cosmology. However, as Jung, Neumann and others have demonstrated, it is still available through the psyche, and a vivid example of this will be given in the following pages.

Thus a dream-in-the-world is a modern phenomenon which depends, to a certain extent, upon psychological development and on the development of ego strength sufficient to undergo the kind of transformation in consciousness that is the hallmark of such an "awakening." This was not necessary in a prior time because the ego was embedded in a sustaining religious consciousness that took mystical realities concretely and literally. Individual consciousness, with its potential for symbolic thought, was only beginning. So we cannot say, for example, that Hadewijch had a "dream-in-the-world," because for Hadewijch, "dream" and "world" were one. Her world was thoroughly infused with medieval Christian cosmology.

Following Jung's model, we could say that a dream-in-the-world contains elements from both personal and collective dimensions of the psyche, or that it is both immanent and emergent. It represents both an inward as well as an outward encounter with "Otherness." Although it may not be particularly personal, a dream-in-the-world arises in the history of a personal life and thus is marked in time as an event, as something that often makes sense out of life for the person who has it. A dream-in-the-world usually transforms the world of the person who experiences it, as well as the way in which that person relates to the world.

Despite being hosted by an individual person, a dream-in-the-world is easily shared, and – in part – its ability to be shared is what maintains it in the world. Not only do persons who experience a dream-in-the world tell others about it, but also others seem to recognize the importance of such an experience for themselves, as if somehow a dream-in-the-world articulates an experience of reality that we can all share beneath and through the differing personal details of our lives. In this sense, hearing about a dream-in-the-world can feel more like a *re*-cognition than a new cognition.

Clearly a dream-in-the-world orients and anchors the personality in whom it arises. At the same time, a dream-in-the-world is being lived through that person, who must balance the effects as best he or she can. As a lens through which to focus attention and gather information, a dream-in-the-world can be used creatively, connecting the dreamer to an experiential core of understanding that makes sense of what is being felt and perceived. We might say that a dream-in-the-world is the embodiment of an individual's guiding idea, or that it embodies the kind of idea that is often called metaphysical, even though "meta" (meaning "beyond") usually implies the opposite of embodiment. In other words, people *live* their dreams-in-the-world. Once it emerges, a dream-in-the-world is ongoing and persistent, and its unfolding within a personality can house the passion of a lifetime.

Mairi's experience of soul that became her dream-in-the-world had a healing effect on her personally. It also transformed her relationships with others in ways that felt healthy and meaningful. In short, the capacity to house a dream-in-the-world is a sign of health in a personality and frequently has salutary effects in the world touched by that individual. Mairi would not have been surprised to learn that in many languages the meaningful root of the word "salvation" points to healing or wholeness not only of the individual *but of the world*,[7] as if the healing of the self and healing of the world go hand in hand, a coincidence of inner and outer reality that we will explore extensively.

The dream sequence

Mairi had an experience of "falling through" into another dimension in which her prior sense of ego-identity felt reduced and relativized in relation to a vast sense of Being. This event was prefaced by a series of distinctive archetypal dreams which I will describe in detail, together with her associations and our mutual efforts at understanding them, in Chapter 2. I believe that these dreams demonstrate the spontaneous unfolding of an autonomous process in Mairi's psyche, something that Jung aptly called the process of individuation.

As the ritual of Mairi's psychotherapy unfolded, the archetypal layers of the psyche slowly opened. Gaston Bachelard (1971: 124) describes archetypes as "reserves of enthusiasm which help us believe in the world . . . each archetype is an opening on the world, an invitation to the world." And as the archetypal psyche unfolded, both Mairi and I were drawn into our shared psychotherapeutic world by these "reserves of energy" (e.g., interest, curiosity, love and hate). Archetypal images precipitated out of Mairi's inner night sky as constellations of collective experience, clouds of imagery pregnant with meaning, even when she, the dreamer, felt dried up, desiccated, and unable to sense significance at all. Veiled (as is any pregnancy), Mairi's archetypal dreams seemed to compensate for her desolate inability to touch the deep-down joy of things by imaging what she could not feel consciously. In this way, Mairi's dreams facilitated healing.

Sometimes Jung referred to archetypal dreams as the voice of the two-thousand-year-old man in us. Mairi and I imagined her dreams as the voice of a sister Shahrazade[8] who offered us another point of view. Spinning stories within stories, Mairi's dreams alluded to inner and outer experiential worlds, pointing to the therapeutic process as well as her life as a whole. The more definitively Mairi became herself, the more clearly her dreams seemed to respond, articulating unconscious aspects of her personality. As the reader will see, both Mairi and I began to feel a kind of mysterious "anticipation" in these dreams for what followed.

At a certain point, all Mairi's dreams stopped. With their cessation, Mairi was catapulted into a waking experience which she described as "falling through" from one dimension of being into another, into experience of soul. I will narrate this experience in Chapter 3. The dimension of being into which Mairi fell I understand to have been a symbol-forming or "feminine" state of being – or better, a state of feminine Being, or what British object-relations psychiatrist D. W. Winnicott refers to as the "female element" of being. These ideas will be expanded over the course of my narration of Mairi's experience in psychotherapy. Chapter 3 includes a review of Winnicott's theory of how early experience of the feminine in the mother–infant dyad prepares the developing infant for an experience of "personalization" and "indwelling" and concludes with my own critique of Winnicott's view of religion as "necessary illusion."

In retrospect, I think that the psychic "downloading" of mostly non-personal collective imagery during the intense period of Mairi's analysis, described in Chapter 2, laid the groundwork for an independent new ego structure, as if a deepened and expanded personality were waiting in the wings, so to speak, for an appropriately containing relationship. Because of the apparent "implicate order" of this material, I refer to these dreams as "Self-directive" dreams, using Jung's idea of the Self in the classic sense of pointing to the existence of a potential wholeness of personality that transcends what we mean by ego.[9] In Chapter 1 I will define more clearly Jung's notion of the Self and elaborate on my own notion of a Self-directive dream, both of which may be unfamiliar to my reader.

Religious experience and the psyche

Having begun her analysis in a state of alienation and depression, Mairi slowly recovered (or perhaps found for the first time) a capacity to experience her life with her whole being – as she reported, "with all my heart, with all my soul, and with all my might." The fact that she described her experience in the language of the first and greatest of the Judaeo-Christian commandments – "Thou shalt love the Lord thy God with all thy heart, with all thy soul, and with all thy might" – is significant. It points to the fact that Mairi's evolving capacity for personhood, or for what I will call "fully human consciousness," naturally seemed to seek a transcendent idiom. Why, we may ask, is this so?

Several contemporary psychotherapists and practitioners of the healing arts (many with a Buddhist orientation) note the appearance of "altered states" (Tart 1990)[10] or "non-ordinary states of consciousness" in an ongoing process of psychotherapy with their clients. Described as "spiritual emergency" (Grof and Grof 1989, Perry 1999), or infusions of conscious-ness or enlightenment (Epstein 1998, 1995), these altered states are gener-ally understood to be intrusions of "higher" forms of consciousness ("higher" meaning not only from above, but of a more evolved refinement) with a beneficial effect. The distinction between these mystical states and bi-polar disorder or acute psychosis has been the subject of several papers (Grof and Grof 1989), as has the distinction between pre-personal and transpersonal levels of consciousness.[11]

Psychoanalysts – with certain notable exceptions (Meissner 1984; Loewald 2000) – have been slow to admit religious experience into the canons of normalcy. Ever since Freud reduced mystical experience to what he presumed were simply the oceanic feelings of infancy, psychoanalytic theory in general tries to free humanity from the "illusions" and superstiitions of religion. Some contemporary "psychoanalytic mystics" (Eigen 1998) are more open to the ineffable as a valid way of knowing, and even in Freud's inner circle, Sandor Ferenczi noted the seemingly telepathic mysteries of unconscious communion in the transference/countertransfer-ence matrix – mysteries that are being explored by contemporary relational theory. Others, such as Wilfred Bion and D. W. Winnicott, emphasize the importance of openness to an unknowable essence of the moment if a true self is to evolve. Michael Eigen (1993a: 109) writes of an "area of faith" in the personality, and James Grotstein (2000) speaks of an "ineffable Subject" in the unconscious as the true deep subject of experience.

But none of these writers acknowledge the crucial contribution of Jung to a discussion of religious experience and the psyche, nor do they acknowl-edge that religious experience may be a separate way of knowing an immaterial reality that stands behind (or alongside) the material reality of scientific psychology – a possibility that Jung took seriously. Jung believed that he had found in the psyche of his patients *a religious instinct* that was just as strong and important as the other instincts. Described as an instinct towards wholeness, the religious instinct is, according to Jung, part of what we as human beings are "given," along with sexuality and aggression, hunger, attachment (kinship), curiosity and a tendency toward creative reflection. "Physical hunger needs a real meal," he writes, "and spiritual hunger needs a numinous content" (CW10: 652–3). If the religious instinct is not differentiated, developed and satisfied like any other instinct, the personality remains incomplete, unrealized, and often ill. Frequently, Jung felt, the religious instinct remains "contaminated" with other instincts, becoming entangled with the ego's will and attachments. In these cases, writes Jung, "a vision of God" needs to be "liberated from the veils of the personal" (CW7: 214). What I am calling fully human consciousness (see below) cannot incarnate in a personality unawakened to this ground of psychological life, i.e., to the soul. This awakening is what happened to my patient Mairi, and on her own account her experience of soul is what finally healed her.

In religious experience, Jung writes, "man[12] comes face to face with a psychically overwhelming other" (CW10: 655) and this encounter has a fundamentally transformative effect. Efforts toward consciousness lead to what Jung calls a "religious attitude," by which he means an attitude that is peculiar to a consciousness that has been changed by an experience of the numinous (CW11: 9). Defining religious experience as "that kind of experience which is accorded the highest value, no matter what its contents may be" (CW11: 106), Jung states that such an encounter "saves, heals, and makes whole" (CW10: 655). Thus Jung explicitly equates imagery of wholeness with regaining what is in essence a religious outlook. In other words, Jung feels that a mature personality cannot fully realize its own potential without finding its way back to, or down to, or into, those eternal issues and ultimate questions that have always been at the center of religion's world view: "Where do we come from?" "What is the meaning and purpose of our lives?" "Does the eternal enter time?"

In our secular, postmodern era, the structures of institutional religion, together with their traditional stories of creation and the cosmos (cosmologies), hold little of the collective numen and significance that they once did. To many of us, they no longer feel believable. Others of us have fallen away from the syncretic forms of religion that *do* remain, turning perhaps to the East or to aboriginal forms, some of which have found their way into "New Age" rituals and even trainings. Thus in the contemporary psyche the religious instinct often has few appropriate objects, and even modern science and the extraordinary achievements of its offshoot, modern technology, cannot fill the bill. Today our culture is replete with desacralized substitute-objects that we idolize or seek addictively but without satisfaction. As Eric Hoffer (1951: 50) once commented, "we can never have enough of what we really do not want, and we run fastest and farthest when we are running from our real selves."

Therefore, in our day and age, despite ritual attendance in church, temple or mosque, or religious rhetoric of every imaginable persuasion, the religious instinct in each person may lie hidden from conscious realization and reflection. As Jung says, this "most important of the fundamental instincts" plays an inconspicuous part in contemporary consciousness because only with great difficulty can it free itself from contamination with the other instincts (CW10: 652–3). Thus labor-intensive hours, often extending over years, are spent in psychotherapy, separating or decontaminating the religious instinct either from the defensive functions of the self into which it has been diverted or from the other instincts themselves in which it may be hidden: in sexuality, aggression, primitive idealizations or attachments – all the major subjects explored in the psychoanalytic consulting room.

When Mairi and I began our work together, neither of us could foresee that a contaminated religious instinct might be at the core of her malaise. In fact, such a formulation would have struck her as preposterous and me as hopelessly intellectual and abstract. Raised in a lower-middle-class, ostensibly Protestant family, Mairi had felt alienated from traditional forms of Christianity for years – enough so that she wondered whether she might not better describe herself as an atheist than a believer.[13] Except for occasional dabbling in New Age readings and dedication to her yoga practice, religion had never been a major area of concern to Mairi, either in her childhood or when she entered therapy. Yet no language short of a mystical, exclamatory and ecstatic outpouring could give adequate expression to her final experience of soul.

Jung's conviction that human beings have an inborn appetite for the numinous – a religious instinct that seeks satisfaction in spiritual experience and conspires towards healing and wholeness – provides us with a revolutionary new model of the human psyche and an important corrective lens through which to view experience such as Mairi's. Throughout this book, I try to show how important a satisfied sense of life's wholeness is for psychological health and for what I call "fully human consciousness," a term which I also elaborate in Chapter 1.

Understandably, many of Jung's critics have been less than sanguine about Jung's claim that the psyche has an inherently religious function. It is not always easy to tell the difference between genuine religious encounters with a numinous reality beyond the ego and certain undifferentiated oceanic states of regressed ego functioning, including the manic inflations that accompany narcissistic or schizoid psychopathology. Both Jung and Freud knew that the unconscious had archaic depths and that its erotic and aggressive energies were daimonic and could possess the person with a weak ego, frequently with destructive consequences. Freud's prescriptive goal for psychoanalysis – "where Id was, there shall ego be" – is not a bad image for the necessary humanization of primitive unconscious affects. Infantile omnipotence is a real thing in early childhood and psychoanalytic thinkers emphasize that if, as we develop, we are to gain an ego that can relate to outer and inner reality, a good deal of suffering and disillusionment is in store for all of us in the process of "becoming real." (As the Skin Horse tells the Velveteen Rabbit, in Williams' charming tale, by the time we become real most of our buttons have been rubbed off, our stuffing sticks out, and we look very shabby! Williams 1971: 17).

But genuine religious experience is not infantile omnipotence or narcissistic grandiosity or manic psychosis, and it was to Jung's credit that he held out for a healthy level of religious experience beyond the early developmental stages and defensive forms that Freud saw. More than that, Jung felt that the capacity for religious experience was a sign of health in a person and also a sign of developmental maturity.

Jung's linking (or re-linking, from *religio*, meaning ligament and connection) the highest aspirations and most transcendent longings of the human spirit with a deep agency in the psyche, is a revolutionary and paradoxical understanding that has many connections to the understandings of modern physics. The idea that there is a spiritual world from which the soul receives knowledge of spiritual things and that this knowledge, while empirical and experiential, is not available through our usual senses, requires a new metaphysics of the mind to complement modern physics' metaphysics of matter, better known as quantum mechanics. This is an area that interests me profoundly, especially since my experience with Mairi. Therefore in another section of Chapter 1, I discuss contemporary notions of the quantum mind and its associated re-visioning of "non-local" consciousness as a way to understand the paranormal features of certain kinds of mystical knowledge that seem to transcend the boundaries of the ego. In this connection, and in order to set the stage for the dream sequence in Chapter 2, I also explore how our dreams may give us privileged access to these subliminal realities.

In the pages that follow, I will attempt to reclaim *territory for the soul in the process of psychotherapy* – territory that tends to be subsumed within the secular idiom of much contemporary psychoanalytic thinking. Long ago, Søren Kierkegaard said we are meant to be a self (in medieval language, a soul) – a synthesis of time and eternity, the finite and the infinite. This is our task, our destiny, said Kierkegaard, but we are not yet selves, and if we are to become such we need to experience an intense encounter between the two natures of this synthesis. Only this can make us whole. Both my patient Mairi and her medieval counterpart, Hadewijch of Brabant, had such encounters. And both women experienced, within and without, a transcendent, reconciling force that they called the Holy Spirit as Feminine Presence (Mairi) and Lady Love or *Minne* (Hadewijch).[14] As I hope the following pages will illuminate, the religious experience of both women speak to a repeatedly emerging value – at times more strongly apparent, at other times, more hidden – of a disciplined integration of the feminine principle[15] *as a symbolic mode of being*. I will discuss this more fully in the commentary on Mairi's dreams and Hadewijch's experience.

Religious experience and the body

My experience with Mairi indicated that crucial to her attainment of her full capacity for experiencing undertaken with her whole being was her ability to *personalise*[16] this experience as it happened *in her body*. As Mairi told and re-told the story of her experience of soul, the telling of it anchored her psychologically and "embodied" her life in a particular way, connecting ordinary dailyness to unique and irreplaceable personal experience. During this process Mairi came to "occupy" herself as never before. Winnicott (1963b) says that in the process of personalization, the infant's mother continually introduces and re-introduces the baby's mind and body to each other, and that through this process "indwelling" occurs. Something analogous to this happened for Mairi in the psychotherapeutic setting.

For some of us, the way to a love that encompasses all our heart and all our soul and all our might comes only through consciously experienced embodiment. Perhaps we may amend the First Commandment to read, "Thou shalt love the Lord thy God with all thy heart, with all thy soul, with all thy might, and with all thy body." Mairi could not have experienced soul without reconnecting to her body. Not only did the emergence of her capacity for fully human consciousness and self–other awareness require both psychoanalytic and religious language, but more than the psychological aspect, the religious aspect of her experience *actualized* her embodiment, making it real to the point where Mairi experienced fullness of Being.

In Chapter 1, I will expand upon the importance of the body as the locus for religious experience. Rooted in the earth of her individuation process, Mairi's experience of soul bloomed into her conscious awareness (ego) out of an organic integrity of *body, soul, spirit and psyche*. These terms are important in the overall argument of the book and therefore I devote a section of Chapter 1 to their explication and differentiation – especially as Jung wrestled with them, and the ways in which my own understanding of these terms may differ slightly from his.

Mairi's work made clear that no matter what form the psychological realization of personality may assume, it can become kin to redemption and salvation only when and as soul becomes explicit. Because, without body, soul has neither home nor form, the bodily presence and bodily participation of another person is necessary for the verification and validation of such an experience of soul. Soul happens in "between." Only two embodied personalities in inter-subjective participation can observe and witness, narrate and give testimony to the soul. As I see it, this is not possible in isolated subjectivity.

A quantum stance

I want to say a word here about my overall depth-approach to the psychotherapy process, i.e., how I orient myself with respect to the patient's presentation and material and how this differs in certain respects from a "classical Jungian" approach. I describe my particular stance as a "quantumstance," by which I mean simply that *how one approaches the patient's material has an effect upon what one sees.* More boldly, I have come to believe that if a therapist is open to *the religious dimension as experienced in the body*, this affects the material she or he gets and also has significant impact on the outcome of therapy for the patient. This attitude requires a kind of binocular vision and becomes what I imagine as *a psycho-religious attitude*, which I call a quantum stance.

Generally speaking, psychotherapists acknowledge that the psychotherapist's personality and the way that she or he works tends to influence the therapeutic outcome. Just as an infant is in-formed by the stimulation pouring into it from environmental and social surroundings, so the psyche and soul are influenced by a method of investigation and the personalities that participate in therapy. While transference and countertransference are implicitly activated in any therapeutic endeavor, these factors may or may not become the center of therapeutic attention, for they are not the only possible descriptions of transitional ligaments between two persons. Were I to write of what happened between Mairi and myself in purely psychological terms, for example, the story would be different: differing perspectives yield different information.

It is my impression that too much has been made in contemporary psychoanalytic theory about the centrality of transference/countertransference, transference interpretation, countertransference disclosure, etc. as the healing factors in the analytic process – as if reparation of early developmental failures via a "transfer" of these wounds to the analyst were the main thing. While in some cases transference analysis is the center of the work, others, such as the case I will discuss, illustrate the central importance of the containing "potential space" (Winnicott) created by the analyst. Transformation happens in this space, but the spark igniting this transformation comes from "somewhere else." This is what the old alchemists must have meant when they prepared their super-saturated solutions and then waited *Deo Concedente* for a transformative moment. The wholeness that "happens" in this moment is a mystery spoken of by the world's religions for at least ten thousand years. People who have this experience feel as if they are given a "second chance" in life – that the universe makes sense for the first time – and that they are suddenly a "child of God," as well as the child of their earthly parents. The psychoanalytic conceit that this second chance comes from the analyst recreating the lost transitional space between mother and infant is just that . . . a conceit. It is just as defensible to think of Winnicott's transitional space as the way the Godhead has arranged for maternal empathy sufficient to provide a "space" saturated enough with paradox to allow the incarnation of God at the core of personhood. A quantum stance keeps these things in mind.[17]

In my work with Mairi I found that my attitude, especially toward her religious experience, had to remain "indeterminate," i.e., radically open and non-interpretive, and I now see this as a general requirement in working with spiritual issues in psychotherapy. By a psycho-religious attitude (or quantum stance) I mean an openness to revelatory experience or to the *soul as an agent of healing*, separate from the psychological factors that we consider mutative within a psychotherapeutic dyad, i.e., empathy, reparative emotional experience, transference and countertransference interpretation, and transmuting internalization of psychic structure, etc.

So, if someone in psychotherapy today has a spiritual or religious experience, I propose that we learn to honor it as such and not interpret it as a derivative of something else. True, we might be tempted to explain such experience by reducing it to primary narcissism and oceanic bliss (Freud), or describe it as a manic defense (Klein) or frame it as a break-through of inflating collective elements into the personal sphere (Jung), or track it within an idealizing transferential field (Kohut) but these inter-pretations psychologize the soul and somehow reduce and distort the patient's subjective experience. The analyst, confronted by a patient's genuine revelatory experience, must say (and feel) more than "I accept that your version of this is real – to you." He or she must communicate that the particular way in which a patient frames his or her experience has its own validity. In other words, the therapist must be open to a dimension of reality *other* than the psychological, by whatever name he or she may call it – God, the soul, the Transcendent, etc.

This therapeutic attitude does not reduce all that a patient undergoes in therapy to psychological projection, nor does it assume that the primary importance of the analyst is to provide a "blank screen" upon which unconscious projections are first made and then laboriously withdrawn. A quantum stance is open to the possible objectivity of otherness, whether of self, other people, historical events, the metapsychological and metaphy-sical contents of consciousness, or the possibly objective otherness of the Real. This means that the analyst must stay open to the possibility that the contents of a particular experience come from the very object of con-sciousness itself: e.g., Mairi's experience of the Holy Spirit as Feminine Presence came from the Holy Spirit, or Hadewijch's experience of God as *Minne* or Lady Love came from God.

Through my experience with Mairi I have come to view soul as that mysterious inner reality through which what we might call a "longing for wholeness" is experienced. Jung called the longing itself the religious instinct. Hence I see the soul as an agency (resident in the body, like the agencies of all other instincts) of the religious instinct. Encountered in the process of psychological work and experienced through the psyche, the soul is beyond the psyche, older by far, and the primary entity. As my work with Mairi taught me, some traumatic events *at the body level* that come to us psychoanalysts for mending cannot be healed by psychological methods alone (including analysis of transference and countertransference) but only as the soul comes into Presence. And, as a state of being, soul is embodied in a way that psyche is not.

I also have come to believe that at its heart, religion is mystical experience. The Buddha under the Bo Tree, Arjuna beholding Krishna's terrible blue glory, Moses in Midian with his flocks, Jesus up to his knees in the river Jordan hearing God's voice, and Mohammed scribbling in his dark cave – each person was responding to something for which words (even the word God) remain poor approximations.

My opening to these understandings in my work with Mairi necessitated a shift in my therapeutic attitude. What I call a quantum stance came to embrace both psyche and soul, and hence its "indeterminate" quality. I like to think that this indeterminacy facilitates an approach to the mystery of consciousness that, like light itself, is partly material, partly immaterial, and never to be grasped by empirical science alone. With reference to Mairi's dreams, I approached her psychic imagery symbolically, but for both of us her experience of soul became an encounter with the numinous that took us beyond the psyche. It was as if the psyche made this encounter possible and even prepared the way toward it, but then stepped out of the way.

A new story of our place in the cosmos

Psychoanalysis was intended to address people who felt alienated not only from themselves and others but also from a meaningful sense of life in the world. A hundred years ago, out of similar feelings about the culture in which they found themselves, Freud and Jung called themselves "alienists," thereby validating the name by which their culture designated psychiatrists as "doctors of the soul" in a world that had collectively lost its soul. The Israeli psychoanalyst Erich Neumann[18] (1953: 81–2) tells us that he ventured into metapsychology because he needed a meaningful picture of the place of human beings in a world of atomized outer reality.[19] My descriptions in the following pages – of Self-directive dreams, a quantum stance, my efforts to demarcate an area of soul as distinct from psyche – and my considerations of how Mairi's dream-in-the-world emerged to augment as well as express fully human consciousness, are also formulated out of need. We need a meaningful picture not only of the place of human beings in an atomized world but of the place of *being fully human* in a culture that exacerbates alienation and atomization. I feel that we need to recover a sense of our basic humanity, of our native capacities to communicate with, understand and accept each other and ourselves. This possibility seems to depend more than we realize upon knowing our place in the larger scheme of things.

Jung felt this too. In a previously unpublished letter to Ruth Topping, a prominent Chicago social worker,[20] Jung points to how all peoples of the world from time immemorial have had a wisdom literature about the irrational wholeness of the world and how human beings filled an essential place in that wholeness. These mythic stories were passed down to the young in the form of holy traditions, celebratory repetition and initiatory ritual. In our scientific civilization, however, this spiritual background has gone astray. We have lost our spiritual containers. In this way, says Jung, "one of the most important instinctual activities of our mind has lost its object. *As these [traditions] deal with the world as a whole, they create also a wholeness of the individual*" (italics mine). Lacking these vehicles, we don't feel whole. Worse still, while we may be aware of missing something in this secular and often religiously alienated culture, we don't know what it is or how to describe it.

One way that Mairi's dream-in-the-world reconnected her to her inner world and her psychological and spiritual roots was by drenching her in a personal experience of some of the core feeling values of the religious background from which her personal life had emerged and, in truth, remained unconsciously embedded. What does a statement like this mean? It was as if the profundity of certain feeling values embraced Mairi *as experience*, rather than requiring her belief. We can recognize foundational feeling values in our Judaeo-Christian culture in the following examples: life is good, in and of itself, and a divine gift; individual life is sacred; and perhaps after all is said and done, the vicissitudes of love are what matter most. Feeling values like these represented the unconscious fundaments of Mairi's relatively unconscious cosmology, but they had been relegated to the unconscious background or overlaid by modern and enlightened atheistic points of view. After her experience of soul, these fundaments of cosmology came to life again in an understanding of the whole that felt religious, but in a more personal way.

A refreshing glimpse of this archaic sense of cosmic connection comes to me with the new story of the world's wholeness that is emerging through a number of recent writers. Among the tellers of this tale is eco-philosopher, geologian and priest Thomas Berry (1988: 195), who reminds us that our bonding with the larger dimensions of the universe is patterned. On a macroscopic scale, writes Berry, we recognize this bonding through the anthropic principle,[21] as we discover that we, as whole human beings, are a mode of being *of* the universe, as well as a distinctive mode of being *in* the universe. Less beings *on* earth than we are dimensions *of* earth, our human mode of being is shaped by and depends upon the support and guidance of a comprehensive order of things. Yet, says Berry, "*the source of this order is so near and its manifestation so immediately intimate that its presence escapes our notice"* (italics mine). When and if we do come to conscious awareness, says Berry, we discover that in addition to being our conscious individual selves, we are beings in whom the universe (and our planet earth) comes to itself in a special mode of conscious reflection.[22] Berry's brave stand against the over-objectification of everything – ourselves, each other, and other species of life, including plants and the planet earth itself – is important in a time which values objectivity and objectifies everything within reach. We are not a gathering of objects, says Berry: we are a sacred communion of Subjects. By this Berry, too, points to Soul. We are ensouled, all of us, and everything that makes up the material world we know. THAT is what we have in common, and conscious recognition of that can re-establish a sacred dimension in life centering a new story of our individual and collective consciousness. As we become ensouled, among a wide community of souls, the world-soul, and the world itself may be redeemed.

The idea at the center of this new story is Heisenberg's thesis that "the same organizing forces that have created nature in all its forms are responsible for the structure of our soul, and likewise for our capacity to think."[23] Therefore, in the very process of our thinking and in our efforts to grasp the ineffable realities that we encounter in religious experience, is it not possible that we align ourselves with emanations of an original Great Spirit present in (immanent in) the primal creative explosion that originated our world as we know it?

Long ago Jung noted that it was no less defensible philosophically to "explain the break-up of the atom in the sun as an emanation of the creative *Weltgeist*" than to maintain that mental phenomena (including the psyche itself) arise from the activity of the glands or the operation of the drives or the neuro-hormonal impulses of the brain. Both kinds of explanation, Jung points out, "are equally logical, equally metaphysical, equally arbitrary and equally symbolic" (Jung 1933: 175). But the scientific spirit of the age derives everything mental (including the spirit) from matter. Huston Smith (2001: 59) calls this irrational position "scientism"[24] and points to the discoveries of modern physics as at least a "crack" in the fortress-like position held by modern science that everything can be traced back to (and explained by) material causes.

Ultimately I believe that religion and science, mind and matter, spirit and body are necessary to our understanding of life on this planet, and that psychoanalysis has a major role to play in our increasing consciousness. But when we psychoanalysts fail to look through the false dichotomies that presently divide our field and see into a larger world view, it should give us pause and make us reflect on this peculiar one-sidedness. We cannot discuss nature or ourselves without seriously reflecting upon the blind-spots that our ways of thinking and seeing create. And I am convinced that one of those blind-spots is our failure to seek – and affirm – that part of our nature that Jung found was expressive of a religious instinct, and a larger world view or cosmology which contains and expresses the fact that encounters with the numinous (like Mairi's and Hadewijch's) are a real and substantial part of human experience. If we are to be fully human in our world, we cannot be content to identify our species as *homo sapiens* only, but must take conscious ownership of our essential being as *homo mysticus*, too.

Notes

1 The *numinosum* is a category of experience described by Rudolph Otto that characterizes humankind's encounter with the *mysterium tremendum* or the *wholly other* (Otto 1958). It is accompanied by the ego's sense of being seized by a mysterious power greater than or "beyond" itself, over and against which it stands in *awe, fascination,* or *dread.* Positive constellations of the numinosum inspire humility, gratitude, religious devotion, and worship, whereas negative experiences inspire fear, dread, and horror. Otto believes that the experience of the numinous, or the holy, is indefinable. It can be only evoked, not analyzed. In encountering the "wholly other," we experience the fact that God is beyond our experience.

2 Mairi's real name was distinctive and her identification with her ethnic heritage formed an important aspect of her personality. I have given her a similarly distinctive name: accented on the first syllable and with a slight Irish lilt, "Mairi" is the Irish version of "Mary," pronounced "May-re." I am grateful for Mairi's permission to discuss her dreams and therapeutic process, disguised to protect her confidentiality.

3 From the beginning, baptism has been recognized as a ritual of death and rebirth or a dangerous crossing from one mode of consciousness to another. Thus we are ritually recognized and often renamed as a child of God in a ceremony that acknowledges a second birth, rebirth, or spiritual birth of the individual person.

4 See accounts in William James's *Varieties of Religious Experience.* According to a report published by The Fetzer Institute, the 1998 General Social Survey showed that some 32 percent of those surveyed reported meditating once a week or more. Approximately 52 percent of Americans reported feeling God's presence in their lives on most days, every day, or many times a day, while 39 percent of people reported having had a spiritual or religious experience that changed their lives ("Frontiers of Research, 36," *Ions: Noetic Sciences Review* 61 (September–November 2002)).

5 Also known as Hadewijch of Antwerp and Hadewijch I, of Hadewijch I and II (Dietrich 1994).

6 See Grof and Grof 1989, for a wide-ranging discussion of "non-ordinary" states of consciousness typical of most mystical experience.

7 The Greek *soteria* is derived from *saos*, the Latin *salvatio* from *salvus*, the German *Heiland* from *heil* (akin to our English "healing"); *saos, salvus, heil* – all mean whole, not yet split, not disrupted, not disintegrated – therefore healthy and sound (Tillich 1981: 14).

8 Shahrazade is the heroine of a collection of Indian, Persian and Arab folktales commonly known as *Tales from the Arabian Nights* (Dawood 1961).

9 Throughout this book I have decided to maintain Jung's use of capital "S" when referring to the Self. I also use capital letters for words which refer to a

transpersonal dimension, such as Presence, Being, or Other. From here on quotations from Jung will be designated in both text and endnotes by CW followed by volume number and paragraph numbers, e.g., CW6: 789–91. See also CW11: 140.

10 Psychologist Charles Tart (1990) has examined many altered states including telepathy, clairvoyance, precognition, psychokinesis, near death experience, etc.

11 Wilber (1999: 217–19) warns against the tendency of New Age adherents to confuse pre-personal with transpersonal experience.

12 A word about inclusive language: when quoting from the ideas or writings of another person, whether author or patient, I will quote them exactly or use their language, as in Jung's use of "man." Of course woman is included in the meaning. Similarly in phrases like Erich Neumann's "mystical man" or Jung's "religious man," what these authors mean by "man" is "human being," and I would prefer to say "human being" myself. However, I feel that it is important to quote exactly in order to give proper credit and correct reference, and I also think that it is important that the cultural context of my references – in which the precise use of language is telling – is not falsified by my re-telling of words and ideas. In the same spirit, I retain the English spelling of certain of D. W. Winnicott's ideas, e.g., "personalisation." In Hart's translation of Hadewijch, Hadewijch refers to God as "Himself," using "Himself" not because she thinks of God as male and excludes the feminine principle, but because masculine reference was built into her language and time. My phraseology will, I hope, similarly reflect the gender-sensitivity that is appropriate to my language and time.

13 Belief is different than faith. Zen philosopher Alan Watts tells us, "Belief is the insistence that the truth is what one would 'lief,' or wish it to be . . . Faith . . . is an unreserved opening of the mind to the truth, whatever it may turn out to be. Faith has no preconceptions; it is a plunge into the unknown," quoted in Johnson 1998: 40.

14 Hadewijch's insistence on referring to God as Feminine (Love, *Minne*) was not new but part of a long tradition. The Church has always been aware of a maternal aspect of God and expressed this in theological formulations, particularly in the notion of providence. A motherly image is attributed to God by Isaiah: "Like a son comforted by his mother, will I comfort you (Is. 66: 13), and attributed to Jesus by himself: "O Jerusalem! Jerusalem! How often have I longed to gather your children as a hen gathers her brood under her wings" (Mt. 23: 37). There is also allusion to "the Father's loving breasts" and to "the milk of the Father" in Clement of Alexandria (Pagels 1976: 302).

15 What I refer to as the feminine principle or the principle of the feminine (after Jung) is one pole of the archetypal couple of masculine and feminine, as basic in both world and personality as "Yin" is in the Chinese philosophical symbol of "Yin/Yang." M. L. von Franz refers to what other writers mean by the feminine principle as the "feminine aspect of the Anthropos," the symbol of whole human *being* (emphasis mine). From a psychological point of view we see today an ongoing re-organization or re-balancing of masculine and feminine aspects of the collective psyche. Among the first to suggest that we understand the "feminine" as a category of being with its own unique values and strengths, Jung tells us that not only does the feminine represent one half of the central psychic polarity of masculine–feminine, but that this particular polarity symbolizes all other psychic polarities in both sexes. Widespread recognition of Jung's expanded ideas about gender, along with the ideas (Winnicott 1966) about "male and female elements of being," or Jungian analyst and theologian and

psychoanalyst Ann Ulanov's (1971: 133) "feminine mode of being," suggests an increasingly collective understanding of the symbolic nature of a feminine principle, i.e., that *the feminine points to a symbolic mode of being* rather than designating gender alone, and that the re-balancing of the objective psyche toward a more radical inclusion of the feminine occurs individually in the lives of *both* women and men. Our collective consciousness resonates with this emergent understanding in a plethora of current, familiar ideas concerning gender equality, a mythic "return of the goddess," and the burgeoning presence of feminist thought and expression in all areas of contemporary Western culture.

16 How my use of Winnicott's concept of personalisation differs from his understanding of what personalisation means will be discussed.

17 If we have gained any wisdom at all in this psychological age, we psychoanalysts know that "analysis" is a surgical technique of the mind, helpful when a gangrenous bond with reality presents itself, but murderous when applied carelessly and for the wrong reasons. Most important, *analysis as such is not symbolic thinking*! Gregory Bateson tells us that the rational part of the mind (left hemisphere) alone is pathogenic and virulent, designed to take things apart, but unable to put anything back together again. This integrative function, upon which healing depends, seems to be the prerogative of the right hemisphere and the older (feminine?) limbic brain.

18 Neumann's early interests included philosophy, his Hasidic Jewish heritage, poetry, and the arts. Once he decided to take up psychology as a profession, Neumann trained medically, which prepared him for studies with Jung, the founder of what today is variously referred to as analytical psychology, depth psychology, or Jungian psychology.

19 "Metaphysics" once meant philosophic or collectively acceptable truths recognizable simply by thinking about them. With the advent of scientific thinking, ideas previously assumed to be true were subjected to validation through experimentation within the materialistic assumptions of science. Physicist Robert W. Wood proclaims that the difference between physics and metaphysics is not that the practitioners of one are smarter than the practitioners of the other, but that the metaphysician has no laboratory (cited by Sagan 1996: 37). To the degree that depth psychotherapeutic work requires the "laboratory" of a therapeutic relationship based upon a body of clinical literature and experience (albeit expressed in "metapsychological" theories), the practical aims of depth psychology may be said to be of a scientific nature, even if the whole undertaking is not.

20 Letter dated November 12, 1959, published in *The New York Times* "Op-Ed" page, November 19, 1993.

21 The Anthropos, or the image of primordial human being, is an archetypal image of an individual's potential unity with the whole of humanity and human experience. Experience of the anthropos is an inner reality, in terms of recapitulating in one's own life a relation to the Divine that is pointed to in Christ's unity with and distance from the Father, or in the Buddha's understanding of the Mind.

22 The Gospel of St. John tells us that in the beginning, all things took form through the Word. Both psychic and personal, the Word was the numinous reality through which all things were made and without which nothing was made. Self-spoken by its own spontaneity, the Word brought forth the universe and established itself as the ultimate norm of reality and value. This Christian vision is in accord with the wisdom of Lao Tzu, the Chinese sage, who tells us that the human models itself on the earth, earth models itself on heaven, heaven

models itself on Tao, and Tao models itself on its own spontaneity (Berry 1988: 196).

23 Quoted in Godwin (1991: 629) who suggests that the most significant discovery of quantum physics is that there is a fundamental realm of unbroken wholeness underlying our perceived (psychological) world of apparent separateness and fragmentation (parentheses mine).

24 "Scientism" (along with other "isms") as a habit of mind indicates unconscious straying from our instinctual roots into the chaotic world of collective consciousness (CW8: 366, 405).

Chapter 1

Theoretical approaches to mystical experience

In order to set the stage for working with Mairi's dreams in the next chapter, here I will outline some of the theoretical ways in which mystical experience has been framed and how mystical experience challenges our usual ways of thinking about the mind, the spirit, the psyche, the soul, and the body. To ground these ideas and prevent our discussion from becoming too abstract, I begin with the actual, lived experience of our two women in their own words. More detailed accounts of Mairi and Hadewijch's mystical experience are found in Chapters 2 and 4 respectively, but brief descriptions of their embodied moments of union follow here.

In later sections of this chapter we will explore some of the ways in which modern theorists (including Jung and my adaptation of his notion of the Self) try to put rational words around ineffable yet concrete, bodily experience in order to organize our thoughts about it in terms of a depth psychology of religion. All these theories and notions represent efforts to square the reality of religious experience as a primary "given" in our lives with what is known of the mind and psyche scientifically. Is there something in our human makeup that provides a way to apprehend an immaterial, "spiritual" reality that surrounds and interpenetrates the material world of our ordinary lives? And if so, how do we sense it, or what is the inner agency of apprehension? Both Mairi and Hadewijch were explicit. They called this inner "agency" the soul.

The body as a locus for religious experience: Mairi and Hadewijch

Mairi's breakthrough experience was mediated primarily through her body. During a period of intense psychoanalytic work (in which her dreams played a large part) Mairi began to report occasional states of what I felt were moments of expanded consciousness or heightened awareness of herself and her surroundings (see Chapter 3). Then, leaving her session one day, Mairi experienced a powerful inner vision during which she felt transparent to herself and realized that she was "of the same substance as everything and everyone around." "Suddenly," she said, "everything in my life made sense. I felt as if all of my history, all of my life, led me to exactly this moment . . . I understood all my dreams . . . a crucial piece of something like a puzzle fell into place . . . All my life I've been heading for this moment and I never knew it . . ."

That night Mairi returned home and without eating dinner (she was not hungry) sat down cross-legged on the floor to calm herself, breathing slowly, all the while feeling "a profound union between inner and outer reality." She felt that something momentous was about to happen. Fear gripped her, and then she was overtaken with a rolling series of spontaneous orgasms, something that had never happened before. Although the energy soon left Mairi's genitals, it continued to rise and fall like light up and down her spine. A short time later Mairi cautiously rose from the floor and began to walk around her living room. "My whole body blazed," she said, "I felt as if I shone, not with fire but with light, blue-white incandescent light, that did not leave as I moved around. I was surrounded by it but light was in me, too. And with me was the presence of another, an Other, like a Queen of Heaven or something – a Presence of enormous Light in the room, everywhere. I knew it was the Holy Spirit, but it was feminine, a feminine Presence. Her Presence blessed me. She knew me, and I knew that It was She."

Mairi's vision of the Holy Spirit as feminine Presence did not fit with anything she had ever experienced before, or learned about in church or school, but was deeply moving and reassuring. That night Mairi didn't sleep. She felt her emotions rise and fall, as if, she said, "I were some kind of little cork, bobbing around in an ocean. Sometimes I wept, tears were copious, endless; solid sheets of water streamed down my face and neck, over my clothes and pillow . . . Sometimes I was swept by huge, silent laughter . . . the joke was on me: God was real and I felt so little, so small . . . so grateful. And someone else . . . some *place* else in me kept witnessing all this because I couldn't. *I* was no more . . . what I used to know as "me" cracked wide open. I let go, but the "witness" held it all . . . not the Holy Spirit, but my soul maybe?"

Mairi's feeling of being "lit up" from within, along with streaming of Kundalini energies up and down her body, lasted for the better part of three days. Slowly the intensity of these infusions abated, but not the sense of Presence nor the conviction that she had been "known" and "seen" by a witnessing consciousness that was not hers, that later she would come to describe as her "experience of soul." The rest of our work together continually referred back to this powerful experience. It changed Mairi's relation to me within her psychotherapy and it changed her in relation to the world outside my office. It became the guiding experience of her life – her dream-in-the-world.

Hadewijch must have been a woman of genuine presence. Her name, meaning "fighting-fit fighter," defines something of her character.[1] Part of her appeal I attribute to her "fierce" spirit, which apparently did not break under suffering. In one of her visions (14: 213) Hadewijch's Voice calls her "strongest of all fighters" (van Baest 1998: 31) or "warrioress," (Hadewijch 1980: 305), depending upon the translation.

Although we have narrated accounts of Hadewijch's religious experience, unfortunately we know about the realities of her actual life, less than we do about Mairi. Certainly Hadewijch was educated, and that was unusual for the time in which she lived. We do not know whether she married or if she ever had children, although many thirteenth-century Beguine women joined the movement after having led relatively normal lives in what must have been the upper classes (because educated) of medieval society. But we do have Hadewijch's journals, her poetry and her visionary accounts, which present her "fruitive being-one" (with God) experiences vividly enough, and in her own words.

Hadewijch's writings had an impact upon those around her in her day, and something of her presence continues in the way her writings continue to "work" in our world now.[2] More than one contemporary scholar has lovingly translated her entire work (Jozef Van Mierlo 1924–52; Mother Columba Hart 1980); others have written about her extensively. Paul Mommaers (1980: xiii), a foremost contemporary scholar of Hadewijch, calls her "the most important exponent of love mysticism and one of the loftiest figures in the Western mystical tradition," as well as a "feminist in conflict" with the social mores of her time (1988).

Unlike Mairi, Hadewijch was overcome by mystical experience from an early age. "Since I was ten years old," she writes, "I have been so overwhelmed by intense Love that I should have died during the first two years when I began this, if God had not given me other forms of strength than people ordinarily receive, and if he had not renewed my nature with his own Being (L11: 10. 69). The vernacular word that Hadewijch used for Love was *Minne*, a word of feminine gender that belongs to the language of courtly love and by which she could mean God, or Christ, or Divine Love but by which essentially Hadewijch meant *the soul's experienced relationship with God*.[3]

> O beloved, why has not Love sufficiently overwhelmed you and engulfed you in her abyss? Alas, when Love is so sweet, why do you not fall deep into her? And why do you not touch God deeply enough in the abyss of his Nature, which is so *unfathomable*? (L5: 28. 56)

> If two things are to become one, nothing may be between them except the glue wherewith they are united together. That bond of glue is Love, *whereby God and the blessed soul are united in oneness*. (L16: 28. 80, italics mine)

Hadewijch's experiences of unity with the divine were also intensely physical. Clearly she was no stranger to desire and its fulfillment. In a vision at dawn (Vision 7: 280) she says: "My heart and my veins and all my limbs trembled and quivered with eager desire . . . such madness and fear beset my mind . . . so that dying I must go mad, and going mad I must die." Her descriptions leave little unsaid about the passionate nature of her love affair with Jesus, but importantly, she refuses to let go of either the divine or the human in her Beloved. In Vision 7, Hadewijch writes

> I desired to have full fruition of my Beloved, and to understand and taste him to the full. I desired that his Humanity should to the fullest extent be one in fruition with my humanity, and mine then should hold its stand and be strong enough to enter into perfection until I content him, who is perfection itself, by purity and unity, and in all things to content him fully in every virtue. To that end I wished he might content me interiorly with his Godhead in one spirit and that for me he should be all that he is, without withholding anything from me . . . After that he came himself to me, took me entirely in his arms, and pressed me to him; and all my members felt his in full felicity, in accordance with the desire of my heart and my humanity. So I was outwardly satisfied and fully transported.

Despite the explicit sexual imagery in Hadewijch's poem, a full reading of her visions leaves little doubt that the union of which she speaks has multiple layers of meaning and ultimately refers to the soul's intimate relationship with God under the aegis of *Minne*, the feminine principle. God's abyss may be masculine and unfathomable, but when "Love engulfs you in her abyss" then you experience the "glue," the "bond," the link between the embodied soul and the "unfathomable" (spiritual) Godhead. "God gives us soul so that we may love God," says Hadewijch (L18: 63, in Hadewijch 1980: 86).

> Now understand the deepest essence of your soul, what soul is. Soul is a being that can be beheld by God and by which again, God can be beheld . . . the soul is a bottomless abyss in which God suffices to himself; and his own self-sufficiency ever finds fruition to the full in this soul, as the soul, for its part, ever does in him. *Soul is a way for the passage of God from his depths into his liberty; and God is a way for the passage of the soul into its liberty, that is, into his inmost depths, which cannot be touched except by the soul's abyss.* (italics mine)

So for Hadewijch it is impossible to relate to God without soul, but even more so without soul's abyss, which resides in the innermost recesses of incarnate being – in the body. This paradoxical unity-in-separateness defines Hadewijch's poetic, mystical understanding of the relationship between the embodied, perishable human and the immaterial, imperishable Divine. Soul is central to her vision: "God gave us his Nature in the soul, with three powers whereby to love his Three Persons" (L22: 137. 97).

Hadewijch reached a point in her psycho-religious development where she grew beyond the ecstasies, visions and supernatural sweetness of her early experiences of "fruitive being-one with God" (which she came to understand as juvenile), to fully embrace the paradox and pain of suffering her Love for God while at the same time recognizing God's infinite otherness. "Love makes the heart taste a violent death and causes it to die without being able to die" (L20: 26. 91). Suffering God's paradoxical presence/absence was how Hadewijch also understood the essential suffering at the core of human existence. She would have embraced Kierkegaard's idea that the self (soul) we are meant to be is always a combination of the finite and the infinite. We cannot approach the infinite without suffering the soul's abyss in the limitations of the body, just as Jesus suffered his humanity in rejection and persecution. Just this suffering brings us closest to the divinity incarnate in the God-man.

Still, for Hadewijch, suffering was never an end in itself. We suffer, she felt, in order to "grow up" ("and all things considered, you have suffered too little to grow up" L239, 249) and once we have grown up or reached "full grownness," our spiritual union with God consists in serving one's fellow human beings, even while being painfully rejected and despised. If we want access to God's divinity then we must live Christ's humanity – his passion for this world – and embrace the consequences.

In the accounts of both Mairi and Hadewijch we see how religious experience boldly claims the body and how central the soul is in this claim. In my years of Jungian training and early therapeutic experience I felt that I gained a fairly deep understanding of the psyche, but even then I missed acknowledgment of the central importance of the body in all therapeutic work. It troubled me then, and it continues to be a revelation. My experience with Mairi, alongside my study of Hadewijch's embodied mysticism, really brought the issue home. I have come to conclude that while the psyche may house a great deal more than my inter-personalist colleagues may give it credit for, it does not house the body, and the soul lives in the body, even if it speaks through the psyche. The importance of the body for the life of the soul has become central to my understanding.[4]

Our culture's massive collective preoccupation with the body easily objectifies it and puts it to use. Through it we feed our appetites. Or we keep it in shape. Or we train as dancers or athletes, honing our body's skills to peaks of expressive power. Most of our bodily disciplines are for ego needs and requirements of self-esteem. This is a far cry from letting what the poet Mary Oliver (1992: 110) calls "the soft animal of your body love what it loves," or living a fully embodied life. As a temple of the soul, the body is hurt, even crushed, by a spirit of perfectionism. Wholehearted acceptance of the body's concrete particular existence seems to be essential not only for living well and fully but for healing. We cannot individuate without it. When our bodies are unloved by others and ourselves, hatred flows in, and shame, and the kind of fear that breeds self-division and emotional illness. What the body knows and where it takes us is navigated from an inner map that is not available to our consciousness. When the dancer Martha Graham spoke of "the house of pelvic truth" she meant that the body is a landscape of truth-telling. An ancient, undivided world lies curled within us with an ancestral memory of unspoiled wilderness. Thus the real experience of the wild is inside us, beyond our ego or mental control, and it has rules and laws that do not obey our human will.

Jung not only honors the body as the vessel in which psyche appears but as the vessel in which reality appears, "all the way down" into matter itself. He writes (CW9i: 291),

> The symbols of the self arise in the depths of the body and they express its materiality every bit as much as the structure of the perceiving consciousness. The symbol is thus a living body, *corpus et anima*; hence the "child" is such an apt formula for the symbol. The uniqueness of the psyche can never enter wholly into reality, it can only be realized approximately, though it still remains the absolute basis of all consciousness. The deeper "layers" of the psyche lose their individual uniqueness as they retreat farther and farther into darkness. "Lower down," that is to say as they approach the autonomous functional systems, they become increasingly collective until they are universalized and extinguished in the body's materiality, i.e., into chemical substances. The body's carbon is simply carbon. Hence "at bottom" the psyche is simply "world" . . . The more archaic and "deeper," that is the more physiological, the symbol is, the more collective and universal, the more "material" it is.

Because nothing in a body's lifetime goes unregistered, wholeness enters through the body's door. Without a body we cannot bring our psychophysiological or biological dilemmas to the emotionally accessible level of felt psychic experience. Without a psychic container within a body self we cannot bridge the gaps in being. This became meaningful to Mairi as she "fell through" psyche into her experience of soul (Chapter 3).

During her days of intense ecstatic experience Mairi felt herself led to what felt like the heart of religious reality, an enormous infusion of energy and light, illuminating her world from within. This substantive experience led Mairi to feel not less embodied but more, and more accepting of her mortality. "I've gone from being in a morality play to being in a mortality play," she said. She felt, from the inside out, that "death has lost its sting." Death was still very real to Mairi, but after her vivid embrace of the reality of her experience the "sting of death" (her fear of it, her bitterness) seemed gone. Instead of "falling" endlessly, Mairi found herself securely held (in Winnicott's terms) not in a mother's arms but in the arms of her embodied soul. Of the role of the body in spiritual reintegration, the Sufi poet Rumi tells us that

> The physical form is of great importance; nothing can be done without the consociation of the form and the essence. However often you may sow a seed, stripped of the pod, it will not grow. Sow it with the pod, it will become a great tree. From this point of view, the body is fundamental and necessary for the realization of the Divine intention. (Bakhtiar 1976: 21)

From the inside, for the person to whom such a revelation is given, a trusting capacity for bodily expression – for creating, enacting, speaking, writing – must be engaged if the experience is communicated to others. This happened over and over for Mairi in her psychotherapy sessions, telling and retelling her central experience. In this way her revelatory experience proceeded out of her body and into the world of discourse and communication. Yunus Emre (1989: 20) a thirteenth-century Bektashi Sufi poet, expresses his understanding of how revelatory experience came into his world:

> We entered the house of realization,
> we witnessed the body.
> The whirling skies, the many-layered earth,
> the seventy-thousand veils,
> we found in the body.
> The night and the day, the planets,
> the words inscribed on the Holy Tablets,
> the hill that Moses climbed, the Temple,
> and Israfil's trumpet, we observed in the body.
> Torah, Psalms, Gospel, Quran –
> what these books have to say,
> we found in the body.
> Everybody says these words of Yunus
> are true. Truth is wherever you want it.
> We found it all within the body.

Symbolically the matrix, mother and ground of our being, the body is our early house, our first environment, the residence into which we incarnate and our most personal experience of earth. The space where the body is is the most intimate space we can know, a place of joy and fear, love and hate, anger and courage, illness and death. To feel our pain, sickness and loss is to enter into the body as the Shadow of Death. To feel joy, inspiration and sanctification is to experience bodily transfiguration, or the Body Blessed.[5]

A capacity for religious experience: quantum mind and the psycho-spiritual senses

In his recent book, *Why Religion Matters*, Huston Smith underscores the importance of feeling and intuition in orienting ourselves to the mystery of religious experience. The received wisdom of science, he says, denies the existence of the Infinite (including the soul) but "that wisdom cannot prevent us from having experiences that *feel* as if they come from a different world" (2001: 29).

> Mystics are people who have a talent for sensing places where life's carapace is cracked, and through its chinks they catch glimpses of a world beyond. Isaiah seeing the Lord high and lifted up. Christ seeing the heavens open at his baptism. Arjuna privy to Krishna in his terrifying cosmic form. The Buddha finding the universe turning into a bouquet of flowers at the hour of his enlightenment. John reporting, "I was on an island called Patmos, and I was in a trance." Saul struck blind on the Damascus road. For Augustine it was the voice of a child, saying "Take, read"; for Saint Francis, a voice that seemed to come from the crucifix. It was while Saint Ignatius sat by a stream and watched its running water, and while that curious old cobbler Jacob Boehme was looking at a pewter dish, that there came to each that news of another world that it is always religion's business to convey.

My patient Mairi and her thirteenth-century counterpart Hadewijch had such encounters with another world and both experienced these encounters as healing. Mairi suddenly felt herself reduced or "relativized" in the face of a vast Being in whose presence she felt infinitely more herself. This was not a narcissistic inflation of her ego but its deflation in the presence of something ineffable and far greater than herself. Her attention was diverted – away from her problems as she and I had addressed them – and towards a new and whole world view (both outer and inner) with depth and intensity. She was left in awe and worshipful acceptance of something beyond understanding that is part of all encounters with the sacred. Smith (2001: 149) reminds us that such epiphanies, with their attendant ego-reductions, constitute salvation in the West and enlightenment in the East. Mairi's experience was primal and beyond explanation; beyond words, yet somehow "known"; not cognized but re-cognized. This was not knowledge that she had acquired in any intellectual or educational process. It was "too big" for that. Trembling with gratitude, Mairi felt that suddenly everything made sense, although she could not articulate the "sense" it made. Having long since "lost" a sense of herself as a person of intrinsic value, Mairi now felt restored to herself, as if something in her had arrived in its true home, which deeply satisfied an inarticulate longing that she had not even identified as "hers."

Smith (2001: 31) accounts for experiences like Mairi's in the following way:

> To say that the pilgrim is not alone in her heroic journey understates the case, for it is the spark of divinity that God plants in human beings that initiates the journey in the first place . . . If there is to be a wooing of God by humanity, it must be God who is the real agent in the wooing, as well as its object.

Smith's formulation is close to Mairi's conviction that her experience was one of inward ensoulment, i.e., that she had been given an inner life for the first time and that this inner life was quintessentially her own. Her conviction did not happen all at once, and clearly her psychotherapy prepared the ground for it, but there was a moment of breakthrough when the numinous reality of a Feminine Presence penetrated her ordinary awareness and incontrovertibly reshaped her sense of herself. If before Mairi felt soulless and without interiority, now she had a soul, for soul took up residence in her deepest parts.

If we are to reclaim territory for the soul in psychotherapy – something which Mairi's experience taught me is important – we may need to re-envision the realm of human interiority in terms of certain dimensions of consciousness that are not accountable through our usual senses or ways of knowing. Mairi's psychotherapeutic transformation was a transformation *in consciousness*.[6] If we are to understand how simply talking to another person about their dreams can profoundly change them – how deep channels of empathy can change even our bodies, or open us up to the depths of religious experience – then we need a new understanding of consciousness, one that requires us to stretch our understanding in the direction of what writers these days call the "quantum mind." Consciousness may be precipitated into the world in the quantum aspect of our very minds: that the transformation of consciousness happens there, and that our dreams can be experienced as a privileged, communicative link with this aspect of our existence, I will attempt to show.

Quantum mind

Mainstream cognitive psychology tends to reduce mind (consciousness) to an epiphenomenon of the body (brain), but many scientists and philosophers no longer accept this simple reduction. They are inclined to think that the true relationship is a mystery and may forever remain one, with the mind retaining the same relationship to the brain that quantum mechanics and its findings has to Newtonian physics and its laws.[7] If this analogy holds true, it makes room for religious experience as a valid, independent way of knowing the immaterial (spiritual) realities upon which our material world depends. Physicists have recently shown (the Einstein–Podolsky–Rosen experiment) that at the micro-level of reality, if you separate two interacting particles, they remain simultaneously in touch with each other no matter how far apart they are. A spin imparted to one particle immediately is accompanied by a reverse spin in the other, even if they are at opposite ends of the universe. These findings define the "area" of quantum mechanics. No simple path of cause and effect can be found at the quantum level, as it can in material reality. This finding alone opens up an "ineffable" immaterial dimension of reality outside space, time and the material world, and these discoveries in non-locality are now being applied to the mind–body problem that has bedeviled science ever since Descartes.

Long ago Freud realized that "the unconscious of one human being can react upon that of another, without passing through the conscious" (1915). Early psychoanalysts explored similar events of unconscious communication and generally assumed that a dialogue of shared unconsciousness[8] was the explanation. Other unexplained findings – telepathic phenomena, clairvoyance, prayer-at-a-distance, and uncanny moments of deep connection or prophetic intuition across distances – tend to be dismissed by mainstream psychoanalysts as unscientific. Often Jung's concept of synchronicity suffers the same fate.

Recently, however, psychologists and neurologists are discussing the idea of non-local consciousness, i.e., the idea of mind not "localized" in just one person (Dossey 2001). This idea is developing into the notion of the quantum mind, and Colin McGinn (1999), Evan Harris Walker (2000) and Danah Zohar (1990) are among those who find this designation useful. These authors generally take as their departure point the fact that consciousness (like the quanta of micro-physics) is not an objectively observable phenomenon. Consciousness is highly subjective, and what we find when we look for it is influenced by the attitude of the observer and the process of observation. Before we had concepts of consciousness – first used by John Locke in 1632 (Barfield 1953: 170) – or even personality (first used in 1768), we had no way to think about consciousness or personality, or consciousness of self, or individual, or person.[9] We simply *were* conscious, without thinking about it.

For example, consciousness is not the same as thinking, but it is the carrier of conscious thought. Consciousness is the blue sky, the sound of wind, the scent of the green firs on the hill, the smell of the sea, the feel of the computer keys beneath my fingers. Consciousness is the child playing down the road, the gull sitting on the post outside my window. It is the sound of things, the feel of things, rain. Consciousness is the experience of images, ideas, words and thoughts that play through my mind as I write, read, and remember. If we are dissociated, or repressed, or unconscious in one or more areas of our personality, or even immature, we may not have all the sensations, emotions, feelings and thoughts appropriate to our state of being. The simple thought, "I exist," is not the same as awareness of my own existence, which involves a dimension of meaning not to be found in purely intellectual life.

Babies undergo a range of conscious states, but it is doubtful that they are reflectively self-conscious. We assume babies have no notion of self at all, at least early on. And animals are similar; they have a conscious life, but they do not aspire to reflect on this fact, meaning that they do not apply mental concepts to themselves (McGinn 1999: 3). In dreams we do not cease to experience, to be a subject of consciousness, but in dreams we are conscious without sentience. So consciousness is not the same as wakefulness, or attention, or perception, nor is it self-awareness, or self-reflection. Consciousness does not need words, or images, or things; the deaf and mute and blind are conscious too.

Yet when consciousness enters, everything changes. It is not a doing, but it is a something. It is not thinking, but it is the existential being that has thinking as its subject (Walker 2000: 175). Consciousness is a fundamental part of reality. Existing in its own right with its own identity, consciousness is both real and non-physical. The non-spatiality of consciousness is connected with its imperceptibility. Consciousness enables us to perceive the world but is not itself a perceptible thing (McGinn 1999: 113). We infer consciousness by observing the behavior of others, and we can examine our own, but neither of these modes of access is a form of sense perception (114). So we are left, says McGinn (51) "with an introspection-based view of consciousness and a perception-based view of the brain staring at each other across a yawning conceptual divide."

According to Walker (2000: 5) the perception of the indeterminacy of consciousness is a kind of doorway to the quantum mind. Instead of obeying normal neurophysical laws (for example at the synaptic junction), consciousness seems to behave in a far more quantum fashion ("on/off," "wave/particle"), more deeply affected by observer characteristics than otherwise expected.[10] Walker even suggests that consciousness itself may be a kind of quantum mind, precipitating non-material reality out of our material brains. And these thinkers imply that we come to a concept of quantum mind – or recognize an aspect of our own human consciousness that works in a quantum fashion – by "growing" into an awareness of this part of our nature, or "evolving" into recognition of our quantum selves, and that this evolution expresses the transformation that occurs within our personalities as we individuate.

As we shall see, this would be one way to describe what happened to my patient Mairi, especially if we equate her experience of soul with an experience of her quantum self as an "agency" that could know God without being able to explain this knowledge in any court of rationality. Mairi's expansion of consciousness opened within her channels for prayer and a deep sense of empathy and gratitude for the world without that felt participatory and non-local. Her experience suggests that for some of us, the process of depth psychotherapy offers access to deeper realities than we believed existed, and which bring sentience to parts of ourselves that do not belong only to "ourselves" at all.

Walker (2000: 138) compares an experience of this new sentient awareness to the ineffable knowledge of Zen Buddhism, finding that in both,

> the revised view of reality in which we see the observer and consciousness as central to reality itself is as significant as if we had found the key to the soul. Perhaps that is what has been found . . . Our quest for the fabric of reality has brought us from religion to science, but science, when asked to show us reality, causes us to look into a mirror to see what we are . . . now we must find out what the observer is and what threads consciousness weaves in creating the quantum mind.

Dreams as portals to the quantum mind

As Jung concentrated on the value of the dream for its own sake he glimpsed something in the unconscious that Freud felt belonged to conscious motivation or rational intent. Jung discovered purposiveness in the psyche itself. He understood this purposiveness to be a principle, by which he meant an inherent tendency implicit in the psyche that strives to undo dissociation and promote further integration. With this realization Jung perceived a spiritual aspect to healing, a dynamic agency which "does" and is different from the psyche, which "is." Because dreams seem to offer a unique glimpse of this autonomous tendency, they have become a central focus of the work I do. Theologian and novelist Frederick Buechner (1988: 37–8) helps us understand why:

> Freudians and Jungians, prophets and poets, philosophers, fortune-tellers, and phonies all have their own claims about what dreams mean. Others claim they don't mean a thing. But there are at least two things they mean that seem incontrovertible . . . One of them is that we are in constant touch with a world that is as real to us while we are in it, and has as much to do with who we are, and whose ultimate origin and destiny are unknown and fascinating, as the world of waking reality. The other one is that our lives are a great deal richer, deeper, more

intricately interrelated, more mysterious, and less limited by time and space than we commonly suppose . . . People who tend to write off the validity of religious experience in general and the experience of God in particular on the grounds that in the Real World they can find no evidence for such things should take note. Maybe the Real World is not the only reality, and even if it should turn out to be, maybe they are not really looking at it realistically.

As naturally as we eat and breathe, we dream (Hobson 1988). Rivers of imagination and memory, thought and vision, fantasy and dream flow through each of us all the time, bathing the roots of our being, nourishing our vitality, and urging us forward through time and circumstance into our unfolding individual and collective lives. Dreaming captures a broad aspect of what it is to be human; thus we can speak of dream imagery as a kind of universal language, a grammar of the psyche that is, in turn, a grammar of the Word. Decades ago we thought that we dreamed only during the two or three hours of sleep that correlate with REM (rapid-eye-movements). Even at that rate, amazingly enough, by the age of seventy we would have spent a tenth of our lives (seven years) dreaming. Ongoing research, however, indicates that we dream throughout sleep (Hobson 1988, Van de Castle 1994), so that within sleep and upon wakening, our awareness of dreaming varies, but dreaming does not. So dreams accompany us throughout our entire lives, expressing the psycho-physiological world in which we dwell.

Unless we speak to others, only we know what we dream. We may not share dreams or even remember them ourselves, but when we are deprived of dreaming, we become disoriented and frayed, even ill. The act of dreaming accomplishes something organic, something cellular, without which we cannot live. Dreaming also accomplishes something psychological. That both our biological and psychological lives are inseparably rooted in dreaming illuminates Jung's idea (CW9i: 291) of a psychoid dimension of reality in which matter and spirit are inextricably bound, a realm in which literally and figuratively we find ourselves.

The quantum theories we reviewed in the previous section affirm an embodied kinship of matter and spirit. No longer conceiving of matter as inorganic, quantum and chaos theories declare that the stuff and logic of the universe are everywhere uniform, and that the same atomic rudiments, chemical constituents, and laws and principles extend from the cellular substance of our blood and bone to the farthest galaxies. Our planet and all life upon it consist of elements forged in the fiery hearts of primordial stars. To know these facts and personally experience the impact of such extra-ordinary analogies and correspondences – what they mean in our lives, how deeply they bind us to our origins, physically, emotionally, psychologically and spiritually – is to feel the psyche in which we live, living itself in us. To attend to our dreams is to begin to connect with all these worlds: to connect to the fact that just as we inhabit them, they inhabit us. Our dreaming contributes to these worlds.

We also know that consciousness circulates throughout our bodies, translating outside to inside and inside to outside. No longer can we imagine that our minds hover somewhere above us, or inside our heads. Current research in physiology affirms that our minds do not dwell in our brains, but "travel the whole body on caravans of hormone and enzyme, busily making sense of the compound wonders we catalogue as touch, taste, smell, hearing, and vision" (Ackerman 1991: xix). What is true for consciousness is true for dreams: they, too, circulate throughout our bodies, drawing upon cellular levels of being. Dream-tears are real enough to wet the pillow. Dream-passion is fierce enough to make our bodies burn. Sometimes we may dream our way to an insight so overwhelming that it startles us awake, and it may haunt us for years. Not until we have grown into and through it consciously does a dream like that disappear.

In order to take all this into account, we need to perceive personhood in a holographic fashion; and in order to do so, we must understand what Jung introduced as archetypal reality. Proposing the hologram itself as a model for Analytical Psychology, Zinkin (1987: 1–2) refers to Jung's understanding of physics and psychology as alternative descriptions of the same reality. In dealing with subatomic particles, physicists deal with entities ultimately as unrepresentable as archetypes. Within certain areas of human interiority, where we struggle to express pre-verbal experience and run a continual raid upon the inarticulate, the psyche and the soul also represent alternative descriptions of the same reality. Perhaps only a quantum consciousness borrowed from modern physics can enable us to grasp this perspective.

Psycho-spiritual senses

A central concern of this book is to reveal some of the ways in which a psychological process uncovers or makes way for something beyond the psyche. What I mean by a fully human consciousness is first and foremost an openness to being penetrated by the otherness of this "something beyond the psyche," whether it comes from within as soul or from without as world. Why some people have this experience in psychotherapy and others do not is beyond my focus (and probably a mystery). But what I want to make room for here is the possibility that the very feeling of conviction about the reality of religious experience to which Smith (2001: 29) refers above may have its origins in the soul. This is to suggest that beyond the ego and its bodily senses, we human beings have interior or perhaps intuitive senses (ways of knowing) that can orient us in the inner world as truly as our familiar bodily senses orient us in the world of everyday reality.

Henry Corbin is helpful here, especially his tracing of what he calls the psycho-spiritual senses available through the Imaginal World. According to Corbin (Bloom 1996: 5) the imaginal realm is an intermediate world that is neither the empirical world of the senses nor the abstract world of the intellect, yet is ever so much more than imaginary. Corbin bases his knowledge of psycho-spiritual senses and what he calls participation in the Imaginal World on his translations of Ibn Arabi's ideas of Spiritual Intelligence (1955). In light of the imaginal realm, experience takes the form of encounter "there" which orients us "here," re-arranging our basic sense of who we are, where we are, where we have come from, and where we are going. This comes close to Mairi's description of what happened to her during her experience of soul, when she "fell through" one dimension of being into another (see Chapter 3).

Corbin suggests that we simply think of ourselves as having more than the five senses of which we know. He calls these additional senses "psycho-spiritual" and they are consistent with the given internal senses of Sufism, all attributed to the feminine principle: common sense (an ability to perceive the form of things), imagination (an ability to perceive meanings), intelligence, memory, and Active Imagination, which consists of an intuitive ability to govern both sensible phenomena and intelligible noumena so that balance (the spiritual Heart) is always preserved (Bakhtiar 1976: 19–20).

Corbin suggests that our inability to conceive of a concrete supra-sensory reality results from giving too much importance to sensory reality alone. With daily life pressing heavily upon us, we seldom realize the way our unconscious attitudes and assumptions actually color what we see. Because we are out of balance (un-centered by the spiritual Heart), we are inclined to reduce the supra-sensory universe to mere abstract concepts, paradigms, and universals. But the figures we may encounter in the *mundus imaginalis*, says Corbin, have nothing to do with universals established in logic.

In our encounters with the imaginal, what Corbin calls our psycho-spiritual senses open. Through these additional senses we encounter subjective experiencing of depths and intensities of Being which are other than (although analogous to) the profoundly silent matrix of our capacities for physical sense. Through psycho-spiritual senses we experience intrusions of Imaginal Reality into our mundane world, intrusions which may seem more irrefutable and coherent than the world we experience with the senses we count upon in our waking lives.

This is what Mairi struggled to describe, and what most people with direct religious experience report. There is the breaking of a kind of perceptual barrier which happens in or by way of the senses, and in this breakthrough, thought tumbles over itself into the inconceivable, i.e., into that which cannot be thought (or perhaps what Christopher Bollas (1987) suggests by his phrase, the "unthought known"). Poet Robert Bly (1996: 214) describes a phenomenon of thinking which implies participation in

Corbin's Imaginal World by using the phrase "vertical thought." Bly means by this, thought that has to do with both our longing and our capacity for spiritual growth. Vertical thought "climbs" and "tumbles." With this kind of thought Mairi tried to express and comprehend her "fall" into an Imaginal World.

Psycho-spiritual senses and the kind of vertical or metaphoric thought that accompanies them have been well known – even cultivated – in monastic communities for centuries. Hadewijch's poetry is full of such expressions. Exploring the spiritual legacy left to us by Hildegard of Bingen, theologian Renata Craine (1997: 43) includes Hildegard's sensual consciousness of tasted intimacy with God as part of her obedience to the Rule of St. Benedict that advised listening with the "ears of your heart." Listening with the ears of the heart, says Craine, refers to a type of contemplative listening by which we become experientially aware of the Divine Mystery in the smallest circumstances of everyday life. Arising from the depths of our being, this kind of hearing or listening is beyond explanation and can only be described by analogy to physical sense experience. Since the time of Origen in the third century, tradition has referred to such forms of contemplative consciousness as senses of the soul, or the spiritual senses, which awaken at certain stages of the spiritual journey. Expressions like "hearing God," "seeing God," "being embraced by God," even "tasting" and "smelling" God are other poetic renderings that point to perception by these senses.

In summary, then, we need an understanding of personal experience and a capacity for a depth of experience that stretches beyond the ego to include another agency of perception. We *do* experience more than a physically sensate nature. We "see" dream imagery, but not with our eyes. If we "taste" an apple but have not eaten one, is this imaginary, or only memory or hallucination? I don't think so. There are times – and my experience with Mairi confirmed this – when personal experience refers us to something more than its perceiving or conceiving subject, experience that overflows its original content. Personal experience can uncover soul. This happens when both our concepts and our sensible perceptions become sources of psychological experience, presupposing not only a perceiving or conceiving subject-as-ego (registering wishing, willing, dreaming, and imagining) but an experiencing subjectivity, or subject-as-soul.

Fully human consciousness: paradox and the capacity to participate

I understood Mairi's experience to be a genuine religious encounter indicative of her emerging capacity for fully human consciousness, a term I will use throughout our discussion of Mairi's and Hadewijch's material. This notion is an extension of Jung's idea that we are not well or whole until we have satisfied the longing that is inherent in the religious instinct. It is also related to my notion of a dream-in-the-world in that fully human consciousness is necessary to truly love the world and to feel at home in the world, i.e., to dream *in the world*. According to this way of thinking, the capacity to house religious experience and evolve a world view that honors its mystical heart is part of what it means to become fully human.

I see fully human consciousness as consisting of three major developmental components. For two of these components I am indebted to object-relations theory, especially to the work of D. W. Winnicott and, more recently, to the inter-subjective[11] analysts, especially Jessica Benjamin (1992). For the third, I turn to Carl Jung,[12] Thomas Berry, and Erich Neumann. All three "developmental" milestones have to do with an evolving tolerance for the reality of Otherness and with the mastery of those fears and anxieties that prevent us from loving and relating to a world of reality outside of our own (inner) assumptions about it. Psychologically speaking, this Otherness comes to us (1) inwardly, as revelation, and (2) outwardly, as discovery. But Otherness is numinous, and the capacity to maintain the tension between inward revelation (dream and experience) and outward discovery (world and experience) requires mediation. Paradoxically, mediation also seems to come from both within and without.

The first developmental milestone required for fully human consciousness is what Winnicott calls "personalisation" or "indwelling," which requires mediation by the maternal figure. According to Winnicott (1963c), the infant's earliest experience is transitional, an "interpenetrating mix-up," in which finding (out there) and/or creating (hallucinating) the object are not to be distinguished and are allowed to coexist for a considerable period. In time this dual unity gives way to hate (as the mother separates) and eventually to integration, in which the child develops a capacity for feeling both love and hate (ambivalence) towards the object who survives this destruction out of its own resources. The infant reaches the "depressive" position, which is a hallmark of personalisation.

During the period of maternal preoccupation leading to personalisation, Winnicott says that the mother is continually "introducing and re-introducing the baby's mind and body to each other" (Winnicott 1970: 271). In this process of mediation, terrifying affects as well as ecstatic states of unity get named and grounded in a shared language which personalises what are otherwise collective energies surging through the baby's psyche/soma. As this occurs, something like a spirit (Winnicott does not specify this any further) comes to "indwell" in the body, and "indwelling" is accomplished. The baby has now reached "unit status." It has a more or less coherent self with a boundary between inner and outer. The object/mother is now seen as other, as separate from the self, and a passionate desire for the object can now be entertained within the baby because the prior dual unity is not present. Winnicott more or less leaves the matter there.

Object-relations writer Jessica Benjamin (1992), writing from an "inter-subjective" point of view, develops Winnicott's thought further. She adds to this layer of developing self–other awareness a second, non-oppositional but simultaneously developing dimension. Right alongside the growing autonomy and separateness which accompany an infant's ability to differentiate self from object, says Benjamin, is a capacity for inter-subjectivity which points *beyond* self–other awareness as such to an increasing ability to recognize the object not only as other, but as an equivalent center of experience, i.e., as another subject. This layer of developing consciousness implies that a similarity of participation in a world of inner experience begins to be recognized in tandem with the recognition of difference. An ability to recognize the object as another subject implies not only a capacity for mutual recognition of an inner world, but a capacity to realize that despite its being shared, mutually recognized subjective experience may feel oppositional and at cross-purposes, as well as harmonious; that another subject may feel differently from the way oneself feels, as well as participate in pleasurably shared understanding.

Benjamin's (1992: 53) elaboration of Winnicott's thought highlights Winnicott's notion of *a reality that can be loved* (italics mine). While an intrapsychic ego feels as if reality is being imposed from the outside, an inter-subjective ego discovers reality in "a continuation under more complex conditions of the infant's original fascination with and love of what is outside, his appreciation of difference and novelty." This appreciation, says Benjamin, is the element in self-object differentiation that gives separation a positive, rather than a hostile coloring, for it embraces "*love of the world, not merely leaving or distance from the mother*" (53, italics mine). According to Benjamin and Winnicott, the development of inter-subjectivity and the recognition of the object as another subject trace the development of our capacities for emotional responsiveness, empathy and concern.

To my mind, fully human consciousness implies the presence of self–other awareness, a capacity for inter-subjectivity, and yet a third dimension, which develops out of the prior two. We might call this third dimension awareness of the archetypal configurations which underlie and overlight all our perceptions, feelings and behaviors, or "participating consciousness,"[13] requiring an openness to being penetrated by the other – either as unconscious within or as world from without. Here we confront a problem in our narcissistic age of which Jung was uniquely aware, i.e., the problem of relating to and loving something both outside the self, and greater than the self. Says Jung,

It is hard to believe that this teeming world is too poor to provide an object for human love – it offers boundless opportunities to everyone. It is rather the inability to love which robs a person of these opportunities. The world is empty only to him who does not know how to direct his libido towards things and people, and to render them alive and beautiful. What compels us to create a substitute from within ourselves is not an external lack, but our own inability to include anything outside ourselves in our love. (CW5: 253)

Our contemporary narcissism is further challenged if we are asked to embrace our own inferiority and limitation by loving a greater or higher reality. Obedience to the First Commandment, "To love the Lord thy God with all thy soul and all thy heart and all thy might" is no longer easy to conceive of, let alone follow, in today's enlightened culture where we are fathoming the mysteries of the human genome and are on the threshold of cloning human beings. Everything miraculous seems man-made. And yet there remains a God-shaped longing in the human heart that cannot be satisfied by any man-made thing. The spiritual, says Jung (CW8: 108),

> appears in the psyche also as an instinct, indeed as a real passion, a "consuming fire," as Nietzsche once expressed it. It is not derived from any other instinct as the psychologists of instinct would have us believe, but is a principle *sui generis*, a specific and necessary form of instinctual power.

The religious instinct is best thought of as our longing for wholeness, and by "wholeness" Jung did not mean simply the integration of the different parts of the self. An awareness of the deep "participation" that fully human consciousness implies requires a paradoxical awareness that the half-material, half-spiritual nature of the universe is matched by the half-bodily, half-spiritual nature of the human psyche. Jung says (CW16: 454) that

> the underlying idea of the psyche proves it to be a half-bodily, half-spiritual substance, an *anima media natura*, as the alchemists call it, a hermaphroditic being capable of uniting the opposites but who is never complete in the individual unless related to another individual. The unrelated human being lacks wholeness, for he can achieve wholeness only through the soul, and the soul cannot exist without its other side, which is always found in a "You." Wholeness is a combination of I and You, and these show themselves to be part of a transcendent unity whose nature can only be grasped symbolically, as in the symbols of the rotundum, the rose, the wheel, or the *conjunctio Solis et Lunae*.

The transcendent unity Jung describes sometimes comes to us as an awareness of one world or the Unus Mundus. A glimpse of this reality comes about when the ego's threshold is reduced (through meditation or the activation of psychic contents in general) so that we participate in a wider field of cognition. We take in what Erich Neumann called "extrane knowledge," knowledge that is otherwise inaccessible to ordinary ego-consciousness.

Erich Neumann (1953) outlined a model of processes through which the religious instinct develops. By describing various planes or stages through which a personality evolves, Neumann's model points to an area of psychic reality where he feels psychological experience and religious life intersect. He calls this area a "reality plane" in which the experience of *homo mysticus* or "mystical man" apprehends the Unus Mundus or One World (1948). "Mystical man," says Neumann, goes through a transformation of psycho-biological intensity – a "shaking of the foundations" in which thought, emotion, body, and psyche join. As my patient Mairi found to her great relief, this "shaking of the foundations" can be "wholling and healing." Neumann's description of "one world" awareness is explored in Eastern traditions as Buddha-like mindfulness or awareness of "mutual arising" (Tao Te Ching). "That the universe would not exist without consciousness, nor consciousness without the universe: that is the principle of 'mutual arising'" (Watts 1975: 43). (See my use of the Buddhist concept of genesis in my comments on Dream #13, Chapter 2.)

A call for the return and recovery of this kind of paradoxical, participating consciousness comes from many quarters. Both quantum physics and philosophy remind us that impersonal or objective knowledge is a contradiction in terms. Ricoeur (1977) calls for a "second naiveté"; Berman (1989, 1990) finds a need for "re-enchantment." Earlier, Polanyi (1962) implicated us as knowers in anything we know, arguing that all our knowing is not really what we think of as "knowing" but takes place in terms of meaning. Even psychoanalyst Hans Loewald finds in the unconscious "a genuine mode of mentation, capable of grasping the unity of experience" (1978: 64), which helps us mourn a "lost original oneness" and "celebrate oneness regained" (1988: 81).

Thomas Berry (1988) imagines that the place where these dimensions mingle, merge and differentiate is the earth's dream, known to former times as the idea, the image, the feeling and the experience of what Plato (*Timaeus*) called the World Soul or the *anima mundi*.[14] When this place emerges in an individual life, I call this place the site of a dream-in-the-world. Centuries ago, Gregory of Nyssa told us that the soul grows by its constant participation in that which transcends it.[15] We might say that a dream-in-the-world emerges by way of participating consciousness.

Weaving itself in and out, up and down, and over and under, a participating consciousness senses the possible presence of One World in the midst of so many. Mairi's transformed consciousness – under circumstances best respected by Corbin's descriptions of encounter within an imaginal world – gave her experiential access to a nexus of individual, communal and ecological realities and helped her see the interrelatedness of all things. Together, she and I affirmed what Jung (CW5: 198) called the "unending All of life" both as a shared sense of soul and as a shared sense of the soul of the world.

In summary, I propose that consciousness, in order to merit the description of being fully human, must include a quality of awareness which overlights passionate human experience relative to the archetypal pattern of the Anthropos, or the Whole Human Being, openness to otherness that encounters the ego either from within as the unconscious or from without as the world. To refer this back to our object-relations paradigm, this is to say that the person must also become aware of the archetypal dimension of her mother complex, for example, or of his unconscious identification with mythic personification or the unconscious *per se*. Fully human consciousness allows us to see *through*. It plunges us into paradoxical awareness and participation in such apparently separate realms as mind and body, psyche and soul, and our environment and ourselves, so that perceptions of separateness give way to a perception of wholeness known in early times, too, as the Anthropos, or the whole human being. Fully human consciousness gives us a numinous, unitive experience: God's gift of the world becomes the gift of God's presence in the world, as well.

Jung's religious terminology: Self (and spirit), soul (and psyche)

In the series of dreams in the next chapter, the reader will see how I oriented myself in relation to the archetypal material that kept pouring forth from Mairi's psyche in the form of Self-directive dreams and dramatic bodily experience. In my struggle to understand and convey my understanding to Mairi, I occasionally used terms from my Jungian training (archetype, Self, psyche, spirit, soul) as well as notions from outside the Jungian tradition (i.e., Winnicott's indwelling, personalisation, etc.). It did not surprise me that Jung's notions served me, because religious experience in psychotherapy was something Jung encountered in his clinical work and, as his autobiography makes clear, he too experienced a breakthrough of revelatory material in his own life. Of all the psycho-religious terms coined by Jung over his many years of practice and writing, two are by far the more enigmatic and important, i.e., the Self (sometimes the Imago Dei) and the Soul (sometimes psyche, sometimes Anima). Because Mairi and I sometimes used these terms back and forth, and the ways in which I use them may be unfamiliar to my readers, I offer brief definitions and descriptions here.

Self and individuation

Many psychoanalytic writers use the word "self" interchangeably with what they mean by ego, as in self-conscious or self-esteem. When Jung writes self with a capital "S" he means something different. By his concept of the Self Jung infers the existence of an entity that transcends what we mean by ego. For Jung the idea of the Self points to a sum total of conscious and unconscious areas in a personality, including processes of the psyche that are present from pre-birth.

Metapsychological (beyond psyche) constructs like Jung's idea of the Self help us to think in a certain fashion. Just as we may understand the idea of "internal objects" as a theoretical construct that is utilized by object-relations writers to explain experience and behavior, we may understand Jung's idea of a Self as a theoretical construct that is meant to express the unity of the personality as a whole. The Self, Jung proposes, expresses itself in drives, images, symbols and behavior that convey wholeness (CW6: 789–91; CW11: 140). To use Jung's idea of the Self in the practice of psychotherapy requires that the therapist regard the whole person of the patient, conscious and unconscious alike.

For Jung the Self was the central archetype of order in the psyche, a kind of "atomic nucleus" that accrues all the imagery that humankind associates with an ordering, coherent and meaning-providing "center" in the universe. In world mythology and many religions, such imagery circles around a central notion of a Creator, Source, Great Spirit, an Intelligence, or God. Hence Jung understood the Self as the medium through which religious experience enters our awareness. He called it the Imago Dei in the psyche, the "place" where images of God accrue and from which they are "projected" into, and simultaneously organize, the chaos of primal experience.

Von Franz (1997: 170) summarizes Jung's notion of the Self as the personality's

> inmost and most powerfully influential center of meaning, and when it appears in myths and sagas and in people's dreams, it manifests as an image of the divine. Expressed in religious language, it is the "divine spark" residing in the depths of the psyche of every human being. From this center also emanate the ultimate resolves of conscience, when a person seeks to be guided not by conventional morality but really by his "inner conscience"; and it is with this center, too, that the problem of self-affirmation is ultimately connected.

Jung's static notion of the Self cannot be understood without his companion concept, "individuation," which can be thought of as the process through which the Self unfolds in an individual's life and produces the ego as its representative agency in consciousness, i.e., as its "affiliate." According to Jung, "becoming the individual you are intended to be" involves the unfolding of a sacred center of wholeness (Self) in the personality as archetypal structures in the unconscious resonate with a strengthening ego. Often this process is envisaged as the unfolding of an implicate order inherent in the personality, analogous to the implicit design of the mature oak tree inside the acorn.

Individuation is Jung's word for the naturally evolving, vital process of psychotherapy which initiates *personality transformation in the process of becoming whole or integrated* (1975: 583). Jung even called his analytical psychology a psychology of individuation,[16] using the word to mean single, or the singular uniqueness of each individual. Jung was an evolutionary thinker, and his theoretical account of individuation articulates a revolutionary process of consciously bringing the archetypal psyche to unique realization and expression in a personal life. Jung's idea involves developing a mature personality, a "well-rounded psychic whole that is capable of resistance and abounding in energy" (CW17: 286), able to choose its own path and self-reliantly remain true to its own inner law (CW17: 295). In practical terms, individuation implies that the more truly we become ourselves the more truly we can relate to others and the closer we can get to them, as we cannot have a genuine relationship with another person until we have, through an inner psychic process of uniting the opposites, become fully ourselves.

The paradoxical reality that we cannot become ourselves without relationships with others (and vice versa) makes analytical psychology more object-related than is commonly thought. Jung is explicit about the centrality of relatedness in individuation: "The unrelated human being lacks wholeness, for he can achieve wholeness only through the soul, and the soul cannot exist without its other side, which is always found in a 'you'" (CW16: 454). Real individuation requires a capacity for self–other relatedness as well as self-realization, differentiating individuation from individualism.

Even so, Jung would not agree with object-relations writers who claim that the self is not even conceivable apart from others, e.g., Winnicott's "there is no such thing as a baby" (without a mother). Because it involves an exclusive adaptation to inner reality (an allegedly "mystical process"), individuation *does* cut one off from personal conformity and collectivity, and the individuant must offer some new value or creative effort as a kind of expiation or ransom for such a radical departure from the collective milieu (CW18: 1095). The offering of new value is how the individuated person relates back to the collective, thereby redeeming his or her absence from the common weave. This suggests that individual consciousness is an instrument, a lens for viewing the world, not a thing unto itself. More broadly speaking, personality, containing the weft and weave of individual consciousness, is also not an end in itself, but a way that individual persons can express the weft and weave of an historic age, a culture, and a moment in time.

The real question is, how can the original sacred potential of individuality (Self) unfold in ongoing ego-development so that an ego–Self axis[17] is maintained? A psychotherapeutic relationship calls the ego out of stasis and into differentiation (of self from other, of ego from unconscious) and that differentiating process both brings about and maintains a link between the ego and its potential development (Self). Erich Neumann understands individuation as a dynamic process which is identical to the development of an ego–Self axis around which the shaping and development of personality circles.[18] A great deal of thought in analytical psychology has gone into understanding the stormy interpersonal process through which ego–Self identity in early childhood gives way to ego–Self estrangement and ultimately to a conscious ego–Self relationship (mature spiritual development). Central in this process is what American psychoanalyst Heinz Kohut describes as "phase-appropriate disillusionment" of the child's primitive idealizations of parental figures who carry (in Jung's language) the image of the super-ordinate Self. The delicate combination of firmness and empathy required for this process has been discussed by many psychoanalysts,[19] and the results of its failure are outlined in textbooks on borderline and narcissistic pathology as well as studies of early trauma.[20]

In contrast to Jung's and von Franz's focus on the Self as a center, Erich Neumann (1954) focuses on the Self as a *field* within the archetypal field. One important difference between working with a notion of the Self as a structural entity as Jung does and working with an idea of a Self-field is that a field implies a different quality of wholeness – not simply "my wholeness," perhaps, but a wholeness involving a link with otherness. Another way to understand this is to say that the Self is transgressive,[21] meaning that it manifests across boundaries and in both outer and inner worlds. Jung refers to this coincidence of subjective and objective happening that is linked primarily by individual feeling value rather than by cause and effect as evidence of, and experience of, synchronicity. Experiences of synchronicity simply cannot be explained causally, at least in the present state of our knowledge. Usually we experience synchronous experience as heart-stopping or alarming or oddly significant. Taking us by surprise, synchronicity interrupts our taken-for-granted sense of cause-and-effect as an underlying explanation of reality. The saying, "the heart has its reasons which Reason cannot know" also points to meaning that exists upon a basis other than logic.

Still a third way to understand this is to remember Neumann's suggestion (1953: 90) that the Self has access to "extrane" knowledge, by which he means knowledge that is more encompassing in all directions than ordinary ego-consciousness. The concept of extrane knowledge is used today in brain research and neurobiological speculations about theories of "emergence" (Tresan 1996: 409–10). Most of these theories suppose an ordering principle extraneous to the ego, whether that principle flows directly from a supra-ordinate being or from the way matter automatically sorts itself out under certain circumstances. Like Corbin's psycho-spiritual senses, the notion of extrane knowledge gives us a possible way to think about experiential perspectives that exist outside of ordinary ego-consciousness with its cause-and-effect or "if–then" thinking. The usefulness of these descriptions will become more apparent as we confront Mairi's experience in Chapters 2 and 3.

Perhaps the most important aspect of extrane cognition to which the Self gives access is the subjective experience of what Jung and Neumann (after Otto) refer to as experience of the numinosum, which brings us back to religion and direct religious experience. Both Jung and Neumann recognized that a numinous experience could be reconstitutive, meaning that it could be of aid to a wounded personality. Jung even called the activation of the archetypal field an "approach to the numinous" and regarded the reconstitutive experience of this activation as the "real therapy." In a letter to P. W. Martin, Jung (1973: 377) writes, "You are quite right, the main interest of my work is not concerned with the treatment of neuroses but rather with the approach to the numinous. But the fact is that the approach to the numinous is the real therapy and inasmuch as you attain to the numinous experiences you are released from the curse of pathology. Even the very disease takes on a numinous character."

Soul and spirit

Jung tended to see the soul and spirit as complementary aspects of the "divine spark" described above by von Franz, hence closely allied with his notion of the Self. One thing alone seems clear, says Jung (CW8: 621),

> Just as the "living being" is the quintessence of life in the body, so "spirit" is the quintessence of the life of the mind; indeed, the concept "spirit" is often used interchangeably with the concept "mind." Viewed thus, "spirit" exists in the same transliminal realm as "living being," that is, in the same misty state of indistinguishableness . . . the doubt as to whether mind and body may not ultimately prove to be the same thing also applies to the apparent contrast between "spirit" and "living being." They too are probably the same thing.

By "living being," Jung clearly means (although he does not name it such) the soul that out-pictures the "quintessence" of life in the body, whereas "spirit" describes a principle of aliveness in the mind . . . "quintessentially." Spirit and soul are therefore complementary aspects of a divine spark in the psychosomatic person that must be acknowledged as such. Humankind does not belong only to the species *homo sapiens* (*sapientia*, knowledge) but also to *homo religiosus* (*religo*, link back, as if to the foundations of Being).

Among primal peoples, Jung reminds us, spirit has been equivalent to "spirits" – ethereal beings, breath-like "presences", light or dark, who dwell with us and exercise invisible yet powerful influence. On a more developed level, transcendent spirit is thought of as supra-natural and trans-mundane, a cosmic principle of order as such. When spirit is given the name of the "Great Spirit" or God, spirit can become a principle of cosmic order that opposes darkness and chaos (like the Self).

Jung was keen to impress upon his readers that the psyche has a religious function and cannot be encompassed by studies of the brain or the hormonal glands; otherwise, Jung laments, we get a "psychology without the psyche" (1933), or worse, a psychology without the soul.

> I do not contest the relative validity either of the realistic standpoint, the *esse in re*, or of the idealistic standpoint, the *esse in intellectu solo*; I would only like to unite these extreme opposites by an *esse in anima* . . . the psychological standpoint. We live immediately only in the world of images . . . (CW8: 624)

And again,

> All that I experience is psychic. Even physical pain is a psychic image which I experience; my sense-impressions – for all that they force upon me a world of impenetrable objects occupying space – are psychic images, and these alone constitute my immediate experience, for they alone are the immediate objects of my consciousness. My own psyche even transforms and falsifies reality, and it does this to such a degree that I must resort to artificial means to determine what things are like apart from myself. Then I discover that a sound is a vibration of air of such and such a frequency, or that a colour is a wave of light of such and such a length. We are in truth so wrapped about by psychic images that we cannot penetrate at all to the essence of things external to ourselves. All our knowledge consists of the stuff of the psyche which, because it alone is immediate, is superlatively real. (CW8: 680)

In these two defining statements Jung identifies the psyche with the "world of images" and imagination, and in this way he conflates psyche and soul, as well as soul and anima. For Jung, the anima (as soul) was the feminine source of these images, i.e., the "projection-making factor" (CW9ii: 20–5). This equation of psyche and soul as imagination has been taken up by Archetypal Psychologists[22] in their discussion of "soul-making," and their writings have become a major trend within Jungian thought. Despite the substantial contributions this movement has made to the world of depth-psychological studies and the humanities, I believe that its focus on psychotherapy as "soul-making" has deleterious consequences. If my patient Mairi's experience of soul is at all typical, soul was far beyond her ability to conceive of or even bring about. More to the point is the poet Keats's characterization of the *world* as a "vale of soul-making." Experience of soul happens, often unbidden. We are not the agents of its appearance.

Jung's conviction that we experience nothing but the psyche and that there is "no Archimedean point outside the psyche" from which to experience anything else has been a bone of contention with a number of otherwise sympathetic followers. My experience of the psyche differs from Jung's and so did Mairi's. I find that while it may be difficult to penetrate to the essence of things external to myself, this is not to say that something of the essence of things external to myself may not penetrate me; e.g., just as fire burns my hand before my mind can conceive of "hot," God can enter anywhere. As Mairi "fell" through psyche into her experience of soul (see Chapter 3), Mairi learned that religious experience is conscious and pre-imagistic. Though the body may be represented in psychic images (symptoms), the body is not psyche; body is weight, heft, warmth and cold, appetite, matter, touch, hunger and sensation, and the body ensouled is the residence of anything we can possibly know as religious experience, particularly in terms of encounter with a sense of Presence, or an Other.

Because of his consistently phenomenological standpoint and his epistemological debt to Immanuel Kant, Jung was hesitant to claim any ontological status for such experiences of Otherness. Thus Jung seldom talks about God or the soul except to say that there is a universal (psychic) image of God in the unconscious (Self), and even an "instinct" for the numinous in the human psyche. He hoped to demonstrate this empirically by noting the remarkable correspondences between individual dream images of a numinous center in the psyche and the central archetype found in all the major mythologies of the world.[23] To be fair to Jung, although he often used the word soul in imprecise ways, he also had a clear idea of what he meant by it. Jung spoke of the soul as an organ of perception. "The soul [not the psyche] possesses by nature a religious function," says Jung (CW12: 14);[24] just as the eye permits us to see light, Jung says, the soul makes it possible for us to perceive God (CW12: 14). After an experience of soul, we can never get away from soul (or God). We know that we do not directly perceive matter but only material things, and we know that we cannot conceive of the mind but only of mental events. Neither can we test directly the existence of the soul. We verify the soul's existence by way of psychological experience, but soul "happens," in much the same way that thought is produced by the brain. And the soul manifests religious experience.

Self-directive dreams

The kind of dreams I call Self-directive (which will be marked as such in the following chapter) first came to my attention in Mairi's archetypal material. I might have called them Self-referring dreams, but their impact seemed stronger than "referring" implies. When first they began to appear late in Mairi's process, I did not understand their portent. From my present perspective I see that they pointed toward an initiatory experience on the brink of happening, a centering which had yet to be realized, that would result in the emergence of what I call a dream-in-the-world, and Mairi would call experience of soul.

Despite their occasional flashes of personal imagery, all the dreams in the series in Chapter 2 are archetypal dreams. They are remarkable for their coherence and vivid content, and much of the imagery refers us to a depth of mythic imagination without personal association. What I call Self-directive dreams are archetypal dreams with a difference. The first difference is that in these dreams, the dreamer as dreamer, whether as ego or imaged body, is dropped from the dream text. Self-directive dreams contain no imaged reference to the dreamer at all, nor images of other people. The witnessing consciousness of the dreamer within the dream (the dream ego) is not pictured. Lacking imagery that symbolizes ego-consciousness, Self-directive dreams may feel unconnected to the dreamer. Mairi's sense that her Self-directive dreams might belong more to someone else or the world than they did to her came about by default: she felt left out. Ordinary archetypal dreams, while they may swirl with collective contents, have some personal reference or associative memory image to indicate that psychological integration might be within reach. But Mairi's Self-directive dreams were full of collective contents to which she felt she had no personal access. Affording no self-reference at all, these dreams left Mairi feeling empty, or "beached" (her words), facing away from herself toward experience in a world of color, animals, roses, and magical jeweled birds. From a spiritual point of view, the loss of ego portrayed in Mairi's Self-directive dreams suggests that she was becoming (as Jesus said) "like a child."

Somewhere Jung calls dreams "hidden doors in the intimate sanctum of the soul," opening into a primeval cosmic night that is also soul, long before there is a conscious ego and far beyond what consciousness can reach. Mairi's Self-directive dreams were such doors, opening both in and out along a long corridor that led eventually to a bigger door both to herself and to the world. She described dreaming these dreams as feeling as if she were being "turned inside out," so that her feeling for the dream itself became her outer environment. By the end of the dream series the relentless procession of Self-directive dreams turned Mairi's attention toward all that she shared with others and the world, stretching her capacity for self–other relatedness and inter-subjectivity to the point where she felt a conscious relationship with or sense of the world soul, or *anima mundi*.[25]

Another difference that I see between Self-directive and archetypal dreams implicates the dreamer's conscious ego and what we might call the depth of the dreamer's subjectivity.[26] We know that archetypal dreams do not depend upon consciousness or subjectivity; they may appear in children, adults, at important junctures of life, in madness, in sanity, before giving birth, and before death. A defining characteristic of a Self-directive dream, then, is that it is an archetypal dream that occurs in the living context of someone who is consciously in dialogue with her individuating psyche. Self-directive dreams take place along an ego–Self axis (Neumann 1954; Edinger 1972), which indicates that in some form, self-reflection (and perhaps individuation) has begun. Self–other awareness is not necessary for the appearance of ordinary archetypal dreams, but the dreamer of a Self-directive dream implicitly demonstrates a capacity for self–other awareness and the beginnings of a capacity for inter-subjectivity.

A closely related characteristic is that the appearance of a Self-directive dream presupposes the existence and importance of a discerning ego that is able to receive the dream and take it seriously. Mairi found it almost impossible to identify with the contents of her Self-directive dreams, yet she felt that they were as much "hers" as her other dreams were. She found their odd nature inexplicable and unusually compelling. Certainly both of us took them seriously and tried to attend to their implications.

As impersonal as an annunciation or an "announcement from above" (or below), a Self-directed dream is like a living painting, beautiful and remote. Once I became aware of this kind of dream I remembered several of my own. Since working with Mairi I have seen them appear sporadically in the material of two other patients, both women. But neither before nor since have I seen Self-directive dreams occur in a series with such gathering intensity. A colleague once told me that a patient of hers (a man) who had suffered a stroke no longer had dreams with a dream narrator, and certainly the lack of a narrator is one aspect of Self-directive dreams. Whether this person's dreams fulfilled other criteria for Self-directive dreams, I do not know.

An important, consciousness-expanding aspect of a Self-directive dream is that in order to anchor it into an immediately personal context, the patient has to struggle with the possibility that her dreams' significance might be greater than she can imagine in her individual life. Mairi's missing or scanty personal associations drove both of us to search for amplifications from cultural and mythological sources, to reach toward what others from other times and cultures might have thought and felt about such imagery. This kind of collaborative search for meaning has a healing effect in itself. The process of consulting the associations of humankind when personal associations are missing carries a potential for opening the eyes of the patient (and analyst) to a wider horizon, to cultural and even religious worlds in which they participate despite their lack of conscious knowledge. While such a technique may be an intellectual defense, especially if the lived feeling experience of the patient in the moment (including personal associations) is overlooked, amplification of Self-directive dreams may be the only way to unlock any insight or feeling at all. Where the occurrence of a Self-directive dream left Mairi feeling stranded, our shared efforts at amplification helped her connect to aspects of her life and nature that she held in common with others, many others, even from times and places that she did not personally know. Thus began her vivid personal experience of belonging to One World consciously.

As we will see in the next chapter, Mairi's Self-directive dreams *initiated* her into the numinous otherness of both inner and outer worlds. Occurring one after the other like beads along a string, each remembered dream constructed a consciously experienced, vertical bridge between unconscious and conscious energy (body and mind), as well as a horizontal bridge between night and day, and self and other. Each dream we discussed expanded the horizons of these bridges, and both directions, vertical and horizontal, defined the three-dimensional structure of Mairi's growing Self-affiliated ego.

Mairi's experience of soul was indisputably transformative. Perhaps the fact that people become more deeply and completely themselves is simply the nature of psychological transformation. Jungian psychoanalyst Murray Stein (1998: xxiv) reminds us that "Transformation is realization, revelation and emergence, not self-improvement, change for the better, or becoming an ideal person. The transforming person is someone who realizes the inherent self to the maximum extent possible and in turn influences others to do the same." During Mairi's initiation into the mysteries of the feminine and the depths of religious experience, I learned much about myself as well. I am grateful to her.

Notes

1 The German name "Hadewijch" consists of two roots, *hadu* and *wich*, both meaning "fighter" (van Baest 1998: 31).

2 Hadewijch has been variously situated in Brussels, Antwerp, Bruges and Nivelles. She wrote in Brabant, a dialect name for a district in Flanders now central to Belgium. The main source for all Hadewijch scholarship is Jozef van Mierlo, who edited her entire corpus, and Mother Columba Hart, my resource for Hadewijch's works in English. All page numbers referring to quotations from Hadewijch's works in this chapter refer to Hart's *Hadewijch: The Complete Works* (Hadewijch 1980).

3 DePaepe (1967: 331) in Hadewijch 1980: 8.

4 William Blake also declares that the body is a part of the soul: "Man has no Body distinct from his Soul; for that called Body is a portion of the Soul discerned by the five Senses."

5 Religious disciplines offer a variety of techniques to suppress, modify, or purify the body in order to attain a state of perfection, happiness, purity or human–divine union. In such disciplines, "body" may be used, subjected, transformed, or improved. The Christian ritual of the Eucharist accomplishes this by infusing something pure into the body. Buddhist disciplines seem to defuse the grip of ego identification. In Soto Zen, the body's breathing is the prototype of *wu-wei* or *Chin*, meaning "non-action." In Judaism, embodiment is explicitly denied as an

attribute of the Creator, who is devoid of any representable content or form. In Hinduism, where differences in embodiment do not define the relation between gods and humans, incarnations abound. The Taoist body is a microcosm of the geographical country, the social and administrative state, ultimately of the whole cosmos. In Taoist thought and practice the body is a central symbol and ritual focus rooted in older traditions of spirit possession, alchemy, and the search for longevity and immortality. In Christianity the Body of Christ incorporates three major sites of religious significance: the human body of Jesus transformed at the resurrection, the consecrated bread whose Eucharistic reception ritualizes a form of symbolic cannibalism, and the Church as the People of God, the community that is the vehicle of God's redemptive activity on earth. "Because there is one loaf, we who are many are one body, for we all partake of the one loaf" (1 Corinthians 10: 17).

6 Most depth psychotherapists stress transformation in the unconscious – whether in terms of ego–Self alignment (Jung) or the re-integration of inner objects (object-relations theorists). This happens, of course, and can be tracked in dream imagery, but religious experience transforms consciousness too, and the experience of transformation takes place *in* the conscious body.

7 See McGinn (1999), Zohar (1990), Smith (2001: 182), etc.

8 See Ferenczi's account (1988) of his treatment of "R.N."

9 The distinction between myself and other selves or self and world is a recent achievement of the human spirit. Barfield (1953: 170) tells us that it began to "light up" in the Middle Ages; we can see it in the etymology of Scholastic words like *individual* and *person*. Consciousness as we know it dawned faintly on Europe during the Reformation, but not until the seventeenth century did the new light really begin to spread and brighten. "One of the surest signs that an idea or feeling is coming to the surface of consciousness," says Barfield, "is the tendency of an old one to form compounds and derivatives. After the Reformation, we notice growing up in the language a whole crop of words hyphenated with *self*; such are self-conceit, self-liking, self-love, and others at the end of the sixteenth century, and self-confidence, self-command, self-contempt, self-esteem, self-knowledge, self-pity . . . in the next."

10 Consciousness is known as an onset phenomenon, meaning off/on, sleeping/ waking. From neurological studies we know that the brain is not inactive when consciousness is absent, even during deep non-dreaming sleep. When we awaken, consciousness comes into being and gives sentience to existence. Consciousness has made a discrete change. It has turned on. The brain has changed its level of activity (Walker 2000: 204–5). A small increase in the brain's activity level gives rise to something entirely new . . . as if some potential of the brain – something that may have occurred before in isolation, as scattered monads of consciousness – now condenses into a whole ocean (of consciousness). We are left, says Walker, with the wave function – the state vector of quantum mechanics itself – as the access route from the physical world into the mind. We must look into the machinery of the key component of the brain, its basic switching element, the synapse (2000: 194). In those minute switches, at the miniscule intersynaptic cleft, that is where the quantitative link between mind and brain is to be found . . . The decision to fire or not to fire constitutes two potential states that the synapse can go into. This opens the possibility for the brain's behavior to be affected by quantum mechanic processes and opens the door for all the observer characteristics of the quantum world to enter as well (219). The observer effect enters physical reality to cause state vector collapse and then it vanishes so that you cannot actually find any outward physical trace of consciousness itself (285).

11 Mental life can be seen from an inter-subjective perspective. Various approaches to inter-subjectivity share the belief that human "being" is interrelated rather than isolated, that the human mind is interactive rather than monadic, and that the psychoanalytic process should be understood as occurring between subjects, rather than within the individual (Atwood and Stolorow 1984; Mitchell 1988). Field workers in anthropology also employ this understanding in studying research and interactions between themselves and people of other cultures (see Jackson 1998).

12 Jung's interest in development lay more in developing a spacious personality rather than in replay and repair along developmental lines.

13 I first came across the idea of participating consciousness in Barfield's *Saving the Appearances* (1965). Bateson (1972) and Berman (1989, 1990), among others, also use this phrase.

14 Jung (CW13: 263) also traces the *anima mundi* to Mercurius, as did the earlier Islamic writer Avicenna: "The spirit of the Lord which fills the whole world and in the beginning swam upon the waters . . . they call (him) the spirit of Truth, which is hidden from the world . . . ." The Holy Spirit as procreator impregnates the overshadowing (*obumbratio*) of Mary.

15 Quoted in Harvey 2000: 32.

16 From the Latin *individuus*, meaning *indivisible*, one only, unlike another.

17 This term originated with Erich Neumann and has been elaborated by Edward Edinger.

18 The idea of an ego–Self axis is of practical use in therapy. Beginning ego–Self axis functioning actually lessens the pressure of unconscious energies upon the conscious situation. A major indication of a functioning ego–Self axis becomes the ability to relate to dream material; to watch for dreams, write them down, talk about them in session. Dream by dream, pressure is released from an impacted intrapsychic situation, particularly where unconscious identification with the powerful energies of the Self are almost inevitable, e.g., in severe trauma, illness, or situations indicative of disordered narcissism.

19 See especially Edinger 1972: 70ff.

20 See especially Kalsched 1996.

21 By "transgressive," Jung means that archetypal energies overlap all kinds of boundaries, with each other and between reality-planes. As in synchronistic phenomena, archetypes "are not found exclusively in the psychic sphere, but can occur just as much in circumstances that are not psychic" (CW8: 137).

22 See especially Hillman 1975.

23 See for example the dream series in *Psychology and Alchemy* (CW12).

24 Tertullian, 310: *Anima naturaliter christiana.*

25 Jung (CW8: 388) defines the *anima mundi* as a natural force that is responsible for all the phenomena of life and the psyche, a collective dream of our lives *in the world* (italics mine) as individuals, communities, and creatures of the earth.

26 By subjectivity in depth I mean what psychoanalysis describes as a resilient and flexible ego, or an "observing ego" or a "conflict-free sphere of the ego," or a "capacity for affect-tolerance." To be sure, we intensify self-development and cultivate self-related subjectivity both in and out of therapy. Many who left records of the kind of experience to which Hadewijch and Mairi refer did not undergo psychotherapy. And many who do not or cannot avail themselves of a therapeutic relationship are not psychologically unsophisticated. When pursued religiously, for example, yogic disciplines bring about a similar cultivation of subjectivity, as do practices like Zen meditation. Samkhya (Reymond 1995: 111–12), an ancient Indian discipline underlying the teachings of the Buddha in Pali,

as well as the initiatic training of the Sufi Mevlevi Dervishes are other practical (meaning psychological) religious philosophies, the practice of which cultivates subjectivity to the point where it affirms the reality of all that is.

Chapter 2

The dreamer and her dreams

Before we turn to Self-directive dreams we need to meet Mairi as a person. Much of this material will be disguised, condensed, and selective. Confidentiality matters, so the following sketch includes only those aspects of Mairi's personal history which are relevant to the appearance of her Self-directive dreams and her transformative experience. However, Mairi's dreams and her vision and the sequence in which everything occurred are as true to life as I could make them, as are her words and the experiences they describe. These I have not disguised.

At the time she consulted me, Mairi was a woman in her late thirties, the single, twice-divorced parent of two children, a boy and a girl. She made her living as a yoga teacher. Tall, slim, blond and fair-skinned, with a quick, winning smile, Mairi readily identified with her Scottish/Irish parental background, from whence came her name with its distinctive Celtic spelling and pronunciation. "I want to understand myself better," she said. "I think I'm depressed. I don't seem to do very well in relationships with men and somehow my life has never really made sense to me. I've got two little kids at home, and their needs are stirring up a lot of stuff that I don't understand about myself. Both my parents died unexpectedly within the last five years, and I've been missing them a lot, lately. It's hard to explain, but my life just doesn't add up. There's something I just don't 'get.'"

Mairi said that she especially wanted to work with a woman rather than a man, although she hadn't always felt that way. "Earlier," she said, "I would have been afraid to talk with a woman, I guess for fear of judgment." Mairi had overcome this fear in a brief but rewarding series of weekly counseling sessions with a woman therapist during her last year of college, when she felt on the brink of "leaving everything and running away . . . I didn't know where, I didn't know why, I just could hardly stay put and finish." With the help of counseling and summer courses, Mairi graduated.

Mairi also worked with a male therapist for a year during her first divorce, so she was not new to therapy. Nor was she unacquainted with her dreams. Amidst sporadic bouts of journal-keeping, Mairi had been recording her dreams for about ten years, ever since she discovered the possibility in a college "dream-class." She was, in other words, interested enough in her inner life to wonder whether her dreams might hold a key to the somehow estranged and painfully mysterious outer life she felt herself living from day to day.

In Mairi's previous counseling no formal history had been taken, so our first sessions were used to gather the shards of early memory and historical realities of Mairi's life into a coherent autobiography. The eldest of five children, Mairi was born in the eastern part of the United States into a white, lower-middle-class suburban Protestant American family. Education was clearly valued by her parents, but her mother and father had been minimally schooled. Clearly intelligent herself, Mairi had "loved school" and studied hard when she was young. "School was where I lived," she said; "books were my refuge, and weekly trips to the library kept me going." Mairi's early intellectual life continued into adulthood and became a vehicle for the rapport that developed between us.

Unusual self-reliance and self-sufficiency were salient features of Mairi's childhood. She earned pocket money by hiring out for yard work and as a baby-sitter before she was ten years old. Later, during the holidays, she sold Christmas cards from door to door. Taught by her mother to use the sewing machine to make most of her own clothing when she was very young, Mairi also made and sold rag dolls. Although this sheer enterprise became a source of mastery and worldly self-esteem for Mairi, the negative to this positive were feelings of having been unable to depend upon her mother. Object-relations therapist Arnold Model (1984: 85–105) comments that, by definition, to have a childhood means to be able to depend upon someone who loves you who can help put you back together again if you fall apart. Regrettably, Mairi became good at holding herself together.

When she was old enough to be hired outside the home, Mairi worked evenings and weekends as a waitress. While in high school, she clerked during the summers and worked as a "wrapper" and department-store salesgirl during the holidays. Continuing evening and weekend work, Mairi put herself through a Bachelor's degree program in the humanities from a local state college. Eventually following her example, all Mairi's younger siblings educated themselves, too. A study of yoga and regular yoga classes entered Mairi's life in college, when she gave up her early dream of becoming a ballerina and settled instead for a minor in dance.

When she and I began our work, Mairi's life in the outer world was fairly stable, albeit depressed. Neither of her previous husbands contributed financial support for the children (one from each marriage) because neither was gainfully employed. However, each of Mairi's parents left at death a sizable insurance settlement to be divided among the five children. Mairi's share enabled her to buy a very modest home with some left over to invest. With the help of proceeds from her small investments and her work as a yoga teacher, Mairi paid her mortgage, her therapy fees, and supported her daily life with her children.

Although Mairi was alone "for the time being," she said that she had made her peace with a single life. She told me that although her sexual life had been fulfilling, now that she was alone, her sexuality was "undemanding." "Sex as sex apparently works fine," she said, but an intimate, loving, and sexually affectionate relationship had eluded her. Despite several long-term arrangements and even a brief try at living with another man, no relationship inspired a third marriage. Mairi characterized her two (also brief) marriages as "each time chosen unwisely. I was so worried about not being able to love someone and 'be committed' that I now see that I jumped in blindly and then had to figure out how to get out."

The idea of divorce was unacceptable to her parents. When Mairi left her marriages, her mother and father were upset, but their concern was for the ex-husbands and the children, with no recognition that either the living situation or the leave-taking might have been difficult for their daughter. Mairi was distressed at what she called "my two failures," but she also realized that each time, more "personal courage" had been required to leave her marriages than would have been required to "stick it out and make the best of it." Mairi did not discover her anger and feelings of betrayal at her parents' lack of empathy and loyalty to her personal situation until late into her therapy. With respect to her own decisions to divorce, Mairi's most immediate worries had had to do with how her actions would affect her children.

Mairi's parents died of heart problems in their early fifties, her father first and her mother three years later. Mairi was attached to both of them. Although the surface relationship with each parent seemed good enough, from neither had Mairi experienced a supporting ground of emotional intimacy that nourished her sense of herself as a child or a young girl, let alone as a woman. Still, she felt their loss deeply, and she pondered their deaths, which occurred suddenly and without warning. "My friends have parents who are still alive or dying slowly," she said; "because they are ill, there is warning and time to say good-bye. My parents' deaths felt like amputations in my life, twice over." A good deal of time during our first year together was spent remembering and grieving their loss.

Mairi's contact with her four siblings (now scattered across the country) was infrequent other than by telephone, but she had acquaintances and a circle of close, supportive friendships with other women and with several couples. She had known two or three of her friends since grade school. And she had her children. She also had her yoga practice and the relationships she formed with students and other yoga practitioners.

As Mairi's personal story unfolded, I found myself thinking of the *I Ching*, Hexagram #3, Difficulty at the Beginning. Even her birth had been difficult. Five months into her mother's first pregnancy (with Mairi), her mother miscarried a twin. "Mum spent the remainder of the term in bed," said Mairi, "trying to keep me from falling out of her womb, too. It must have been a difficult time for her because as she lay in bed, my father was shipped off to military training for the Korean War in a different state." Her solitary mother, Mairi said, was "anxious about daddy's absence, about the war, about giving birth to me, and about how she would manage alone." Her mother told Mairi that labor had been long, painful, and dangerous. Mairi's grandmother (maternal) took care of Mairi and her mother in her home in a nearby town for the first few months when they left the hospital. Her father was absent for her birth and the early months of her life.

Mairi was never breast-fed. Because her mother's milk "failed to come in," Mairi was formula-and-bottle-fed on a rigid schedule from birth. While grandmother took care of mother, infant Mairi was placed in the hands of a day-nurse for several weeks and then into the care of a child-care person for several months. When Mairi's mother recovered enough to begin caring for herself and her new baby, the child-care person was dismissed and Mairi and her mother went home. Mairi never knew whether her miscarried twin had been identical or fraternal, nor could she speak of her own birth without feeling responsible for her mother's difficult pregnancy, delivery, and pain. She felt guilty for having survived, while her twin had not.

Her mother told Mairi that she had been born with a "caul," a waxy covering formed from the amnion that sometimes covers the head of a child at birth. Under the caul Mairi had "a full head of straight blond hair which stuck up like the mane of a pony." Mairi's Irish (maternal) grandfather told her that in Celtic lore the saying that "one born with a caul will never drown" comforted many a fisherman through a stormy sea, since most of them had never learned to swim in the first place. "Maybe," said Mairi, "that caul protected me in the womb. I didn't drown, but my twin did."

To further burden her beginnings, Mairi was allergic to whatever she was fed. "From day one, I had raging eczema all over my body. I was told that finally I had to live on tea and goat's milk for several years. Everything else affected me violently. Mum said that as a toddler I rolled around on the rug in agony, trying to scratch myself." Mairi continued to have severe food allergies until she was four. Gradually the allergies decreased and by now she was relatively untroubled. When she was two and a half, Mairi's father finally left for Korea "for the duration. I'm told that I cried myself into a fever because he didn't say good-bye," Mairi said, "although I don't remember that."

To add to the difficulty, Mairi's eczema and recurrent food allergies required her to wear arm braces for several years, to prevent her from scratching. As we reviewed her early history, Mairi concluded wistfully that she could not have been often or easily held in her mother's arms. This led her to say that she had felt uncuddled and restrained from natural spontaneous movement and expression for most of her early life. She showed me a poignant snapshot of herself at the age of four, an awkward little girl, arms in braces, in a white flower-girl dress at a relative's wedding. She stood facing the camera with a sign that said "Please Don't Feed Me" hung around her neck "as if I were an animal at the zoo."

"I had to wear the placard because of my food allergies," Mairi explained. "Mother had to make sure I didn't eat something which would make my skin break out, and I liked to eat everything. I was always hungry. I don't remember, of course, but probably this picture describes not only how I looked, then, but how I felt." Mairi hastened to assure me that both then and later her mother had done her best to make up for this early "physical restraint." "But," she said, "surely I was difficult. How can you want to touch or hold a child whose skin is all broken out, or whose arms are in braces? Who can't eat anything you give it? Even if you wanted to, you couldn't reach out to a baby like that. That is what I felt: untouched most of the time, and unreached for."

Following her soldier husband first from one job to the next and then from one training camp to another until he was sent overseas, Mairi's mother had constantly moved herself and baby Mairi from one makeshift place to another – trailer parks, rented rooms, and small apartments. In one of these places her baby brother was born, when Mairi was three. Mairi remembered almost nothing of her brother's birth, but she remembered scattered elements of the places she had lived in: a pencil-drawing of a ship with clouds behind it on a piece of board hung on a wall in a house-trailer; the way filmy white curtains blew in on her head in a hotel bed; feeling frightened and lost in a small woods behind a beach cottage. These "glimpses of place" and the memory of a small green wooden trailer piled high with household belongings and topped with her rocking horse, pulled behind the car her mother drove when they moved, along with two brief dreams which happened while she was under anesthesia for a tonsillectomy at the age of four or five, formed the core of Mairi's earliest memories.

When Mairi was six years old her father returned. Wounded in the leg, shell-shocked, and too troubled to settle back easily into family life, he took a sales position in a nearby town which required that he be on the road most of the time: so another move was required, and then another. Finally Mairi's father took a lasting job at a nearby gas station, and when Mairi was seven her first sister (the third child) arrived. Mairi did remember hoping that this new child would be a boy so that at least she, Mairi, would be "the only girl," but other than that, she remembered little of her mother's pregnancy. Peculiarly unaffiliated with relatives, near neighbors, or a lasting sense of place, Mairi felt little familiarity with her surroundings or friends. A sense of "being at home" was oddly lacking.

As I listened to Mairi's history I realized how deeply all that "moving about" had affected her without her awareness. Feeling solitary despite the company of her mother and siblings wherever she went, uprootedness had become for Mairi a way of life. Perhaps in some deep psychological place such a traveling child need not feel quite as estranged as Mairi had, for if all the world is alien, then everywhere can also be home, if only "with mother." But at the beginning of our work together Mairi had little appreciation either of herself in the context of the world, or of her early nomadic experience.

In keeping with these frequent and at times drastic environmental changes, Mairi had no early memories of her father. "I knew we were a family," she said, "and when daddy first came home from the war he still wrote notes to mum and sometimes me while she managed alone with the children – just the two of us (herself and little brother) then. I never saw my mum with anyone else, that's for sure; but until he started living at home with us and running the gas station, I hardly remember my father as a person."

In addition to environmental and family disruption, when she was four years old (after the birth of her brother) Mairi was sexually violated. Using the old ploy of "little girl, would you like some candy," a teenaged boy had lured her into a garden shed down the block from her house. There he held Mairi by the back of her neck, forced her mouth over his penis, and ejaculated. Stuffing a peppermint candy into Mairi's mouth the boy then let her go. She wandered back out onto the street and into a neighborhood that she no longer recognized. She remembered that she cried for a long time as she stood in sunlight on a street-corner, not knowing how to find her house. Finally a passer-by took her by the hand and led her home.

Somewhere around our fourth or fifth therapy session Mairi remembered this incident with great emotion. "I've never told anyone before," she said; "I couldn't, then, I did not have words to say it, to describe what happened. But I remember *everything* – what I was wearing, how afraid I was, how I could hardly breathe when he held me by the back of my neck, and the taste, the stuff in my mouth. I lost my way home from nursery school where I had walked just that morning, only a few blocks away. I forgot how to get home, which way to turn at the corner. I remember how bright the sun was, almost blinding, and the tall old man who took my hand, asked me my address, and walked me home."

The sudden irruption of this memory surprised us both. Mairi was just as surprised by the realization that she had forgotten all about it for so many years. Telling me about it brought relief as well as tears. When I asked why, despite her lack of articulate descriptive words, she had indicated to no one that something frightening had happened, Mairi replied, "Mum wouldn't have believed me anyway – I doubt if she'd believe me if I told her now." Reflecting further upon her four-year-old self, she added, "also Mum was busy nursing my brother and I wasn't supposed to bother her. And I was proud of being able to walk those two blocks back and forth to nursery school all by myself every day. I was ashamed of forgetting my way home."

Summarizing Mairi's early difficulties, we might say that her primary experience was of psychosomatic disruption: pre-birth trauma, difficult birth experience, skin inflammation and body braces, early feeding problems, and lack of bodily holding by the mother after birth. To this we add both cumulative and violent disruption of the emotional holding environment, i.e., of nascent self–other experience in terms of maternal attachment, and to that a poverty of emotional and psychological mirroring or consistent "playback" in a context of continuous environmental disruption and change. Mairi learned to cope with these early deprivations through a variety of self-care defenses ("all by myself") and by dissociation in her emotional life.

Despite Mairi's "together" presentation of herself and her stated desire for "self-knowledge," I sensed that underneath (from an emotional point of view), Mairi was in despair. This was visible to me in the way she held herself, and audible in the lack of animation in her voice when she spoke. Too far removed from the reality of a feeling life even to know what kind of trouble she was in, Mairi's very remoteness paralleled, or indicated, a cut-off-ness that I sensed at the core of her being. An absence of feeling took the place of an active sadness – a numbness, like the ice over a pond, or the growth of colorless, unfeeling scar tissue over old pain.

Clearly during her early years Mairi's developing ego and growing personality compensated for this core of painful, pre-verbal somatic experience. Even now Mairi did not act despairing. Although she knew that her mother had thought of her as a "sickly child" (and had been memorably annoyed when a pediatrician referred to Mairi as "high-strung"), Mairi remembered herself as active and eager. She recounted memories of exuberant play with little friends whom she gathered around her wherever she could, and later, play with siblings. After the family settled into one place, Mairi remembered beloved dancing lessons ("to make me strong"), along with piano lessons, hours of swimming in a nearby public pool, and horseback riding on a neighbor's horse. Over many years her prolonged fascination with dance gradually gave way to a devotion to Hatha yoga, a physical discipline which is embedded in a body of psychological, philosophical, and religious expression emerging from another culture, another country and the dim beginnings of time.[1]

Mairi's non-religious life existed in exile from twentieth-century religious communities. Having grown up in a vaguely Protestant atmosphere, Mairi belonged to no church and claimed no particular religious affiliation. Her religious education consisted of cultural references to Judaism and Christianity gleaned from secular studies in the humanities, while her personal reading had given her familiarity with a smattering of Hindu, Buddhist and Christian philosophies. Mairi's interest in Hatha yoga expressed her individual spiritual practice and discipline, and yoga studies formed the core of her professional teaching. Her community was a circle of supportive friendships and relationships formed with students and other yoga practitioners. Although Mairi had become acquainted with the religious and philosophical aspects of yoga, she had never joined a meditation group or sought a guru. She studied under several yoga teachers and changed from one to another when the spirit moved her. After her experience of soul, however, Mairi felt that she belonged to the world and others in a remarkably different way. Whether or not she ever becomes a member of an institutionalized church, Mairi came away from therapy feeling (to her surprise) that she was more Christian than anything else. Practically speaking, Mairi sought companionship among groups of people who seemed to "find each other" on an affiliative basis rather than on the basis of institutional belonging or even geography. Here her experience brought her close to the communal attitude expressed by Hadewijch toward her beloved Beguines.

During Mairi's adolescence each parent confided in her about his or her emotional life and problematic "feelings" about the other parent. Mairi's ability to be a confidante and keep family secrets isolated her from an emotionally free childhood among her younger siblings who were not so chosen. Clearly Mairi functioned as the "first-born" in a somewhat dysfunctional family. But her parents stayed together. Mom took care of the children and Dad worked hard to make ends meet. Mairi, the oldest, was of all the children the "good child," with high academic achievement and "compulsive mothering" (her words) of her seldom appreciative younger siblings. She felt herself to be her father's "favorite."

Always helping out and – above all – helping her parents keep up the appearance of being "one big happy family," Mairi grew adept at what family therapists call "doublethink." As we worked, Mairi gradually began to understand how she could use her feelings of guilt to defend against and distract herself from deeper, mostly negative feelings about her real situation, about those upon whom she depended, and about herself. Schooled in how to not "rock the boat," Mairi learned too well how to understand, forgive, forget, and surrender her will to those she felt were in power. She also learned to "trance out," which she described as losing awareness of her body so that she would not feel the unending yet inescapable intrusion of the psychological demands and needs of so many others upon her, or (my observation) her instinctively negative reactions to those demands and expectations. "Trancing out" led Mairi into disembodied behavior and altered states of consciousness in which, in her later life, unconscious feelings were "acted out" rather than experienced consciously. Her marriage-choices, for example, had little to do with Mairi consciously relating to a partner and much to do with "behaved," unconscious ideas and expectations of both herself and others.

With this brief sketch of Mairi and her background in mind, let us look at her dreams. Over the five-year span of her treatment, Mairi and I worked with dreams in an ordinary fashion, gathering her associations and memories, using my memory (did this dream bring to mind earlier dreams, motifs, or situations?), using our mutual speculations about the immediate context of each dream (what happened yesterday? last night? did this image seem to come from Mairi's psyche mostly, or in response to an outer situation?), and so forth. When in the dreams archetypal material intensified, I took note. When Self-directive dreams appeared, both of us found them difficult to understand. Only in retrospect did many of our associations and amplifications to the following Self-directive dreams become clear.

A word about my method of dream selection: I selected the following series of twenty-three dreams and a vision out of hundreds. Many of Mairi's dreams were ordinary and prosaic, concerned with personal complexes and issues of daily life. But as we proceeded, vivid archetypal dreams occasionally punctuated this orderly procession of ordinary dreams. Eventually, Self-directive dreams arrived, although I didn't recognize them as such until after Mairi's transformative experience of soul, to be described in the next chapter. The notion of Self-directive dreams came to me simply because I did not know how else to think of them, or what else to call them. The other dreams I chose by noticing which among the many "stood out." Others were arresting also, and as I wrote I remembered still more, the relevance of which is now clear. But there had to be a limit. Most of Mairi's psychological material orbited around the same major themes, images, and unconscious ideas, as is often true in a depth psychotherapeutic process.

The following individual dreams are barely edited. I have maintained the sequence in which the dreams occurred, but there are varying gaps of time between one dream and another. The duration of these gaps lessened near the end of the series, when Self-directive dreams began to appear relentlessly, one after the other, with little intermediate dream-experience between them. As I present the series I will indicate the time of occurrence relative to the entire five-year period.

Seen in series, Mairi's dreams illustrate what Erich Neumann (1958) describes as a figurative process of "coming to earth," a kind of psychological tumbling head-over-heels into bodily being and soulful life in the world. Tumbling so, Mairi's religious and psychological experience intersected in a way that led her through a major personality transformation which Mairi called experience of soul, and I came to think of as the emergence of her dream-in-the-world. The dream commentary, consisting of Mairi's associations and occasional amplifications as well as my associations to her previous dreams and her life history, enriches the text of each dream and indicates something of the tone of transference/countertransference interactions.

With the exception of the single waking vision that occurred during the time of this series, each dream is numbered sequentially. Regular archetypal dreams appear in plain type, the vision appears in *italicized* type, and Self-directive dreams appear in **bold** type. As mentioned above, the Self-directive dreams cluster together near the end of the series, where they appeared rapidly, one right after the other, just before all dreaming ceased and Mairi was ushered into her experience of soul.

DREAMS, AND VISION, WITH COMMENTARY

1. Red circus tent

I am standing with a friend, a man. In the distance we see a large red silk circus tent with people and animals around. My friend suggests that we enter the tent but I say no, there is too much pain.

This dream, appearing about two months into Mairi's analysis, articulates emotional ambivalence toward something that just begins to appear on her psychic horizon. Fearing to approach the bright red circus tent – an arena of unbearable (to her) psychic pain – Mairi disagrees with her male friend (companion? analyst? adventurous spirit? psychotherapeutic process?), who indicates his willingness to approach and suggests entry, for which Mairi is unprepared. Who wants to revisit pain?

Mairi was not surprised at her reluctance to attend a circus. When I asked why, she said it troubled her to laugh at clowns along with the crowd. "I feel odd," said she, "when I can't laugh at things everyone else laughs at. I know it is just a clown-act, but I can't laugh easily when someone looks hurt or embarrassed, or sad, or is making a fool of themselves." Yet Mairi was known as (and knew herself to be) something of a clown, so that her reluctance pointed toward feelings about herself, too, that she hid by clowning around and amusing others. "Clowning" is a ploy to throw spectators as well as oneself off the track of feeling whatever sorrow or pain hides beneath or behind the laughter evoked. Clowning tips into laughter and away from tears, both of which distance a sober ego from self-reflection. And a manic defense is contagious.

High-wire acts, too, Mairi did not like because they put her on the edge of her seat, fearful that the tightrope walker might fall, the animal trainer be bitten by the tiger. "In a circus, everything is too close and too exciting. When I was little, though," she said, "I liked the circus, especially the animals." These associations, full of identification with hurt or humiliation (projected onto clown or trapeze artist) suggested significant trauma in Mairi's emotional life of which she was still relatively unaware. Her unconscious pain appeared as a hypersensitivity to the real or imagined pain of others.

When I questioned Mairi about the man in the dream, she said she didn't know him but he reminded her of a male artist friend who had just completed a large oil painting of a hanged ballerina. When she saw the painting, Mairi was upset ("I don't find beauty in death, especially in the broken body of a dancer!"). But the painting was admired and was to be hung in a museum, and her friend was proud. However "spirited" the adventurous attitude of this dream might appear (personified by her friend), its thrust was oriented primarily by aesthetic values that conflicted with Mairi's emotional sensitivity, which was emerging into consciousness.

Collectively, circus people are categorized with gypsies and other traveling nomads. I thought of the wandering Mairi had experienced in her early life. Like gypsies, circus people tend to live on the edge of ordinary respectability, spreading their tents on the outskirts of town. People flock to see the show and then go home, seldom wondering about what goes on behind the scenes. The red circus tent full of animals around which people gather indicates a panoply of liminal space and imaginative activity, everything in motion. We will see the motif of enclosure and the color red in many of Mairi's dreams.

After this dream Mairi's first year of psychotherapeutic work proceeded apace with little movement into depth on the part of the unconscious. Meeting weekly, we became acquainted and established a good working relationship. Her dreams accompanied our work on her personal complexes and her daily life with two small children. A year later another dream indicated a big opening to deeper levels of the psyche and surprised us both.

2. Flaming angel

I am standing alone on a low hill in a bare, seemingly empty landscape. It is evening and I look out into an almost-dark sky. I have been waiting for a long time. Suddenly in the distant sky I see what looks like a moving light, bright red-orange and yellow. I see that it is an enormous being of light, entirely made of flame. The angel alights on the hill beside me; I am filled with awe. The angel is hermaphroditic, a woman with great flaming wings and garments, yet with a penis. It wraps me in its arms, folding us together in its wings. Its penis penetrates me and I am finally warm again, all the way through, inside and out. I talk and talk, telling the angel everything.

The open night sky "encloses" this dream, a container on a vast dark scale, echoed and contrasted by the warm, close embrace of a flaming angel. A dark, emotionally barren landscape underlying the conscious normality of Mairi's daily life shows through. Feelings of emotional poverty are woven from loneliness, hopelessness, longing, emptiness, and feelings of being without resource. Into the night sky of this empty world streaks a bright, flaming object, and the affective world moves toward Mairi in the form of a red–orange–yellow-flaming angel. Mairi's first numinous dream was powerful. Filled first with awe and then by an extraordinary opening of feeling and a bodily sense of herself, Mairi felt embraced, penetrated, warmed, and wrapped in the all-embracing wings of the angel, whereupon she "talks and talks, telling the angel everything" in a moving "re-union."

Mairi had few conscious associations. To angels – "Saying 'Now I lay me down to sleep' when I was little," she said, "and I liked to imagine that I had a guardian angel, maybe." She repeated how relieved she felt to be able to "talk about everything. I feel warm talking with you, too," she said, and she wondered that the angel appeared out of "the nowhere of a night sky. I somehow knew it would, though," she said, "because I remember waiting – and waiting – and waiting." Mairi also remembered "pieces of fire" which scattered on the dark earth around the angel, long drops of flame like feathers falling from the angel's wings, "but nothing burned."

Remembering Mairi's sense of being underfed, unreached-for, and unheld as an infant, I understood the barren landscape to be that part of Mairi's emotional world which felt without life: a cold, dark earth, a barren matrix. In ancient Greece the hermaphrodite was the child of Aphrodite–Venus and Hermes–Mercurius. A mythic figure, the image of the hermaphrodite embodies the twists and tangles of love and lust united in a single being. We find this image in earlier prehistory along with other cosmogonic creator gods of a bisexual nature. Jung (CW9i: 192) reminds us that Plato understood the hermaphrodite as a symbol of the essence of wholeness. Likewise, the alchemical hermaphrodite indicates a union of strong and striking opposites: above and below, male and female, sun and moon. But this image also indicates a primitive state of mind where differences and contrasts are barely separated or still merged, i.e., an archaic, primordial stage in the evolution of consciousness. With an embrace which Mairi felt brought her "back to life," the winged image bridged the emotional barrenness of Mairi's inner world with a sense of the natural unconscious and the wholeness of a more primeval time.

With this dream an experience of primordial being became the distant goal of Mairi's self-development, an experience that Jung would term "a union of consciousness and the unconscious, personally experienced" (CW9i: 293). Usually in mysticism, says Jung (CW9i: 295), the primordial image is sublimated on a lofty plane, *only occasionally approaching the physical sphere in emotional intensity*. Mairi's dream-image definitely includes the physical sphere in its emotional intensity, and because the physical sphere is included rather than remaining an object of psychic preoccupation, this dream directly addresses Mairi's native capacity for mystical experience.

As we worked with this dream I thought of many things: Psyche, offered in a marriage of death to an invisible dragon-demon, was saved by her numinous love for Eros. Psyche's penetration by the winged herald of another world resulted not in rape but in eventual fulfillment. Images of the Annunciation also came to mind: in painting after painting, Mary is depicted being summoned into revelation of her destiny by a presence that breaks through her abstraction (usually she is shown reading a book) and her immersion in ordinary time. Mairi's hermaphroditic angel both heralded transformation and penetrated her. Certainly with this dream something primordial irrupted into Mairi's consciousness and into our shared therapeutic context, and our mutual reflection on this image and its archetypal content became a major referent in Mairi's subsequent therapy.

I was impressed by how wholeheartedly Mairi's dream-ego met the angel's embrace. She opened to that which came to meet her with welcome and relief. The result was life-giving. The British psychoanalyst Neville Symington (1993: 3) proposes that as infants or children we become narcissistically disordered when we make an unconscious choice: either we choose toward what Symington calls the "lifegiver" (our capacity for authenticity and spontaneity), or – choosing to disavow the "lifegiver" – we turn to magical pretense in order to evade psychic reality and avoid external reality. Symington believes that narcissistic disorders always emerge from trauma, and in concentrating upon our unconscious acceptance or rejection of the "lifegiver" he reminds us that each of us has an individual *response* to trauma that is separate from the traumatic event itself. Our individual response to trauma – not the event itself – determines whether or not we forfeit our true selves and become narcissistically disordered.

James Grotstein (in Symington 1993: ix) suggests that Symington's image of the "lifegiver"[2] personifies Eigen's (1993a) "act of faith," pointed to by the capacity for an all-out, no-holds-barred way of experiencing, of which Mairi was to become increasingly capable. Ultimately, Mairi's latent receptivity to the reality of the psyche opened her to her transformative experience of soul and the emergence of her dream-in-the-world. Although she wrestled with symptoms of disordered narcissism, Mairi did not fit the diagnostic picture of narcissistic personality disorder. Her dream image of the angel "gives life," and Mairi "chooses" to receive it. Despite early trauma, Mairi's unconscious choice tended more "toward" than "against" her authentic self. Mairi was not starting from ground zero: once, some-where, she had bonded with something or someone whom she passionately missed, longed for, and for whom she could wait and welcome on return.

Of course later injuries and what Masud Kahn (1963) calls "cumulative trauma" were relevant also. Juxtaposed to Mairi's experience in the dream – "I talk and talk, telling the angel everything" – I thought of three-and-a-half-year-old Mairi's jammed-up silence after her sexual abuse by the teenaged boy, her inability to talk or tell, as well as her precociously developed self-sufficiency. However, the psychic presence of the flaming angel holds the possibility of a passionate engagement with life that Mairi misses, even unconsciously. When she is embraced by the possibility of passionate engagement, Mairi responds. Then the angel enfolds her like a fiery womb.

3. Snowy mountains, two children

I walk alone in snowy mountains. In a distant valley I see what looks like a church. Deep snow covers the roof and piles up along its walls. Two small children, a boy and a girl dressed in red and blue clothing (from this distance I don't know which is which), play beneath the eaves. I hope the snow doesn't melt. I am afraid that the children might fall through a thinning snow-crust along the walls of the building and hurt themselves, or be trapped or crushed.

This dream appeared in the second year, a depressing time for Mairi. Here again she is solitary, up high and observing, but this time dressed for the cold, alone on a mountaintop in bright daylight. Snow blankets the mountain like the thick cover of frozen affect stretching between Mairi's experience of herself now and what in the distance catches her attention: two young children, a boy and a girl, playing beneath the snow-covered eaves of a church. The hermaphrodite has differentiated into male and female, though from this distance Mairi can hardly tell.

Spontaneity and play reside in the children ("not my own, I don't know these children") dressed in red and blue, opposing colors often indicative of soul and spirit. What does Mairi feel? Interest, yes, and anxiety and fear, similar to her fear of entering the silk circus tent in Dream #1. A too-rapid thaw of frozen-over affect might endanger unsuspecting young life, might trap or crush it. After the angel's powerful entry into her inner world, Mairi's re-entry into the outer world needs to proceed slowly. But a stronger dream-structure suggests possible containment of the numinous content. A church is the container in this dream, instead of the night sky or a circus tent, and the colors red and blue each clothe a child.

Associating to "church," Mairi told me a story: "When I was little," she said, "I used to ask God please to not make me have to take a nap. I was sure that God would rather I be outside playing, and mum always made me nap in the afternoon. I guess "God" was in my room, but God was also in a church we sometimes went to; I knew that because of the silence and the way the candles smelled. Later I forgot about God, even when I went to church. Once I joined a youth group. When kids talked about believing in God I piped up to say that I had never experienced God so how could I know whether I believed in God or not. Later the youth group leader said that maybe this wasn't the right group for me. I felt rejected and stubborn, and I never went back." From that time on God and church seemed incommensurable and Mairi forgot God even more.

When I asked her about feeling trapped or crushed Mairi told me another story: "When I was four, or five, we lived for a short time near the ocean. On the drive from our house to the beach there was a patch of land along the road which mum told me was 'quicksand.' She explained what quicksand was and I was terrified that I would open the car door, jump out, and run into the quicksand. From then on each time we passed that spot along the road I hid in the back on the floor of the car so I wouldn't run into the quicksand and drown." Why had Mairi felt and feared unconscious self-destructive impulses when she was so young? Apparently she had been struggling with despair for a long time. Three months later, Mairi dreamed:

4. Ordeal by spiders

I see two feathery black spiders, one in each side of a figure eight turned on its side – an infinity sign that is actually formed by the slightly lifting pages of an opened book. I know that I must let each spider come out and bite me on the back of my hands, where they will leave four small red scratches in the shape of a pound or number sign. I am afraid, and I can do this only if I kneel in the presence of someone I can trust. I must undergo an ordeal.

This dream introduces the archetypal motif of initiation, with inevitable apprehension, dread, and fear of an "ordeal." Yet initiatory ordeals point toward the possibility of deep psychological transformation. Again the affective world moves toward Mairi, this time alive with negative feelings. Fear, even terror, center around the two black, feather-legged spiders, often a symbol of the darker side of Mother issues. Here the image is doubled: two spiders emerge from a book opened on its back so that the pages lift and bend together, forming a figure eight on its side, the sign for infinity. Jung writes about the number eight as (1) a double quaternity, indicating psychic processes concerning individuation, and (2) a final equilibrium (psychologically, the Self), arrived at through a process of development (CW9ii: 351ff.). The appearance of the number eight formed by pages, and implicit in four red (for affect?) scratches on the back of each hand indicates a potential for psychic wholeness or an experience of the Self, and the infinity symbol confirms it.

Black spiders reminded Mairi of poisonous black widow spiders which lurked in the dark corners of a garage near an army base outside the southern Nevada house in which she had lived briefly as a child. To her relief, these dream spiders "with feathery legs" (like her winged Angel?) had no red hourglass marks upon their bellies. To an open book Mairi associated the Bible, the dictionary, and the encyclopedia – all "spilling over with words, as if," she said, "hidden in words, hidden between the pages, is something frightening, something scary that I have to let bite me and get into my system, but not too much. This has to happen with someone I trust. That's you, I guess."

Another association: before the births of her children, Mairi had spent a month in an ashram in Southern India. She was undecided about whether to stay, whether she was seriously ready to "live a yogic life." One hot afternoon as she lay swathed in mosquito netting trying to nap, she glanced up at a portrait of The Mother (the woman who headed up this particular ashram) that hung on the wall at the foot of her bed. In the lower right hand corner of the portrait she saw an enormous black spider the size of a hand. "With that," said Mairi, "I knew I didn't belong there. In that moment I decided to leave." Here again the co-appearance of frightening black spider and "Mother" indicated that we were in the realm of a negative mother complex.

To the red pound-signs the spiders were to engrave on the backs of her hands Mairi associated "cross, and double-cross, and tic-tac-toe. Double-crossed by life . . . double-crossed means feeling betrayed." It also means twice marked, or twice crucified. "The sign means weight, too, something heavy I have to carry with me in the world. Red is like blood. I have to risk wearing the sign of double-crosses on my hands out in the world, like Hester wore her red sign in *The Scarlet Letter*."[3]

Over time Mairi's complex came to focus on the difficult emotions she had experienced in relation to her personal mother, a woman somewhat remote by nature. Mairi first understood her own situation from her (imagination of her) mother's point of view. "She had me before she wanted to and before she felt ready to handle a sickly infant," she explained. Mairi had a hard time unearthing her own feelings, buried beneath understanding and empathy for her mother. Mairi had been told of a time when she "talked back" to her mother: "I was little – they delivered milk then, and sitting on the porch was a bottle almost as high as I was and too heavy for me. Trying to bring it inside, I dropped it and it broke. I cried even before mother scolded me: that's what brought her attention. She told me that as she leaned out the window and yelled at me I looked up through my tears and said, "Can't you say thank you for trying?"

"'Cheeky,' my mother called me, when she told that story. I liked hearing that I spoke up, though," Mairi laughed, "even though *she* didn't." With vivid feeling Mairi remembered another time "first hand": in the midst of being scolded by her mother (for what, she could not remember) five-year-old Mairi sobbed out, "Don't you love me anymore?" to which her mother snapped "You are my child, of course I love you. But I don't *like* you. I mean I don't like your behavior."

These words struck terror into Mairi. "I wanted to go where love was," she said, simply. "From then on, for years, every night after climbing into bed I called out to mum sing-song down the hall, 'I like you and I love you!' Floating from the dark bedroom through the door ajar, 'Mommy! I like you and I love you!' That was my bedtime ritual," Mairi said. "I couldn't go to sleep unless I called that out to her. She would call back to me 'Good night, sleep well.'"

"I don't know how many years I did that but it was a long time. Once I said it I could sleep, but not till then. Eventually I forgot about the whole thing." This story began a slow process of shouldering previously unrealized (therefore unfelt) negative feelings toward her personal mother – feelings un-owned by Mairi and probably projected onto "mum", locked away not only during her childhood but throughout an unusually repressed adolescence, during which Mairi occupied herself in "mothering" her younger siblings in order to help Mom out. Peeling away Mairi's early identification with her mother and her mother's needs and attitudes was laborious work. Slowly Mairi realized that her own negative attitude toward herself was one thing, while her mother's attitude towards her was something else.

We talked about the difference between love and like, and what that difference might have meant to little Mairi. "I was too young to hear it," she said; "all I heard was that mum didn't love me." This memory opened other perspectives. "Mum and I wouldn't have liked each other had we met later, say in college," Mairi was able to say, meaning that she was begin-ning to imagine that sometimes she – Mairi – had returned her mother's dislike. "We were too different," she went on. "But when I was little, I feared her dislike, even when it didn't come directly at me."

Mairi's mother had an older sister, Louise, an unmarried career woman who traveled extensively, lived abroad, and ended up in New York City. Louise became an "Auntie Mame" figure to Mairi, glamorous and exciting, sender of boxes of second-hand clothing unlike anything her mother ever bought for herself (or Mairi) from the Sears catalogue. Aunt Louise was also Mairi's godmother, so sometimes she paid attention to Mairi, too. "She sent me the best gifts from New York City," Mairi remembered enthusiastically, "once a little red umbrella with my initials on the handle, another time a little pearl ring. I never imagined such fine things, and treasured them for years."

But Aunt Louise was troubled, and Mairi's mother had mixed feelings about her older sister to begin with. Over time Louise's life became chaotic. "She had affairs, and she began to drink, until she had to see a psychiatrist and ended up in a state mental hospital. Nobody in my family had affairs, or drank, or went into therapy, let alone into a mental hospital. Or at least no one talked about it, if they did. Or at least I didn't know about it. When I was little – seven, eight, early teens – for years mum walked around muttering to herself about Aunt Louise's 'selfishness.' 'If she would just think about somebody other than herself for a change, Louise would be alright,' mum would say. 'I don't know what's the matter with her. She never thinks about anybody but herself!' Eventually Aunt Louise jumped out a window of Napa State Hospital and died.

"After Aunt Louise died granny never mentioned her again, at least in my hearing," said Mairi. "But mum commented on granny's silence, too. What this has to do with mum and me," Mairi continued, "is that when I was little and mum was mad at me she would call me Louise instead of Mairi. She would look straight at me and say 'Why don't you ever think about anybody but yourself, Louise!' Or, angry, she would yell 'Louise! I mean, Mairi!' It sounded confused. But what I heard was loud and clear. Mum didn't like Louise much. And when she called me Louise, she didn't like me either."

All this personal history was relevant, but the dream imagery of ritual initiation seemed bigger. Initiation is an archetypal pattern of experience. To become an initiate, to wear a sign of initiation into adulthood in the world, Mairi needed to find the negative feelings that she herself carried, not just those she could attribute to her personal mother or to her own experience of being mothered, or even to her experience of being a mother and mothering her children. This session led Mairi to muse upon aspects of her own mothering as she had directed it toward her mother, her siblings and herself, as well as the negative feelings she had toward her own two youngsters. She began to see how neglectful she could be toward herself as she overdid "good mothering" toward others, and how difficult it was to find time and space for a life of her own. No matter how much she loved them, living alone with two young children was hard. She realized that she could *hate* being "stuck with this life with my kids all alone," no matter that she also enjoyed and accepted it.

Mairi also reflected upon the part she had played in her two "failed" marriages. "I married for my own needs, I guess, I wasn't discriminating. I needed to feel loved more than I could love anyone else. I didn't pay enough attention to who the other person was that I was loving, who seemed to love me. Really, I didn't know either one well enough to know whether I loved him or not," she said. "That's hardly loving another person, is it? Under it all, I was afraid of being alone. And my fear that I wasn't a loving person was a kind of caul around my better judgment. I never should have married the men I did."

These affirmative releases of negative feeling were freeing. Mairi began to realize her own inner darkness, her own negative aspect of the archetypal Great Mother, and to realize that whatever her mother had done to her, she also did to herself. The Sufi poet Rumi[4] writes of "night travelers" who search the darkness instead of running from it, a companionship of people willing to know their own fear (Chodron 1997). Mairi was becoming a night traveler, accepting that what she feared as negative judgment from her outer mother was more truly a source of living energy inside herself: that she, too, could personify a negative mother. This is to realize that the dark, life-denying, life-suppressing "night-mother" is not only a negative factor that attacks us from without. As a constituent element of archetypal reality, this inner darkness has to be realized as an inner factor too, especially for women (like Mairi) who tend to be too accommodating and understanding for their own good.

Remembering Mairi's time in India I mentioned the image of the Feminine Divine portrayed in the dark Hindu goddess, Kali. Mairi was intrigued. She researched Kali and we discussed what she found. In India black Kali has inspired fervent devotion and surrender for over ten thousand years – the world's longest unbroken tradition of worshipping the divine as feminine. *The Chandi*, a classic Indian goddess text, describes Kali emerging from the goddess Durga's "third eye" to vanquish demons that no other god or goddess could overcome. Garlanded with a necklace of severed heads, a belt of human arms dangling from her waist, one of her four arms holding a sword and another a severed head still bleeding, her tongue hanging out of her mouth[5] as she dances on the body of her lover, Kali presents a truly horrific countenance. The nearest analogy in our Western tradition is the petrifying visage of the Medusa.

But far from finding Kali's wrathful appearance threatening, worshippers discover in her a warrior goddess, a big black angry woman who likes to "play." They see in Kali a form of the Divine Mother and find in her many faces the power and wisdom to contend with the multiple demons, outer and inner, of our world. Kali's appearance, so shocking, also makes sense: her swinging sword cuts off the head of ego and the grasping hands of our clinging nature (with which Mairi, for example, clung to those she did not love). In the Kali Temple in Dakshineswar, Kali is worshipped affectionately as Kali Ma, "Mother Savior of the World." Some see in her image their own rage at the devastation and suffering of all life caused by the oppression of the feminine. Some see in her outrageous unconventionality and sexuality and her wild and limitless energy a freedom and power they seek to internalize. Others come to Kali as children come to a mother, finding in her a never-ending source of wisdom and bliss.

Behind Kali's demonic appearance Mairi and I found the sense of a true warrior, a woman who, while inspiring fear and anger, is herself at home with these emotions, knowing how and when to use them.[6] Warrior Kali breaks down violence as well as petrifaction (stony lack of expression or the freeze of fear); she calls for a deeper, stronger kind of compassion. Although Kali is called the Destroyer, ultimately her powers are beneficent, for what she destroys calls for destruction. Jungian psychologist Marion Woodman (1996) suggests that the chaos that Kali embodies is a shattering of rigid categories. To refuse to enter into Kali's dance of creation and destruction is to risk getting stuck in a one-sided view of reality, stuck in destruction without creation. The chaos we fear (represented by Black Kali) may be the very thing that can free us. Kali also teaches her devotees to be kind to themselves, something much more challenging, said Mairi, "than thinking about abstract spiritual theories that I read in books [in which spiders live?]."

Talking about her past relationships and failed marriages, Mairi pondered her poor choices. Had she been more than a little "in love with death?" Before my eyes Mairi's long-suppressed self-assertiveness and aggression filled her up, until together we could laugh and joke about "growing fangs" and "clearing the air." Suddenly Mairi felt more at ease with her anger toward her mother, her children, her friends and ex-husbands, toward me, and her children's anger toward her and with each other.

Returning to her dream, we reflected upon the ritual initiation pictured so clearly: the sacralizing nature of the initiatory ordeal is conditional upon her ability to kneel trustingly in the presence of another. A similar trust characterized Mairi's embrace of the angel in Dream #2. I thought of Mairi's experience of being held by the scruff of the neck, "kneeling" before the teenaged boy in the garden shed, her naive trust then ("would you like some candy, little girl?") leading her astray. In trustfully submitting to her dreams and relating to me in the therapeutic situation, perhaps Mairi – without denying her fear and pain – could recover some trusting ability to relate not only to the otherness already negatively constellated in her life but to what in this dream was represented as "ordeal by spider-bite" – trust in a kind of vaccination by her own venom against further self-betrayal.

Mairi wondered whether she could overcome her "unbending [un-kneeling] pride." She remembered stubbornly leaving the church youth group. When teased unmercifully by her brother or father or lovers, or facing painful conditions, Mairi remembered saying to herself, "They can't get to me, I won't let this get to me, I can always *die* before I give in." While Mairi thought of the "sin" of pride, we looked at how pride defended her against unbearable humiliation. Until Mairi could give up "pride" and feel the shame beneath, she would remain self-sufficiently aloof, feeling that she needed no one. Psychic images of linking inner and outer elements imply a dawning hope for a trusting relationship with another. In my own mind the "feathery" legs of the (twin) black spiders within the Book of Eternity corresponded (even if negatively toned) with the winged image of the flaming hermaphrodite in Dream #2. Spiders, too, belong to both heaven and earth.

5. "Two-ness" beneath the ocean

I am with a man friend, strolling on the ocean bottom. We are both breathing naturally as we walk hand in hand, looking around. As if it were a sunny day, I am wearing a large beribboned hat. My friend points out to me that "two-ness" has existed from the beginning. Sure enough, every-where I look I see two of every living thing, as if the ocean itself were some kind of Noah's ark.

In this dream, about six weeks after Dream #4, Mairi is as deeply submerged in the collective psyche as she was high above everything else in the snowy mountains of Dream #3. The whole ocean is her milieu. I did not know what to make of this scene: people do not usually breathe, converse together, or even wear hats underwater. Relatedness is a major motif, repeating the motif of two from the spider dream (#4) and the two children near the church (#3). Does all this two-ness have to do with Mairi and her unborn twin, or an archetypal statement, or both? At least here a principle of self–other awareness lurks in the depths, though not yet ready to emerge into the light of day. I concluded that some kind of central transformation was taking place underwater in terms of self–other awareness (including Mairi's awareness of me in the transference). Again Mairi is companioned by a man, unknown but friendly. This time, rather than disagreeing with Mairi (the circus dream), her companion holds her hand and teaches her something important: two-ness has existed from the beginning.

Mairi was amused by an underwater dream. From her brief experience of snorkeling she described how the underwater world was truly "other." A blue world, I thought, where people communicate beneath language, and other senses flower. Jung relates his concept of shadow-integration to this watery world:

> The shadow is a tight passage, a narrow door, whose painful constriction no one is spared who goes down to the deep well. But one must learn to know oneself in order to know who one is. For what comes after the door is, surprisingly enough, a boundlessness full of unprecedented uncertainty, with apparently no inside and no outside, no above and no below, no here and no there, no mine and no thine, no good and no bad. *It is a world of water, where all life floats in suspension; where the realm of the sympathetic system, the soul of everything living begins;* where I am indivisibly this and that; where I experience the other in myself and the other-than-myself experiences me. (CW9i: 45, emphasis mine)

The collective unconscious appears in the archetypal imagery of the previous dream, but this dream pictures Mairi in the collective unconscious *per se*. Mairi had no personal associations. Her companion, she said, was a stranger. Like everything else in this watery underworld of "twos," she and her friend proceeded hand in hand. Many summers ago, while she was still in college, Mairi had seen brightly beribboned hats on native peoples in Chiapas in southern Mexico, during "a month that I just took off and I made my own way, before I married, before I had children, it was a lovely freedom." On hats she commented, "My other grandmother (father's mother) loved hats and taught me to wear one in the sun."

The allusion to Noah's ark reminded us of the biblical story. Noah survived the flood sent by Yahweh because of his obedience. Faithful even though those around him thought him mad, Noah obeyed God's instructions. But Noah wasn't underwater to begin with. Edward Edinger (1972: 184) makes the point that the number two is the first real number, since two symbolizes the act of creation and the emergence of the ego from an original state of unity. With two is born opposition, as well as the possibility of consciousness, which always involves "knowing with" someone else. Mairi's self–other awareness is at stake here, with transference and countertransference implications. Submerged in a necessity for consciousness while she is still underwater, Mairi's dream indicates that at least all the basic ingredients are there.

Because Noah obeyed God's command to build an ark, he and his family and all the animals were not submerged two by two in the flood. Portending a capacity for an expanded consciousness (i.e., knowing with another), the point of Mairi's dream may be that for her (at this moment, at least), being submerged in the collective is not only bearable, breathable, and pleasant as a sunny day, but educative. I thought of the psychologist Ernst Kris's phrase, "regression in the service of the ego." Yet being *in* the collective unconscious is not simply ego-regression. "Being" in the collective unconscious comes close to being submerged in something like a dream of the world itself – a world that is yet to be realized. Jung (CW9i: 46) reminds us that

> the collective unconscious is anything but an encapsulated personal system: it is sheer objectivity, as wide as the world and open to all the world. There I am the object of every subject, in complete reversal of my ordinary consciousness, where I am always the subject that has an object. There I am utterly one with the world, so much a part of it that I forget all too easily who I really am. "Lost in oneself" is a good way of describing this state. *But this self is the world* [emphasis mine], if only consciousness could see it. That is why we must know who we are.

Mairi's dream suggests that at certain times a degree of submersion in the collective unconscious might be necessary and beneficial, even healing. Her lesson in two-ness indicates possible compatibility, companionability, and the mutual acceptance of an "other" both within and without.

Perhaps this dream also alludes to a different quality of consciousness, or a different way of "knowing," a consciousness that participates knowingly within the realm of the unconscious. Consciousness that is at home with the unconscious rather than in opposition to it depends less upon a dichotomy between two opposing mental principles than it does upon mutual reliance and inter-penetrability. As I remember, the creatures of the sea are not mentioned in the biblical story of Noah. But I assume that they, too, survived God's flooding wrath, if not by means of obedience then by submerging themselves in the watery sanctuary of the sea, two by two.[7]

In her third year of analysis Mairi had her first Self-directive dream. In contrast with the archetypal dreams above, her Self-directive dream contained no dream-ego and no persons. With a lack of "personal access," it is difficult to come up with personal associations. In the following dream, either Mairi is not in it or she is so far into it that as Mairi, she disappears. Like a vision, the dream is singular, immediate, and real. Unlike a vision, however, it is clearly a dream. This is why Self-directive dreams can feel to the dreamer as if they are being dreamed for someone else, for the world, perhaps, rather than for oneself. With no dream "persona" with whom to identify, the dreamer feels like an envelope, or a radio antenna.

6. Artichoke dream

An enormous green artichoke: each artichoke leaf is overlaid, engraved as intricately as a Chinese ivory carving. Each carving depicts a different human relationship – mother–child, lover–beloved, old–young, father–son, friend–foe – actually, each leaf depicts aspects of loving and hating with all gradations in-between.

Artichokes are not simply the large, round, many-leafed green vegetable we see in grocery stores or eat at table, but the many-leafed bud of a purple, thistle-like flower. In this dream, each leaf in the entire bud was overlaid as if with green ivory carving, yet carving and bud were of the same substance, as if each leaf had been separately carved and the bud re-assembled, all of a piece. Emphasizing the two-ness of Mairi's previous dream, each leaf was engraved with an archetypal dyad, a singular form of human relatedness: mother and child, man and woman, friend and enemy, old and young, neighbor and stranger, father and son, and so on. While every imaginable aspect and variety of collective human relatedness was pictured in a single organic image, Mairi's dream-ego was missing (her personal singularity?). That was the dream.

Mairi did have sparse associations, mostly positive. She was fond of artichokes and liked to eat them. She knew that each leaf had a small sharp thorn on the end and that the prickly-thistle-bit nestled in the heart of the artichoke had to be removed carefully before the heart itself could be consumed. Several years earlier she had planted an artichoke that had grown taller than she. The large purple thistle, the flower of the artichoke, was borne upon a tall, feathery (like spider-legs and angel-wings?) green plant that impressed her with its size and beauty. She kept some dried thistles from that plant in a pitcher on her kitchen shelf and sketched them. That Mairi found value all along a spectrum of "artichoke possibility" – awareness of thorn, the plant for food, the thistle for beauty – suggested to me that symbolically, Mairi could appreciate both thistle and thorn as part of what becomes real nourishment.

With regard to the ivory-like carving of each leaf, Mairi remembered seeing Chinese carvings in a museum collection of Asian art. Entranced at the intricate "entire worlds depicted in miniature," she was impressed with the time and patience it must have taken to achieve such fine work. I reached for cultural amplifications: in Greece, artichokes belonged to Aphrodite and were thought to incite lust (Bishop 1990: 49). The color of this dream was as striking as the object itself, so Mairi and I amplified "green": Aphrodite's color, yes, and older still, the color of Osiris, the re-born Egyptian god. Green is also the color of Sophia and the Holy Ghost, the color of life, procreation, and resurrection (Jung 1930–1932, 1932–1934). Hildegard of Bingen writes about the *benedicta viriditas*, the "blessed greenness," as a time when the world is blessed with grace. Hildegard's notion of fecundity, *viriditas*, tells us something about the mothering nature of God in whose image and likeness we are made (Craine 1997: 47) but it also tells us something about ourselves, made in God's image. The color may point to an emerging greenness in our time, a strikingly feminine mode of being (Ulanov 1971, 1981), a capacity to personally receive, embody, and relate to the mystery of God which more and more insistently presents itself for our attention.

This passage from Jung in which he too recognizes the implicit affect in the color green speaks to the hidden stirrings of the still-unconscious emotional implications of Mairi's Self-directive dream:

> The state of imperfect transformation . . . hoped for and waited for, does not seem to be one of torment only, but of positive, if hidden, happiness. It is the state of someone who, in his wanderings among the mazes of his psychic transformation, comes upon a secret happiness which reconciles him to his apparent loneliness. In communing with himself he finds not deadly boredom and melancholy but an inner partner; more than that, a relationship that seems like the happiness of a secret love, or like a hidden springtime, when the green seed sprouts from the barren earth, holding out the promise of future harvests. It is the alchemical *benedicta viriditas*, the blessed greenness, signifying on the one hand the "leprosy of the metals" (*verdigris*), but on the other the secret immanence of the divine spirit of life in all things . . . Green signifies hope and the future. (CW14: 623–4)

I think that this green dream, depicting the organic depth and variety of human relatedness, began to compensate for Mairi's deeply alienated feelings. Although she had not imagined or thought of herself as despairing when she started working with me, I had seen her so. By this time Mairi was no longer satisfied ("at peace") with her aloneness. She wanted to feel her way back into the world and into the hope of a new, intimate and loving relationship. This dream gave her a vision of possibility. Each artichoke leaf, although separate and different from any other, grew in relation to and was linked with all the other leaves through a central core at the heart of the flower.

Here the psyche was ahead of Mairi, leading her on. Moved by imagining both dream and possibility, Mairi began to imagine emotional life stirring. She denied ever feeling suicidal, or even times ("after adolescence") of being deeply depressed. Yet Mairi lapsed into long stretches of time when she was unaware of an active desire to live. In striking contrast to the dark barren earth on which nothing grew (Dream #3), this dream burgeons with organic possibility. "O blessed greenness, which generates all things!" cries Mylius, the author of the *Rosarium* (quoted in Jung CW14: 623–4),

> Did not the spirit of the Lord, which is a fiery love, give to the waters when it was borne over them a certain fiery vigour, since nothing can be generated without heat? God breathed into created things . . . a certain germination or greenness, by which all things should multiply . . . They called all things green, for to be green means to grow . . . *Therefore this virtue of generation and the preservation of things might be called the Soul of the World*; herein lies the reason for the hidden joy, which might otherwise be difficult to justify,'

continues Jung; in alchemy, green also means perfection. (emphasis mine) Mairi's Self-directive dream refers us to an inherent component of this "collective world dream," a greening reference to the Soul of the World, the *anima mundi*. The fact that Mairi even had this dream might be attributed to the generative and preservative qualities of the Soul of the World depicted therein. Jung's comments made me realize how full of the elements Mairi's earlier archetypal dreams were: earth, air, fire, water, sometimes people and animals, but few, if any, plants. Plants bridge the mineral and animal kingdoms, and images from the plant world express the mystery of life emerging from the elements. So the vegetable soul has a connection with dark downwardness, as well as associations with melancholy, dirt, and depression. The old alchemists worked to create not only a philosopher's stone but a "vegetable stone," as well; the *lapis vegetabilis*, the *quinta essentia*. At least in part, Mairi's Self-directive dream indicates soul in a vegetative state. The very idea of a vegetable soul draws us into a twilight zone in which only imaginatively can we separate soul and body, psyche and soma, mind and matter.

Correlating vegetative greenness with the Holy Ghost, Jung comments on parallels between the quiet rooted-ness and immobility of vegetable life and the many injunctions toward a calm abiding which are found in Eastern yoga and meditation. In Eastern or Tantric yoga, consciousness is imagined as originating in the lowest chakra, the Muladhara, "which is the darkness where things begin. There the green shoot or bud is Shiva," writes Jung (1932–1934: 335). After the mineral world, the vegetable level of the psyche is the deepest realm of the unconscious. To go deep, to descend into the deepest levels of the unconscious, is symbolized in terms of an increasing engagement with the body. A profound and fundamental life-energy originates at the roots of the self.

Peter Bishop (1990: 197) reminds us that the color green and the alchemical vegetable soul indicate more than the presence of blessed hope and joy:

> Weaving their way through the idea of the vegetable soul are ideas about the body and nervous system; nourishment, digestion, circulation, and reproduction; a fundamental substratum of consciousness; a sense of dwelling, of having roots, of being grounded; a reverie and repose that takes us back to childhood, to the beginnings of things; an anima involvement in the sensual world; an all-pervading cosmic life-energy, and so on . . . but also profound melancholy, returning us downward into our own root concerns, and to the vegetative tragedy facing us today in the world.

Vegetative tragedy visits individual bodies as well as the body of the world. Shortly – but not immediately – after Dream #6, came the following:

7. Lightning strike

I am standing inside a large white tent on a mountaintop. My father and my infant son are with me but we are in shock: an enormous bolt of lightning strikes the earth where we are and tears the top of the tent wide open to the night sky. My father, clearly hurt, sits on a bed on one side of the room, holding his head in his hands. My son, knocked from my arms and lap to the floor, lies in shock near the other wall. I am stunned, my body unable to move, my heart torn between them.

This was a shocking dream. The archetypal father (Zeus, Father of the gods), symbolized by lightning, strikes Mairi's world, tearing open her enclosure, hurting her, her father, and her small son, all three at once, and out of nowhere. In contrast to the distant red circus tent of Dream #1, which Mairi would not enter, here the tent is white and she is inside it with three generations of her family – father, self, and son. Again the night sky opens, the sky of the flaming angel of Dream #2. Perhaps the "too much pain" of Dream #1 is being pictured. Whatever this lightning bolt represents will become central to understanding Mairi's suffering and despair.

As in Dream #3, Mairi is on a mountaintop. The torn tent is laid open to the elements from above. The premonitory sense of organic elementary wholeness depicted in Mairi's artichoke dream (#6) is broken through, blasted open, this time by Father material (Zeus, her father, and her infant son). Perhaps a glimpse of potential wholeness in the artichoke dream was necessary before Mairi could experience a dream which opened such traumatic material. I thought of Masud Khan's idea (1972) that not all dreams can *be* dreamed – that first one must develop a capacity for dreaming. Before he could tell her good-bye, Mairi's personal father (shipped out overnight) left for the war. He left her again when he died abruptly of a stroke. When Mairi's now eleven-year-old son was five years old, a slow-moving car hit him and broke his leg as he ran across a shopping mall parking lot. But this, too, had occurred years before this dream. These were associations to Mairi's personal father and her young son, but clearly this dream alluded to something more than Mairi's conscious experience. Lightning is impersonal. Both the impersonal and the transpersonal enter this dream.

Sacred to Zeus and a universal emblem of royal power, sometimes lightning is called "the finger of God." When we imagine that being hit by a bolt of lightning comes from a tyrannical, dark side of God, we impute a quality of personal intent, even if negative, to the awesome and "strikingly" impersonal nature of lightning. But lightning itself cannot be domesticated. For Heraclitus, Lightning was the third Person of a Trinity of Zeus, the Logos, and the divine Fire, or Lightning (Hymn to Zeus of Cleanthus). There, lightning is not an instrument of coercion but a fire that arouses voluntary consent and obedience. It is therefore Love, a servitor, an eternally living Presence, hence a Person. And in the New Testament, fire is the symbol of the Holy Spirit.

Before the eighteenth century lightning was thought to emanate from the earth or the friction of clouds rubbing together. In fact, lightning is a profound collision of opposites, colliding hot and cold. Being hit or touched by lightning refers more closely to what we imagine as destiny or fate than it does to an encounter with deity personified. Job argued with and eventually engaged the God who nearly destroyed him. But who can speak with lightning?

In this dream it is as if a stroke of fate tears open a protective enclosure, exposing "father," a man holding his hurt head, "son" (a six-month-old infant, not Mairi's eleven-year-old) fallen to the floor, and Mairi herself, petrified with shock, with a torn-to-breaking heart. This is the first major appearance of what I call an "undefended body" motif. Mairi finds herself paralyzed and helplessly exposed to the elements. Shock comes in the form of what might be felt by a six-month-old infant flung to the floor – dropped, abandoned and un-rescued (herself at six months, un-reached-for?) – or a man struck by a bolt out of the blue who, even while sitting, staggers to contain his pain and disorientation, or a woman who is torn from her baby and her father simultaneously, so paralyzed by pain that she cannot move to aid herself, let alone those whom she both loves and needs.

Mairi's eyes darkened as we talked about this dream. Her whole demeanor sobered and slowed, as if shadowed by earlier shock and numbness. Memories of pain, helplessness, abandonment, and disorientation were laid bare, even if specific incidents were unclear. These are sequelae of early trauma. I wondered whether her father's precipitous death had revived Mairi's earlier loss of him when she had cried herself into a fever. Possibly her own infant-trauma with her mother was surfacing through this dream, too: but why now, and why through lightning? Two months later came the following:

8. Silver fish kiss

I swim aimlessly in a large rectangular indoor pool. In the water with me are a red lobster, a white crab, and a silver fish. A game ensues: I try to keep away from the three water creatures. I swim around and around, keeping ahead of my pursuers with great effort. Then somehow I climb outside the pool and stretch myself over it, suspended by my hands in two corners of the room and my feet in the other two corners, like a giant X. From there I gaze into the surface of the pool, which clouds over as if I am looking down into a milky sky. Suddenly the silver fish leaps fully out of the water, strikes me (kisses me) smack in the middle of the forehead between my eyes, and calls out "I won!"

Here aimlessness and solitude are a context in which "play" enters the dream. In Dream #3, children play beneath the eaves of a church and Mairi worries for their safety. Here, Mairi plays. The space is the aquatic space of a pool rather than ocean of Dream #5. We are a long way from the mountaintop of Dream #7. The atmosphere is less elemental, it is daylight and the enclosure is secure. The pool contains a red lobster, a white crab, and a silver fish – alchemical colors all. It also contains Mairi. In this dream Mairi's solitude is transcended by the structure of a game that links all four dream participants. The motif of the undefended body (so hurt in the dream above) appears in Mairi's strenuous swimming, as if what followed were to be churned into being by her efforts – an alchemical *circumambulatio*. Then it appears again, no longer underwater.

Emerging from the pool, Mairi stretches fully – all out – bracing her hands and feet in the four corners of the room, "just like" she said, "the picture of the naked man in a circle, like the one we sent into a space-time capsule [Leonardo's picture of the Anthropos?]." I thought about the

Egyptian goddess Nut, the night sky, arching over Geb, her partner, whose body is the earth. Nut symbolizes all imaginable space differentiating itself from time (the earth). Mairi's posture was similar, but limited and more human: she braces herself against the four walls of a room. Perhaps finding herself "enough" to fill a room enables Mairi to raise herself out of the water and relate to it (look at it from a distance rather than being immersed in it) even though this takes great effort from "all of herself." Like Nut, Mairi arches over and spans what lies below.

By suspending herself, spread-eagle, over the watery medium in which the game occurs, Mairi elevates herself above the unconscious with its native creatures, something she often did defensively in her mind. She then uses the surface of the water – the reflective nature of the unconscious – as a sky-like mirror into which she gazes.[8] The water clouds over. Unable to see herself or the three other creatures of the game ("through a glass darkly"), Mairi assumes that they continue their pursuit of her beneath the surface. Then to her complete surprise, the silver fish leaps through the milky surface of the water and into the air ("through the looking glass") to smack Mairi "right in the middle of my forehead, with a hard, wet, kiss."

Calling out "I won!" the leaping fish disappears and its kiss ends the game. Victory goes not to the ego – to Mairi's sense of herself – but to a content of the unconscious, to something completely outside the ego's purview. I remembered Mairi's earlier dream (#5) where she and other water creatures left out of Noah's plans nevertheless survived the flood. As with Pisces as the Christ symbol (to which this silver fish also points), Mairi does not catch this fish: the fish catches Mairi. In so doing, the kiss of the silver fish links her head-ego (with its tendency towards dissociation) to the lunar (feminine) aspect of the unconscious.

In general, the psychological meaning of the image of the fish points to an autonomous content of the unconscious (CW5: 290 n. 47) with links to the upper world. Fish often possess a hermaphroditic aspect (CW9ii: 237) and bring about magical animation. This fish animates Mairi's mind, surprising her with a smack in the middle of her forehead as well as with its miraculous speech. The symbolic fish indicates a renewal and rebirth of libido or psychic energy, which returns into the unconscious from whence new contents constellate and are brought to the surface. From here the symbolism of the fish leads us to the symbolism of the Self, the central unconscious content *de profundo levatus* (CW9ii: 285), a phrase used by St. Augustine of Christ, meaning "drawn from the deep"; when Augustine invokes the image of Christ as "Ichthys" (fish), he is referring to something that has arisen from the depths. Jung (CW9ii: 285) names the fish symbol as the bridge between the historical Christ and our psychic nature, wherein the archetype of the Redeemer dwells. "In this way," Jung writes, "Christ becomes an inner experience, the 'Christ within.'"

Jung further comments that we now have a new symbol in place of the fish: a psychological concept of human wholeness:

> *In as much or in as little as the fish is Christ does the self mean God.* It is something that corresponds, an inner experience, an assimilation of Christ into the psychic matrix, a new realization of the divine Son, no longer in theriomorphic form but expressed in a conceptual or philosophic symbol. This, compared with the mute and unconscious fish, marks a distinct increase in conscious development. (CW9ii: 286, emphasis mine)

Mairi rubbed her forehead as she told me this dream: "I really felt something hit me here, hard, right in the middle of my forehead – my 'third eye' place." I thought of earlier dreams in which physical contact between Mairi and a strange or miraculous creature was portrayed – angel, spiders, even a bolt of lightning. The impact of this hit was more beneficent than the lightning strike. Like feathered spiders and the winged angel, this leaping silver fish breached and united opposing elements: water and air, body and mind, linking from below different dimensions of psychic reality. Mairi herself linked the lunar, silvery fish to her knowledge of the masculine, solar third eye upon which she meditated in the breathing discipline of Hatha yoga (sun–moon yoga) practice. These meditations also were meant to unite the opposites, by which she meant the left and right sides of her brain. Lunar process and solar intent came together in Mairi's surprised sensation of a fish's kiss, smack in the middle of her forehead.

A single eye has ambivalent significance; less than two, it can imply something subhuman. But given its location in the forehead above the place designated by nature for eyes, a single eye also alludes to the kind of extra-human powers which mythology depicts in the Cyclops. So an eye in the middle of the forehead is also linked with the idea of destruction. The same applies to the third eye in yoga, which is linked with Shiva (Cirlot 1962: 95).[9] Thus the image of the third eye also symbolizes the superhuman or the divine.

The element of play in this dream needs comment. Winnicott once remarked that until a child could surprise itself in play, real healing did not happen. I wonder if something similar might be said about surprise in dreams. That someone other than Mairi won this dream game was unexpected; in playing, Mairi's silver fish blessed her with surprise. One other personal association: a friend, upon hearing Mairi's dream, reacted with horror: "No doors, no windows: you're trapped in there! I would be afraid of suffocating!" But Mairi said that she had felt no such thing. She found comfort in this dream, as if the inner world were simply itself, containing her; as if – for the time being, at least – connections had to be made *within* that space, rather than opening her inner world to outer scrutiny. This was not a Self-directive dream in which "being" in the dream or not was an issue. This dream seemed meant for Mairi.

Although I did not comment at the time, I noted that Mairi told this dream first to someone other than myself. This was not her habit. In retrospect, I think that this small gesture of "breaking the therapeutic vessel"[10] – standing alongside the introverted comfort provided by the dream – indicated a turning deep within Mairi's psyche, as if the psyche were readying her to relate to the outer world again, this time from a place of personal spontaneity which heretofore had been relegated to "shadow," probably because Mairi wanted me to think of her as a "good patient."

During her fourth year of analysis Mairi had her first waking vision, simple, and profoundly effecting.

I saw on the wall in front of me an enormous eye, looking at me

A vision is not a miracle of the mind only; the body is its crèche and the flesh is its manger.[11] In telling her vision, Mairi's words fell all over themselves. The vision had come to her in vivid color against the white wall of her bathroom as she stepped out of her shower. Mairi stressed that her perception of this vision was concurrent with physical sight: she did not experience this vision in unconscious ecstasy. Hildegard of Bingen might have said that Mairi perceived her vision by hearing with her soul, referring to perception that occurs when the senses of the soul point to a newly awakening quality of perception, an in-breaking of a contemplative awareness that perceives all reality illumined and suffused by God. The spiritual senses are graced with tremendous potential. But with no conscious awareness of such sensibilities, no such words came to Mairi's mind. She scrambled to make sense of her vision. She had already had her first Self-directive dream (the Artichoke Dream, #6), but this vision was Self-directive in another way.

"I was immensely excited," she said; "I saw something like a white star shining in the center of a black pupil, surrounded by a brown iris, and an eye, the whole thing against a dark-blue background. A pun on 'eye' and 'I,' a star in the pupil of the eye and a star in the heart of the pupil (as in student-pupil) kept flickering in my mind."

Here was an image clearly related to the third eye of her previous dream #8, "smack" in the middle of her forehead. First I asked Mairi how she felt about feeling seen so intimately and abruptly. Had she wanted to flee or hide? Had she felt persecuted or pursued? Apparently she had not. "I looked right back," she replied; "I was awed, but I was so excited. The eye was not unkind. It saw everything."

Marie Louise von Franz (1980) writes about the eye as a symbol of insight: the moment at which insight is "ripe" depends on the archetype of the Self, of inner wholeness, which controls the equilibrium of the whole psyche and corrects the ego attitude through dreams. "Another, inner subject watches us in dreams," says von Franz (1980: 165–6); "it sees us as too anxious, too reckless, too immoral, or too anything else that seems to be a deviation from the norm of wholeness."[12] When we understand a dream or some other spontaneous product of the unconscious, our eyes are opened: hence the eye motif. Von Franz understands the words of Paul, "For now we see in a mirror dimly, but then face to face" (1 Corinthians 13: 12) in this sense: "at first this eye from the Beyond sees us; then through this eye we see ourselves and God or the unfalsified reality (1980: 166). Jung says, "The mandala is indeed an 'eye,' the structure of which symbolizes the centre of order in the unconscious . . . The eye may well stand for consciousness . . . looking into its own background." At the same time it is also the Self, looking at us (quoted in von Franz 1980: 166).

I wondered about the symbol of the Eye of God, the All-seeing. Edinger (1995: 65) comments that the Eye of God refers to the experience of being seen and known by an "other" in the unconscious. Psychopathology of the Eye of God refers us to the basis of paranoia, when the Eye of God is projected into the environment so that the ego has the experience of being watched, listened to, or persecuted (67). Another way to imagine the essence of the image of the Eye of God is to listen to Plotinus, who tells us that the eye would not be able to see the sun if, in a manner, it were not itself a sun (Cirlot 1962: 95). Given that the sun is the source of light, and light is symbolic of intelligence and the spirit, the process of seeing represents a spiritual act and symbolizes understanding.[13] Here, intelligence does not mean reason or discursive thought as we think of it but intelligence as an organ of direct knowledge or certainty, a pure light of intelligence that goes beyond the limits of reason alone. The theology of the Eastern Orthodox Church (in particular Maxim the Confessor) calls this organ the *Nous*. The Sufis would say that the real seat of the intellect is the heart, not the brain.

But Mairi focused on the star in the pupil of the eye more than she did the eye itself. It reminded her of being "starry-eyed," as did the dark-blue background. I thought of the night-sky Nut (Dream #8) and the angel's dark sky (Dream #2). Mairi had read how the Bushmen of South Africa believe that each individual person has a star in the sky like a heavenly twin.[14] I thought of this eye "seeing everything," like Mairi's "talking and talking and telling the angel everything" in Dream #2, and I thought of Mairi's lost twin, miscarried before her birth, somehow alive as her "other self," found again in night sky or shadow. I also thought of the star of Bethlehem, guiding the wise men to the birthplace of Jesus, the manifestation of deity. Because they followed that unusual star, three oriental kings were drawn out of personal preoccupations and into a significant destiny.

Trying to tell me what she meant by a "pun on 'eye' and 'I,'" and "'a star in the heart of the pupil,'" Mairi said, "I was always a good student, but it took me years to understand that being a good student was not the be-all and end-all of learning." Here she searched for words: "I realized something with this pun," she continued, "I realized that no matter how bright it is, no matter how beautiful it is, a star is also a stone. And a stone, even a diamond, has no place in my heart. Even a diamond-like star in my heart would be hard and hurtful, cold as a shard of ice, like a piece of stony grit in soft oyster flesh."

Mairi burst into tears. "Somehow my heart has to melt," she cried. "I need a real, beating, human heart again. The scars I carry in my heart from whatever happened to me are far worse than whatever the original events were. They make a caul over my feelings, over my heart. I feel as if I am always cramped up in the middle, as if I can't stand up straight yet. Scar tissue doesn't yield, or feel. How can scar-tissue disappear?"

In her weeping lay some of the yield and melting for which Mairi longed. With her tears what she called the caul of scar tissue began to peel away. As Mairi and I sat together holding her pain in the space between us, with my mind playing over this rich imagery of eye, star, heart, and pupil, I was reminded that Jung considers the eye to be the maternal bosom and the pupil its "child" (Cirlot 1962: 96). In Spanish this Jungian idea is also expressed as a pun, as "niña" means both daughter and pupil of the eye. The phrase "Niña de los ojos," like our phrase "the apple of one's eye," gives something of the feeling of this pun. Was Mairi remembering what it felt like to be seen as the apple of someone's eye and then to lose this connection? Was this connection being restored through the witnessing function of the transference? In light of this symbolism and Mairi's associations, we could say that like a lost child, Mairi's hurt heart sought food, comfort, and renewal at life's maternal bosom, mediated by the maternal container of our connection.

I understood Mairi's "cramped up in the middle" feeling as a "psychological cramp" in her as-yet unrealized "fully human consciousness." In Dream #8, with her body stretched over a pool, Mairi was beginning to be able to feel towards and about her "whole self" (depicted by full-body extension), but only "horizontally," suspended, and held up by her own efforts. As for "standing alone and tall with her feet on the ground," Mairi still felt "doubled over" (doubled as in twin? doubled as in dissociated? doubled as in split, bodily? doubled over in pain?). She wanted to be able to straighten up, "but I can't, quite," she said. "Straightening up" to a vertical, grounded posture is certainly an image of full "here I stand" self-acceptance, and Mairi was not there yet. But "vertical" also means something else, namely a spiritual dimension, and I wondered if Mairi's desire to be able to stand up straight might not also be a longing for spirit. Jung comments on the vertical "spiritual" outlook we have lost in our modern scientific and secular world:

> When the spiritual catastrophe of the Reformation put an end to the Gothic Age with its impetuous yearning for the heights, its

geographical confinement, and its restricted view of the world, the vertical outlook of the European mind was forthwith intersected by the horizontal outlook of modern times. Consciousness ceased to grow upward, and grew instead in breadth of view, as well as in knowledge of the terrestrial globe . . . Belief in the substantiality of the spirit yielded more and more to the obtrusive conviction that material things alone have substance, until at last, after nearly four hundred years, the leading European thinkers and investigators came to regard the mind as wholly dependent on matter and material causation. (Jung 1933: 173–4)

During a slow process of becoming conscious of a vertical dimension, it was as if Mairi's unconscious psyche stopped being like a mass of pick-up sticks (i.e., chaotic affects and images) and began to align itself, becoming centered. Jung describes this process (1955b: 258) as an

endless approximation. The goal of this approximation seems to be anticipated by archetypal symbols which represent something like the circumambulation of a centre. With increasing approximation to the centre there is a corresponding depotentiation of the ego in favour of the influence of the "empty" centre, which is certainly not identical with the archetype but is the thing the archetype points to. As the Chinese would say, the archetype is only the *name* of Tao, not Tao itself. Just as the Jesuits translated Tao as "God," so we can describe the "emptiness" of the centre as "God." Emptiness in this sense doesn't mean "absence" or "vacancy," but something unknowable which is endowed with the highest intensity.

In light of Mairi's subsequent experience of soul, the meaning of her Eye-vision takes on an added dimension if we consider it in terms of Nous, the "organ" which goes beyond the light of the intellect to become the "eye of the soul." From the writings of the early Church Fathers, Robin Amis (1995) gathers multiple definitions of the nous. In addition to being the "eye of the soul," Saint Theophan describes the nous as "awareness" (52). According to Clement of Alexandria, Saint Paul defines the nous as "non-verbal intelligence that perceives direct experience and symbols as equally 'real'" (69). Saint Anthony calls the nous the part of the mind that dis-criminates, which may at one time be filled with thoughts and images but at another time be free from all that – "The body sees by means of the eyes," Anthony writes, "and the soul by means of the nous . . ." (183). Saint John of Karpathos gives a lovely imaginative account of the nous in the *Philokalia*

The moon as it waxes and wanes illustrates the condition of man. Sometimes he does what is right; sometimes he sins and then through repentance (*metanoia*) returns to a holy life. The nous of the one who sins is not destroyed (as some of you think), just as the physical size of the moon does not diminish, but only its light. (1981: 1. 299)

Writing from the second century, Gregory of Nyssa links the parable of the sower and that of the tares by saying that the field in which tares grow is the human heart, linking this to soul. Quoting his sister Macrina as his teacher, Gregory also calls the nous the garden in which the man plants the grain of mustard seed that becomes the kingdom of heaven (Matthew 13: 31). It is also the field in which treasure is hid (Matthew 13: 44). The eye of the soul as the human heart becomes the nous that is the whole background to the drama of what Amis (1995) calls esoteric or inner Christianity.

To continue the odd punning of Mairi's experience, perhaps we could say that within her vision of God's Eye or "I," Mairi's nous – the eye of her soul – opened her to healing, addressing the issue of the "caul of scar tissue" around her heart described with such longing. According to the Church Fathers, healing the nous leads to illumination of the nous (cure of the soul),[15] and this develops the hidden potential or talents of the individual, described by St. Paul as the gifts of the Spirit. Among the gifts Paul lists are teaching, prophecy, healing, and apostleship (1 Corinthians 12: 8–11). Both Mairi and Hadewijch were teachers.

Neither tent nor church of earlier dreams, this vision was organic (as was the artichoke, Dream #6), but it points to the human realm, rather than a plant. A living enclosure, the eye opens like a flower to light, envisioning light, love, and Mairi herself. The eye indicates human receptivity, as opposed to a place or a space that has been blasted open or rent. As in her first Self-directive dream (#6), Mairi is not "within" this vision, but outside and separate; her only access was through the nous itself, our relationship, and her associations to star, pupil, and stone.

9. Burning stone

A large gray stone is embedded in the earth. Suddenly the right side of the stone bursts into brilliant yellow-orange flames that reach high into the air, clearly visible in the daylight.

Mairi's second Self-directive dream followed close upon the heels of her vision, perhaps a month later: again, no dream-ego, no persons, and few personal associations. Mairi felt as if this dream were a visual koan, a puzzle or a teaching that she wanted to understand, a collective issue that concerned her because she dreamed about it, but not her alone.

To the large gray stone embedded in the earth Mairi associated the star-stone embedded in her heart and all the emotion that had erupted around the image of her vision. Here stone, ignited, undergoes transformation, its right side bursting into flame. Mairi commented that when Moses saw the Burning Bush at least he saw something that *could* have burned: the miracle was that something that could have burned to ash did not. For Mairi (in this dream) the miracle was that something that does not burn – stone – does.

Often the image of a stone, or a jewel or crystal appears to represent the Self. Von Franz (1997: 336) muses that perhaps stone is so suitable a symbol because its nature is most completely expressed by pure "suchness," pure being-as-it-is.

> The stone symbolizes a form of consciousness that is just pure being, beyond emotions, fantasies, feelings, and the current of thoughts that characterize ego consciousness. It is a unity that merely exists, that was and is always there, unchanging. In this sense the stone symbolizes perhaps the simplest and at the same time most profound experience of the eternal and immutable that a person can have. (336)

The universal appeal of stones must have its roots in the immutability von Franz describes. Who resists picking up unusual stones from travels, beaches, mountains? We erect stone monuments to the memory of famous people and events, and we place stones on the graves of our dead. Jacob marked the site of his dream with a stone. For Muslims the most sacred stone is the black stone in Mecca, the Kaaba, to which pilgrimage is made at least once in a lifetime. The Inuit mark the "presence" of human beings along Canada's most northern shores with lifelike figures made of stones called *inukshuks*.[16] In the symbolism of the Church, Christ is "the stone which the builders rejected" (Luke 20: 17), or the "spiritual Rock that followed them" (1 Corinthians 10: 4). Medieval alchemists seeking the secret of matter in order to find in it God or God's actions saw this secret embedded in the philosopher's stone. The alchemical stone, the *lapis*, symbolizes something in us that cannot be lost and cannot dissolve, something eternal, equated by many with the experience of "God within us" (von Franz 1997: 336–7).

But stone also holds the meaning of petrifaction. In this dream, perhaps something begins to happen to "stoniness," quickened by flaming energy. Becoming radioactive, the flaming stone indicates activation of a nuclear issue in Mairi's life, her embedded-ness in gray depression. Unlike the descent of fire in the angel of Dream #2, here fire flares from below. The burning stone reminded me of the fiery angel's falling feathers, flame falling to earth that consumed nothing. Mairi was not ignited in the embrace of the fiery angel of Dream #2, and that was remarkable. She might have burned. But her earth was as barren as this gray stone was cold.

Self-directive dreams are often numinous. Their self-enclosed nature fascinates and their appearance feels like a visitation. Luminous with archetypal imagery, the impersonal nature of a Self-directive dream lends itself to an atmosphere of statements from elsewhere, or announcements "received from on high." With this dream Mairi felt as if she were dreaming a revelation, if only she could understand. There is a remarkable, little-known tale (recounted by Marco Polo)[17] about a stone presented by the Christ child to the three wise men in exchange for their gifts. Not realizing the value of the stone, the wise men cast it into a well as they journeyed home. A fire from heaven descended into the well and the kings repented, realizing that it had a great and holy meaning. They took of the fire, and carried it into their own country, where the people kept it burning and worshipped it as a God: such were the beginnings of Zoroastrianism. In this story the stone that burns or creates fire is linked to the Christ child, i.e., Christianity's pre-eminent symbol of God's penetration of this world – the spirit's fiery incarnation in matter and flesh.

The natural order of things is reversed in this dream of burning stone, as it was in the angel dream (#2) and the dream of walking under water (#5). These paradoxical images bring to mind the alchemical description of the *opus contra naturam*, which is how the alchemists characterized their labor: a work against nature. Though it emerges out of nature, alchemical work yet works against nature: out of nature must come nature's cure. The alchemical light of Dream #9 comes from nature – from below – to burn inflammable matter and cure nature. Here is what alchemy describes as the light of nature as opposed to the light of revelation, the *lumen* as opposed to the *numen* (Jung 1974: 406–7):

> According to alchemy, we, like other animals, have a natural light, an inborn spirit innate to our nature, an invisible light given to the inner body (breath-body) that illumines our consciousness. Paracelsus characterized *lumen* as a "light that is lit from the Holy Ghost and goeth not out . . . (it is) of a kind that desireth to burn . . . therefore *in the light of nature is a fiery longing to enkindle*. (emphasis mine)

Paracelsus, the great sixteenth-century physician, alchemist and philosopher, tells us that we "learn" the *lumen naturae* through dreams: "as the light of nature cannot speak, it buildeth shapes in sleep from the power of the word [of God]" (quoted in Jung 1974: 405–6). Paracelsus says that just as we cannot exist without the divine numen, so we cannot exist without the natural lumen. "A person is made perfect by numen and lumen alone," he writes, "everything springs from these two and these two are in human beings, but without them a person is nothing, though they [numen and lumen] can exist without human beings" (quoted in Jung 1974: 402). Paracelsus is referring to two sources of knowledge: the light of revelation (numen) and the light of nature (lumen) (CW13: 111).

In my experience, what Jung calls the light of nature and what Neumann (1959) refers to as "gathering the lumen" become evident as the self-knowledge we gather during a therapeutic process becomes heart-felt. In order for something to become heart-felt, access to feeling and emotion is necessary, but that is not sufficient. The attitude with which we "gather" matters, too. Because love springs from our capacity to be, it does not depend only on how we feel, nor is it something that we must do. We learn to permit love. Openness counts, and humility. So do receptivity, trust or faith in something other than what we already know, and hope for eventual meaning. When something becomes heart-felt, we have become seriously engaged.

Mairi had no consciously held faith to depend upon as she gathered lumen. But perhaps faith is not so much a binary pole (faith – lack of faith) as it is a kind of quantum state which tends to indeterminacy when closely examined. Unlike the fixity of a belief, faith is like an illumination, and illumination is what flamed forth from Mairi's Burning Stone. An experience of emerging faith is a bit like falling in love: after that, you change, you act differently, with faith. One is confident, one acts *con-fidere*, with faith. Psychoanalyst Robert Grinnell (1973: 89) calls this "psychological faith." Unlike religious faith, psychological faith is not a belief *in* something, but confidence in a process that permits, sustains, and vitalizes our experiences of belief. Psychological faith keeps us intimately connected to both the psychic depths and the image-making process. Faith in the value of her dreams and in our relationship kept Mairi connected to "gathering lumen."

Psychological faith is not the prerogative of the ego or the rational soul, but it can be found at every level of the psyche and soul. It is a gift. In some sense, *dreaming itself gives evidence of psychological faith*.[18] The devotion that Mairi displayed in gathering lumen through her dreams, and her faith that puzzling images were not meaningless, even when she could see no meaning, opened her heart to the deep things of God. When our hearts open – whether in heartbreak or in love – hard-won words and images "fall in," not to be lost again. Stone burns. The old alchemists describe the philosopher's stone as "fire-tried."

10. Three angels

Three angels in white descend from the sky to stand on the earth: A man, a woman, and a child.

Mairi's third Self-directive dream followed the dream of burning stone by about three months. Here the single great angel of Dream #2 has become three. The fiery hermaphrodism of the first angel falls to earth to become two clearly gendered beings and a child, whose potential definition is to develop. White robes are common angel garb, but perhaps they also refer to the *albedo*, the alchemical stage of purification, purification of the angelic archetype (mediator, messenger), and integration of that originally flaming descent. From a psychological point of view, "whitening" is akin to "washing," which refers to a stage of wringing the complexes dry of unconscious emotion. "Washing" the complex of Mairi's birth trauma might point to her possible rebirth – "on earth," this time, "as it was in heaven."

In this dream an earlier, primitive organic unity (also depicted in the artichoke dream #6) differentiates from archetypal duality (two-ness) into three-ness, or an archaic trinity. With the enlargement of consciousness an archetypal patterning of two poles once experienced as conflicting opposites begins to be viewed as compensatory or even complementary – as polarities, or opposites reconciled. The realization that one opposite cannot exist without the other mediates the tension of this conflict. The single symbol of the Chinese Tao consists of recognized opposition, embracing male and female, white and black, movement and stasis, warm and cool, and light and dark.

But in Dream #10 differentiation is the issue. In light of Mairi's psychological situation I understood three-ness as making space for an awareness of body, along with mind and spirit. In retrospect I would say that it also made room for Mairi's experience of soul alongside ego and psyche. I say this because the organic unity imaged in the artichoke dream (#6) implies soul in a vegetative state, and because the undefended body motif of the lightning dream (#7) and the bodily effort depicted in the swimming and stretching of Dream #8 both point toward the human dimension which began to emerge with Mairi's vision of the Eye. In these dreams and in her vision, body and soul seem to be coming into focus.

Mairi's comment on the three angels was that angels did not have gender. As far as I know, this is true, although I seldom think of Raphael, Gabriel, and Michael as feminine. Mairi's angelic dream figures *were* gendered, as male, female, and child. Certainly something about "family" is here – man, woman and child – as if an archaic wholeness of family were being addressed. Mairi's personal experience of family unity had been sorely hurt.

In light of Mairi's musings upon how difficult it seemed to "stand up," I noticed that these three angels "stood." On the mountaintop of Dream #7, after being struck by lightning, Mairi, her father, and her infant son were thrown into various positions of distress: sitting hurt, standing paralyzed, and thrown to the ground. In contrast, this dream depicts a man, woman and child descending safely to earth. Descent from the sky to the earth almost always points to descent into the body, i.e., to incarnation. And an experience of trinity marks a progressive realization of faith in an incarnational god. Here a Self-directive dream (#10) pictures the archetype of primitive family unity as alive and well, as if a spirit of organic, collective unity were landing on earth. This dream presaged Mairi's eventual ability to "come to earth," to fully straighten up and stand up for herself, and to embody a collective unity, free from the cramp of her personal family complex.

11. On the beach, naked woman, fiery skin

I am walking along the top of some dunes near a beach with friends at night. Looking down the dunes I see a naked woman walking along the sand next to the water below us. Her head, shoulders, and entire left side seem to be filled with fire, flickering orange, red and yellow below the surface of her white, translucent skin.

For the first time in this series Mairi is with "friends," rather than alone or with a companion, her solitary state beginning to give way to potential relatedness. On the beach below, solitude is embodied and personified by a naked woman (undefended body, again) who walks along the water's edge. Her head, shoulders, and entire left side are translucent (as opposed to the right side of the stone, Dream #9). Flame flickers beneath the surface of her skin. We might say that "body," for which space is being made (Dream #10) does not yet belong to Mairi, but is "in the shadow." But "body" is human now, a woman's body, neither mythic, nor hermaphroditic, nor angelic. The light beneath the woman's skin suggests internalization of warmth, humanization of the influx of passionate energy from both above and below depicted in the flaming angel of Dream #2 and the burning stone of Dream #9. The woman's head, shoulders and left side glow, the ignited element no longer stony. Flesh, rendered transparent, is lit from within. This dream points to lumen, the light of nature, and heralded Mairi's later experience of bodily illumination.

The naked woman's glowing body made me think again of Mairi's birth caul. Perhaps the waxy coating with which she was born smothered the same area around her head and shoulders, but it could not have covered her side as the light did in her dream. Could the glow on the left refer to a side of Mairi's small body which felt lost – the space-place her missing twin once occupied, nestled near within the womb? Or might it signify illumination of "body" from the left, the left side indicative of the unconscious itself? Perhaps both.

Mairi said that she loved to walk along the beach, any beach at all, and did so as often as she could. She did not recognize these friends as personal acquaintances, nor did she recognize the solitary woman. The time of this dream is evening, neither day nor night but a liminal "time between," when "on the shores of endless worlds, children play" (Tagore). Evening is a time of edges blurred, a third space between opposing light and dark. Beaches, too, bridge land and water, earth and sky.

12. Four colors

Four quarters of colored space, each quarter [implicitly forming a cross] brilliant: yellow, red, blue and green.

After the warmth of being among friends on a beach (#11), the impersonal nature of Mairi's fourth Self-directive dream left us with little to say: no human touch anywhere. Mairi did a watercolor of the four quarters and brought it to our session. We felt that a completed spectrum was probably the point of the dream, a mandala made up of what Jung (CW14: 390) calls the "color *quaternio*," expressive of the emotional range and full spectrum of feeling that was seeping into Mairi's awareness.

Color is a vibrant medium in which to portray a psychic spectrum of subtle differences in emotional tone and intensity. Color occurs when archetypal energy (white? like lightning?) is refracted through the prism of the body, leading to a spectrum of affect and emotion. Jung (CW14: 389) tells us that in alchemy the *lapis* is said to contain or produce all colors and is related to Iris as goddess and rainbow, as well as to the iris of the eye (e.g., Mairi's vision). The alchemical image of the Peacock (the *cauda pavonis*), whose gloriously colored tail expresses all possible permutations of emotional and feeling experience, is also thought of as the bird of Hermes, which alludes again to the blessed greenness and the Soul of the World and is a symbol of the Holy Ghost (CW14: 391). Leaving Mairi's personal reality aside, this Self-directive dream presents an abstraction of feeling wholeness.

I did not ignore the mandala aspects of some of Mairi's Self-directive dreams (e.g., this dream, the artichoke dream #6, the vision of the Eye), but neither did I emphasize it. While working with a dream there is little to be gained by reducing it to universals. Once a mandala format has been remarked upon, further comment can diminish the significance of the personal aspect of such an experience, which is always more promising than another version of the same old story, and Self-directive dreams have no personal aspects to begin with. Mairi's painting of this dream was personal, and therefore important. Her personal effort enabled her to link her vision of the dream to paper, and it enabled me to link my vision of her dream to what I understood to be her personal effort to honor it.

Mairi herself noted that her vision of the Eye was mandala-like: "a human mandala," she called it. In contrast, the four-color spread of Dream #12 was abstract. From her yoga studies Mairi was familiar with mandala-like *yantras*, images used for meditative centering. She knew as well as I that the centers of mandala formations were to be meditated upon in preparation for a transformation of consciousness. I noticed that with the exception of her waking vision of the Eye and the dream of herself as a swimmer braced over the pool like Leonardo's "man" (#8), many of

Mairi's mandala-like dreams (the artichoke, Dream #6), this dream of four quarters (#12), later the rose (#16) and the globe of the earth itself (#13), though highly mandalic in form, were not particularly marked by centers. This was true of all of Mairi's Self-directive dreams.[19] Even her watercolor depiction of Dream #12 had only the thinnest of separations between vivid areas of color, each section differentiated more by essence than by line, existing side by side with the others round a wheel. From another perspective, however, I could see that images of artichoke, eye, rose and earth consisted almost entirely of "centeredness," depicting an "essence" of center. In contrast to more highly structured, definitely centered and sharply differentiated mandalas, Mairi's Self-directive material displays a diffuse, overall-aspect of organically portrayed wholeness in which center is implicit rather than explicitly displayed. In retrospect, I wonder whether this paradoxical feature of Mairi's mandalic material points to transformation of the quality of Mairi's consciousness, becoming more lunar than solar, or more feminine than masculine. Shortly after the Four Colors dream came the following:

13. Buddha with a globe

To my left, standing tall in yellow robes, the Buddha faces me, holding in his hands the globe of the world. Though he is silent, I understand that I must submerge myself in a pool of red blood that is on the ground in front of me. I prepare to do so.

This dream moved and fascinated Mairi, as numinous material does. That the Avatar of all her yogic practice, the Buddha, appeared in her dream made Mairi aware that something of transcendent importance was happening in her life and her analysis. It made her feel "special," part of something larger than her earthbound ego. In this dream something "came down" to dream in her – in this case, a dream of the world, held in the hands of the great God-man of the East. Mythological figures that appear in dreams can be understood to indicate a paucity of life happening in consciousness. At this time, although Mairi could imagine coming to life emotionally, she experienced little of this in reality. Living quietly, teaching, seeing old friends, her newly awakened feelings essentially remained contained in her analysis.

The mandala the Buddha holds is the earth itself. And the Buddha stands tall, where Mairi cannot. This time her descent is to consist of self-immersion in a pool of blood. Baptism suggests initiation, and a bloody baptism suggests again an initiatic ordeal, as in Dream #4, where black spiders were to bite red double-crosses on the backs of Mairi's hands. The Buddha stands to Mairi's left, where the left side of the naked woman walking the beach in Dream #11 glowed, perhaps bringing alive Mairi's long-ago body sense of her missing twin. Does Buddha here stand for the "missing other," who will keep Mairi's world safe while she submerges herself? Or can we suppose that the Buddha represents a kind of consciousness that, in its witnessing capacity, sustains Mairi's world as she prepares for immersion?

To Mairi, the Buddha in her dream was as silent as the scriptural depiction of the Buddha when in reply to questions about enlightenment he stood before his disciples holding up a flower. That posture, that gesture, that silence, was Buddha's answer to all questions. In Mairi's dream the Buddha holds the earth. To what question does that gesture reply?

Like the law of impermanence, the Buddhist doctrine of not-self is not a product of philosophical speculation but expresses deep religious experience, affirming that contrary to what we may think, we are not merely bodies or minds. If we are not either or both, what are we? Stemming from his experience of enlightenment, the Buddha's answer shatters not ego but the ego's unconscious pretensions: "In truth I say to you that within this fathom-high body, with its thoughts and perceptions, lies the world and the rising of the world and the ceasing of the world and the Way that leads to the extinction of rising and ceasing" (Kapleau 1995: 7).

Enlightenment is not abstract, it is always enlightenment *about* something. I asked Mairi if this dream frightened her. She said no, that it felt like a "just-so story." She had been immersed before, she laughed, though always in water. Then she punned on Socrates' dictum, "Know thyself": "For a Buddhist," she said, "'Know thyself' means 'No thyself,' but that isn't what I've been doing here. I've been trying to find myself." I suggested that perhaps not-self was not the same thing as no-self, and she agreed. Rather than viewing ego-development as all-important, Buddhism proposes that we see the ego as a necessary fiction. But a necessary fiction does not *not* exist, as in Mairi's pun. The image of the Buddha pointed to her yogic studies and her sometime-practice of Zen, but I felt that the image of immersion in blood was more relevant and we wondered what that might have to do with her. Clearly submersion in blood indicates a deep encounter with her own suffering – a vivid evolution of the image of the red circus tent (Dream #1) into which earlier she could not enter, fearing an experience of "too much pain."

Writing from both a tradition of meditation and an object-relations point of view, psychiatrist Mark Epstein (1998: 102) tells us that

> Both the ancient tradition of Buddhist psychology and the modern one of psychotherapy recognize that recovering the capacity to feel is crucial to their disciplines. There can be no wholeness without integration of feelings. The paradox is that while we seek to integrate feelings, the only way to access them is through a state of [what Winnicott calls] unintegration. We need a state of reverie to know our emotions. This

reverie both gives us space, as Winnicott described, and allows us to take in others' feelings, as therapists have discovered. As the psychologist and writer Gregory Bateson used to say, "It takes two to know one."[20]

Pondering Mairi's pun on No-thyself, I thought of Winnicott's (1962: 61) observations on the necessity in adulthood to discover – or to rediscover – the ability to "lose oneself," or to create an environment in which it is safe to be "nobody," because only then can we begin to find ourselves. I wondered if this were part of the attraction Buddhist thought held for Mairi. I also wondered about the seeming paradox of the Buddha attending a baptism by blood, which is specifically a Christian image. While a Buddhist counsel of detachment from self is useful for self-exploration (Epstein 1995), the Christian counsel of baptism in blood implies the opposite of detachment: an immersion to extraordinary depth in the great passions of bodily life and death. Though both religions emphasize the great value of com-passion, I wondered if they mean the same thing by this word, or if there is a difference in the quality of compassion, somehow. Perhaps Buddhist compassion is less personal than Christian love? I wasn't sure. Perhaps Mairi's dream suggests that the kind of detachment which had become necessary to her from her ego's point of view might not apply to dimensions of soul or body.

I understood Mairi's necessary immersion as part of the initiatory ordeal referred to above in the feathery-spider dream (#4). A plunge into a pool of blood points toward Jung's metaphor for individual religious experience: "warm, red blood, pulsating today" (CW11: 88). Within the compassionate mind of the tall, yellow-robed Buddha and in my presence, Mairi was to undergo not only trial by fire (Dream #2, Dream #9), but trial by blood, risking complete submersion and trusting that she would emerge again, transformed.

14. Statue of a woman

I am in a museum looking at a reddish earth-colored clay statue of the body of a woman, posed in movement, maybe turning, with her arms slightly raised. I hear a voice that says "This is your shadow."

Here the red (blood) of the previous dream appears in the reddish earth-body of a woman in motion, arms extended upward. Affect has progressed from flaming fire to pooling blood and now to reddish earth, as if passion itself were undergoing coagulation (an alchemical coagulatio) or gradual incarnation. This earthen statue reminded Mairi of early Neolithic goddess figures in a celebratory or dance position – some of the earliest images of the feminine in Western civilization. A voice says, "This is your shadow," i.e., the *body* is your shadow. If the body is one's shadow, what can integration of the shadow mean, other than integration of the body?

Our culture affirms the manipulation of our bodily nature over developing an ability to dwell responsively within it, so this dream points to collective shadow, too. While Mairi's reddish-earth woman's body is not yet animated, and her dream-ego is still in an observing role, there is definite movement from the abstract (archetypal) ritual implied in the Buddha-dream into the body. Just as Adam, the original "red man," frequently represents the aboriginal self, here is an actual beginning of incarnation.

Mairi said in response to this dream, "When I heard the voice I realized that for me, being in my body has always seemed like being in the Valley of the Shadow of Death. I'm terrified of dying, although I used to boast that I was not. That was part of saying that nothing could get to me. Underneath, the fear of death penetrated me to the marrow of my bones. That's how I've been able to treat myself as if I were a statue."

Thinking about a statue's rigidity, I remembered the months spent in arm braces in Mairi's early infancy, as well as the physical and psychological discipline of her years of dance and yoga training. I also thought of the mysterious role played by the statue in ancient alchemy: from the heart of a statue is extracted the water of life (CW14: 560), or the heart of a statue hides a precious substance (564), or it stands for inert materiality which needs an animating soul (569).[21] I also noted the appearance of a voice which spoke and was heard in this dream, in marked contrast to the visual and aesthetic configurations more resonant with Mairi's detached, observing attitude.

Neumann (1969) suggests that the appearance of a heard voice in a dream marks the achievement within a personality of what he calls a "second" level of consciousness, a level beyond pure conformity. Contrasting "conscience" as the authority by which the collective ethic imposes sanctions on us as individuals with what he calls the "Voice," which represents an individual expression of psychic truth, Neumann ties the development of this second level of consciousness to shadow integration. On the basis of compliance with or conformity to outer requirements, Mairi's previous life had been lived almost entirely in the collective. Now a second level of consciousness with an inner Voice indicates that Mairi has access to an inner compass, a new, inward source and affirmation of individual value and personal values.

Acceptance of the shadow means acceptance of all that has been sacrificed by the developing personality in order to form an acceptable persona or public mask. Thus integration of the shadow is "the essential basis for the actual achievement of an ethical attitude towards the 'Thou' who is outside me," writes Neumann (1969: 8). Integration of the shadow in Mairi's situation (meaning her achievement of an embodied awareness of her animating emotional suffering) relates to Mairi's growing capacity for self–other awareness. This integration is not easy. With it, says Neumann, the decisive ethical authority shifts from commonly accepted, collective values of good and evil and a conventional conscience to the experience of an inner Voice which is often in conflict with collective values. When the inner Voice leads to a rejection of collective morality, it challenges one's individual decision and responsibility to the highest degree. Acceptance of the Voice does not involve indiscriminate approval of everything which comes from inside, however, any more than acceptance of the negative side of something implies acting out negativity without resistance (Neumann 1969: 110). Discriminative judgment is imperative.

Mairi's dawning realization of personal as opposed to collectively sanctioned responsibility for her own life showed in an observation she made during a session after this dream. Sailing with some friends in the popular resort area of a large nearby lake, she said that she had been startled by a sign in the middle of the lake which read, "You Are Responsible For Your Wake." "Always before I saw that sign in terms of a boat's wake," she said, "which is, of course, what it refers to. But last Saturday I read it in terms of my life, as if it were speaking to me. I am more responsible than I have known, or can easily say, for what has happened around me unthinkingly, and for everything in my life that has affected and upset others."

In addition to Neumann's developmental slant on the Voice, I saw Mairi's hearing of a voice in this dream as a call to a larger, deeper, more integrated and embodied life. What Neumann calls "second consciousness" I think pointed again to Mairi's emerging capacity for a participating, symbolic consciousness, perhaps similar to Neumann's second conscious-ness but not identical. As we will see in Hadewijch's material, a voice calls both Mairi and Hadewijch to account for *fearing the fullness of life*. Facing the results of her emotional dissociation, her paralyzed instinctive behavior, and her unconscious fear of death, Mairi struggled to integrate how deeply she had feared all of life, including the religious dimension. Her pro-gressively deepening capacity for self–other relatedness demanded that she take into full account the effects of her behavior and attitudes not only on herself but on those she left "in her wake" – her family, her ex-husbands, her children, her friends.

From here on all the dreams are from Mairi's fifth year of analysis. The next dream occurred within two months of Dream #14.

15. Swami B. is dancing

Swami B. is dancing, whirling like a dervish.

This brief dream was vivid, "like looking at a whirling top." It is not a Self-directive dream because it contains a person, even though the person is not

Mairi. In striking contrast to the motionless statue in Dream #14, this dream portrays a person in motion, embodied as her yoga teacher (and teachings), fully engaged in ecstatic movement.

Mairi simply identified Swami B. as her yoga teacher from Southern India. She had avoided becoming part of his community of followers, so she did not feel that she knew him personally even though she had studied Hatha yoga with him for several years. Before coming to America Swami B. taught yoga to political prisoners in India, managing to keep them fit and well through years of incarceration. Badly crippled as a boy, he no longer bore any indication of his early disfigurement. Knowledge that he had healed himself moved Mairi, and she associated him with healing hurt bodies.

We were impressed with the intensity Swami B.'s small white-be-turbaned, flying figure conveyed, whirling round and round like a Sufi-dancer. Dervish dancing refers to the circling of the spirit around the cycle of existing things, receiving the effects of unveilings and revelations (Bakhtiar 1976: 70). This is the state of the mystic. "The whirling is a reference to the spirit's standing with God in its Secret . . . the circling of its look and thought, and its penetrating the ranks of existing things . . . And his leaping up is a reference to his being drawn from the human station to the station of union . . ." (70).

In their whirling, dervishes refer to their soaring spirits as the falcon, flying towards God. Sufi dancing is a far stretch from the careful sustained discipline with which Mairi practiced her yogic asanas, or the calm medi-tative attitude yogis strive to cultivate. This little dream suggests contra-diction: to escape yogic (yoke-like) discipline means no longer to be inhibited (incarcerated) or controlled by the mind's intent. Mairi's spirited capacity for a spontaneous, authentically embodied life turned toward ecstasy. I thought of Rumi again. Like Mairi with her yogic discipline, Rumi's discipline of music and whirling dance (*sema*) dramatically declares the body as the necessary vehicle for the kind of mystical realization that will correspond with Mairi's experience of soul. When one has experienced this state, says Rumi, one knows that life has meaning, one knows that love and joy transcend all sorrow and that nothing is absurd because, as he puts it, "man is infinitely greater than man" (de Vitray-Meyerovitch 1987: 12). With this phrase Rumi points toward his personal experience of Universal Personhood, or – as a Taoist might put it – his experience of True Man, which touches upon what Jung called the Anthropos, an experience of universal man or Whole Human Being.

Reflecting on this dream and Mairi's progress, I was struck again by how transpersonal dimensions of the psyche mediated in the analytic situation address trauma. We do not have to go back and abreact everything, or recover all memories. It is as if some transpersonal center gathers every-thing up into an integrated whole and presents it in emotionally moving images: or is it that this center holds everything together so that we can enter the world feeling as if someone else (another, the Buddha? Rumi's "Beloved?") will hold the center for us, in case we fall apart?

16. Rose dream

An enormous red rose, each petal carved or engraved with a version of human relatedness – friend–friend, friend–enemy, brother–sister, mother–child, lover–beloved, husband–wife, neighbor–stranger, etc. The petals of the rose are so vivid they tremble, as if each petal were made of blood or some other liquid about to spill over the rim of itself.

Following close upon dreams that emphasized body and Mairi's increasing capacity for a wide spectrum of emotional experience came this one of a full-bodied rose. Strikingly like Mairi's first Self-directive dream (green artichoke, #6), this dream consisted of a single organic image, an enormous, full-blown, deep red rose, "so full of color," Mairi stammered, "that the petals brimmed like blood about to spill." As in the artichoke dream, each petal was engraved with a form of human relatedness – every imaginable kind of relationship. So vivid was the dream that the rose seemed fragrant, reminding Mairi of scents she had inhaled on hot summer afternoons when as a child she stood barefoot in the warm brown dirt of her grandmother's rose garden. It also reminded her of a perfume she liked to wear. Both these associations were body-based, anchored in memories of scent and touch, our most intimately personal senses.

I have imagined that Self-directive dreams presage or herald the emergence of a capacity for an all-out, no-holds-barred way of experiencing oneself and life in the world. This way of experiencing encompasses all the unconscious emotional experience which up until now could not have been tolerated, consciously encompassed, or borne, and represents experience which has not been metabolized by the body of one's incarnate life. This Rose, this Self-directive dream, does more than simply compensate for rigidity and restriction, deprivation and numbness. The proportions of the capacity for experience to which this image points are intense and wide, necessary for a soul that has been lost to body. This numinous image moved heart and mind together, fascinating Mairi with the sudden revelation that her existence consisted of something more than the existentially "blighted bud" of an unlived life. Out of an un-bruised rose of individual consciousness flowers not isolation and self-absorption, but union with God and the world, a union which is mystical and eternal in a way that other unions based on either mind or body cannot be. Thus we can see it as part of a prolegomena to the full retrieval of Mairi's soul into her body.

The dream was visually and aesthetically compelling. Neither Mairi nor I could anchor it in circumstances of daily life. As warm and trusting as our therapeutic relationship felt to each of us, these feelings paled before the emotional intensity of this dream. I thought of Jung's cautionary reminder (CW16: 454) that although an experience of wholeness fully depends upon the relationship of one person with another, essentially the principle of self–other awareness or wholeness is the product of *an intrapsychic process*. Mairi's and my therapeutic relationship might pave the way for her individuation, but in itself our relationship neither caused nor gave proof of the psyche's movement toward healing, nor of Mairi's conscious trans-formation. For Mairi, neither healing nor transformation would occur outside of soul.

Mairi and I talked about the color red again, appearing here "full-blown." Red had moved from tent and fiery angel to flaming stone and pool of blood, to reddish earth and blood of the rose. Again I reached for cultural amplification. Fossilized wild roses have been dated as far back as 40 million years, so roses were already considered ancient when the Greek botanist Theophrastus (270 BCE) wrote about "the hundred-petaled rose" (Ackerman 1991: 35). In Greek mythology, the red rose (Aphrodite's flower), once white but stained by the blood of Aphrodite when she caught her finger on a thorn, declares love for eternity. The mystery and beauty of the archetypal feminine is the focus of Mairi's dream.

Unlike Dream #6, a green artichoke of possible food and flower in bud, this rose flowers passionately, declaring to the world that it is beautiful, open, available, and desirable. Its vivid color ignites dramatic emotion and heartfelt desire, reminding us of life-blood, rich and warm. In vestigial ways, its fragrance reminds us of fertility and vigor, and the optimism, expectancy, and passionate bloom of ardent youth, particularly ardent feminine youth. In Jean Cocteau's film, *Beauty and the Beast*, everything begins when the daughter – promised whatever she wishes – asks her father for a rose, a single rose from her father's hand being her sole desire. Mairi also knew this film and its father/daughter rose.

"For years," said Mairi, "I puzzled over how in the world Beauty could have come to love the Beast. One day I realized that the most important thing that happened was that Beauty finally left her father and his promises, even if he had fulfilled them. Her father loved Beauty, but he was old and ill and wanted her at home. Beauty loved her father, but she had to leave him even if he were dying in order to keep her promise to the Beast. Only after the split with her father could Beauty *feel* her love for the Beast, which allowed the Beast to become human. Funny, isn't it, how the same story can mean one thing at one time in your life, and something else at another?" I agreed. From Mairi's observation on the shift in her own understanding I understood that her deepest sense of spiritual authority had been transformed. A changed understanding of this tale reveals a shift of Mairi's psyche from residence under the aegis of the Father (as father's daughter) – even the negative Father (Zeus, Dream #7) – to residence under the aegis of Eros, as Mairi claimed allegiance to a growing sense of her feminine self – albeit in relation to a beast.

Yet the red rose bespeaks more than passionate love. The rose is also the symbol of the Virgin Mary.[22] As an image of the unseen shaping of the Self, the rose is an image of the soul, as well. Alan Watts (1954: 116) tells us that Saint Bernard said of the Virgin that she "was the Flower who willed to be born of a flower, in flower, in the season of flowers"; so Christ is the Fruit of the Flower, the Mystic Rose. I thought of the lovely hymn "Lo, how a Rose 'ere blooming." I also remembered what Owen Barfield (1953: 127) refers to as "that strange 'Rose' tradition" which is preserved to us in Chaucer's translation of the *Roman de la Rose*: apparently there grew up during the thirteenth and fourteenth centuries a small, special vocabulary, defining the landmarks in a new region of the imagination which the poets and even the scholars of Europe were just discovering, called the region of devotional love . . . devotion remaining purely theological until as late as the sixteenth century.[23]

Henri Corbin (1953: 15ff.) tells us that the Persians thought of flowers as the *prima materia* of the resurrection process. Every angel and every divine power possesses its own special flower, and the Daena – the divine anima of the man – has the rose of a hundred petals. A daena is a daughter of the cosmic Sophia, the man's celestial alter ego or anima image, the mirror of his earthly likeness formed from his good deeds that originate in his active imagination (out of his good thoughts). A daena is actually the religious visionary organ of the soul itself, "the light it throws and which makes it possible to see" (Corbin 1953: 28, 36, 42).

Meditation on a flower like this rose makes possible an epiphany of otherworldly divinity within the archetypal world. The feminine principle of Eros is a god not only of *coniunctio*, but of destiny, as well. "The fire and the rose are one," sings T. S. Eliot's *Little Gidding*, mingling heat and heart, passion and love in mystical prose. Mairi's dreams indicated movement from the green beginnings of the alchemical opus to the final stage, the *rubedo*. At the stage of *rubedo* life is to be lived passionately and fully in the world. From a psychotherapeutic point of view, at this stage a patient becomes able to bring insights and capacities gained in therapy back out into life in the world. This dream-rose is a full mandala, symbolic of totality and an image of the center. It brought Mairi smack into an imaginative experience of Eros, archetypal love, and an undefended heart. As a symbol for the heart, this rose blooms at the heart of any matter, whenever love is at issue – not love in the abstract, but love in relationship.

As I wrote my comments on this dream, I recalled three occasions on which Mairi told me about incidents in the world in which she "noticed" herself (became aware of her own consciousness) in an unusual fashion. The first time happened near the beginning of therapy. Mairi told me that once after a session it felt as if "one part of my brain touched another part, and I thought Oh, *that's* what they mean by the Virgin Birth!" When she told me this, I understood her to mean that she had experienced in a sensate fashion the undoing of a previous dissociation (one formerly dissociated part of her mind – or self – touching another). The second incident, perhaps two years later, formed part of a narrative of "what happened last night": "We (she and a friend) were driving along a country road at twilight," Mairi said; "I was looking out the window. I saw something along the side of the road, and I felt my mind so clearly form the gestalt of the head of a cow – which, as we came closer, turned out to be a mailbox!" This occasioned laughter and Mairi's comment, "I really felt myself 'seeing things.' I mean, I knew at the time that what I saw couldn't be the head of a cow," she said, "but I could feel my mind making it into one."

The third incident happened when Mairi was in the Southern Hemisphere. She looked up into the night sky at stars she had never seen before "and I felt my mind making connections between the stars, finding forms, and I felt my imagination begin to weave stories about what I was seeing." *Feeling* this instinctively imaginative activity surprised her. "I had no idea how I depended on knowing the constellations, on their familiarity, until I saw a sky that I didn't know at all. My disorientation made me into a primitive sailor at sea; I could feel myself having to make sense of anything that was around me in order to find direction. How odd. That must be how the stories about the constellations happened in the first place, a long time ago."

Telling me these three incidents, Mairi was interested in *what* she perceived. I was *as* interested, if not more so, in *how* she perceived what she perceived. Each occasion seemed to speak for Mairi's unusual growing capacity for apprehending, even sensing, her mind/body engagement in the world around her. It was as if she were beginning to feel herself think, or think about what she felt, simultaneously.

Perhaps these incidents came to mind with regard to the image of the great red rose because this dream implicates the *rubedo*, the final stage of the alchemical process – taking what has happened in therapy out into the world again. At the time of the rose dream Mairi was moving into her life with an expanded quality of self-awareness which included physiological as well as psychological insight.

The remaining dreams in this series followed one another within several weeks. All were exceptionally vivid and succinct. All had an emotional impact on both of us. Not all the dreams were Self-directive, but many were. As usual, the Self-directive dreams were vastly impersonal, dreams of spiritual transformation (#17), purification (#18), and what I understood as a statement of relationship between fully human consciousness and the world (#22). Those which were not Self-directive (#19, 20, 21, 23) depicted Mairi's personal self-emergence, her new relatedness to archetypal reality from both a lunar (feminine) and a solar (masculine) point of view, and –

emerging from the psyche's rebalancing – Mairi's conscious entry into full embodiment.

17. Bird with jeweled wings

A great brown bird (a falcon?), its head turned to the side, looking back over its folded, bejeweled wings which are outlined in shining colored precious stones. A voice says, "There is a shift in the order of things."

This dream returns Mairi to a new version of mediator or messenger between the worlds, a bird with attributes of both heaven and earth: wings like angels (#2, 10), yet red-brown as the earth of the clay statue in Dream #14. The image of a falcon brings to mind powers of spirit: wind, height, wings, and a capacity to hunt and kill as well as seize and carry. Mairi was more impressed with the voice in this dream than she had been with the voice of Dream #14, announcing the statue-body as her shadow. But she did not know what to make of the message, "a shift in the order of things."

An authentic connector of height to depth, the falcon mediates between heaven and earth. Flaming angel and lightning stroke, three angels above and fire from below, coalesced into the image of a single bird, an archaic but consistent symbol of the soul since the time of the Lascaux cave paintings some 30,000–80,000 years ago.[24] Perhaps this falcon symbolizes Mairi's capacity for keen-eyed vision "come to earth." The great brown bird of a high-flying, flaming intuition is dreamed into transformation and pause: Spirit becomes spiritedness. In *The Seed Market*,[25] Rumi writes,

> This giving up is not a repenting.
> It's a deep honoring of yourself . . .
> A perfect falcon, for no reason,
> has landed on your shoulder,
> and become yours. (Ayliffe et al. 1992: 806–7)

Relative to the still-being-washed, white-garbed angels of Dream #10, this earthy brown falcon conveys a sense of integrated shadow. Nevertheless, this bird is not of nature, for its wings are rimmed with jewels. Precious stones reflect the colors of the once-ignited, "fire-tried stone" (Dream #9), taken to flight. The quadrated colors of Mairi's emotional spectrum (Dream #12) have hardened into flashing jewels. I understood the phrase, "a shift in the order of things" to refer to what Neumann (1953) calls "a change in reality planes." Here something ordinary, even common (matter, body, soul, emotion) is elevated to regnancy, uplifted and bejeweled.

The great brown bird looks back over its shoulder in a posture of reflection different from the reflection embodied by Mairi as she peered down into the pool in Dream #8. The falcon stands as an image of instinctive, creative self-reflection, perhaps alluding to Jung's affirmation of an *instinct* toward self-reflection, which is as real when it is functioning as an instinct to survive.

The image brought to mind the story of Horus, a major figure in the founding myths of Egypt. Son of Osiris and Isis, Horus also experienced being "double-crossed" (see Mairi's initiatory ordeal by spider-bite, Dream #4): Isis, his mother, changed her allegiance to Horus' rescue mid-stream in order to align herself with her own dark brother, Set. In the myth, Horus dies, but resurrects. As he prevails, his capacity to see – symbolized by the "eye of Horus" (an image of a wounded eye or an eye with a tear-like configuration in its corner) – broadens to encompass both the sun and the moon. Gifted with both solar and lunar vision, the resurrected Horus represents an ego related to both light and dark, tempered by suffering life's adversity. For the Egyptians, Horus' solar and lunar vision united Upper and Lower Egypt. In Hatha yoga, a union of solar and lunar vision indicates the opening of the third eye.

This falcon-headed Egyptian god is one of our earliest symbols of the wholeness of life resurrected in the wake of painful dismemberment and crucifixion. I also remembered Mairi's vision of the Eye. The dream of this falcon, implying double-vision and solar and lunar integration gained through emotional experience ranging from death to resurrection, was part of a process of cleansing the nous, or eye of the soul. It parallels melting "the stone in the heart of the pupil" of Mairi's vision, right down to the tears.

As a symbol of the soul, however, this falcon is distinct. Falcons are hunters and raptors, falcons are strong of wing and keen of sight, flying high in order to dive swiftly to the kill. To find that one's soul bird is a falcon differs from envisioning one's soul bird as a dove. Falcons have a fierceness and freedom about them which is foreign to doves. Bird of the Virgin Mary as well as Aphrodite, doves bill and coo, soft and white. Doves do fly (a dove brought an olive branch, signaling to Noah land above water after the flood), but they tend to keep to the ground. In contrast, falcons soar and fall, living and dying in a world of flesh and blood, predator and prey. Mairi dreamed of other birds, too: once an owl, also a raptor, captured a white rabbit to the distress of a boy child; another time a white gull with black stripes on its wings flew in the sun ("He earned his stripes," Mairi said, "he doesn't look pure and innocent anymore.") But her Self-directive dream of a falcon was the most striking of all.[26]

Here again a voice pronounces something of note: There is a shift in the order of things. In light of Mairi's subsequent experience of soul, perhaps this falcon points toward the transformation of archetypal spirit (Zeus, Dream #7) into the Holy Spirit. Mairi had little else to say except to comment upon bejeweled wings. Were they heavy when the great bird flew? Mairi lightly lifted her shoulders (her "wing bones," as she called them), smiling as she spoke.

18. White elephant on a white sea

A great white elephant stands on a white ocean: this is the centerpiece of a white altar, which is inside a white cathedral.

This Self-directive dream gave Mairi and me another way to picture both transformation of the spirit and spiritual transformation. For all the possible lack of emphasis on a "center" in the other Self-directive dreams (with the exception of the Rose, #16, and the Artichoke, #6, which seemed to be all center), this dream is purely centered with an animal soul (Elephant), and everything is white. I asked Mairi how she could see white on white. She replied that each thing was so distinctly itself and alive that of course she could tell an elephant from the waves beneath its feet, from the white altar, from the cathedral walls around it. For all its "sameness," this is a vision in depth.

I saw this dream as a dream of the animal-self (the Self in animal form) and as a companion-piece to the dream of the blood-red rose (#16). Alchemically speaking, while red is the color of passion, sulfur (the masculine) and the *rubedo* stage of transformation where one takes one's insights out into life, white is the color of purity and salt (the feminine). This white dream links to Mairi's earlier dreams – snow threatening the safety of two children (#3), the white garb of three angels differentiating unreflecting unity into three-ness (#10). Here white takes us fully into the *albedo*, known as the great process of purification. During the process of *albedo*, we go over and over our complexes, washing away our identification with them (and sometimes they are hard to let go). White is also the color of the pure, un-refracted Spirit, before its incarnation into the rainbow and its covenant with earth, i.e., before it relates to other-than-Itself.

Again Mairi was dropped from the dream-text altogether. Personal associations, few and far between, were of little help. We turned to symbolic magnification of the elements (e.g., the elephant) in order to make any sense of the dream. Although such practice (amplification) can be an intellectual defense against memory, personal imagery and lived life, with Mairi's Self-directive dreams, this was not the case. There was no alternative. Because Mairi knew much of the following Hindu amplification already, she and I were able to talk about this extensive material together. In that way, at least to some degree, we personalized the dream.

In the Hindu system of chakras (experience of which is reached only by way of the body), elephants carry the gods. Elephant-headed Ganesha[27] rules the first bottom chakra, the Muladhara (meaning Foundation), whose element is Earth. According to Harish Johari (1987: 52) worship of Ganesha involves accepting him as remover of obstacles: Ganesha subdues the rational mind or left hemisphere (analytical and critical in nature) and frees the right hemisphere (emotional), which is needed for any spiritual venture. "One who is put off by external form cannot admire the internal beauty of Ganesha," writes Johari (51), "but one who penetrates physical reality can see in Ganesha the union of love and wisdom, Shakti and Shiva."

In the fifth or throat chakra, Vishuddha chakra, meaning Pure, the image of the elephant returns. Vishuddha chakra relates to knowledge of the human plane (Johari 1987: 71) and points to the vulnerable joining of head and body, so often imagined as the location of our western mind–body split. Our phrase, to be "hung-up" on something, graphically describes an image of a flailing person hung as if by a hook by the back of the neck, unable to get its feet on the ground. In Mairi's situation, perhaps being held by the scruff of her neck by a sexually molesting neighbor boy had left her "hung-up," unable to save herself or speak of what had happened. But that had not been the only cause of her depersonalisation.

The ramifications of Vishuddha chakra point toward the tremendous importance the throat and voice have in bringing together a mind–body split. As Mairi became conscious of herself by talking with me in the "talking cure,"[28] she became less hung-up. Eventually she freed her personally expressive voice as well as the voice in her dreams (#14, 17). Johari (1987: 71–3) tells us that

> the fifth-chakra person comprehends nonverbal messages, for all energy has been refined . . . Spoken words come from the fifth chakra, *giving voice to the emotions within the heart. The voice of a fifth-chakra person penetrates to the heart of the listener. This pure sound affects the listener by changing the space of mind and being.* (emphasis mine)

The more rapidly Mairi's Self-directive dreams occurred, the more deeply affected I became by Mairi's words as well as her dreams as she related her experience to me. Vishuddha Chakra with its elephant presence is the center of *dreams in the body* (Johari 1987: 74) and embodies *chit*, or cosmic consciousness (75). Here the elephant Gaja, supreme lord of herbivorous animals (still cloud-colored, gray) indicates confidence and knowledge of nature and the environment as well as consciousness of sound. As a teacher of patience, memory, self-confidence and *an enjoyment of synchronicity with nature*, Gaja carries knowledge of the entire past as well as knowledge of earth, herbs and plants. Generally symbolic of air (which in the chakra system belongs in the region of the heart), in both first and fifth chakras the elephant stands for the animal that *dies for touch* (emphasis mine) (Johari 1987: 93).

Whether from the point of view of Hindu chakras or from an alchemical perspective, the image of a white elephant in Mairi's Self-directive dream indicates something both sacred and taboo. As body, perhaps it was indicative of Mairi's big "animal self": imprisoned behind food allergies, eczematic skin and arm braces, it knew what it was to "die for touch." As psyche, perhaps it was the small being (soul?) who barely survived birth into a body and an anguished infancy, not to mention later cumulative trauma.

In this dream a central symbol of the Self (the elephant) is purified (white). It stands rock-solid on the restless surface of a common symbol of the collective unconscious, the moving, moon-pulled sea. These symbols make up a white altar enclosed within a white cathedral. Was this an elaboration of the imaginal impact of Mairi's forehead kiss by the lunar (feminine) silver fish (Dream #8)? Perhaps it points to what now is safely internalized in the earlier dream (#3) of the red- and blue-dressed children playing beneath the eaves of a dangerously snow-covered church. However we understand it, this dream sanctifies the container of body and body as a container, whether as a sacred animal, a manifestation of the collective unconscious, an altar, or a cathedral. Sanctified by purification (alchemical "washing"), Mairi's early memories of body-and-blood experience now feed into her renewed experience of self and other, just as the religious symbolism of Christ's body-and-blood sanctify a communion of bread and wine.

Many opposites alluded to in this dream are thus contained: animal and element, large and small, earth and water, inside and outside, sacred and profane. In the West we do not think of the elephant as the East does – as laborer, familiar, and carrier of the gods. But we know the elephant for its prodigious memory, for having a tough hide despite an exquisite sense of touch, smell and hearing (*not* keen vision), for its loyalty, longevity, intelligence, courage and size, and for its communal behavior and presence.

Mairi wondered whether "white elephant" might not have a double meaning. On one hand a white elephant is seen as sacred and taboo either because it is different, as in albino, or because it is rare, as in royal or one of a kind. On the other hand a "white elephant" is something you cannot give away because no one wants it. Mairi felt that on occasion – treating herself like a "white elephant" – she had tried to give *herself* away, emotionally and physically, not because she felt that she had something valuable to offer but because she felt worthless. She gave herself away in order to get rid of herself (her two failed marriages). When she did so, that another person might want her surprised her, for underneath it all she herself did not.

I had never imagined a white sea. I *had* imagined that we are changed (symbolically transformed) by immersion (baptism) in the sea, yes, but not that the sea may be changed (or purified) by our psychic transformation.[29] But I remembered another Hindu image that I had seen in a painting called "Churning the Sea to Milk." On one side of a milky sea demons stand, engaged in a tug-of-war with the gods on the other side. Each team pulls on either end of an enormous snake which is wound around a pillar in the middle of the sea. Back and forth, back and forth they pull, until out of white-frothing sea-foam milk comes, and out of the churning milk comes butter, the nurturing gold. Perhaps Mairi's growing ability to carry her share of shadow material had a purifying effect on the collective unconscious, churning it to milk (remember the milky pool above which she suspends herself, in Dream #8). As if in response to her efforts, the depths themselves precipitated out "from the other side," as Mairi's dream of a transpersonal symbol (the elephant as the Self), which is as precious to a psychological culture as an experience of the mothering aspect of Vishnu might have been for an Indian sage.

19. Self-birth

I see myself lying on a couch, naked, laboring to give birth to myself. As I emerge from between my legs, I am the same size and age as I am in real life, both as I give birth and as I am born.

This odd dream, archetypal but not Self-directive, intensely personal but realistically impossible, puzzled us both until Mairi grounded it with an enormous burst of weeping, reminding me that neither of her two children had been born naturally. On each occasion, and for no foreseeable reason, birth by cesarean section was necessary. Consciously, Mairi could not help but appreciate medical help and she gratefully found herself nevertheless very much a mother. Now she expressed regret and remorse at how mercilessly butchered she felt her birth-giving experience had been and wondered what kind of damage cesarean birth implied with regard to the birth-experiences of her two children. Had they missed some essential experience because of her frailty? Had everyone missed out because of "destiny"? "It was no one's fault," she sobbed, "nature's, I guess. But I felt as if I were at fault, if anyone was, as if I were hopelessly unnatural, as if this proved that I wasn't meant to give birth in the first place, even more so the second time. I *know* those unnatural births hurt my children, too. I wasn't able to see them or bond with them for several days, or even to nurse right away." This full-blown experience of a negative mother complex was remembered vividly and released into the here and now.

Mairi then recalled how several weeks earlier a friend of hers told her about her natural child-birth experience, describing feelings of triumphant achievement as the birth took place despite long hours of painful, uninterrupted labor. Upon hearing her friend's story, said Mairi, "I realized that I have never had that kind of feeling. I've never felt triumphant over something I got through, or achieved. I knew I would never have a chance to feel that sense of deep-down, individual achievement through child-birth, either, the way she did."

Mairi's deeply emotional response to this dream made me consider it in a new light. The imagery points to the possibility of achieving exactly that capacity to undergo a deeply instinctive, bodily life-giving process with pain that Mairi felt that she had missed in her real-life birth-giving (and that her personal mother had probably missed, too; so Mairi had not undergone the process from within her mother's body, either). "If I could have given birth like that, I don't think I would have felt so badly about myself for so long," she mourned. "Maybe I would have come to trust myself, somewhere deep in the middle."

How much of this belonged to Mairi personally and how much of it belonged to her still unconscious identification with her own mother was difficult to tell. "Deep in the middle" did describe the missing something, however, the place where Mairi felt cramped and unable to "stand up straight." Yet the image of giving birth to herself in this dream implies the achievement of a capacity for an all-out, no-holds-barred experience of a woman immersed in psychological, emotional, and physiological processes that are much bigger than her ego. These processes are deep, older even than trust and reliance upon others (doctors, a midwife, a mother, an analyst) to help us if we are in need. I thought again of Mairi's missing twin whom she had never known. Did this dream give birth to a part of herself that had been missing since before her own real birth? Did the loss she mourned include beneath her conscious memories of mangled birth-giving and poorly-birthed children – as well as her loss of an experience of natural birth and mothering – grief for a lost other, miscarried before Mairi was born? The motif of giving birth to oneself also points to no-mother, or pre-mother. What kind of survivor guilt might have lurked in a tiny psyche torn from another while still in the womb, in the tiny body left behind? Did this image picture a benign aspect of Mairi's self-sufficiency?

When the storm of tears passed, Mairi and I looked at the dream in terms of a doubling motif (twice-over) as well as the birth of a new attitude toward herself, a new stance in the world, unafraid of the pain involved in the process. Some kind of culmination was at hand. In this dream Mairi not only gives birth to herself (full-grown, at that) but gives birth unassisted and without anesthesia. Radically embodied birth pain may be key to a kind of deep suffering that can midwife ensoulment. Our work on this dream gave us a sense of an instinctive, spontaneously achieved body-aliveness that was deeper than Mairi's ego (or mine) could fathom. Despite an apparent return to two-in-oneness, the birthing process as a wondrous third holds birth-giver and the newly born in the three-ness of new life.

The next two dreams, neither one Self-directive, came one night apart.

20. The lunar tree

I am standing alone in a deep-blue night looking at a silver tree. The tree has two limbs, both of which have been broken off, one a little longer than the other. Neither limb has branches or leaves. Yet the tree is still alive and it shines as if it were the moon.

In the dark, Mairi said, the shining tree looked like a silver Y, with the left arm shorter than the right. This was a lunar tree. I can think of no better image to express a state of hurt feminine being than a silver tree with amputated limbs. This dream portrays the image of a feminine person (Mairi's dream-ego) gazing at an archetypal symbol of wounded feminine Being itself. Feminine *Being* is maimed. Among many other aspects, the tree symbolizes the mother and devotion to nature. Mairi's lunar tree is an even more archaic depiction of the feminine mode of Being than an image of an archaic goddess. I thought of the leaping silver fish (Dream #8), hitting Mairi's forehead between her eyes.

Both Jung and Neumann characterize ordinary ego-consciousness as masculine, in that it is focused, clarifying, differentiating, and of a solar (light and consciousness) nature. In compensatory or complementary fashion, chthonic or lunar feminine nature characterizes the dark matrix of our conscious minds: body, soul, and psyche, too.[30] Even if this is over-simplified, when we are searching for a general sense of the human body's contingent and ineluctable existence, the masculine–feminine differentiation can be helpful. I also find it useful when I try to define the participating quality of consciousness that accompanied Mairi's experience of soul.

The dream of the lunar tree gave Mairi and me a chance to explore the feminine mode of being both from the point of view of Mairi's personal associations and from culturally amplified perspectives. Usually I think of the feminine in terms of "female elements" of being (Winnicott 1971), and "feminine modes of being" (Ulanov 1971: 81). To contrast masculine and feminine modes of being, take for example the act of dreaming. As we sleep, dreams are visited upon us. When we dream we are in what Ulanov calls the feminine mode of being, for we are subject to dreams. We do not make a dream or do a dream, we are given a dream, we undergo a dream. Dreaming, we experience night after night in a natural rhythm a deep feeding from the living source that Freud called primary process and Jung called non-directed thinking. Dreams bloom within us, flowers of the inner world stirred into life by the ongoing activity of our organs and nervous systems, the life in our bodies even as we lie unconscious. Ego-less when we dream, yet still experiencing, we are feminine in our receptivity to generative, penetrative activity on the part of the psyche, the voice of nature within us.

As we awaken and seize upon dream content, however, the feminine mode of being changes places with us; the imaging psyche becomes the receptive servant, mediating to us the Being behind its presence. Consider-ing a dream or telling it to someone else employs an ego-consciousness more focused than that in which the dream occurred. As we give the dream form, we take form, moving out of a receptive feminine mode into an instinct-backed, more masculine position of activity – the desire to capture a dream-experience and relate to it. Describing the dream to someone else, we relate to the images by attending to them. We work to understand. We elaborate, associate and amplify, immersed in conscious processes that are more assertive (masculine) than the diffuse consciousness that accompanies feminine being. Simultaneously, we remain close to consciousness, even intimate, hoping to record our primary experience of the quivering surface of the unconscious mind itself. Sensitive to what happened in the dream, to what we really experienced and to what that might bring to our consciously inquiring selves, we fish for dreams as delicately as if we were casting hand-tied flies into the dappled waters of a favorite stream.

In meditation we also experience what comes up, to us and in us: emotions, memories, fantasies, and thinking "monkey-mind" itself. Here also we draw near to a feminine mode of being, receptive and quiet, holding and containing, waiting upon something other than our conscious minds. The image of "waiting upon" implies service and attending, as well as patience and receptivity.

Ulanov (1981: 72–89), like Jung, stresses that the presence of a feminine mode of being belongs to all of us and to the world. She fleshes out her idea of a mode of feminine being with what Winnicott tells us is associated with the female element in all of us, both male and female,

> a sense of being-at-the-core-of-oneself, which involves a capacity to be, to be there calmly, at rest, sensing one's "self" as somehow found, given and reflected, instead of achieved, created, or manufactured . . . a capacity to feel alive, real, possessed of unique personal existence. (77)

Being-at-the-core means being open to one's feelings of vulnerability.

A second major characteristic of the feminine element of being precedes our being able to exist as individuals, as well as "doing" of any kind. It grows from an experience of being-at-one-with that lies far beneath our achieved distinctions of me and not-me. Winnicott (1963c: 84–9) places being in "quietness and an inexplicit togetherness" in the mother–child relationship. A. Ulanov (1981: 78) reminds us that the fundamental at-one-ness that precedes any sense of a separate self can occur in other significant experiences, too: in love, when we discover something of a true image of ourselves mirrored back in the face of a lover; in religious experience, where we find God's being-at-one-with us; and in therapy, where the therapist repeatedly reflects back the self that the patient brings to her.

At-one-ness also can happen between our conscious ego and the unconscious. I once saw a Chinese drawing of a sleeping sage leaning against a sleeping tiger. To me this image pictures a peaceful relationship with the unconscious. A. Ulanov (1981: 80) reminds us that our ego-identity is also reflected back to us through the figures of the unconscious that face us in our dreams: these are "others" who lead us to an experience of the integrating center of the psyche that Jung calls the Self. When, as in Self-directive dreams, self-reflective dream figures are missing or utterly unfamiliar, they might well be "in another world." But that, too, comments on our ability to experience at-one-ness. It is paradoxical: at-one-ness requires two-ness in order to take place. Do Mairi's Self-directive dreams imply her inability to feel at-one with the world?

When hurt, the feminine mode of being does not react angrily. When it is wounded it lacks a healthy struggle for redress or even revenge. When the feminine mode of being feels hurt it feels maimed, like Mairi's lunar tree. It feels not whole, or missing. It feels disfigured and incapacitated. When our capacity for elemental Being is hurt our capacity for "doing" (including thinking) is also hurt, becoming somehow irrelevant, if not impossible. This way of feeling hurt (feeling maimed instead of angry) applies to the feminine mode of being whether we address it in body or soul, psyche or ego.

As soul itself, say the Sufis, the feminine principle has its own kind of containing activity. From this point of view the feminine mode of being has an active receptivity within which the masculine principle lies, just as Christ the Spirit lay within the Virgin Mary (Bakhtiar 1976: 22–3). Spiritual transformation occurs when the container of Being (body, soul, psyche) has been made receptive through spiritual practices, so that spiritual possibilities (the archetypes) are conceived, and develop and grow. Suffering the pains of birth, the Virgin within gives birth to the spirit. In Sufi thought, the First Born is masculine, while the process of birthing is feminine. In spiritual transformation and rebirth, then, the masculine principle is born (Christ is born in the heart), while the feminine principle is the heart in the process of birthing itself.

Likewise, our ability to "do" (including thinking) depends upon, lies within, and is contained and conditioned by our capacity to be. Among the many facets of Mairi's feelings of loss were feelings of personal, physical, psychological, and emotional maiming. As she uncovered her hurt experience of being mothered she became aware of how her maimed feminine nature in turn displayed itself in a hurt capacity to mother others. Her birth-giving experiences left her feeling remote from her children and unfulfilled herself. Recognition of Mairi's innately detached mode of mothering herself as well as her children helped us to bring the feminine mode of being into focus with regard to Mairi's body and soul.

Traumatic experience – experience that maims – is visited upon a particular, unique body, whether that body be male or female, the body of a child or the body of the earth. As bodies, we do not "do" pain, illness, childbirth, or death, we are subject to them. Body suffers these experiences, just as it suffers joy or bliss. Where perception and expression depend entirely upon blood, nerve and bone, striving and muscular ego or mind-directed activity become useless and irrelevant. So when Winnicott (1988: 80) writes that "Probably the greatest suffering in the human world is the suffering of normal or healthy or mature persons," he is speaking not only of emotional pain; he is reminding us that a great deal of vulnerability and hurt is implied in living a bodily life. When we connive to deny suffering, we try to flee our bodies, or we long for escape. But when and if we do escape, we deny vulnerable, passionate embodiment.

When the body is hurt or opened helplessly, muteness is revealed. Usually the body's pain is wordless. I thought of little Mairi rolling on the rug, scratching her excruciatingly suppurating skin. The body mediates to us painfully personal experience of the depths of real Being to which Jung points by calling it "psychoid." But we cannot always stay with what incarnate Being offers. Who cares what an afflicted skin symbolizes, or where eczema comes from, when the wish to shed your skin becomes so acute that you scrape it off like a little animal, clawing its way out of a body trap?

The four-year-old child-body of Mairi was "hung up" by the back of her neck, suffocated in oral sexual molestation, and terrified to the point that the psyche engraved itself into an image of stunned shock (Dream #7). A still younger Mairi, rigid arms in metal braces, stiffened until the spontaneity of her psyche could imagine bodily suffering as a lifeless statue (Dream #14). From this depth of feminine Being, archetypal imagery arises in our dreaming bodies. From this depth of feminine Being, the psyche breathes forth imagery that expresses and explores still other states of Being. For Mairi, the living glow of her maimed silver tree summed up an experience of Being too deep for words to tell. Rooted in a silvery earth, she stood and gazed upon a lunar tree, shining back upon her like the moon.

The dream of the silver lunar tree related Mairi to the wounded of her being and modes of the wounded feminine. It helped her recognize her experience and step away from it, for in her dream, Mairi and the tree are two. Mairi is not the tree, the tree is not Mairi. She and I had many thoughts about the amputated, uneven limbs, themselves expressive of a maimed "two-ness": I thought of the shining tree as the cross, as suffering transformed. I thought of Mairi and Mairi's mother, the miscarried twin and Mairi. I thought of Mairi's two arms in metal braces; of Mairi's two failed marriages; of Mairi's two butchered experiences of birth-giving; of the two abrupt deaths, like amputations, of Mairi's parents.

Wounded but alive, the lunar tree glows. Maimed, it stands in darkness unhealed and disfigured, the effects of trauma evident, as if to remind Mairi that she can not go back and live her life another way. She would not be three years old again and "do it right, this time," never hear "thank you for trying." She would not again be four and hear that her mother loved her and liked her too. No amount of the long, hard work we put toward finding ourselves changes the fact that the completeness we seek inevitably includes pain and sorrow, loss and lack. Yet by symbolizing a feminine mode of being, the silvery lunar tree implies a *self-acceptance* that acknowledges scars and deficits, failure and weakness, and loss and misery, as well as strength, endurance, perseverance and courage.

According to this dream, a mode of maimed feminine being has undergone an alchemical change. Alchemically speaking, silver symbolizes a purity of soul, something which is entirely human both in the individual and in humanity in general. A. Ulanov (1994: 39) tells us that in the Psalms, the word of God is compared to silver, as is the Virgin Mary. In the philosophical tree of alchemical metals, silver represents the cross of Christ. "Washed," whitened, and silvered, what a different light this lunar tree casts over Mairi and the night of her dream, as compared to the red-orange flame which ignited the night-sky of her first angel dream (#2) or the bolt of white lightning which parted the heavens themselves (Dream #7). Standing alone, gazing at this singular, silver tree glowing in the night, Mairi became calm and unafraid. Its moon-nature spoke to her, and awakened her own.

21. The solar tree

I am standing at the foot of a giant sequoia or redwood, gazing up at its immense height. Above my head I notice in the trunk a scar which seems to be weeping. As I look at the scar, tears come to my eyes and I blink, which makes my tears glitter in the sunlight and makes them mingle with the weeping scar. I blink again, look, and see that the scar in the trunk is healing over. Soon the tree is whole.

Years ago Mairi had wandered among a grove of giant sequoia in Oregon. She was awed by their majestic nature and by evidence of a fire which had not destroyed them but had blackened their roots with ash. "They were enormously tall," she said, "the tallest living things I've seen in my life. Just as I did in that grove, in this dream I threw back my head so that I could see to the top of a tree. As I slowly looked up the trunk, I noticed the scar in the bark, maybe three feet above me. The sun was behind the tree. Tree-tears flowed from the scar, and caught the light and glittered. I guess tree-scars are not completely lifeless. I began to tear up, too, and blink. I felt less sad than simply accepting, of the tree weeping tears, of my own scars, of the inevitable wounds and scars of life. My tears and the tree's tears merged in my sight. I had to blink again, to clear my vision, and when I looked, the last of the tree's scar had healed over."

This tree was different from the lunar tree of Dream #20, yet it is a variant on the same motif: the suffering, injured tree, this time healing. From the beginning of time we have looked to trees to feed not only flesh, but spirit. Adam and Eve ate from a tree, and Jesus' tree was both cradle and cross. Beneath a fig tree the Buddha had his night of illumination. Then he meditated for seven days under the bo tree, and for another seven under a great banyan. For a third seven days the Buddha meditated under the

Tree of the Serpent King, who dwelt among its roots, before setting out on his mission.

Like the elephant in Dream #18 (King of the Animals), the majestic sequoia (King of the Trees) can symbolize the Self. While the elephant portrays the Self in animal form, the giant sequoia – like the Rose and the Artichoke (Dreams #6, 16) – points us toward the Self in relation to a vegetative soul. And vegetative imagery summons us to a symbolic awareness of our bodies from a cellular level of being. All healing and transformation begins in an earthy darkness.

Concerning the images of plants in dreams, Jung (1932–1934: 402), writes "The life of the plant is in us . . . in us it becomes the symbol for a non-biological quality, for what we call spiritual." Elsewhere, Jung (1932–1934: 403) comments that

> plant-like growth . . . represents an entirely different psychological experience from that which we are used to, for we ordinarily think of our psychology in terms of warm-blooded animals . . . (plants) represent impersonal life, life beyond one's own psychology.

Like the sequoia which is truly impervious to fire, the vegetative aspect of the Self may be relatively impervious to personal anguish. Yet it was affected. Nevertheless, this dream implies that given tears, sunlight, and time, even Self-scars heal. With regard to the imperviousness of the sequoia to fire, von Franz (1986: 80) tells us that some Greek alchemical texts explicitly state of the end result of the *opus* that the stone of the wise (the *lapis*), which is often symbolized by the tree, is *pyrimachos*, "able to withstand the fire." The stone of Self-directive Dream #9 to which Mairi had no personal access also ignited, though it did not burn. Mairi's sequoia (to which she had personal associations both within and outside the dream) was scarred, but not consumed. As Mairi deepened her capacity for a spirited, spontaneous life in the world, these elements changed progressively, from one dream to another.

Solar and lunar trees (#20) picture different states of being. They allude to two sides of Mairi's psychic reality, the maimed yet still standing feminine aspects of herself, and a strong, healing, spiritual, solar side. Both sides are real. Neither can be denied. Jung (CW13: 304–482) speaks of the tree as a symbol of the alchemical *opus* itself. A symbol of the Self – and, like the Self, evidence of its own organizing activity – the tree is an unseen shaping more than it is leaves or bark, roots or branches, cellulose or fruit. As it enters into relationship with elements of earth and air, rain and sunlight, a single tree organizes millions of operations. From mythology we know of other doubled trees: the Manichean Tree of Life and Tree of Death, the Judaeo-Christian Tree of Life and Tree of the Knowledge of Good and Evil. Last year I heard an old Celtic Christmas song called "Jesus Christ the Apple Tree." The image of Christ as the Apple Tree pairs the Tree of the Knowledge of Good and Evil from which Eve ate the fateful apple with Christ Himself. Is this an early, round-about envisioning of the religious destiny of what today we call female elements or a feminine mode of Being?

22. Hands holding the Earth

The planet Earth, held gently and firmly between enormous woman's hands, which emerge from the folds of a deep blue robe, as if she were looking down on the globe from above.

"Humm," said Mairi. "She's got the whooolle worrld, in her hands!" We both remembered Dream #13 where the Buddha held the globe of the earth while Mairi prepared to plunge into the pool of blood. Now "She" (whoever She was) held the world, the planet itself, between her hands. Mairi did not seem to feel that these hands were hers, nor, when I questioned, did she think that She held the world as if it were an infant. "Unless," Mairi said, "She's like a mother looking down on her child's head. Maybe that is what it's like, as if She cradles the earth between her two hands, as precious a vessel as the head of a child . . . unbroken, safe, un-dropped . . . *held*."

Perhaps Neumann (1994) was the first to suggest that the mandala may be a concrete image of the earth itself (as it was in the hands of the Buddha, Dream #13). By now, most of us have seen pictures of the earth taken from the moon. By moon-view our planet shimmers, a blue-green globe floating in the darkness of outer space. Neumann did not live to see this sight, nor did Jung. Today when we actually have a collective vision of the whole earth as a mandala, it seems fitting that it is from a lunar perspective. The vision of the earth as a seamless whole is a lunar gift, a gift through the lens of feminine being, a glimpse that may be as important to our collective consciousness as photographs of the moon itself.

So have space exploration and the moon landing lent material substance to ideas of the symbolically feminine nature of psyche, soul, body, and Gaia, the earth itself. From a lunar feminine point of view our earth is immensely vulnerable. Our atmosphere – which makes the earth inhabitable to us – is a thin wrapping only ten miles deep, a distance most of us could walk to the end of in hours, were it laid out before us. As a small single planet supporting an awesome, lonely phenomenon of organic life, the earth's aura of at-one-ness is heart-breaking. And an awareness of this vision of our earth has been born, if not torn, from earth's own body. As it emerges into collective consciousness, this awareness exemplifies the virgin birth of a consciousness which perceives the entire universe as interrelated. Perhaps this new consciousness[31] will illuminate the darkness in our being that prevents us from perceiving the presence of Divine Mystery in everything: in body and soul, in nature and history, in pain and in joy. Born from a dramatic breakthrough into the deepest realms of conditioned (collective) consciousness, this new awareness is emerging with a play of passion so intense that opposites are bridged: male and female, God and human, light and darkness, body and spirit, heaven and earth, focused and diffuse consciousness, compassion and confrontation, and outer and inner worlds.

I asked Mairi if she could sketch this dream but she did not want to. She said suddenly "You know that Albrecht Dürer sketch of two hands praying? I used to like that sketch a lot. The background was light blue. I think this dream is a companion to that sketch. There, a monk's gnarled hands are pressed together in prayer. Here, Her hands are full of something precious, given, received. Her robe is not the color of the monk's spiritual light blue. Her robe is a deep, deep blue, as blue as an evening sky, or the dark, dark blue behind the Eye of my vision." And that was the end of our conversation.

23. Cowlick and re-entry

I see the cowlick on top of my own head – as if I were outside myself, looking down on my own body from above.

As if by change of octave, instead of "She" looking down on a planet or the head of a child, this dream pictures Mairi herself observing the cowlick on top of her own head. "My grandmother used to tease me about this cowlick," she said, touching the top of her head with one hand, "and when I was little I believed her, that a cow came along and licked me there, making my hair grow into a whorl. She said that is what happens to all babies, that that is how cowlicks are made."

I began to think of Hathor, the Great Cow-Mother aspect of Isis, the Goddess of Egyptian mythology. But Mairi exclaimed "This is where the *sipapu* is!" Mairi then told me, "Hopi Indians believe that the soul enters and leaves through the sipapu, and they build a symbolic opening into the top of their ceremonial dwellings for that to happen."[32] It is also, I thought, the spot where at birth the soft skull-bones of an infant have not yet knit together. Called the fontanel, this is a space of built-in "give," so to speak, so that the brain within the fragile skull is not damaged irreparably during a convulsive journey down the birth canal. The fontanel symbolizes a difficult passage into life and an imaginal portal in death.

This dream implied Mairi's centering, finding her way back from a long journey elsewhere, from a state of dissociation or depersonalisation or both. The inner journey is not linear. It is an uncharted, meandering descent through layers and layers of consciousness and being in which we are intermittently tossed backwards or sideways like a diver in a current, as much at the mercy of life as a child in birth. But the purpose of the journey is to travel the whole circle, as does the world.

As in Dream #19, in which Mairi gave birth to herself, in this dream Mairi's dream ego is doubled. In the first doubling, Mairi, in the act of birthing, experienced her other self subjectively. In this doubling, Mairi's objectivity toward herself is striking. Also striking is how shamanic this dream image is, how literally it references the archetypal pattern of the solitary personality who – in searching to heal another – leaves the body in search of soul. This whole dream implies such a journey and return. As she aims for re-entry through the sipapu, an inherently built-in "give" in her personality, Mairi "heads" back into embodiment, reborn. How literally and unconsciously had Mairi been living out the archetypal configuration of the shaman?

Von Franz (1997: 150) observes that when (as in many myths)[33] the feminine part of the androgynous Anthropos figure is lost in matter or plunged into darkness (either "lost" in the unconscious or not yet found) *the feminine aspect of the symbol of the Self becomes lost through projection.* Apparently one's sense of soul is one of those "lose-able" aspects of the feminine, as is one's sense of one's body. And if we lose our sense of soul in matter, that's where we will find it again – in the space where the body is, the most intimate form of matter we can know. If, as I said before, the body responds to "what is," and the soul deepens the body's response to "what is" into a meaningful experience, if the body cannot psychologically *metabolize* its response to "what is," soul may be lost too, along with the body's experience. Such was Mairi's condition when therapy began.

Von Franz's observation also points to the fact that in collective thinking, the principle of masculine Logos tends to prevail one-sidedly (its archaic understanding usually translated as *verbum*)[34] at the expense of Eros, meaning at the expense of a relationship to feeling (1997: 151). As long as Mairi remained embedded in externality and collective thinking, this described her state of mind, as well. Once it becomes clear that an archetype has been constellated because of some serious psychological stress, says von Franz, it remains an open question as to what will happen with regard to consciousness. Although a masculine consciousness (in man or woman) will try to bring about a comforting closure into a sense of causality – e.g., this comes about (or does not) *because* of that – we cannot infer a causal chain, says von Franz, *because consciousness itself is what correlates and organizes all other goals into a meaningful whole*; the most we can say is "that something might happen when an archetype is constellated; and if something does happen, then it will have the same meaning as the archetype. But we cannot predict this with certainty – it might happen, it might not" (von Franz 1992: 27, emphasis mine).

Thus *the restoration of feeling* by way of (1) transference and counter-transference feelings and value; and (2) expression of the unconscious wherein the feminine principle was lost (e.g., dreams as a whole, but especially the Flaming Angel Dream), and (3) the consciously felt and experienced personalisation of Mairi's feeling values (e.g., the transformation of too much one-sided Logos, meaning collective and personal habits of mind, empty words or words unexpressed) that brought about Mairi's capacity for a participating consciousness played a central role in the healing emergence of Mairi's dream-in-the-world – but it might not have happened that way. With the old alchemists I also add *deo condedente*, meaning "God willing."[35]

Psychoanalyst Harold Searles (1972) suggests that all of us have the desire to heal, that this is a general need within us as human beings. Yet to seek wholeness by healing another is also a general (and very good) indicator of an activated religious instinct. Searles suggests that this desire to heal an outer other symbolizes the inner task that we all face, which is to bring the different parts of ourselves into unity, an emotional as well as a religious task. I will end this chapter with an example of how Mairi's early life experience illustrates von Franz's idea as to how the feminine part of the Anthropos may be lost and recovered.

As I came to the end of the dreams I selected for this essay, I found Mairi's two earliest dreams, something for which often I ask at the beginning of therapy. I had listened to these dreams when she and I began our work but had not thought about them since. Now I read them with different eyes and a different understanding. To the best of Mairi's memory, these two dreams occurred together when she was between four and five years old, under anesthesia for a tonsillectomy:

(1) I see lying in the grass a little jeweled dog harness. As I lean down to pick it up, all at once I am looking up at the Big Dipper in the night sky, as if the earth and sky and day and night changed places. The little dog harness and the Big Dipper have the same shape.

(2) A wooden pole with an iron ring through the top of it stands like a hitching post embedded upright in a street that is paved with brightly colored stones.

Another therapist to whom Mairi told these dreams commented that the little dog's harness implied that Mairi would undergo the "harness of necessity." I thought about the arm braces she had discarded by the time of this dream, and the early harnessing of her small animal spiritedness. I also wondered at the unusual juxtaposition of near into far, earth into sky, and day into night in this dream. A dog's harness implies containment and control: a constellation marks position in infinity. Dante came to mind again: in the *Commedia*, Virgil leads Dante into the depths of Hell, the place where an *enantiodromia* of the cosmos can occur. *Only as the worlds revolve* (e.g., transformation of the reality planes) does Dante begin his ascent into Paradise. At the least the extraordinary juxtaposition of opposites imaged in this little dream suggests a capacity in the dreamer for experience of immense scope, a stretch that might dishearten and disorient the bravest traveler, let alone a child.

Now I speculate that Mairi's earliest material contained archetypal reference that pointed to (or now recovers) the psychological moment that the feminine aspect of the Anthropos became "lost in projection," i.e., one of the early times when she lost touch with soul. Her first remembered dream indicates a constellation of Feminine–Mother–Soul issues imaged in the pattern of Ursa Major, the Big Dipper, the Plow in the Sky, Demeter the Earth Mother, or the Sign of the Great Bear Goddess – the tail of which points to our "true north" and Jung's process of individuation. "Is it the wind, or rainstorms, or the sea / repairs a soul," sings the poet John Burnside, "or is it magnetic north / that brings us true, knitting the cut flesh / smoothing the creases / in dreams? (Burnside 2000: 70). Ursa Major is considered to be the ruler of the stars and the protectress of the *axis mundi*, the Pole of the World, marked in heaven by the North (Pole) Star at the center of the small circle described by this constellation, which for centuries has oriented entire cultures in time and space, on land and on sea. And according to our oldest traditions, the Pole or the World Tree was female. Historian Barbara Walker writes that as a symbol of the milk-giving tree of the Finno-Ugric peoples (from Mesopotamia),

> . . . The tree is the source of unborn souls, which would give birth to the new primal woman, Life (Lif) in the new universe . . . Its fruit could be given to women in childbirth "that what is within may pass out." The spring at the tree's root was a fountain of wisdom or of the life-giving fluid *aurr*, which may be likened to the "wise blood" of the Mother – that much mythologized feminine life-source likened to the Kula nectar in the uterine spring of Kundalini [or the blood of Kali] as if the maternal tree upholding the universe were the Mother's spine with its many *chakras*. (Walker 1983: 59–60)

Perhaps this describes that aspect of the Celestial Feminine that precipitated out of the cosmic realm to transform – eventually – into Mairi's embodied soul.

The second little dream of "brightly colored stones" (see Mairi's dream of similarly "bejeweled falcon wings," #17) implies the opposite of what we mean by "hitch your wagon to a star." A hitching post ties animal energy into time and place. The "ground of being," to which this small spirit needs connecting, the earth itself (the street), is bejeweled with stones, glowing with beauty and color – full of emotional presence and precious. *And this is a Self-directed dream.* Apparently Mairi's potential for experience of soul dwelt within her psyche from early on, in accord with her earliest dream images. Her dream-in-the-world would blossom in full accord with an earlier archetypal situation portrayed by a psyche under stress (the physiological and psychological effects of surgery and anesthesia at a young age), if not "determined" by many other factors and the forces of the stars themselves.

Notes

1 Broadly speaking there are six traditional systems of yoga: Hatha, Raja, Tantra, Jnana, Bhakti, and Karma. Hatha yoga starts with the body. Hatha is derived from the roots *ha* (sun) and *tha* (moon): hatha implies the equalization and stabilization of the sun breath (flowing through the right nostril) and the moon breath (flowing through the left nostril). Hatha also means violence and force. Through the regulation of physiological processes Hatha yoga forcibly releases the dormant energies of the human personality.

2 Grotstein (in Symington 1993: ix) understands the "lifegiver" to be an internal, phantasmal, transitional-like object composed of aspects of the self and of the external life-supporting object.

3 In this story by Nathaniel Hawthorn, Hester wears a scarlet letter "A" pinned to her breast as public punishment for adultery.

4 Jalal al-Din Muhammad (1207-73), known as Rumi, the Sufi poet who founded the Mevlevi Whirling Dervish order: Rumi's writings helped reshape Islamic thought. Several archetypal images in Mairi's dreams brought to mind Islamic, Persian or Sufi amplification, and aspects of Rumi's experience of the Beloved – intensely felt in his body – bear similarity to Mairi's experience of soul and Hadewijch's experience of *Minne*, or Lady Love.

5 Bright red (like the red-rimmed eyes staring from her black face), Kali's extended tongue repeats her representation as a tantric symbol, the inverted triangle as the yoni or cosmic vagina.

6 The image of a woman warrior will appear again in Hadewijch: in vision a voice addresses her: "O strongest of all warriors! You have conquered everything and opened the closed totality . . ." (V1, Hadewijch 1980: 305).

7 On a wall of Salisbury Cathedral in England I saw the following comment: "To the Fish: In what dreadful majesty, in what wonderful power, in what amazing providence did God Almighty distinguish you among all the species of creatures that perished in the universal deluge! You only were insensible of the mischief that had laid waste the whole world" (St. Anthony of Padua 1195–1231).

8 This is an interesting feature: despite finally recognizing himself in his reflection, mythic Narcissus *never sees the water into which he gazes*. I understand Mairi's conscious recognition of the medium into which she looks in this dream as indicative of her dawning capacity to recognize the reality of the psyche.

9 Cirlot (1962: 95) explains this by reference to a facet of the symbolism of the number three: if three can correspond with active, passive and neutral, it also applies to creation, conservation, and destruction (as does Shiva).

10 When dream work is part of depth-psychotherapeutic treatment, patients often are instructed to keep their dreams for their analysis (keep them in "the vessel"), or at least discuss them first with the therapist before telling them to others.

11 Visionary experience happens also in creative work. Marion Milner (1979) cites William Blake, referring to a state of "fear and trembling" while creating visionary designs (14); she quotes Cézanne describing the loss of self involved in

authentic response to painting: "[A painting is] an abyss in which the eye is lost" (25).

12 The inner eye of self-recognition mediates a different view of ourselves. Gerhard Dorn, a pupil of Paracelsus, described it as the real essence of the alchemical *opus*: "But no man can truly know himself unless first he see and know by zealous meditation . . . what rather than who he is, on whom he depends, and whose is he, and to what end he was made and created, and by whom and through whom" (von Franz 1980: 165).

13 Hence the Divine Eye of the Egyptians (the wounded Eye of Horus) denotes "He who feeds the sacred fire or the intelligence of Man" – Osiris, in fact (Cirlot 1962).

14 Commenting on Jung's (CW6: 755) statement that our essential individuality has an *a priori* unconscious existence, Edinger (1972: 159) suggests that this notion is expressed in the idea that each person has an individual star, a kind of celestial counterpart which represents his or her cosmic dimension and destiny.

15 Referring to the light in the darkness of the unconscious, Jung writes about sparks and seeds of light. When these points of light gather in the psyche, says Jung, the effect can resemble what the early Fathers meant by "illumination of the *nous*."

16 From an Inuit word pronounced in-ook-shook, meaning "in the image of man." Along treeless horizons inukshuks serve as directional markers guiding those who follow. Despite their rocky, solitary nature, inukshuks remind us of our dependence upon one another and symbolize the importance of friendship and human presence.

17 Recounted by William Dalrymple (1990: 9–10), who refers to Sir Henry Yule (trans., ed.), *The Book of Ser Marco Polo*, 3rd edn (2 vols, London: John Murray, 1929) and Paul Pelliot, *Notes on Marco Polo*, 3 vols, Paris, 1959, 73.

18 Mohammed tells us that prayer is a healing, not that "it heals." Prayer cannot heal and does not give health, but *is* health: one senses the refreshing breath of greatness. Likewise dreams are a healing. Dreams do not heal, but demonstrate a healing expansion of imagination and consciousness (Ceronetti 1993: 167).

19 Jung spends a good deal of thought on the circle and the square, three and four, and the star, the precious stone, child, lotus, and seed, all symbolic of the central, centering space of various mandala formations (CW11: 109–13). This is interesting in light of his comment upon the "empty center" (Jung 1975: 258).

20 Quoted in Nachmanovitch 1990: 94.

21 Quoting the alchemist Mylius, Jung (CW 14: 80 n.) tells us, "It is a great mystery to create souls, and to mold the lifeless body into a living statue."

22 Originally, rosaries consisted of one hundred sixty five dried, carefully rolled-up rose petals darkened with lampblack as a preservative (Ackerman 1991: 36).

23 Umberto Eco's novel *The Name of the Rose* refers us to this same time in history. There Eco tells us that if a pledge were made "under the rose" (a rose actually held or tied above a conference table), those who made it were understood to be sworn to secrecy.

24 See especially "The Well Scene," the Lascaux cave painting of a stick figure with a bird-pole lying before a wounded auroch (mammoth), interpreted by H. Kirschner (1952) as a medicine man in the throes of an ecstatic trance (cited in Bataille 1955: 140), thought to date from the Upper Paleolithic Age.

25 Rumi Book IV, Stanzas 2611–25, trans. Coleman Barks (Ayliffe et al. 1992: 806–7).

26 *The Living Symbol* (1961), Gerhard Adler's beautifully crafted case study of a woman's process of individuation, is full of bird-dreams. *Vis-à-vis* symbols of

both bird and fish (see Mairi's Dream #8, above) Adler comments (380) that on the deepest level of the psyche the bird and the fish represent two polar aspects of the psychological self.

27 The seat of Kundalini Shakti, the vital life force, is in the Muladhara Chakra. There Indra, god of the firmament, rides on his elephant Airavata, whose skin is the soft color of clouds and whose seven trunks form a rainbow of seven colors.

28 Recent attention has been given to how specifically "therapeutic conversation" actually changes the structure of brain, mind, and body. See Vaughn 1997.

29 Although individuation cuts us off from personal conformity to collectivity, Jung (CW18: 454–5) reminds us that individuation and collectivity remain a pair of opposites, two possibilities or divergent destinies which are often related by guilt and discord. Because of this inescapable connection, conscious work toward individuation by way of shadow-integration must affect not only ourselves but those around us and society as a whole. This is like having the collective sea changed by individual transformation.

30 This perhaps too-facile designation lends itself to turmoil in gender-sensitized discussions, although the designation is not as simplistic as it sounds. Even within the context of Jung's work on the ego, we can think of consciousness as feminine relative to input from the Self, while it remains masculine relative to self-expression.

31 The widespread birthing of this new consciousness may be as surprising and shocking to us as the New Testament story was to its time, what A. Ulanov (1994: 9–10) calls the "startling stepping into history and time and space of the Holy One who brings all images and religions to an end."

32 Von Franz (1986: 61–2) notes that "the Hopi Indians of North America believe that the soul of the deceased goes through a small square cavity, the so-called Sipapu, which leads to the Kiwa buildings. The cavity has the connotation of a sacred place and is regarded as the place of origin, that opening through which the Hopi tribe came up from the depths to the surface of the world."

33 For the Ophite sect, Sophia initially belonged, as a female holy spirit, to a celestial trinity of primordial man and son of man (von Franz 1997: 150); in the system of Valentinus, Sophia was abandoned in the lower world of darkness and seeks her way back to the light of the primordial father, which corresponds to the idea of the exile of the Shekhinah in the Kabbalah (151). Today the feminine aspect of the Anthropos tends to be recognized in distorted collective (therefore archaic) forms.

34 A modern mystic, Simone Weil, feels that the very fact that Logos is translated by *verbum* (word) shows that something has been lost, for "Logos means above all relation, and is a synonym for *arithmos*, number, with Plato and the Pythagoreans: relation, that is to say, proportion; proportion, that is to say, harmony; harmony, that is to say, mediation. I would translate as follows: In the beginning was Mediation" (Weil 1974: 138).

35 An apt analogy to what von Franz suggests lies in current research concerning our genetic inheritance: although we may have a genetic predisposition (an activated archetype) toward some kind of illness, without two or three "hits" (e.g., traumas or constellating events) during a lifetime, a genetic predisposition may well remain latent; however, with two, three or more hits, a predisposing genetic constellation may (or may not) swing into operation: cancer appears, or diabetes, or a particular character configuration.

Chapter 3

"Falling through"

Experience of soul

What Mairi would come to call "experience of soul" began at the end of an ordinary session about two weeks after her last Self-directive dream (#22). Three days later Mairi telephoned to request an extra hour. When we met she said, "Last week when I sat here across from you gathering myself together to leave, I leaned my head onto the back of the chair for a moment, closed my eyes, and suddenly had a kind of 'inner vision.' Instead of looking at darkness or at the inside of my eyelids, I was gazing up into a dark-blue, starry night sky.[1] Two enormous invisible streams of energy emerging from below my vision whooshed up into infinity, crossing before me like a giant 'X.' Had they been visible they would have criss-crossed the night sky like search lights. But they weren't visible; they were like palpable streams of 'aware energy' of enormous power.

"Suddenly everything in my life made sense. I felt as if all of my history, all of my life, had led me to exactly that moment, that time, that place. I felt as if I understood all my dreams. A crucial puzzle piece of something fell into place – a piece of my life? A piece of myself? I don't know. I've never felt like that before. I felt as if I were part of something very big, and that there was a natural place for me in it. When I opened my eyes the feeling of that deeper reality stayed, although I was spacey and light-headed, and overwhelmed with a feeling of the rightness of everything that had ever happened to me – all of it. I couldn't speak to you then. It was the end of the hour, I knew I had to leave. Also I was too surprised to say anything. So I just said good-bye and walked out the door, and felt as if I were swimming through air.

"As I walked along the sidewalk outside my body felt loose and easy, moving on its own. I stood still for a moment just looking at everything around me, the people, the traffic, the buildings, the trees, and I had an extraordinary sensation – not of union with everything and everyone, not as if everything were transparent – but of being transparent to myself and realizing that I was *of the same substance* as everything and everyone around me. I kept walking home – both my kids left for summer camp last week, so the house was empty – and I began putting things away and puttering around, absently thinking about supper. All the while that feeling of rightness, of a wondrous being in place, persisted. I "swam" out of your door at our last session because the air was full of wonderment. I felt as if I'd fallen into a pool of wonder, the air as thick and dense around me as water. *That* feeling stayed, too: the atmosphere was palpable and shimmering."

Previously unaware of the moment of Mairi's "inner vision" at the end of her last session, I listened carefully. She had changed. Her presence was heightened and intensified. She said she was "full to overflowing" with so much to say. As she tried to tell me what was happening to and in her, she said she needed to know that I would "be there." She had telephoned for extra time because talking to me helped her feel grounded. We decided to double her weekly sessions and I made a third hour available to her if she wished.

By the clock, Mairi and I spent only seventeen or eighteen hours talking together in session over the next two months, so I was not present in person for most of Mairi's experience of soul. Our communion of conscious and unconscious feeling, thinking, imagining and sensing about Mairi's experience had been forged out of whatever interpersonal understanding we had managed to reach in an enduring, five-year psychotherapeutic relationship. Out of that context, along with what Mairi told me, I will try to relate my impressions of what was happening to her.

Occasionally – between earlier sessions – Mairi had begun to write to me, keeping notes to read aloud during the next hour. This supplemented regular journal-keeping, writing dreams, and other "organizations of my life," as she called them, including imaginative sketches, lists of books, things-to-do, and things-to-remember. While writing to me Mairi felt that she "kept herself company" well enough to formulate her inner experience when she was alone. Reading these notes aloud to me represented keeping me up to date.

The enormous influx of psychic energy released in Mairi's experience of soul made use of this ready-formed channel of expression, but the tenor of her note-taking changed, along with how she used it. At home, Mairi wrote and wrote. With me, she now used her notes only to remind herself of what she needed to cover in our time together – no more reading as if from a script. Unlike Hadewijch of Brabant, Mairi was no poet. However, Mairi's note-writing, like Hadewijch's poetry, now became not only *about* something, but written from *within* whatever it was she was going through. This is to say that as Mairi's inner experience intensified, the way she related to me changed, too.

In our next sessions Mairi talked and talked, stumbling over words and phrases, righting herself and continuing. Alternately flushed and pale, excited and reflective, Mairi wanted to tell me *in person* everything possible about what she was experiencing. Obviously I was no stand-in for Dream

#2, where Mairi "talked and talked, telling the angel everything," but a similarly warm, all-enveloping presence seemed to be with us in the room during the next few hours. I do not think Mairi was remembering her dream, but I did.

The immediate major motif running throughout Mairi's narration was her shattering recognition that something (or Someone) had been revealed to her. Astounded, Mairi encountered this presence as holy, feminine, and abiding. "She cares about me," Mairi kept saying; "I feel it, through and through. It is the Holy Spirit, but feminine, She is with me and I'll never be the same. I feel as if I have died and been reborn. At first I felt as if a floor had fallen out from under me, but somehow the free-fall was a threshold, disguised. I crossed – or It – or She – crossed to reach me. There is no going back. I will serve Her the rest of my life. How can this be?"

In my understanding, revelation unfolds in a four-fold fashion. Primarily, revelation is self-revealing. By way of the intrusion of another dimension of reality the presence of "elsewhere" into the here and now, *revelation reveals itself* as an experiential phenomenon. We *encounter* revelation. Opening to another dimension of Being, revelation knocks us to the ground (Saul on the road to Damascus). It throws us into chaos like being hit as lightning tears through a tent (Dream #7). It opens us to another world (Corbin's *mundus imaginalis*). Pictures of Gabriel's Annunciation to the mother of Jesus often depict Mary with books: Mary looks up from a manuscript, a book is nearby, or a book has been thrown aside and fallen to the floor. The image of book-reading hints at magic and secret knowledge, and in some paintings (such as Antonello da Messina's beautiful Annunciation, without angel)[2] Mary's face is lit with obvious inspiration as if to indicate that her state of mind (thinking, reading, reflecting) were suddenly interrupted by a completely different state of being.

Gabriel's annunciation invades Mary's ordinary thinking mind, announcing the possibility of new life and new Being by way of a conception which is bodily rather than mental. Encountering this angelic annunciation, Mary accedes to a self-fulfillment so personal that her body bears an "other" life, inexplicably new. Simultaneously, *revelation reveals the experiencing subject as a locus of revelation*, a being or a soul upon whom revelation impacts. The soul is often understood as the inner site of revelation.[3]

A third aspect of revelation is *the content of revelation*, its realized message, meaning the something that it makes real. The Virgin Mary became pregnant. Terrible to look upon, Moses brought down from the mountain the Tables of the Law. Mairi was "reborn." While revelation is not confined by the psyche, the psyche coagulates around it, lending revelation time and space, form and image, and story.

The fourth important aspect of revelation is that *revelation reveals spirit*. Revelation reveals spirit to soul, as soul receives spirit in all its forms, whether it is constructive or destructive. Insofar as spirit is a force that cannot be easily described, much less represented, we sometimes experience spirit as God or the Holy Spirit.

Mairi's narration contained a dense orchestration of these four aspects. Listening to her, I too stumbled, my mind and senses struggling to provide Mairi's "musical score" with an answering "staff" of comprehension. Still coherent, Mairi continued her story of what had happened to her for the three days after she had left my office. She had decided not to eat supper that evening, after all; she was not hungry. Instead, "to still myself, I sat down cross-legged on the floor. I felt as if something momentous were about to happen. Suddenly I understood how the psyche of my dreams wasn't really out there somewhere, or even in my dreams, but part of me. I mean I *experienced* the psyche, instead of just knowing about it. Once you quoted an old alchemical saying: 'as above, so below.' That's how I felt – 'as without, so within' – every thing is one. I stayed very still on the floor, thinking these thoughts, breathing slowly and deeply, and then I began to have spontaneous orgasms, over and over. I've never had an orgasm alone without touching myself, except in a dream."

The energy soon left Mairi's genitals but it continued to "rise and fall like light" up and down her spine. A short time later she cautiously rose from the floor and began to walk around her living room. "My whole body blazed," she said. "I felt as if I shone, not with fire but with light, blue-white, incandescent light, that did not leave as I moved around. I was surrounded by it but light was in me, too. And with me was the presence of another, an Other, like a Queen of Heaven – a presence of enormous Light in the room, everywhere. I knew it was the Holy Spirit, but it was a feminine Presence. Her Presence blessed me. She knew me, and I knew that It was She."

In the telling, Mairi's presence radiated her experience. Her face glowed. But she was also bewildered. The Holy Spirit as a Feminine Presence did not correspond either to what she had imagined as a child or heard as an adult about the Trinity in terms of Father, Son and Holy Spirit. Her experience did not "fit." I replied simply that perhaps her formulation came from another tradition. Inwardly, I thought of the Gnostic Sophia.[4]

Mairi laughed. "Thank goodness," she said; "I can't – I can't even think right now, let alone make sense." She sighed. "At last," she continued, "at long, long last." Long silence. Then, "This is not like my vision of the Eye," she told me. "I don't see the Holy Spirit like I saw the Eye. I just know She was – is – there. Here. I feel Her Presence right now; I *am*, in Her Presence. She does not embrace me, She is far greater than that, but She is *with* me. Myself – what I always thought of as my 'outside' – has suddenly turned inside out. Inside there is such space between my breaths. Nowhere is Now Here. How do I say this? Inside and outside, without and within.

"I don't have the words to talk about this." Mairi slumped in her chair. "I want to keep trying. The Holy Spirit hasn't gone away, though She is farther from me than She was three nights ago, than She was yesterday evening. I didn't sleep, that first night. I tried to rest. My body was empty . . . light? tired? I couldn't eat. I wanted to lie down. I thought I ought to sleep. But even when I closed my eyes, something in me, a witness,[5] took in all that was happening, an unchanging background, not She, not the Holy Spirit, but my soul, maybe? Some other kind of consciousness.

"My emotions rose and fell in great waves and I felt as if I were a cork, bobbing in an ocean. I thought about those two scowling, ferocious Japanese Guardians of the Threshold at the Metropolitan Museum (we had discussed these earlier): fear and anger, I named them then, no wonder they looked so horrendous. Now I see them as Denial and Pain, *in me*. As they moved aside, I fell through the middle. Sometimes I was swept by huge, silent laughter. Clearly the joke was on me: God was real, had always been real, had never *not* been real, after all. When I wept my tears were huge, copious, endless; solid sheets of water streamed down my face and neck, over my clothes and pillow. But mostly I felt joy, relief, and gratitude: such a great recognition of my infinite littleness. I was so small. And someone else, some *place* else in me kept witnessing all this because *I* could not, *I* was ended, what I used to know as 'me' had cracked wide open. *I* let go, but the witness held it all, unmoved and unmoving, something attending nothing and everything, always. I felt the force of its attention: clear, open all the way through. Eyes open, eyes closed, moving, lying still, awake or asleep, I was never alone. She was with me, Royal. Splendid. Immense. Am I crazy? If this is crazy, then being normal is a huge disappointment. This feels right and good. All my life I have been heading for this moment and I never knew it."

As I write Mairi's narrative now, a translation of one of Rumi's sayings comes to mind:

> I have lived on the lip of insanity
> wanting to know reasons, knocking
> on a door. It opens.
> I've been knocking from the inside!
>   (Barks and Green 1997: 36–7)

Rumi conveys something of what I imagine Mairi was discovering then, finding beyond a feared crossing (a threshold) the Holy, and finding herself there too: a *real* self, relative to what she remembered of self-experience before. Describing a transformation in her self-image, Mairi's capacity for an all-out, no-holds-barred kind of experiencing drew itself into a pattern of self–other relating that called her into fully human consciousness. She gained a completely different perspective on who she had been and how she had lived earlier.

Mairi continued: "All night long I heard voices in the streets outside my bedroom window – voices, one boy calling another, 'Angel, Angel!' And traffic going by, and a late-night quarreling couple right beneath my window. All night long my mind crawled, weaving itself, textured with what I could not possibly see or know about outside my walls. Yet I seemed to see and know about everything *and* the deep, silent night behind it, behind the world, behind all. I don't think I slept. Inside my room, lying on my bed, I was full of myself, everything going on inside me, flotsam and jetsam, scraps of music floating by, lights and colors, words and phrases flashing through my mind like shooting stars. I could feel myself strain for inner coherence. I could practically see my brain forming gestalts. But I felt as if I were looking *in* on all this, enveloped in a darkness as dark as outer space is outside, that existed in-between my thoughts. In the empty space between stars, as if between constellations, my imagination rested and could leave everything alone."

She took a deep breath. "I was terribly afraid before the orgasms came, but when they stopped, fear left, too. Instead, I was enormously relieved. At last I was *in*. I was "in" someplace where I knew I belonged but have never before been able to reach. This whole experience fits. To have this experience is why I've been through everything I've ever been through. All of me suddenly makes sense."

Still slumped in her chair, Mairi struggled with words, struggled to tell me what had happened in her mind, in her heart, in her being. Though her body was quiet, it too was involved. She bore not the slightest resemblance to a lifeless clay statue (Dream #14). Imaginally, emotionally, and physio-logically released from her former sense of self, Mairi's body spoke from depth. Her face glowed beneath a faint sheen of perspiration, shining as if lit from within. Eyes wide and fixed, she looked like a Sumerian seer, her inner vision as engrossing as whatever (or whoever) was before her. "Something other," urgent and of supreme importance, was present. What seemed to push Mairi urgently from within was Presence seeking passionate embodiment, seeking another (i.e., me) in Mairi's passionate need to speak to another person all that she possibly could of the thoughts, feelings, sensations and memories that rushed through the fabric of her being. Clearly she was breaking out of her self-sufficiency impelled by an inner need to relate everything she felt to another person. Energy transparently ebbed and flowed within her. I remembered the woman on the beach of Dream #11, transparent to a fire within.

I had never seen Mairi like this, simultaneously utterly open with me and completely and unselfconsciously engaged in her inner experience. I thought of a remarkable picture I once saw in the Library of St. Gall, in Switzer-land.[6] In black and white, the picture depicts the head of Christ gazing upward, his brow crowned with thorns, blood and sweat falling in great drops down his neck. What is extraordinary about this picture is that it is made entirely of words. In squiggly, fine medieval German script, writing both outlines the figure and tells the story of the passion of Jesus. Incarnate flesh is outlined by story, a body rimmed with words. Both beneath and by means of these words, the presence of Christ's passionately embodied Being burgeons forth, shining through both meaning and embodied human form. As I watched and listened to Mairi, a similar thing seemed to happen. She, too, moved into a capacity for passionately embodied being that was beneath, because of, and beyond the words and meaning of her personal story. Telling me about her burgeoning embodiment grounded Mairi's transforming consciousness into a relationship to otherness that she could express outwardly and inwardly at once.

Mairi continued. The next day she had tried to continue her yoga practice. "I thought that it would hold me together," she said, "calm me down." But she noticed a difference. Any posture, any asana, seemed effortless. "I felt as if I weren't even *doing* the postures," she said. "They took me over. I had no resistance at all." This she found eerie and frightening. "Before I thought it through I just followed all the postures I knew, riding the energy. It was so strange. It was as if all my body armor disappeared. I never knew what body armor meant before. Now I do. Mine was gone. No one I know – except maybe Swami B. – can do all the asanas that way normally. Achieving them effortlessly is not even the point of doing them in the first place. Then I was afraid that I had torn my muscles or hurt myself. But I guess not. Afterwards I wasn't even sore. When I was little I was limber but even so I couldn't have done what I did. My bones, muscles, limbs, simply didn't resist. The asanas bent me in and out of themselves as if I were a piece of warm candle wax. *I* didn't 'do' them, they 'did' me, and they almost did me in."

"When I finished, I was high, like on drugs," she said. "It was scary to be so spaced out. To ground myself I went into the kitchen and made myself eat: meat, eggs, heavy food, even sugar, things I don't eat often because of my practice. That helped. Gradually I came down. I feel a little more solid now. But I'm not going to do yoga anymore for a while. I hope this energy rush stops soon. It is exhausting."

Mairi and I initially framed her experience in the language of awakening kundalini[7] energy. Earlier Mairi worried that perhaps I would analyze away her philosophical interest in yoga, or that depth psychotherapeutic work would somehow belittle how much her discipline meant to her. I had assured her that her yoga practice in no way contradicted the kind of psychological work we would do, for I knew that work with chakras can often correspond with psychological work as a path to the Self (Judith 1996), each enriching the other. Once Mairi felt that I had accepted her interest she told me that her Muladhara chakra was the one that she felt was most in need of attention and healing: the chakra that rooted her into her body, the physical world, and earth.[8] Within Mairi's conceptual frame-work, trauma to this particular chakra could embrace birth trauma, poor physical bonding with the mother, and feeding difficulties. Its developmental stages were thought to be the second trimester to the end of the first year. "In fact," Mairi commented, "I'll bet my need to work on Muladhara drew me to Hatha yoga in the first place, years ago."

At first, Mairi's familiarity with the language of yoga served her well. "Kundalini rising and falling" described some of her physical sensations, and the sense of an opening Muladhara helped us think about the abrupt illumination of many issues to which that chakra pointed. She was also aware of "tantric" energies and some of our discussion circled around this ancient concept and practice.[9] But in truth, Kundalini teachings and practices point the practitioner to what cannot be taught, or even practiced. As Mairi's experience continued, the significance of these concepts and the symbolic system to which they referred began to pale: they did not seem "big" enough to enable her to express herself fully. As Judith (1996: 468) reminds us,

> The main thing to remember (in working with chakras) is that body, soul, mind, and spirit, together with the seven chakras, are all one indivisible whole. Even when working with a part, all the other parts are present and participating. The whole must be kept in mind at all times as the guiding archetype of the Self.

The presence of an indivisible whole kept making itself felt. Because the actual activation of kundalini implies that all the chakras undergo simultaneous illumination, and because at this point neither Mairi nor I were able to sort out the illumination of any one chakra from the illumination of another, I began to think of alternative models for the sensations of an "opening Muladhara." Her experience seemed to fit what Neumann (1953) called "the transformation of reality planes," through which, as he suggests, "*homo mysticus* apprehends the *Unus Mundus* or One World" (1948). Equally relevant was Corbin's idea of *encounter within the imaginal world.* According to Corbin, just as we think of our physical senses as fantasy-prone, we may think of our psycho-spiritual senses as encounter-prone. Corbin's descriptions imply an encounter within the imaginal realm, a bodily apprehension . . . a sign, an intimation, an announcement that is finally the soul's annunciation to itself of itself" (Corbin 1953: 12).

From a psychological point of view, we can say that whenever the magical dimensions of the psyche open, everything becomes illuminated. Every discipline becomes a language of meaning. Meditation, Aikido, Tai Chi – the mysteries of any discipline in which we participate are illuminated in a new light. Mairi's understandings of her dreams, her yoga practice, and the puzzles of her personal life were suddenly transformed, back-lit by that which underlay them. A great illumination in the background of her heart and soul, the psyche and the transpersonal, opened and acted like a depth-charge upon Mairi's embodied being, including her sense of self-understanding and her capacity for self-acceptance.

Mairi seemed to have an urgent need to differentiate her experience of soul from the psychological work we had been doing, and she spoke of "soul" rather than "the soul" because she felt utterly immersed in soul and was unable to objectify that in which she felt immersed. Her personal discovery of being-in-soul acted like a body-shaped life raft in the midst of chaos. Soul was something different from all the psychological material we had processed together – her dreams, her feelings, her self-representations as she interacted with others. Soul was concrete, an undeniable *something real* into which Mairi felt herself fall, and out of which Mairi felt herself become. As if the inner light of embodied Being, soul was something that Mairi *was* not, but that contained her; she *experienced* soul; she did not think about it.

Mairi was telling me that she could suddenly feel soul inside herself, as if it were an all-but-indescribable second self, or perhaps a parallel of herself, more pure – almost as if her experience of soul defined her opening inner world. More than the sum of her intelligence and emotions, more than the sum of her bodily experience, soul seemed to run like veins of a rare substance through all three. For Mairi, soul was an inner faculty that recognized the animating mysteries of the world because it (and she) were of the same substance.

Mairi's gradual understanding of her experience of soul mapped out her physiological, psychological and emotional transformation. Whereas the concept of soul was neither new nor particularly interesting to Mairi, *experience* of soul was a bulletin from beyond. Deeply receiving its message, Mairi felt nested into her body from the inside out. Sometimes this differentiation of soul from psyche comforted and relieved her. "This is so different from anything I've known before," Mairi said. "What I fell into is so much older and bigger than anything else."

As I sat with rapt attention listening to Mairi's impassioned narration, I experienced something of a revelation of my own. I realized that the psyche as I had come to know it from my Jungian training had led us this way and that, like a butterfly fluttering ahead of a child.[10] By following the images of her dreams, we glimpsed something else – something totally "other." Previously psyche had meant *image* to me – images in dreams, images in imagination, images in life. Mairi was telling me that images are not experience of soul, even if images had led her there. Images are channels, maybe, but they're not the way through. It dawned on me that *psyche is part of soul*, not the other way around. Spirit may enter psyche, but God enters the soul.

As I thought this through I began to realize that while the psyche remains attached to the soul, soul is the primary entity. Mairi's experience of soul became something like experiencing the inside of her body – the indwelling flesh of the matter that she was. For Aristotle, the soul was the "form" of the body. For Mairi, it was as if her soul had dreamed, her psyche had *imaged* what her soul dreamed and reflected it back to both the dreamer (Mairi) and her soul. From this point of view, the psyche becomes the soul's expressive and apprehensive organ. Psyche works for soul, partners soul, and pictures soul . . . and when the psyche becomes imageless or trans-lucent, soul alone shows through as a state of being. Occasionally Jung himself defines the soul (rather than the psyche) as an organ of perception. The soul, says Jung,

> has the dignity of an entity endowed with, and conscious of, a rela-tionship to Deity . . . indeed the very intimacy of the relationship between God and the soul automatically precludes any devaluation of the latter. It would be going too far to speak of an affinity; but at all events the soul must contain in itself the faculty of relation to God, i.e., a correspondence, otherwise a connection could never come about. This correspondence is, in psychological terms, the archetype of the God-image. (CW12: 11)[11]

Apparently, even in dreams the soul itself is not imaged by the psyche, neither as substance nor body, person nor "anima" figure.[12] If soul is to be conceptualized or imagined at all by the conscious mind, it must be felt, imagined, and remembered as embodied experience. Spirit is imaged in dreams by the psyche as personified images and conceptualized in psycho-analytic circles as a mysterious animating principle that "indwells" in the soma during what Winnicott calls the process of "personalisation." But *like all truly religious experience, soul comes to presence and takes place in consciousness.* Soul can be thought about as a bodily event, perhaps, even as a *transfiguration* of the body (all that light!) occurring during a trans-formation *of* consciousness, *in* consciousness. This is why the psyche's dreaming imagery gave way for Mairi's conscious experience in her body of soul welling forth from the depths of soul's abyss.

Perhaps we could say that the psyche as image is closer to the dreaming mind, while the soul, resident in the body, is closer to the dreaming flesh. I tend to think of the soul as genderless, or as masculine and feminine both. But overall, soul seems to point toward what we think of as female elements of being: toward darkness and coolness, reflective and receptive, something like the indwelling particularity of *this* person's body, incarnate in flesh. While soul can embody a uniquely personal relation to God, psyche cannot.

Another way to understand imaginatively how the psyche functions as an organ of the soul is to consider that when the psyche becomes "virgin," meaning free of images, we may experience a kind of fall through that image-communicating medium into its substratum, soul, which is home to psyche's embodiment as well. Theologian Michael Sells (1994) uses this understanding of the psyche as he explores gender implications in Meister

Eckhart's apophatic writings, wherein a symbol of a virgin wife becomes the symbol for a mystical re-conception of the virgin birth. Sells (1994: 137) looks closely at the words of one of Eckhart's Sermons: "Now, then, pay close attention to this word; it was necessarily by a virgin that Jesus was received/conceived. 'Virgin' designates a person who is free of all foreign images, as free as he was when he was not yet." Switching then to the first person, the voice in the sermon speaks of being as free of images "as I was when I was not" – the theme of reversion to a pre-created state, which we find in Hadewijch, as well.

Sells points out that by combining both intellect and will in his notion of foreign images and refusing all images and attachment to images, Eckhart finds the soul free and virginal. Here, to be virginal implies valuing intactness, or being in touch with itself. At this point the soul is ready to receive the impression that Eckhart compares to the fruit which the soul bears. In our words, the soul becomes vulnerable and open to direct religious experience. The soul becomes virgin, god-bearing, and bearer of the possibility of fully human consciousness. In Hadewijch's words (see the next chapter), the soul is readied for an experience of "fruitive being."

Mairi's experience of soul knocked her previously half-conscious but deeply held assumptions about herself, her dreams, the psyche, and our psychotherapeutic work into a cocked hat. I chased after the anger that I heard. Was she angry with me, as if to say that after all the years she and I had spent attending her psychological struggles I hadn't told – or warned – her about the sustaining Presence she now felt? I asked. No, she replied. When she thought about it, she could not imagine how I could have told her if I wanted to, or how she could have understood me even if I had. Nevertheless her anger and shock were real, and directed at something. Things were so much simpler than she had thought.

I thought about the shadow of depth psychotherapeutic work in general. A profession that justifies its existence and methods of practice on the basis of unconscious pain and suffering cannot deny a sizable chunk of darkness. Mairi's anger reminded me once again how the frame of therapy is particularly difficult for those who deal with early trauma or pre-oedipal, pre-verbal issues and how the relationship and setting re-constellates memories of early deprivation. While my approach to Mairi had been anything but reductive, nonetheless our focus on her early life had highlighted her psychological illness, magnified her hunger, and fostered illusion in the name of more consciousness, healing and personality development. Emotional and physical deprivation are inherent in a therapeutic situation. Often we practitioners are no better persons than were the original parents or caretakers of our patients, and sometimes we are worse. As neurotic and fallible as others, and sometimes more so, we need to recognize that the depriving frame has a protective function, too, serving our patients as well as ourselves.

Although Mairi's therapy transformed her consciousness, the rigor of our work offered little to her immediate hungers of skin, blood, bone, brain, and soul. No matter how consistently reliable our meetings were, Mairi's and my relationship offered no answer to her longing to be held or her starved need for bodily touch. Perhaps I as a person within the psychotherapeutic frame had been as remote as Mairi's original mother. Wherever Mairi's erotic desire or hunger for early nurture, touch and holding was constellated (other than the symbolic comforts of the therapeutic relationship), I had offered Mairi no ease.

But apparently my physical and emotional absence outside the therapeutic frame was not the point. She had no desire to be held or touched in other than the casual or appropriate ways that had occurred: my hand brushing hers as I helped her on with her coat, or as we handed back and forth papers or a cup of tea. Any overtones of desirousness specific to our personal interactions had woven themselves into our shared descent into the erotic roots of consciousness itself. Whatever it was that surprised and angered Mairi had less to do with me than with her radical experience of the soul's otherness . . . a cosmic simplicity that cleared everything else up in the "fall."

Relative to her therapeutic process, I thought perhaps Mairi's irritation referred to a gradual awareness of a "knot in the psyche" or the "misconstruction" (Lacan 1949: 1–7) of a mistaken early self-representation.[13] But this proved not to be the case. *Image breaking*, more than an image of a particular kind, seems to have been what freed Mairi into experience of soul and the Holy Spirit as Feminine Presence. In Mairi's experience, Presence was the *absence* of inner images, the presence of what *is*: "I am that I am." Mairi's experience of soul *and* of presence arose from a place of old, silent knowledge divorced from (or perhaps never married to) the possibility of inner self or object-representations or even of symbolic language.[14]

I also thought about how Mairi had described her birth caul as a "caul" around her heart (in her commentary on her vision of the Eye) and how she was aware of an early separation of herself from herself. Now it seemed the falling away of what "caul" represented was abrupt. A massive inrush and expression of energy was released as a membrane between Mairi's consciousness and unconscious psyche simply thinned and disappeared; with this the "caul" disappeared, too. Perhaps this thinning also explained the cessation of her Self-directive dreams – indeed, of all dreaming – for awhile. This disappearance accompanied Mairi's fall into a "shimmering atmosphere," the stuff that had textured the imagery of her dreams all along. Stripped naked and reborn bare, Mairi felt extremely vulnerable.

All of our "thinking" about her experience seemed to miss the point. Mairi's self-reflection separated her from Presence, and while the comfortable house of self-reflection provided a necessary container for the fear she felt and defended her (and me) from the terrors of her free-fall into the abyss of soul, none of our explanations or efforts at psychological understanding did justice to what she had just experienced. Mairi was not angry with me. She was appalled at her previous unconsciousness and at the revelation of a world of Being of which she had had neither conscious experience, nor memory, nor idea.

Only a religious language seemed to suffice. "Love broke in," Mairi said, "and I was no longer alone." "God's presence came into my loneliness and healed my despair."[15] "From where I am now," she said, "my whole past looks like an obstructed conduit to the Holy. *I* had to dissolve enough to receive what has *always* been there, always been there, trying to get through. I feel like I have been reconciled with God."[16] "I am the one who turned away, long ago," she said. "I am the one who forgot. God didn't leave me. I left God." In experience of soul, Mairi both saw and felt seen through: "God had to get through to me somehow," she mused. "I was not easy to reach." "Something had to break down – me I guess – before I could receive what was offered."

Mairi's enlarged capacity for passionately embodied being was ignited by her experience of God as Holy Spirit, more than as Creator or Savior. As Feminine Presence and the presence of Feminine Being, the arms of the Holy Spirit held her. With her fall Mairi was thrown into an unusual awareness of the contingency both of her "being" and Being itself; of the "thrown-ness" of body and soul, the "just-so-ness" of matter and spirit – of being as "two-ness from the beginning" (Dream #5), as feminine (the Holy Spirit as Feminine Presence), as self–other awareness – of Being as God. All of her life held meaning now. Each hitherto bewildering occurrence suddenly made sense in light of her experience of soul.

Mairi was describing an experience of extravagant intimacy with the inner world. Closer than close, the Holy Spirit comforted Mairi in a manner that might have (but does not) put to shame our human desire to comfort one another. I say this because Mairi's flow of inner self–other awareness lent a similar intimacy to the awareness that flowed between her and me. I wondered aloud whether any persons she had known – her lost twin, her mother, her father, anyone who had loved her or whom she had loved – had, from this point of view, fulfilled her unconscious search for this "nearest and dearest" (her earlier words) presence.

"Yes," Mairi replied, "They did. So I misused them too. I didn't mean to," she continued, "now, I understand how unconscious I have been. I mistook them for that 'nearest and dearest' and I didn't love them humanly. I am so sorry. I'm appalled at how I loved people before. My love wasn't a real, human love for other real, human beings; my 'sin' was doubled-edged (double-crossed?) – against the Holy for not recognizing God as such, and against people I cared about because I loved them so blindly. I loved them wrongly, not for themselves but instead of God. I don't think I've ever had a conscious relationship in my entire life."

I remembered then Mairi's words after we talked about her vision of the Eye. She needed a human heart, she had said, a heart that was neither hard nor scarred, but real. As she spoke now I felt immensely close to her, as if nothing separated us. Yet "nothing" has a reality of its own and an organizing power, too.[17] Mairi's description of "nowhere is now here" fitted my sense of our presence together, a co-presence, as of a shared shifting of figure and ground. I wondered how to name it. Probably more than she, I felt that Mairi and I shared soul as the locus of what was happening to both of us. But I wanted to *think* about what was happening, too. What was this "nothingness" become Nothingness between us? A Buddhist concept came to mind: that of *interbeing*. In Buddhism, the birth, growth and decline of things depends upon multiple causes and conditions, not just a single one. The presence of one thing (dharma) implies the presence of all other things. Experience of this realization is referred to as *interbeing*, or genesis (Hanh 1995: 41). And I did not remember the Buddha of Dream #13 until I wrote this chapter. Did the Buddhist concept of "interbeing" hold the world for both of us as Mairi plunged into a pool of passionately embodied emotion? Did I fall in, too?

Mairi and I were in a state of interbeing. We were not interrelating: we saw each other twice a week, and except as analyst and patient our personal lives were not intertwined. We did not have the same thoughts, dreams, or experiences simultaneously, as if revisiting *participation mystique*. Mairi bore living witness to Eigen's proposal that the capacity for an all-out, no-holds-barred way of experiencing points to an "area of faith." As the contents of her experience of soul flowed into the relationship between us, filling her life and our hours together, I understood my own experience of descent and return. As my awareness of Mairi's ability to reach passionately embodied being deepened, my companioning her experience of soul returned me to a genesis of my own self–other experience, co-mingled and complete.

What allowed for Mairi's extraordinary capacity for intimacy? As one of twins, had she from conception been born into unusual intimacy, albeit interrupted? Was her "permeability" the result of early trauma, lived bodily? Known by her friends to be "intuitive," Mairi had an extraordinary sensitivity to the "being" of whomever was with her – to the physical, emotional, and psychological presence of another, whoever that other might be – in both outer and inner world. I felt this sensitivity too. But now it was as if a previously "inferior" sensate function was manifest down to cell and bone.[18] Previously unconscious body experience was metabolized in Mairi's personal experience of soul. For a few days, small patches of eczema appeared and disappeared on her upper arms, as if in memory of her body's memory of agonized alienation.

"Everything is the same, yet everything is different," Mairi said. "All the old clichés make sense. Death is still here, a fact of life, but 'death has lost its sting.' To 'walk through the Valley of the Shadow of Death' just means to consciously be in my body. Somehow I had to die in order to get 'in.' Now that I've been through death, I'm not so scared. That's what that means: 'Death has lost its sting.' And so many 'rebirths' – one after another! Like being stuck in a Xerox machine, or peeling away layer after layer like the skins of an onion!" Mairi laughed. "One time when I emerged, I found myself imagining what I wanted on my gravestone. This is what I want: 'She Loved THIS Life.' Isn't that odd? Only by dying could I uncover my love of *this* life: not an afterlife, or another life, but *this* life."

This statement moved and interested me enormously. It brought to mind a short essay by Jacques Derrida, 1992, discussing the ideas of the Czech writer Jan Patočka, in which Derrida states that "the origin and essence of the religious" is found in a changed attitude toward death. This changed attitude (from death as fearful enemy to death as gift) comes about as "the demonic secret and the orgiastic sacred" are surpassed (or outstripped, or outmoded) within experience. If we think of Mairi's kundalini release as an experience of the "orgiastic sacred," we can then understand the widening of this experience into what she called her experience of soul as a kind of psychic mutation into a mature religious experience which was marked by the transformation in her consciousness. Her ability to personalise her experience becomes indicative of her growing ability to make that mysterious, sacred energy subject to herself as she, in turn, freely subjects herself to the "wholly and infinite other that sees without being seen" (Derrida 1992: 2), meaning the Holy Spirit as Feminine Presence.[19]

Derrida goes on to say that this process that he calls "becoming-historical" is intimately tied to the experience of the *mysterium tremendum* and the trembling that seizes one *at the moment of becoming a person* (emphasis mine) and the person can become what it is only in being paralyzed, in its very singularity, by the gaze of God. Then it sees itself seen by the gaze of another, "'a supreme, absolute and inaccessible being who holds us in his hand not by exterior but by interior force'" (1992: 6). Derrida also verifies that *psyche is not concerned with death* in the first place. *Only the soul so distinguishes, separates, assembles, and wakes itself into consciousness through a concern with death*, (italics mine) thereby becoming individualized and interiorized to the point of its own invisibility. Says Derrida, "the psyche as life, as breath of life, as *pneuma*, only appears out of this concerned anticipation of dying" (1992: 5) – and, I would add, may disappear as it did with Mairi's experience of soul only to reappear accompanied by Mairi's transformed consciousness and changed attitude toward her mortality and death. She spoke as if she had been given the secret of death, or a new experience of death.

If we think of soul as that which is highly genuine and unique in each of us, Mairi's paradox was that without personalisation of her body, her soul had no place to dwell. Mairi spoke out of a new sense of herself as an embodied person. The witnessing consciousness that she discovered in her experience of soul companioned her back into the world to make itself heard as Mairi's *personal* voice. Embodied, she began to give voice to personal points of view about herself and her experience, about her dreams and me, about psyche and her life as a whole: about her children, her friends, her society, her culture, her world, and her God. In sensate terms, Mairi personally experienced the life energy dwelling within her very cells. She experienced orgasms, energy coursing through her body, a "blooming, buzzing confusion" that made her senses feel extraordinarily alive. Infant Mairi's skin and bones had been touched by her experience of paralysis in braces, afflicted by skin disease, and traumatized by sexual abuse. These impingements surely disorganized her awareness and her bodily spontaneity. Bracing herself against these experiences, she also had braced herself against feeling fully alive, wished she had no skin, and fled an embodiment that left her feeling disoriented and awry. With me, Mairi revisited an emotional attachment to another without immediate bodily contact or comfort. Before her fall, Mairi could not have known how often her psyche, unconsciously remembering, recapitulated the throes of passionate emotional bonding with others without personal touch.

When the unconscious archetypal (mythic) core of the negative mother complex (which masks traces of pre-verbal terror experienced in the face of a mother "possessed" by archetypal rage) severed from the personal body (Mairi's body) of the complex, a well of energy is released: the frozen, stone-like, expressionless-ness locked within the core of personality is freed: Pegasus, the great white winged horse, soars up from the severed connection, his hoof striking open a spring of living water in the body of the earth, an upwelling from the depths of the archetypal core of being itself. In archetypal language, this is at least one way to understand what happened to Mairi. But nothing addressed Mairi's hunger or anguished skin and bone, at least nothing that could be explained as psychological. Perhaps only religious experience can do this. Out of dream, The Comforter entered Mairi's reality, to hold and warm her through and through. As God came to be with her, Mairi discovered soul at home. Her personality rediscovered what her soul had known well enough to miss – achingly – but she herself had forgotten: the presence of the Divine. Touched by the presence of the Holy Spirit, Mairi moved into an all-out, no-holds-barred capacity for self–other awareness. Her passionate attainment of embodiment relativized not only what she knew of herself, but all that she could remember of how she had related before. In the light of this Love, Mairi could mourn both a lack of love and her lack of loving. In Hadewijch's language, "fruitless" Being ceased for Mairi, and "fruitive" Being bore new life.

"I have a religious life, now," Mairi said, "though it's still an odd one. I could not say exactly who or what God is, or what the word God means. In fact I haven't the slightest idea. But nowhere do I see God's absence, even if

I'm unaware in the moment. Even now, I can't believe that God is confined or explained by how I experienced the Holy Spirit. God helped me find my soul in order to find God, too."

Another part of Mairi's new life consisted of a new relation to her bodily reality. Her incarnate relation to the fact of her embodiment changed. She described it as going from "having a body" to "being a body." Her repeated reference to finally "being in" almost seemed to refer to the inside of her body, as if her bodily interior contained soul . . . outlined soul? . . . was soul's habitation? As Mairi's body retrieved soul, the Holy Spirit illumined both. From a psychological point of view, Mairi traced the psyche's return to the formative roots of the architecture of her dream in the world. Religious experience tends to put an end to egoism, and Mairi's experience of soul addressed in particular those aspects of unconscious egoism that are initiated somatically, e.g., as body armor. In Mairi, these defenses had defined themselves somatically and remained in bodily form, becoming the symbolic matrix of that early, unconscious, primordial identification with an image of "I-alone" that shattered with Mairi's experience of soul. Just as Mairi's rigidity, numbness, depersonalisation and psychosomatic symptoms peeled away from her sense of bodily being, a caul of unconsciousness seemed to peel away from her capacity for an adult awareness of self and other, body and soul. Mairi remained conscious throughout her experience of soul, although she felt fragmented, and clearly her hard-earned consciousness was working overtime. With her own self-discipline and a nod from the spirit, the disordered remnants of Mairi's narcissism seemed to fall apart at the seams. As her unconscious defenses gave way, Mairi emerged, feeling reborn, as a new person in a new world with new life ahead of her.

One way to frame this psychoanalytically would be to say that Mairi's therapy re-constellated her primary narcissism while rendering her narcissistic defenses unnecessary. Disassembling and reassembling Mairi's psyche, therapy took the depths of her personality neatly apart in order to put it together again. Heightening the structures and vicissitudes of primary narcissism, the therapeutic process analyzed it up to a point, while then making way for another process, a widening, more inclusive consciousness. Subsequently the impacted psyche seemed to reassemble itself under its own impetus. This shifted the central thrust of the personality away from self-regard toward self–other awareness. In the myth of Narcissus, unconsciousness moves slowly into self-awareness: only when the reflecting image is *re-cognized* can obsessive self-regard die.

While certain aspects of such intimacy with interiority may echo the fruitlessness of self-love, real religious experience reaches beyond it. So deeply was Mairi startled into new life that feelings of "all shall be well, all manner of things shall be well" rang from her heart, not because Mairi had read Julian of Norwich but because – as joyously surprised – her heart resonated in company with all those who catch a glimmer of "One World" beyond the ego, so long lost. Immediate or direct religious experience can leave us feeling utterly changed. What seems to clear up is perception or awareness itself. Liberated from the filters of attention and image, it can assault us with rare intensity. When "free-fall"[20] becomes the freedom to feel fully ourselves, we reach to feel fully alive. "The glory of God is *the human person, fully alive*" (emphasis mine), says Irenaeus of Antioch, a second-century philosopher and theologian. From a psychological point of view, to be "made whole" in this manner means to see the world whole: to see all that is offered – light and dark, good and evil, flux and permanence, greatness and triviality, freedom and necessity – even God and the World – and not feel split in two by them.

Because she no longer felt "split" Mairi now began to feel the heaviness of being singular and alone. Sorrow followed joy. The tone of her discourse darkened. "Have you gone through this too?" she asked. And again, "I mean, have you felt like this? Oh, I know you can't really know what I am going through from the inside. But I wish I felt less alone." This cry came often as Mairi's experience of soul began to fade. While in the presence of the Holy Spirit, Mairi had felt anything but alone. But as the ecstasy dimmed, the pool of wonder darkened, and sorrow came to swim, along with pain. Harrowing may belong to hell, but it also belongs to heaven. I answered Mairi's cry as best I could. My experience of "soul" was not the same as Mairi's, but I, too, had worked hard to open up defenses that had kept me from living fully in the world, and I knew that the process was difficult, and painful, and long.

As the presence of the Holy Spirit waned, physical and emotional exhaustion overshadowed Mairi's experience of soul. She was burned out, or even burned up. Flooded by energy and feeling that formerly had been blocked from awareness, her body was spent. Nevertheless, although Mairi could not stop the feeling of "losing touch," or feeling alone, lost, sad and regretful, now these feelings stood *in relation to* her earlier experience. A formerly empty (depersonalised) sense of body was now engraved with soul's memory of being. Although the Presence of the Holy Spirit diminished, soul stayed. Mairi's sense of her soul's visitation faded, but her memory of it remained: she felt born again[21] and gifted with a "second chance." A "second chance" at what? A second chance at living, a second chance at a newly embodied life: a *personal* life, this time, different from before. Mairi's experience also offered her a second chance at *loving* life. After great unconscious loss, Mairi found herself. Being given again into her own keeping felt like landing on the coast of a new world, a world in which everything was both the same but different, including herself.

In each session following, we attended to the most immediate aspects of Mairi's personal life in the world. The children returned from summer camp: how were they, how was she with them? After weeks of ragged sleep and a wildly fluctuating metabolism Mairi had lost nearly fifteen pounds.

She looked thin, haunted, and strained. How was she eating? Had she begun to sleep? How long did she sleep, how well? Had she begun to dream again? How did she manage the details of daily existence – her work, friends, driving, chores? Inquiring into the "dailyness" of things brought Mairi "in and down" to focus upon her personal needs and responsibilities. Gradually, her sense of herself, as well as the psyche, began to coagulate. Where the whole experience of soul took three months, Mairi must have spent five of those thirteen weeks "putting herself together again."

What *did* it mean, that the Holy Spirit had appeared to Mairi as Feminine Presence? Over these last weeks we discussed this, too. References to God's feminine aspects were not hard to find, whether they were rooted in Gnostic thought, in "Mariology," in feminist theology, or Sophia and the wisdom tradition. However we looked at it, the intimately personal terms forged by the audacious emergence of Mairi's dream-in-the-world made her experience of the Holy Spirit as Feminine Presence into something that rooted her, willy-nilly, into the depths of her personal feminine nature.

Mairi had thought about the Feminine as a category of Being before – especially through "New Age" reading about the "Goddess" – and she had thought about herself as a woman. But "thinking about" the feminine and *experience* of the feminine point to different dimensions of psychic reality. Perhaps the feminine as a symbolic mode of being can *only* be experienced, before it can be understood as such. When we began our work, Mairi had spoken of the feminine with reserve and bewilderment. Sometimes resentful and often mystified, she did not like to think of herself as a feminine person. To her, the feminine meant a dangerous vulnerability of unthinking and unknowing. It meant goallessness, and an uneasy lack of concern with achievement. Although her ambition was relatively unconscious and unclear, Mairi knew that she had some, and to her, the feminine implied acceptance of uncomfortable limitations of her body, mind and self, as well as the limitations of circumstance and other people.

Before her experience, to be "in the feminine" meant to Mairi feeling as if there were no particular place to go and nothing much to do. It meant easier laughter and quicker tears. The feminine meant slowness and listening, and having little to say. It meant being, rather than doing, dreaming, rather than thinking, dwelling in chaos over having a sense of order, or resting with chaos rather than attempting to create order. The feminine meant submitting, rather than initiating, pondering, rather than understanding. It meant being present, rather than being prepared. All of this Mairi had found difficult (if not terrifying) in the past, and none of these feelings were easy to approach in the present. Although she had progressed beyond fears of "being like" her mother, shadows of having been mothered, as well as pain, regret, and fear about her own experiences of being a mother, remained. In attitude and memory, Mairi's conscious relation to the feminine mode of Being had been dubious and pinched. But until she could welcome the feminine, she could neither receive nor welcome all of her sense of herself.

Mairi's lunar dream (#20), seemed to mark an unconscious hinge in the psyche, a turning-point. Whereas her earlier relation to the feminine had been tentative and frightened, in Dream #20 Mairi was at peace, as open and accepting of all the feminine principle portrayed, as It seemed to be, of Itself. And her experience of soul changed Mairi's relation to the feminine completely. She bore no terror of "mother" or even the "Mother," in the presence of the Holy Spirit. Entry into the feminine as a symbolic mode of being completely reversed the Kali-esque negativity of Mairi's "mother complex," black spiders and all.

In a lovely passage, A. Ulanov (1988: 99) tells us that – like imagery of God come into and born of Mary without a human father – religious experience implants itself and gestates in us

> in and through the feminine mode of our being. It comes through the matrix of the unconscious, unfathered by any conscious skill, neither created nor authorized by any cultural intent or anything else that we could claim as our doing. It comes through the dark mothering unconscious of our being. It comes through the feminine as one-in-herself, as virgin, that capacity in us to receive the transcendent each time as for the first time.[22]

Finding herself ushered into a sense of the Holy Spirit as Feminine Presence empowered Mairi's relation to the feminine principle. We will find this phenomenon in Hadewijch, too. In Poem 2:47, 51[23] Hadewijch tells us that "woman is the strongest, woman who is humility," describing "woman-being" as being like the Virgin Mary whose humility and submission tumbled God from sublimity to birth within her womb.

I am suggesting that Mairi's "fall" into a new relation to the feminine principle *personalised* her newly ensouled body and her newly embodied soul. In contrast to someone for whom a realization of personality may not include experience of soul, for Mairi soul became explicit, correlating with an archetypal inclusion of the feminine. And I suspect that the feminine aspect of Mairi's experience of soul had less to do with the gender of her analyst (me) than it had to do with Mairi's inherent nature (and gender) and with the access to the feminine by way of dreams, imagination, and bodily participation that attended our therapeutic relationship. Mairi might have come to experience the Holy Spirit as Feminine Presence while working with a male analyst as well, were that man open to feminine elements of being in himself.

After Mairi got her feet on the ground we returned to once-a-week sessions. She (and the psyche) continued to consolidate. Both of us knew we would soon stop working together, for I was preparing to move in the next year to another city. Mairi did not wish to begin therapy with someone else unless she felt the need. Some essential question had been answered truly from within. I suppose that Mairi's question was a version of Jung's (1963: 300) essential question, "Are we related to something infinite or not?"

Encountering the "infinite" as *experience* of soul helped Mairi release a formerly perilous introjection that somehow had not only hidden her from a sense of being ensouled but prevented her full embodiment. On the one hand, from a strictly personal point of view, Mairi was undergoing separation from her internalized image (identification) with someone (her mother) who meant the presence of life itself. On the other hand, she was sorting a sense of herself out from an archetypal mother-imago representing merger or unconscious incest with the daimonic matrix of the unconscious. From a religious point of view, the presence of the Holy Spirit freed her from this unconscious identification with "another," allowing her to experience It for the mighty, impersonal presence that It is – the Holy Spirit as Feminine Presence. Only by differentiating herself from this presence could Mairi recover her soul.

Mairi once described her experience as "an immense generosity of Spirit overflowing its own geography." Tumbling in its roiling currents "like a babe in a body-shaped basket" (her words), Mairi found that she was both mother and child to herself (Dream #19). Because she no longer felt depressed, her self-preoccupation lessened, and so did her hunger for self-knowledge. Nor was she inspired to take her religious life into a community or church. She entered into what I think of as a very loosely affiliated group of individuals who participate in "religion-less religion." People who live with an awakened, consciously attended religious sensibility are seldom contained within a religious institution, although they may draw freely upon religious tradition without identifying particularly with one or another historical manifestation of it. "Now that I can let God be God," Mairi said, "whether in my soul or anywhere else, I'm less interested in myself or even in Who or What God is supposed to be like. I feel connected to God. I know God is present. I love God and I think about God always, beneath my other thoughts. That is the important relationship, even if I can't describe the 'Other side,'" she concluded. And then, smiling, "Loving *this* life feels like the best possible way to be grateful."

Mairi and I resumed a tightly-knit dialogue around all the inner and outer experience Mairi could gather. Gradually she regained weight. She resumed dreaming, although her dreams were brief and we paid less attention to them than we did to the details of her daily life. More to the point were Mairi's feelings about herself as a person. Often early trauma makes a person unable to give of themselves in a way that might allow soul and self to feel reborn through a human communion of spiritual and sexual love. But with her "caul" dissolved, Mairi became less understanding (i.e., "less good girl and good mother") toward others. A sense of body-backed personal judgment began to emerge and she used it sensibly. What she could now recognize as her "personal" feeling began to seem possible in a new relationship with a man ("a person in his own right") whom Mairi found more and more interesting. Mairi felt that he treated her as a person, too, with little expectation of roles. Old patterns of relating remained, of course, but Mairi felt that she was "in relation" to those patterns rather than identified with them. She imagined that she might maintain a sense of personal integrity through whatever might lie ahead, and she was excited. Maybe she would not live alone forever. It felt good to be in a relationship.

Gradually Mairi resumed her yoga practice at home. She began teaching again professionally and broadened her practice by forming beginning yoga classes in an after-school program with African American and Latino low-income students. In an opening class for fourth graders Mairi found that their biggest fear was to take their shoes and socks off because "they think their feet are ugly!" Younger children grew to love her classes, especially the animal postures.[24] In a high-school class, she discovered that the hardest thing for students to do was to close their eyes. "They can't let down their guard," she realized; school is not a safe place, nor is being in a group together, even in a class. And when they breathe deeply," she said, "so much emotion comes to the surface. They could begin to work with their feelings, but they have so much anger, fear, and frustration! And they're not used to letting this stuff out."

"In fact," she said, "though it looks as if I'm teaching yoga, I really spend most of my energy creating a 'safe place,' and now I think of that as a place for body and soul." Within a few months Mairi found her work tremendously valuable. She grew to love these classes and her students, even when parents had to be assured that yoga lessons would not contradict their religious beliefs but were for calming the mind and taking stress out of their children's lives. Excited about the new scope of her work, Mairi described it to me: "What I'm teaching these kids is that we – they – people are not all that different," she said. "Everyone breathes, everybody has a body, and everybody's mind is out of control. We all suffer illness and pain, stress and death. But my inner city kids suffer more than most from social and emotional isolation. And they are terrified to feel alone. For a lot of them, silence is an enemy, because it means the absence of people and no music. Silence is lonely. I'm trying to teach them that silence is not empty. I help their bodies learn how to assume "ancestral modes of being" (the animal *asanas*). I teach them that bodily silence unfolds into a feeling of presence, rather than absence. I say that yoga is linking body and breath together. I don't tell them that breath is God. It isn't. But I do think that breath opens the door to soul. Maybe God is like the Breath of breath. But stuff like this can't be taught, so I don't try. They'll discover it themselves. I just try to teach them that bodily silence can give them a chance to be with soul."

To my knowledge Mairi never wrote about her experience of soul – certainly not as I am doing here, as her dream-in-the-world. But a dream-in-the-world doesn't have to be written about to exist and be effective. A dream-in-the-world lands us in being, even a Void in the midst of being: Jung's "empty center," Mairi's "cramp" that would not let her stand tall, and Hadewijch's "abyss" of soul. All these "places" point to a vacancy, a void opening onto the depths of despair and anxiety, all of which must be borne until something breaks through from the other side. When that breakthrough happens, it is as if a God-shaped space appears in the psyche and the roots of being open and full. Hadewijch overflowed with her love of Lady Love, and Mairi shone with gratitude at the presence of the Holy Spirit.

As I mentioned, Mairi *lived* her dream-in-the-world in a fashion similar to the way in which Hadewijch and her Beguines freely "lived Love." I imagine that Mairi continues to spend her time teaching and raising her children and growing in her ability to love and receive love, whether that be with a partner, or friends, or her students. Probably she continues to read and think and feel connected in varying ways to a loose-knit community of individuals who through bonds of personal experience and shared values rather than similar social, political or religious identity are affiliated, even if they seldom meet. By many social and cultural standards, Mairi was an ordinary woman and her outward, or conscious life story was not dramatic. But having learned to "let God be God," Mairi was also released from caring whether she was ordinary or not. Personhood is what she listened for, personal life is what she came to value, and personality is what she finally achieved.

Psychological commentary

To round out this chapter I will offer some reflections of Mairi's experience, on her Self-directive dreams as initiatory experience, and on her discovery of personhood through what Winnicott describes as personalisation and indwelling. In the course of this discussion we will focus on the "second chance" Mairi felt she got through her numinous experience. Clearly Mairi's increasing capacity for affect set the stage for her experience of soul, but in and of itself her passion was insufficient. Crucial to her attainment of a full capacity for experience undertaken with her whole being was her ability to *personalise* this experience as it happened. Only by experiencing her soul as her own *in her bodily senses* did Mairi become the person she did. In the process, ordinary daily life *in her body* became much more important. Body here means that her personal being became real and ordinary. Mairi *felt* the Being that underlies all life, in her *particular* being. In recognition of a necessary reconnection to body in religious experience, Jung himself wrote that any search for "living being" whose existence is postulated beyond experience (spirit) consists of a search for the *"quintessence of life in the body"* (CW8: 621, emphasis mine), and perhaps that is as good a psychological definition as any.

The body is the mind's bone house, the heart's door. Our bodies are sources of deep revelation for us; they are how we come to know both great pain and great pleasure, and they help us recognize ourselves in one another. Mairi discovered that the body is also how God gets to us, at the most intimate and universal level imaginable, and this discovery revealed that everything in her life mattered, after all – that all that had ever happened to her by way of her concrete, physical experience had had an impact upon her soul's integrity. This realization helped her resume her life in the world.

To the best of my awareness, the consciousness with which I participated in Mairi's experience heightened my awareness of my body as well as hers. It intensified my capacity for direct experience, allowing a deeply imaginative participation. I encountered Mairi's presence and her capacity for passionately embodied being as she encountered the presence of the Holy Spirit, while between us wove the Buddha-net of "interbeing" (Dream #13). Participating in a mutual realization of genesis, Mairi and I entered a shared heart of experience, descending to the bottom of reality, apprehensible and non-apprehensible, of all that is and all that could be, where everything is not just part of an infinitely complex web of interdependence but a moving web, a pattern of flowing, a never-ceasing in-flow and out-flow of being and love. Earlier I reached for a Buddhist understanding to explain what was happening; in Christian terms, Mairi was "twice born" (James 1902), initiated into a new capacity for abundant life and a new sense of Being.

Another way I perceived Mairi's experience of soul was as an unexpectedly great flood of tenderness released in her mind toward her heart, rather than the other (more usual) way around – from heart to mind. This flood carried her into love of her body and herself, washing away conscious and unconscious self-judgment. When asked what releases a mother from her need to be a near-perfect mother, Winnicott (1949: 245) answered that it is the infant's understanding. Winnicott implies that we do not really *need* perfection, even an idea of perfection. We need a mind that is capable of generosity. Somehow Mairi's mind became generous. Commenting on Winnicott's suggestion, Epstein (1998: 114) says that most of us have minds of judgment instead of minds of tolerance; we experience these minds of judgment as beyond our voluntary control, as if much of the time our minds have "minds" of their own. The Buddha gave his original teachings to counter this condition, says Epstein: to heal the split we feel from our own minds, to permit the mind to take on its inherent capacity for tolerance.

Mairi's abrupt and extraordinary intimacy with the inner world transformed her ego-position, her habitually conscious stance in the world, and her conscious attitude toward her life. From being an observer of herself, her dreams (e.g., her person-less Self-directive dreams), her life, and other people, Mairi became a *participant*-observer.[25] This transformation arrived within an archetypal configuration of inclusivity and integration, which anchors itself in the feminine: soul *and* body, psyche *and* dream, mind *and* spirit, earth *and* heaven, life *and* death, self *and* God. Prefigured by Self-directive dreams, this shift deepened Mairi's appreciation of and access to the unconscious, heralding a change in the texture of her consciousness as well.

Self-directive dreams and initiation

In the midst of an open field in Gitskan, British Columbia, in a row of many others, stands one tall totem pole that is unique. Where all the other totems are solid, this pole has a beautifully carved oval hole cut clear through it. This opening, placed five or six feet above ground level, perhaps three feet tall and almost as wide as the pole itself, "frames" another world – thought to be beyond, behind, perhaps before – the world in which we stand. Surrounded by carved human/divine figures, the oval is also simply empty space. "Through it" we see the open sky, trees, the meadow behind the poles, as if to reach up and crawl through the opening, to enter a "world beyond" is a real possibility. The world into which we would emerge would not be so different from the one we left, but we would be different because of our bodily experience of clambering through, or emergence from one world into another.

This unique (and probably initiatic) totem pole reminded me of Mairi's Self-directive dreams and their seemingly initiatory function. Each dream, like this opening, provided a glimpse into the presence of another world, beyond, behind, and before "this" world. Linked to that other world, the psyche coaxed Mairi's consciousness toward conscious experience of it, dream by Self-directive dream. In Chapter 1 I suggested that Self-directive dreams are archetypal dreams, which point to a process of psychological centering, an experience which, in Mairi, was on the brink of a personal realization in her body. Looked at this way, they described an objective process – like pregnancy – that aimed at the birth of her conscious realization of the archetype of the Self through the individuation process. But for Mairi this was too abstract.

We could say that as a woman, Mairi experienced the soul aspect of what the Self can convey. Before Mairi's experience of soul, her dreams addressed a particular aspect of her personal psychological situation, portraying specific holes in the psyche or in her personality as areas to which Mairi had no personal access. Through the "holes" of these personal wounds, gaps, or traumas, were glimpsed aspects of trans-personal (collective) reality – archaic elements of humanity's inherent surroundings: Roses,

Artichokes, Burning Stones, White Elephants, a Woman's Hands, cradling the World. By mirroring this kind of objective environmental surround, Mairi's Self-directive dreams provided archaic[26] garments (imagery) with which to clothe the *lacunae* in the fabric of Mairi's personality. We could say that these empty spaces portrayed exactly where the kind of all-out, no-holds-barred way of experiencing with which we are concerned was manifestly impossible; facets of her developing experience that were un-companioned, un-mediated and therefore un-humanized.

Like flash exposures, Mairi's Self-directive dreams collectively imagined the world itself "beyond" her personal experience – elements of the environment serving as mother-nature and matrix, container and womb, in the absence of personal mother and her physical and psychological con-tainment. Like miniature paintings they depicted where Mairi, as person, did not yet live, where even the psyche seemed motionless (perhaps in shock), unable to personify *or* personalise. They "stood in" for gaps in Mairi's experience of on-going bodily life.

Another way to say this is that through the gaps in Mairi's personal experience, she was *initiated* into another world, and through this experi-ence, *into another dimension of consciousness*. One of the most powerful image-patterns in the collective psyche to address transitional processes across such "gaps," is that of initiation, so it is no surprise that Mairi's dreams contain many images which resonate with initiatic ideas and images.

Perhaps the most explicitly initiatic dream in the sequence we reviewed in Chapter 2 is #4, "Ordeal by spider-bite," to be undertaken as Mairi knelt in the presence of someone she could trust. Then, after dreams had paved the way, Mairi underwent a primordial experience of falling into that liminal "space" toward which her dreams had seemingly directed her: she experi-enced an actual, sacrificial opening in ego-consciousness which seemingly aimed at reconnection with the erotic beginnings of consciousness itself. Opening like the oval in the initiatic totem pole, this reconnection involved a kind of death or surrender of her known ego with its ordinary con-sciousness, and rebirth as a person with a transformed awareness and a new-found relationship with an Other, encountered as feminine Presence.

Jungian psychiatrist Joseph Henderson (1967: 6) characterizes this emo-tional suspension of ordinary consciousness as the essence of the initiation archetype. He suggests that initiation is primordial and archetypal before it is social or cultural, and that initiation freely "re-creates itself forever anew out of the mysterious underworld of history, changing, as it does so, the prevailing fashion of conscious belief" (12–13).

Just as there are different aspects of life into which the archetype of initiation initiates us, so there are different kinds of initiation. In puberty rites, whether for men or women, initiation spans the step from childhood into adult sexuality and social maturity, carrying us from a psychological mother-world into a psychological father-world, meaning society and the world at large. Later in life, another initiation may carry us out of an extroverted, primarily achievement-oriented adaptation to our social world into an introverted, psychologically integrated sense of life which becomes personally meaningful as well. Illness and the approach of death may initiate us again. We are carried toward ways of taking leave, ways of letting go, and intimations of return. Still other rites and rituals of initiation promote an individual discovery of what other cultures knew as religious mystery. It was this latter initiation that Mairi experienced. In terms of our earlier discussion we could say that *her initiation clearly restored the vitality and health of her religious instinct.* If previously contaminated, her religious instinct was restored to its appropriate object, and her world view, which had previously been narrowed by an overly rational and outer-directed consciousness, suddenly expanded to include "mysteries" never dreamt of in her previous philosophy.

Into what was Mairi initiated? In therapy, Mairi revisited (recapitulated) an attachment to another person with whom she felt safe and where the atmosphere was one of non-interfering, devoted, and loving attention to her inner world. Apparently this "potential space" set the stage for what was to follow as archetypal and Self-directed dreams unfolded. When the dreams stopped, Mairi fell into her experience of soul and for three days was transported or infused with energies that felt as if they were from another world. During this time, physiologically, she was initiated into a depth of embodiment and a personal experience of the energy of life surging within her cells. Emotionally, Mairi "fell" into an encounter with an Other (the Holy Spirit as Feminine Presence) which gave her a soul to call her own. Socially and interpersonally, Mairi was initiated out of a bond of blood kinship (mother–child), separated from clan kinship (family–tribe), and ushered into her individuality.[27] And spiritually, let us say that Mairi was initiated out of one category of being and into another – out of a compulsive outer-directedness into an inner world where she encountered and "re-cognized" a mysterious Presence that lay "beyond" herself and to whom, paradoxically, she belonged. As a background to this world, The Holy was unveiled.

In initiation, at certain times of crisis, something familiar is lost (not the least of which is the sense of familiarity itself) as something of greater value begins to be found. In the wide arc of initiatory experience, life slowly becomes transparent to deeper values, and truer to itself. We forge a new relationship with the unknown, turning to an inner compass rather than an old blueprint. Despite her earlier experiences of suffering and loss, gradually Mairi came to trust life more. The realization of meaning which accompanied her archetypal experience was not a simple acquisition of information or of knowledge, but rather "a living experience that touches the heart just as much as the mind" (von Franz, 1992: 257). And the body, too.

During initiation, the very nature of the unknown changes. Our sense of wonder increases. When initiation is successful, the unknown no longer frightens us. It becomes mysterious rather than terrifying. It becomes something to move toward, rather than avoid. Every initiation proves a strength of soul, and any initiation can be a messenger of grace. In part a quest for vision and new eyes, initiation offers entry into an indeterminacy of psyche and soul, as well. I remembered Mairi's vision of the Eye (the Eye of God or *Nous*, or both), which prefaced her initiation into her own new eyes, into her heart's eyes that could see the opening of soul. Mairi's experience was marked by a deep sense of gratitude and an emerging sense of the possibility that is ever-present in life. Despite her history and limitations, despite her smallness and her unconsciousness, Mairi bore witness to the fact that here and now, in this very world, all was well. Offered the freedom to feel fully herself, Mairi accepted it wholeheartedly.

Slowly, over the course of our work together, Mairi's Self-directive dreams had begun to appear like solitary sentinels along the outermost rim of her psychological horizon, inukshuks of her inner North. They marked a passage through which Mairi would progress consciously, a threshold of initiation over which she would fall into an unknown country she would come to inhabit. As compensatory dreams, they attracted her attention and mine, deepening her conscious imagination and broadening the reach of her intelligence. Without our mutual non-judgmental attention – our "psycho-religious attitude," they would have been useless for building psychic structure except for providing maps of where psychic structure was not: maps of "empty lots" and an uninhabited territory of soul. Their emptiness prompted an acute awareness (on both our parts) of Mairi's "disembodied" state. In order to detach to the point where she could use *both* psyche and soul as principles of observation, Mairi had to assume a kind of "quantum stance" toward herself. She had to recognize (consciously, and in the presence of another person) that she played a part in all that she observed, while at the same time she did not create (or even co-create) her world. A physicist does not create the light she sees, even though she beholds both particle and wave.

Self-directive dreams gave Mairi a glimpse of what later she felt in the flesh as part of her experience of soul: a way of being in the world which was of the same substance as everything around her – the earth, people, plants and animals, stars. To glimpse profundity may feel awesome, but to "become" profundity can feel like death: to feel kinship with the stars in the cells of one's own nature is a wondrous experience, but to lose a human frame of reference portends terrifying alienation. Feelings of danger (from both memory and instinct) accompany an active awareness of one's vulnerability. And knowledge of subhuman and suffering aspects of matter that point to helpless and destructive aspects of human embodiment may be no longer hidden. In experiencing her bodily reality to such an extreme, Mairi discovered that she was not "dead matter," as she had unconsciously presumed (or unconsciously remembered being treated as if she were). Of one substance with all, Mairi, along with everything else, consisted of "star-stuff," and now this realization meant something to her that it had never meant before.

We could say that Mairi came to embrace herself as someone in whom collective consciousness and the depths of the collective unconscious had been vitally connected. She discovered that as a kind of "medial personality" she had unconsciously put her life in the service of living out what Jung describes as the "living function of a genuine symbol" (CW6: 824). But a symbol isn't human, and can have no personal life. Uncovering this archaic tendency in her nature, Mairi found herself literally "fighting for her life." As she dissolved in what Jung calls an experience of the Self, Mairi's experience of One World threatened to overwhelm her. I think that she might not have made it, had the Holy Spirit not claimed her. Some of my psychological colleagues think I am exaggerating here. They protest my claim that the Holy Spirit enabled Mairi in her extreme experience. But perhaps what Winnicott calls the "true self" and what Jung calls the "individuated self" is exactly the self that God *does* call, bless, and claim. This, at least, was so for Mairi. This is not to say that God abandons the false self or turns from the less-than-individuated personality, but it does suggest that a certain amount of psychological honesty and "stripped-to-the-boneness" enables us to *receive* God's blessing and call, when and if God chooses to extend them.

As our work progressed, Mairi's Self-directive dreams paralleled her conscious position, heightening her consciousness to a point of transparency. They "thinned" ego-awareness (or revealed its thinness), much as the surface tension of water in a glass rounds higher and higher past the rim until it finally spills. With the tension of over-spill, personalisation and indwelling became necessary. As if she had fallen through a trap door and foundered her way through underworld fields of archetypal imagery, Mairi emerged with the sense that soul was far more extensive than the inner life of its personally embodied partner, meaning herself. A sense of the *anima mundi* entered her world, illuminating soul's part in our time and place.

Jesuit theologian Pierre Teilhard de Chardin[28] tells us that beneath the surface of our experience, *all* of us can detect the soul of the world: "Whichever road we follow," says Chardin, "we cannot withdraw from the superficial plane of day to day relationships without finding *immediately behind us, as though it were an extension of ourselves, a soul of the world*" (quoted in Cousins 1992: 171). Plotinus, in his *Enneads*, gives us a definition of the doctrine of the World Soul, which, says Cousins (167), resonates with the holistic, earth-centered spirituality of primal peoples everywhere:

Now to understand how life is imparted to the universe and to each individual, the soul must rise to the contemplation of The Soul, the soul of the world. The individual soul, though different from The Soul, is itself no slight thing. Yet it must become worthy of this contemplation: freed of the errors and seductions to which other souls are subject, it must be quiet.

Silent and quiet contemplation became much more valued in Mairi's life. She would have agreed with Simone Weil (1974: 131), who reminds us:

When the intelligence, having become silent in order to let love invade the whole soul, begins once more to exercise itself, it finds it contains more light than before, a greater aptitude for grasping objects, truths that are proper to it . . . these silences constitute an education for [the intelligence] which cannot possibly have any other equivalent and enable it to grasp truths which otherwise would for ever remain hidden from it.

As I noted earlier, all Mairi's dreams stopped prior to her "fall." This puzzled us both, and I remained puzzled until years later, when a passage came to my attention in which Jung (1976: 473) describes how sometimes the Self *undoes its own symbolism* (emphasis mine). Jung (CW5: 198) also describes the purpose for which the Self does such a thing:

When the great swing has taken an individual into the world of symbolic mysteries, nothing . . . can come from it unless it has been associated with the earth, unless it has happened when that individual was *in the body* . . . if your soul is detachable, as in the primitive condition, you are simply hypnotized into a sort of somnambulistic state or trance, and whatever your experience in that condition is, is not felt because it has not been *experienced in the body* . . . you were not there when it happened . . . individuation can only take place if you *first return to the body, to your earth*, only then does it become true . . . the reason why the whole structure of the symbolism is being pulled asunder is that the Self wants its own destruction as a symbolic form, in order to dismiss the individual so that it can get lost in the earth. She (the patient) must go back to the earth, *into the body, into her own uniqueness and separateness*; otherwise she is the stream of life, she is the whole river, and nothing has happened because nobody has realized it . . . individuation can only take place when it is realized when somebody is there that notices it; otherwise it is the eternal melody of the wind in the desert . . . (emphasis mine)

Personification, personalisation, and "indwelling"

In this discussion, I will try to address the process through which Mairi became "ensouled" as an individual personality. This great mystery has to do (in general) with the process through which impersonal (archetypal) elements of being become part of a finite, limited, unique embodied person, i.e., the extent to which they are "personalised." It seems that this human-izing process is simultaneously each individual's opportunity and respon-sibility. And the extent to which the process is mediated by human persons seems to have a great deal to do with the outcome, at least in the view of inter-personal (object-relations) theorists, especially Winnicott. Jung had slightly different ideas about this, and Mairi's experience of soul gave me a few of my own.

That the psyche spontaneously "personifies" has long been taken for granted. We experience personification nightly in our dreams, dreaming of persons, of people we know and people we do not know, of strangers and people from long ago, and sometimes of people we have yet to meet. The psyche personifies affects in our dreams and so we think of personification as the nature of the psyche. Jung even tells us (CW9i: 514) that because the unconscious spontaneously personifies, he intentionally personified his psy-chological terminology-Shadow, Anima, Animus, Great Mother – wishing to remain true to the spontaneous speech of the psyche.

We, too, personify. We consciously make "persons" of the animals we live with. We personify our imaginations and memories in order to bring imagination and memory to life. Archetypal psychologist James Hillman characterizes the psyche's tendency to personify as an "epistemology of the heart, a thought mode of feeling," wrongly judged to be "inferior, archaic, or appropriate only to those allowed emotive speech and affective logic – children, madmen, poets and primitives" (1975: 15). Both Hillman and Jung find personification to be the natural expression *of* mythic conscious-ness *to* mythic consciousness. We personify in order to enter myth, and the act of personifying carries us there. To mythic consciousness, however, persons of the imagination are real. And where imagination reigns, personification happens.

Aside from psychic personification, which happens whether we want it to or not, personification in our conscious lives becomes problematic if we recognize reality only in persons of the imagination, or if we compulsively "make mythic" the persons we meet in everyday life. Finding the right words to express our emotions is notoriously difficult and unsatisfactory. Most of us find it easier to deal with emotion at one remove, endowing others with mythic dimensions or even dealing with emotion non-linguistically in behavior, or in music or dance. Expecting our emotions to behave logically is equally unsatisfactory. Often the best we can do is collect painful evidence as to the patterns of their behavior: the emotional patterns of the Beloved, for example, or the behavior of the Clown. We call someone a witch or a siren, a diva or a hero and think little of it; hopefully, we use such metaphor consciously.

I go to such lengths about personification here for two reasons: (1) in order to differentiate personification – which belongs to psyche – from personalisation which I feel belongs to soul; and (2) because of how resolutely Mairi's Self-directive dreams *lacked* personification, apparently to a purpose. Mairi's Self-directive dreams, containing no personification at all, tipped Mairi out of what I now think of as psyche's world of imaging into a world of inner and outer presence. Being pushed through an imagistic text of psyche into a text of body and soul demanded of Mairi that she differentiate herself from the personification that the psyche does naturally. Mairi had to *personalise* archetypal energy, seeking incarnation by way of flesh and bone. Mairi encountered lights and sounds, insomnia, spontaneous orgasms, unusual bodily flexibility, and an extraordinary Presence of The Other.

The emotional impact of the unifying force of life, stripped to its barest essentials, devoid of purpose other than that of maintaining itself, yet instantly recognizable as that which drives you, too, can be shattering: "I am that I am." The ramifications of such an experience are so miraculous as to fill a lifetime with wonder. But the experience must be personalised. Von Franz (1997: 200) characterizes what I discuss as personalisation as "a common primal form of religious behavior" which attempts to safeguard the human boundary with the numinous. In von Franz's understanding of personalisation a certain humility must prevail which functions as "a self-disciplined protection of oneself from *one's own emotion* [panic, fear, ecstasy] and from the emotion of deity by preventing [one from] getting affectively entangled with it; and an awe-conditioned letting the divine be as it is" (200). In von Franz's words I find both an understanding of Hadewijch's struggle to detach from Love whom she continues to love, and Mairi's ability to "let God be God."

Neither Jung nor Hillman addresses the differentiation of personalisation versus personification directly. As we have seen Jung identifies the psyche with images; "Image *is* psyche," he says (CW13: 75; 11: 889, 769); "The psyche consists essentially of images . . . a 'picturing' of vital activities" (CW8: 618). Hillman (1975: 23) takes Jung's point even further, suggesting not only that psyche is image (including personified images), but that *being* is imaginal: ". . . our psychic substance consists of images," he writes; (therefore) "our being is imaginal being, an existence in imagination." By contrast, Freud said being is instinctive drive and the imagination serves these drives. Although this makes imagination secondary and derivative, at least it includes the body as well as bodily limitation and particularity. In my view personalisation is crucially important to developing individuation because it articulates a process of internalization or metabolization which makes something small instead of mythic, makes experience personal, individual, and "close to me." One problem with the therapeutic concept, "personification of the archetype" is that the archetype is *always* pre-human, and personification of it does not ameliorate this issue. Personification remains locked in image, never mediating what personalisation and indwelling accomplish toward an aspect of life that hitherto mediated archetypal energy in an impersonal fashion.

Winnicott's personalisation and indwelling

Mairi's Self-directive dreams pointed to *a void, a gap* in psyche's spontaneous activity of personification – something Jung does not discuss as such. When, in Mairi's situation, the void opened into personalisation and indwelling, her dream-in-the-world emerged. Winnicott's notions of personalisation and indwelling are highly suggestive of the religious notion of incarnation in which spirit comes to be embodied in flesh and blood, time and space (history), and – my addition – flesh and blood come to be ensouled.

By personalisation, Winnicott means "the inherited tendency of each individual to achieve a unity of the psyche and the soma, an experiential identity of the spirit or psyche and the totality of physical functioning" (1964: 112). Winnicott (1970: 261) uses the term

> as a kind of positive form of depersonalisation . . . various meanings are given to "depersonalisation," but on the whole they involve . . . loss of contact with the body and body functioning, and this implies the existence of some other aspect of the personality. The term "personalisation" was intended to draw attention to the fact that the indwelling of this other part of the personality in the body and a firm link between whatever is there which we call psyche, in developmental terms represents an achievement in health.

As a developmental process, personalisation happens during the "holding stage" of infancy, when the infant, utterly dependent upon its environment, needs to become comfortable *in its body* while changing from states of unintegration to integration and back again to unintegration. Trust (in the environment) develops as the infant repeatedly experiences unintegrated states restored to integration by a "good enough" mother. The reverse of becoming comfortable with states of integration and unintegration is disintegration of the nascent personality (trauma). This leads to psychotic levels of anxiety, mental illness and exaggerated "splitting" of psyche from soma, body from mind, and self from others.

Disintegration of being threatens an end to being altogether and becomes a descriptive definition of death. During certain crucial developmental crises, deprivation of environmental care can threaten an infant with cessation of being, with a "privation of being" which the infant experiences as overwhelming. To an infant, a state of disintegration may threaten as severely as Augustine's description of the adult apprehension of evil.[29]

Reliable (environmental) care of an infant who spontaneously experiences integrated and unintegrated states over time allows the infant to attain what Winnicott refers to as "unit status" (1960: 44). The infant becomes *a person in a body*, an individual in her own right, albeit unconsciously. During this time the infant's psychosomatic existence begins to take on a personal pattern, whereby, Winnicott says, the psyche "indwells" within the soma, linking motor, sensory, and functional experience with the infant's new state of being a person (1960: 45). Further, there comes into existence what might be called a limiting "membrane," which to some extent (in health) is equated with the surface of the skin and takes a position between the infant's "me" and "not-me." The infant comes to have an inside, an outside, and a body-scheme (1960: 45). At this stage the ego is essentially a body-ego, and not at all a matter of intellect.[30]

For Winnicott, personalisation and indwelling are spontaneous developmental processes that occur pre-consciously in the psyche long before a conscious registration of personalisation becomes possible. These processes form an individual weave of body and ego, and psyche and spirit, which determines how each of us is knit together from the start. But for Winnicott, personalisation and indwelling do not happen autonomously. They are enabled by, and occur within the environment of the embodied presence of another, meaning a care-taking environment or "environmental mother."

Winnicott tells us that by how she handles the infant's body, the mother of an infant is forever introducing and re-introducing the baby's body and psyche to each other (1970: 271). As this happens over time, personalisation and indwelling come about. When because of accident, illness, or maternal deprivation personalisation and indwelling fail to occur, psychosomatic illness and depersonalisation result. Under these circumstances, the infant's *mind*, which under optimal conditions is integrated with psychosomatic experience, tends to become a "thing in itself" (Winnicott 1949: 246). This constitutes a "usurpation of environmental functions by the mind (which has developed precociously) and the result is a "mind-psyche," which is pathological (247). Certainly this is one way of imaging what takes over in states of depersonalisation: a precocious mind. Jung has another way of approaching this phenomenon, and I will suggest a third.

For Jung, what takes over in states of depersonalisation is often a possessing "spirit," or an archetypal image. When traumatic experience is severe enough to cause unbearable affects, Jung suggests that the resulting split goes deep into the collective layer of the psyche, completely shattering the ego complex and substituting for it a personified image which is often demonic and alien.[31] Says Jung, "irruption of these alien contents is a characteristic symptom marking the onset of many mental illnesses. The patients are seized by weird and monstrous thoughts, the whole world seems changed, people have horrible, distorted faces, and so on" (CW8: 587–91).

A third way to envision what occurs in states of depersonalisation is to imagine that depersonalisation indicates the presence of a "disembodied soul." When Mairi broke through her depersonalised state and entered her body, soul was there to greet her. This implies that a process of personalisation and indwelling that is faulty in infancy might happen later; that becoming ensouled might constitute a "second chance" for someone – a chance mediated by a presence other than that of the actual mother. The ego still undergoes personalisation, but what for Winnicott is the infant's unconscious achievement of "unit status" was for Mairi the discovery of an ensouled body and an embodied soul. It is as if soul can become the missing link between a sense of personal body and an indwelling spirit. Soul is what allowed Mairi to *encounter* spirit, rather than being *possessed* by spirit. She found, as it were, a "moon" to reflect the "sun," a soul to reflect the spirit's intensity. Without a moon, Mairi might have burned.

If the body-ego is analogous to a limiting membrane that allows an infant to have an inside, an outside and a body schema, and this in turn is analogous to the body's skin, then a linking membrane that allows a person to have personal as well as impersonal experience of how we incarnate and embody life in the world (reflected by personal and collective levels of the unconscious) may be the best analogy to soul. Soul is not a body-ego, but like the body-ego, soul links us to an embodied state, a body location, a state of being that allows us to orient ourselves in the midst of mighty impersonal energies which, for want of a better word, we call archetypal.

As a kind of inner skin, perhaps soul even grows. Just as in organic phenomena growth takes place *under* the skin (and how the outer skin, the membrane, grows at the same rate as other organs we cannot explain), soul may grow in life and depth beneath the psyche. Just as the phenomenon of organic growth within the body is a major message pertaining to the presence of life in the body, the growth of soul pertains to a quality of life *in* the body. Outer skin receives and heals over wounds, changing with changes within the body. As an inner skin, soul also receives and suffers wounds, physiological and psychological. As body responds to "what is," soul deepens the body's response into experience. In suffering, soul deepens into meaning and significance.[32]

Soul, then, is that embodied "place" in us which registers the spirit. Before entering her body Mairi felt soulless and numb, "stuck," empty, and unable. We might contrast Mairi's experience of herself in experience of soul with her earlier self-image as it was portrayed in the lightning-strike dream (#7). There Mairi sat, stunned as a bolt from the blue tore open the ceiling of the tent, threw her infant to the floor and hurt her father's head. In this archaic, revelatory scene, explicit soul is missing: Mairi sits paralyzed, although emotionally torn in two. Perhaps Mairi's capacity to have this dream in the process of our work together marked an important entry for the possibility of soul. In her psychotherapeutic relationship, created in space and molded by space to matter, Mairi's dawning sense of herself cracked wide open with a realization, which had the impact of a bolt of lightning. Dream #7 gave us a mirror that reflected images of archetypal energy that had been unbearable. Already lightning had struck, as if even the psyche could not depict its actual occurrence. The impact of this "strike" spread into imprints of transcendent energy in other dreams – angels, the Buddha, a bejeweled bird. The progressive evolution of this image may be understood as soul's literal coming-into-life, reflecting Mairi's capacity to be in a state of Being. In Mairi's final breakthrough experience, however, the Holy Spirit was neither an unimaginable abstraction, nor an imprint of the transcendent. It was a life-renewing, palpable *Presence*. Encounter with this Presence healed, renewed and blessed Mairi in Person.

Beyond personalisation to personhood

In adulthood, the soul holds the process of personalisation much like an infant's mother does in Winnicott's developmental metaphor. For Mairi, it was as if experience of soul took the place of a missing "good-enough" environmental mother of her infancy. Loaning Her Presence to Mairi (just as She loaned Herself to Hadewijch), God enabled Mairi to undergo something she had not previously undergone. Mairi never claimed that she had "reached God," or that she had "chosen God" (CW11: 156). Hers was a blessing unasked-for, unearned, and undeserved. Personalisation and indwelling occurred as part of Mairi's initiation into the Feminine, and the presence Mairi "knew" was the Holy Spirit.

When Winnicott defines health as the relatively free capacity to move back and forth between internal psychic life and external reality, he means that we experience emotional connections with internal objects as well as emotional connections with external objects, and that the two enrich each other. This process leaves us with a three-dimensional interpersonal world. Only with a sufficient weave of self-integrity can we relate to others in a personal fashion, out of potential space within the psyche as well as potential space within the interpersonal world. First created by the infant's experience of the presence of another (mother) *as an environment* rather than as an object with needs of its own, potential space means space which is open for psyche, for play, for symbol formation, and for other kinds of transitional objects that Winnicott tells us "substitute" for the body of the mother. Winnicott models his idea of "therapeutic space" between analyst and patient on his idea of potential space between infant and mother, which in turn models potential space between persons. Thus, the potential space of therapy becomes the safe space of an environmental mother's "presence." Perhaps I provided this "presence" for Mairi.

When Winnicott writes about therapy in terms of an emotional "regression to dependence" (upon the analyst), he is envisioning a slow, incremental indwelling and personalisation of a true self that is infused with bodily aliveness. This replaces a false self frequently identified with the mind and its abstractions. Viewing these processes through the lens of developmental theory, Winnicott proposes that therapy can reproduce "good enough" mothering. I would like to suggest that another view is possible.

Winnicott's paradigm of mother–infant, yielding personalisation and indwelling, suits Mairi's overall situation well, for her experience of soul emerged from and flowed into "potential space" out of an environment of potentiality created within our relationship over time. But Mairi found room for adult religious experience in this potential space, and her conscious experience of psyche *and* soma differed from Winnicott's hypothesis of unconscious experience during infancy. So while I have no quarrel with Winnicott's developmental point of view, perhaps it cannot account for all psychological phenomena or for the entirety of religious experience when it occurs in a psychotherapeutic setting. Discussing the results for an infant of an experience of "transitional space" which is satisfactory enough to result in the coming-about of a beloved and irreplaceable "transitional object," for example (the teddy bear, the blanket), Winnicott says that we cannot ask the infant, "Did you make it, or did you find it?" But adult experience is open to inquiry, and opens to different dimensions of Being. In no way did Mairi "make" the experience that encountered her. Even the question would have held no meaning for her.

We can only speculate on what causative factors were involved in Mairi's early eczema and other childhood illness. Whatever they were, at an early age either Mairi had gone "into hiding" or "out on a limb," depending upon one's imaginal point of view. At the time of therapy her symptoms resembled those of mild depersonalisation more than they did active manifestations of psychosomatic illness. From either end of Winnicott's spectrum, Mairi's inherent tendency to achieve a unity of psyche and body had been impeded. Re-entering her body became her therapeutic task, and her quest to regain a sense of passionately embodied being pointed the way.

Psyche was introduced to soma over time in Mairi's therapy in dreaming and Mairi's attention to her dreams, if only to record and think about them. Psyche also was introduced to soma in her yoga practice, away from therapy. Encouraged by consistently reliable therapy sessions to slip easily in and out of states of integration and relaxed unintegration (analogous to the difference between consciousness and dream), Mairi's belief in and reliance upon her inner processes grew. Yet I would insist that neither I, nor our slow work together introduced Mairi's soma to her psyche, as did her dramatic experience of soul. To call her experience a "regression to infancy" does not fit all the facts. Mairi's experience was primarily progressive. It was, in Hadewijch's terms, about achieving "full-grownness," which is beyond simply growing up.

One could say that our relationship symbolized an "environmental mother," and that psychotherapy was the real matrix of potential space in which Mairi sought and found a sense of herself in an unplanned, unthought-out fashion. But with the cessation of Mairi's dreams an entirely different quality of experience introduced her body to her awareness. There was no particular crisis in the transference and no particular separation/individuation crisis in our relationship. Instead, Mairi simply fell into mysterious depths of the soul out of which the Holy came to meet her *"in Person," as a person.* The emergence of her dream-in-the-world became Mairi's personal discovery of (1) mysterious depths of soul, (2) the Holy Spirit, (3) herself as a person, and (4) me as a person, as much as was possible within the therapeutic relationship.

Mairi's experience of soul interrupted what Winnicott might call her "mind-psyche" with sensations of body (soma) that rendered mind from psyche and psyche from soul. Like a lightning bolt of Dream #7, spirit uncovered body and laid soul bare.[33] For Mairi, *differentiation of soul and psyche, and spirit and body, made room for the indwelling of all four to occur.* As she personalised an illumination of her body as experience of soul, Mairi felt like a whole person for the first time. Apparently it could not have happened otherwise.

From a psychological point of view, Mairi's psyche, hemorrhaging at a level of creaturely survival (all those archetypal dreams!) was held and personalised in the feminine holding environment provided by the transference and manifest as divine feminine presence. Yet this feminine holding environment was far greater than the transference and it covered dimensions of reality that accompanied Mairi wherever she was. From a religious[34] point of view, even though the Holy Spirit came to her, Mairi did not become the Holy Spirit *or* Feminine Presence, nor did I. Nevertheless, in the presence of Her Feminine Presence, Mairi felt *re*joined, *re*vitalized, *re*united, *re*juvenated, and *re*deemed.

What we imagine as personhood has been deeply informed by our Judaeo-Christian heritage not only through the dogma of Trinity but by biblical text. When the Bible tells us that God came to us in the *person* of Jesus of Nazareth, it refers us to Christ's incarnation in human form and to the embodiment of spirit as this occurred once in history in a particular, gendered, and individually limited human body of flesh and blood. In experience of soul, Mairi discovered her own incarnate, gendered, and individually limited human body of flesh and blood in a very new way.

Reflections on psyche and soul

Mairi's experience of soul housed not only the Holy as Other but herself as other than she had known herself before. Encountering "The Other," Mairi became herself in the presence of the Other. Relative to a new reality shining from the background of reality, psyche waned. Its mythic, personifying constellations dimmed like stars fading out of sight in the light of a full moon. The psyche of image and personification waited in the wings while indwelling personalisation came about. It was as if experience of soul took Mairi below experience of privation to rebirth and a second chance for life as a person.

Later – cleansed, broadened, and no longer mistakable for soul – psyche returned, offering Mairi imaginative, feeling, thinking and sensing ways to articulate her experience of that other reality. Here Mairi's dialogue with me helped. Slowly her psychological world re-formed. In fits and start, she began to dream again. The following tiny scrap of a dream, thin as a new moon, pictured (in her words) her inner situation: *a tempest of light pours over the face of the earth. Small whirlwinds of light burrow into every crevice and hole, into every abyss, clearing, cleaning, scouring.* "Everything is starting over," Mairi said of this dream. "Everything has been scoured clean."

As Mairi's experience of soul was illuminated from within, psyche thinned to reveal the presence of the Holy Spirit as Feminine Presence. Thus, part of soul *as soul* participates in psyche, as well as in mind and body. Of mind, body, psyche and soul, *I have come to see soul as the fourth, uniting factor*. Soul is not the thinking, willing, wishing subject, nor is it the perceiving, material body: *soul is the experiencing subject*, and, at least in part Mairi's experience of soul was as much a discovery of herself as an experiencing subject as it was the presence of the Holy Spirit. In a manner that echoes Winnicott's description of the mother's role in introducing the infant's body and mind, Being held Mairi. In the middle of her crisis, she was held in Being by the presence of the Holy, Who introduced body to soul and soul to body. As feminine presence, the Holy Spirit introduced not psyche to soma (Winnicott), but Mairi to body by way of soul, and hence to personhood.

Mairi would not have agreed that the presence accompanying her newfound embodiment was merely an "inner object" or even "a God within" (which would direct our attention back to psyche and image as well as Jung's well-known equation: Self-image equals God-image, and God-image points to God[35]). For Mairi, the Holy Spirit was an objective, non-psychic reality that might or might not have reached her through the psyche, or might or might not have touched her through the Self, not merely a psychic content of great value (Jung). While experience of soul opened her to encounter with the inner world, this invisible world existed *within the visible world around her*, not "elsewhere." For Mairi, soul was *of* psyche but *not* the psyche, and her revelation of soul was body-backed: God was *in* soul, but *not* soul, and if anything came from "elsewhere," God did.

Limitations of Winnicott's view of religion as "necessary illusion"

Winnicott's fundamental respect for religious experience stems naturally from his ideas regarding illusion and transitional phenomena. From Winnicott's perspective, illusion is an important, positive aspect of human involvement in the world of experience, which is at one and the same time objective and subjective. As mature expressions of transitional experiences (which occur with environmental mothering in potential space), Winnicott suggests that both religion and art help keep the human personality from slipping into schizoid isolation and despair. Both are valuable means of establishing and attaining a sense of self. Winnicott was no enemy to religion, though he distrusted any imposition of belief and tradition, including coercive acceptance of dogma. He saw religion as he saw other transitional phenomena: as an essential illusory experience that is indispensable to selfhood. He says, "we can share a respect for illusory experience and if we wish we may collect together and form a group on the basis of the similarity of our illusory experiences. This is a natural root of grouping among human beings" (1971: 3). Winnicott might even agree that Mairi's experience of soul could stand as an adult perspective on the personalisation and indwelling he had observed as unconscious processes during infant development. Nor might he have objected to understanding Mairi's experience as a valid expression of fully human (mature) consciousness. But now we come to a problem of language, for neither objectively nor subjectively could Mairi describe *the effects of the contents* of her experience of soul as "illusion." For Mairi, the whole point was how *real* her experience was and how the Holy Spirit enabled the reality of her essential personhood.

For Winnicott, illusion is not necessarily "unreal" or insubstantial, but it is not concrete, even though *evidence* of illusion may take on concrete form (e.g., the teddy bear or a work of art). Pushed to consciously personalise soul and soul's indwelling in a body come alive meant for Mairi a differentiation of soul from the psyche (Winnicott's "illusion"). The psyche became for her (*and* me) more like the soul's organ of expression and perception – that which produces image, or concrete form. If, looking at a clay statue sculpted by Mairi (Dream #14?) Winnicott were to say, "this concrete image gives evidence of the psychic *illusion* which helped your personality avoid disintegration," Mairi would have replied, "Well, what really kept me together was not sculpting the statue (body), but the feeling in my hands and the sensations in my back as I bent to mix the clay. Soul inspired my body to move, and the psyche pictured to me soul's inspiration."

Mairi had an experience of the body's bare, autonomic faith. Once our body moves (is infused with energy), any of us can submerge into an unthinking, unfeeling unconsciousness that links the roots of thought and emotion without distinction. This state of being precedes thought and feeling, often so distinct and separate. This is a state of pre-thought and pre-emotion, the embodied unconscious itself, and almost unreachable by definition. Yet it is there, and we visit it under certain conditions. In the way that it is almost impossible to describe the *impact* of a dream (not the image), it is almost impossible to say what goes on in unconsciousness. At this level of being, without conclusions, the architecture of the self seems to air itself with an opportunity for reorganization. To this place Mairi "fell," and from it she emerged, into her experience of soul. Not psyche, but soul was the embodied home of Mairi's "I," her (non-illusory) body open to the Holy from the "inside" as she opened her attention to others without.

Again, all of this suggests that *if* in infancy, what Winnicott describes as "good enough mothering" does not introduce psyche to soma, or if the process is interrupted or distorted by illness or trauma, *personalisation and indwelling may happen in adulthood.* When this is so, we do not have to think in terms of regression to dependency upon another (the analyst) in order to discover a real self-dwelling in bodily aliveness. As Mairi did, we can think in terms of religious experience and recovery of soul. We even can think in terms of re-balancing the psyche toward the feminine. Notions of dependence on another, past or present, fall through a reality of psyche into a reality of soul, which actively relates to an indwelling Feminine Presence of the Holy and a state of personalisation.

Winnicott's and my views of personalisation and indwelling indicate two ways of understanding psychological experience. One makes less room for religious experience and the other extends the possibility of renewed faith. A realization of personality that explicitly acknowledges soul (as happened with Mairi) can bridge the fields of psychology and religion. "God in the picture" suggests that in some situations of personality realization, more than individual development goes on.

I feel that my point of view has implications for psychotherapy because I am also convinced that we observe phenomena to the degree that we participate in them; that we observe what happens in therapy to the degree that we fully participate in what happens with fully human consciousness. Just as we cannot arrive at spirit if spirit is not there to begin with, we will not experience soul if soul has no place or significance in our lives. Just as the unconscious reflects to consciousness the face that consciousness displays to it, soul reflects the values and qualities of a soulful life. Numbness and blankness, despair and nothingness – these are the qualities of being that reflect an absence of soul to a soulless life. If a therapist is unaware that soul underlies and animates the psyche, soul's manifestations may be missed. The therapist will not be attuned to experience of soul, no matter to whom, in whom, or with whom, it occurs. Likewise, when theologians deny soul's underlying reality, they will identify with spirit and find psyche irrelevant, an unnecessary bother. While revelation and experience of soul rest upon individual perception, information and self-witness, the companioning and verification of revelation and experience of soul will always rely upon a companioning participating consciousness, as well as upon human observation and a conceptual system which makes such observation possible to begin with.

Differing fundamentally from Freud's view of illusion as a distortion or contradiction of reality in the service of wish-fulfillment, Winnicott tends to emphasize the positive, creative aspects of religious experience. Winnicott did not wish that psychoanalysis would eliminate through enlightenment the hold that the Church has on believers. Rather, he hoped that psycho-analysis could "save religious practice from losing its place in the civil-ization process" (1963d: 95). Instead of reducing the religious impulse to defensive compensations or disguised substitutes, at times Winnicott (1935) even turned the Freudian legacy on its head by pointing to how *intolerance of religion* [emphasis mine] might serve those functions instead. He wonders whether part of our own manic defense is an inability to give full signi-ficance to inner reality (1935: 129).[36] I wonder what Winnicott would say about Mairi's experience of soul.

Winnicott distinguishes faith from processes of introjection and inter-nalization. But for Winnicott, faith means a capacity for belief *in . . .* something else, someone else, someone Other. To have faith, Winnicott says, is to have a degree of fearlessness. Faith *refers* to that capacity to experience with one's whole being, all-out, with "all one's heart, with all one's soul, with all one's might" (and all one's body, too). Eigen agrees with Winnicott that a capacity for "belief *in*" evolves from transitional experiencing with the actual mother, but he implies that something more is involved. Consistent with the hypothesis that I am developing here, Eigen (1993a) suggests that the primary object of creative (and religious) experi-encing is not the actual mother or father, but what he calls an "unknow-able ground of creativeness as such." What is at stake in transitional experiencing, says Eigen, is not mainly a self or an object (mother) sub-stitute (although he agrees with Winnicott that it does not happen without these), nor even a principle of self–other awareness as such, but *the creation of a symbol symbolizing experiencing itself* (Eigen 1993a: 135, emphasis mine).

Like Hadewijch, who experienced an "abyss of soul" (L18: 1. 63), Mairi's experience of soul opened her to what Eigen (1993a: 133) describes as a "wholling tendency that thrives on coming through tendencies toward depersonalisation and dispersal, (thereby bearing) witness to the category of mystery as a basic dimension in which we live." But Mairi's experience of mystery had *content* that Eigen does not engage. Inclusive of our world yet not our world, for Eigen this inexpressible ground of creativeness is what literally and figuratively supports us. For Mairi, it is God.

Perhaps Mairi's Dream #22, of a Woman's Hands Holding the Earth, depicts the psyche's version of what Eigen means by being supported by an inexpressible ground of creativeness or what Winnicott implies by a capacity for "belief *in*" (being held by another?). I suppose that Eigen (and Winnicott) might suggest that experience of soul was Mairi's "creation of a symbol symbolizing experience." But I do not know how these authors would characterize Mairi's encounter with the unknown and unknowable behind the Holy Spirit as Feminine Presence, out of which Mairi's dream-in-the-world was precipitated. Winnicott might describe how Mairi's experience of soul came into being within the reliability of her therapeutic situation, and Mairi, in effect, might agree. But Mairi would also insist that nothing could have happened had the Holy Spirit not approached her from the other side. Mairi might have said that her experience of soul was the creation of a symbol symbolizing a capacity for "symbolizing" experience – for writing *about*, for speaking *about*, for singing *about*, even for experiencing experience itself – but compared with Mairi's experience of the Other as Subject, Eigen's concept of an "unknowable ground of creativeness" as such (1993a: 135) does not fill the descriptive bill.

From Eigen's side, the inexplicable autonomy of the spirit may be understandable from his description of "an unknowable ground of creativeness as such." From Jung's side, the autonomy of the spirit resides in his supposition that beyond perception and cognition there exists "the uncomprehended absolute object which affects and influences us" (1963: 351). Both psychological formulations contrast with Mairi's experience of soul, in which her "symbol symbolizing experiencing itself" was not visual (psyche, image) but an *encounter with sensed, felt Presence*, not of an object but of a Subject which required her active personalisation of body and soul. Mairi encountered neither an unknowable ground nor an uncomprehended absolute object, and I think the difference is important. The difference has to do on the one hand with Mairi's capacity for personalisation, and on the other, with what Teilhard de Chardin calls the "inherent capacity of God to be the personal (and in spite of the Incarnation, transcendent) summit of a universe on the road to personalisation" (Cousins 1992: 177). When Mairi encountered the Holy Spirit as Feminine Presence, Jung's absolute Object turned out to be a Regnant Subject. I, too, "God willing," was able to participate in Mairi's experience of soul, and personally companion her personalising immersion in the fiery furnace of passionately embodied being.

Notes

1 Von Franz (1986: 89) observes that the entire *opus* of transformation "culminates in the production of the so-called *caelum*, the inner sky." This goal or

telos is "*the extracted quintessence of the life of the body*, the inner truth which, as God's exact image, lies hidden in the innermost recesses . . ." (emphasis mine).

2 Palermo National Museum, Palermo, Sicily.

3 Theologian Paul Tillich suggests soul as the locus of revelation. Masterfully charting the revelatory spirit that soul receives, Tillich mentions soul only a few times in the three volumes of his *Systematic Theology*: "Life as spirit is the life of the soul" (1. 250); soul "bears the life of spirit" (3. 26), has infinite value (305), and has a quality that transcends temporality, though it is not immortal (410–11).

4 In his work on the *Apocalypse, The Secret Book of Revelation* Gilles Quispel (1986: 3–5) says that Gnostic formulation is intrinsic to all religious experience that goes beyond ephemera to some permanent wisdom: "Gnosis is based on the idea that there is something in man, his unconscious spirit, that is related to the ground of being. In order to restore the wholeness it has lost, the deity has an interest in redeeming this spiritual principle in man. The figure that incarnates wisdom in the Apocalypse is a Lady [Sophia] who might be called the 'world-soul' . . . she who adds darkness to light . . . who signifies the marriage of opposites . . . who reconciles nature and spirit . . . the Lady is the Holy Spirit, as it used to be for all Jewish Christians."

5 The concept of "witness" as an aspect of consciousness separate from ego-consciousness is found in many religious traditions. The Sufis call it the Fair Witness.

6 *Die Passion Jesu ist in Haare, Bart und Dornenkrone eingeschrieben*, by J. M. Buchler, 1650.

7 "In Hindu mythology, Kundalini is a serpent goddess who lies asleep at the base of the spine, coiled three-and-a-half times around the first *chakra*. Her full name is Kundalini-Shakti, and she represents the unfolding of the divine Shakti energy, the energizing potential of life itself, a living Goddess who enlivens all things. Under certain circumstances the Kundalini energy awakens and begins to rise through the body, piercing and opening the *chakras* as she moves in her undulating snake-like fashion. As she releases stored and blocked energies her movement can be quite intense, sometimes painful, and often leads to mental states that seem out of this world. Circumstances that stimulate Kundalini awakening are many and varied, but are usually triggered by such things as extended periods of meditation, yoga, fasting, stress, trauma, psychedelic drugs, or near death experiences . . . Kundalini is a condensed, primal force, similar to the potential energy found in matter. Kundalini can also be seen as the result, rather than the cause, of the *chakras* connecting with each other . . . Kundalini is basically a healing force, though its effects can sometimes be quite unpleasant. Such effects may last for minutes, days, months, or even years" (Judith 1996: 469–70).

8 To bring *Muladhara* to consciousness means to bring awareness to our roots, to uncover the past, to delve into and examine it. Returning to our roots brings us into singularity, simplicity, and the commonality of collective union. It brings us home to earth. Judith (1996: 52–3) lists the attributes of the Muladhara chakra (under the title, *Reclaiming the Temple of the Body*) as follows: *Purpose*: foundation. *Issues*: roots, energetic grounding, bringing consciousness into the body (essential for forming healthy boundaries): a downward current of consciousness connects with body and meets the field of sensation, the edges and boundaries of physical reality; learning how to be present here and now, focused, dynamic; nourishment, trust, health, home, family, prosperity, appropriate boundaries. *Color*: red. *Location*: base of spine. *Identity*: physical. *Orientation*:

self-preservation. *Demon*: Fear. *Developmental Stages*: second trimester to twelve months. *Developmental Tasks*: physical growth, motor skills, object permanence. *Basic Rights*: to be here and have. *Balanced Characteristics*: good health, vitality, well-grounded, comfortable in body, sense of trust in world, feeling of safety and security, ability to relax and be still, stability, prosperity, right livelihood. *Trauma and Abuses*: birth trauma, abandonment, physical neglect, poor physical bonding with mother, malnourishment, feeding difficulties, illness or surgery, physical abuse/violent environment, inherited traumas (meaning parental survival fears). *Deficiency*: disconnection from body, fearful, anxious, restless, can't settle, poor focus and discipline, financial difficulty, poor boundaries, chronic disorganization. *Excess*: obesity, overeating, hoarding, material fixation, greed, sluggish, lazy, tired, fear of change, addiction to security, rigid boundaries. *Healing Strategies*: reconnect with body, physical activity, lots of touch, bio-energetic grounding, Hatha yoga, look at earliest relationship to mother, reclaim right to be here. *Affirmations*: it is safe for me to be here, the earth supports me and meets my needs, I love my body and trust its wisdom, I am immersed in abundance, I am here and I am real.

Relative to the psychological material of a woman with whom he worked, Jung (1931a: 147) also comments on the Muladhara, characterizing this chakra as the experience of complete unconsciousness or complete mystical identity with the object. "The yoga process," he writes, " is really something that happens on a different plane, as it were, and there are dangers and risks that do not attend the usual development of consciousness . . . should one, for instance, reach the lowest place, Muladhara, one might be caught in the roots. . . . it is associated with the dangers of insanity because insanity really is that attachment to the roots of consciousness . . . therefore a typical case of insanity might be called a yoga experience that had gone wrong." "The Muladhara is the earth all around, in its manifold aspects, not only as the soil from which life springs but also the place to which life returns . . . These two aspects of the earth are mixed in religious Christian language, where the flesh is also the grave and decay; and in Buddhism the world has a double aspect, on the one side the birth place, the cradle, and on the other, the burial ground, the place of specters and carrion . . . we need this double aspect . . . because the patient herself is concerned with her actual transition into the world. And the world is *Muladhara*, the root world, the place of death and birth, of construction and destruction, all at the same time" (1934a: 452–4).

9 Tantra, often understood only sexually, is actually about weaving. The word *tantra* means loom, and the verb *tan* means *to stretch*. Tantra is the spiritual practice of harmoniously weaving together primordial opposites: the upward and downward energy currents of Shakti and Shiva, male and female, mortal and divine, spirit and matter, Heaven and Earth. As a subset of Tantra, sexuality as a sacred act embodies this union physically. The ultimate balance of these two forces, however, occurs when they are woven throughout all the chakras and balanced in the heart. Tantra seeks enlightenment not by renunciation but by embracing the full experience of living. Delighting in the senses, desires and feelings, tantra focuses on an expansion of consciousness that comes from a dynamic, sensate connection to life (Judith 1996: 474–5).

10 See the lovely images of winged Psyche in the ruins of Pompeii preserved in the Palermo National Museum, or Louis Simpson's poem which begins, "She is on her knees pulling weeds . . ."

11 In a footnote (n. 6) to CW12: 11, Jung says that it is "psychologically quite unthinkable for God to be simply the 'wholly other,' for a 'wholly other' could

never be one of the soul's deepest and closest intimacies – that is precisely what God is. The only statements that have psychological validity concerning the God-image are either paradoxes or antinomies." Jung is caught here in the nature of his language. Paradox and antinomies exist and are constructed within the mind. Mairi differentiates between what Jung would have called a God-image and what she experienced as imageless Presence – between psyche, that is apprehending and expressive of image, and soul, which for Mairi was more bodily apprehension than visual perception.

12 This point of view is contrary to that of "Archetypal Psychology" which equates anima and soul and speaks of "soul-making".

13 Lacan writes about a failure to recognize, or a "misconstruction" in the psyche formed primarily through unconscious identification (which means "to assume an image") and visualization. Upon seeing its own image in a mirror or seeing another baby sometime within the first six to eighteen months of life, a child unconsciously forms a self-image deep in the psyche and identifies with it as an ego-ideal.

14 Neurobiologist Benjamin Libit (1989: 184) demonstrates that the neurobiological organization that gives rise to our subsequent subjective experience of behavioral intention actually takes place approximately 0.5 seconds after behavior is initiated. It is then automatically referred backwards in time (1989: 182) to when the behavior actually began. Contrary to what object-relations theorists purport, internal representations neither precede nor accompany action: objectively, they follow action, disaffirming the proposition that behavior is intentional and driven by internal representations.

15 In receiving Spirit (Acts 2: 4) the Holy touched Mairi literally, immaculately and bodily, in a manner and to a depth no human therapeutic situation could assume.

16 2 Corinthians 5: 19.

17 Jung (CW8: 920) acknowledges the reality of nothingness: "Nothing is evidently meaning or purpose, and it is only called Nothing because it does not appear in the world of the senses, but is only its organizer."

18 In his early work Jung tells us that intuition proceeds by way of the unconscious. Usually we define intuition as an immediate apprehension of a truth, fact, or situation independent of any reasoning process, as if intuition were a kind of keen, quick insight. But in a later letter (1960: 50–7) Jung tells us that intuition proceeds by way of endopsychic perception, which I would understand in Mairi's situation as introverted sensation or a sensation function become conscious as the "fourth."

19 Patočka tells us that the new mystery of the soul refers us for the first time in history to the immortality of the individual, since it is interior and inseparable from its own fulfillment (Derrida 1995: 12).

20 Dante alludes to a similar reversal of direction (*Divine Comedy*); only when he descends to the depths of hell does the cosmos *reverse itself*, so that by continuing (rather than by turning around), Dante ascends to heaven.

21 John 3: 7.

22 Virginity is consistently associated with the power to heal. This is why a virgin spring is a place of healing (as in Ingmar Bergman's film by that name). We may understand virginity as a full experience of selfhood and identity and the recovery of a capacity to know by direct experience of the world. Virginity can also be understood as "singleness of heart" – a state of being that can return to God in a wholeness not of having experienced all, but of something preserved,

reserved, and reclaimed for what it was made for – an ability to stay centered, with oneness of purpose.

23 Of *Poems in Couplets* (Hadewijch 1980: 320).

24 Translated into English, many asanas describe animal postures, e.g., up- and down-dog, cobra, cat, camel, crow, eagle, frog, fish, locust, crocodile, dolphin, even "dead bug" (known as "happy baby" in California).

25 Quantum physics describes this as the stance of a "disturbing" observer who consciously participates in the existence of whatever he observes. Hence we develop "participating consciousness" backed by an attitude of willing participation in the experience of experience. Awareness of being a "disturbing observer" points us toward a quantum stance and an indeterminacy of psyche and soul.

26 The Greek word we translate as *arche* (as in archetype) really means origin, the center of a circle, the origin of an arc, rather than the beginning of a line of time, as the English word suggests.

27 This meant that she broke an unconscious identification with a mother-imago so deep and primal that, before her encounter with the Holy Spirit, the unconscious existence of that imago meant to her the presence of life itself. Selfless to a fault, the over-responsible daughter in her original family, care-taking her siblings and even me in therapy when she could, Mairi's breakthrough experience shifted her awareness away from patterns of relatedness between community and world to patterns within interiority. So embedded was she in externality and so medial in her efforts to "mother" herself, her children, and her friends that one could say she was identified with the archetypal image of the healer or shaman with its odd, unstable inflation and sense of self-sufficiency. Having fallen through this identification, she now appreciated the energies of this archetypal constellation she encountered them in the form of the Other who came to presence in her experience of soul.

28 In "The Soul of the World," in *Writings in Time of War* (1918), 182.

29 Winnicott's idea of "privation" (as in de-privation) links with Augustine's notion of the *privatio boni* or evil as the lack or absence of Good. Privation also leads to depersonalisation, suggesting a lack of personalisation: just so, Augustine imagines evil as a "privation" of being.

30 Jung (CW8: 78–83) also sees the ego as dependent upon the body and says that the combination of all body sensations is what holds the ego together. With strong emotion the body changes, weakening the ego's coherence and sometimes leading to ego-dissociation.

31 See Donald Kalsched (1996) for a vivid description of these possessing images as the archetypal defenses that take over in the psyche in the form of a self-care system that aims to protect what he calls the "personal spirit" of the individual.

32 Christianity has an affinity to the suffering body that is unique in religion. There, the "body" refers to a soul that is resident in a multidimensional body that experiences selfhood and relationships through it. Through our body we are, we change, and we die. A crucified Jesus is a bodily Jesus.

33 Whereas Jung tends to merge psyche and soul, in observations on infant personalisation and indwelling, Winnicott (1964: 112) tends to merge psyche and spirit, e.g., "experiential identity of spirit or psyche and the totality of physical functioning."

34 From *religare*, meaning experience that unites and binds together, religating to presence and image that which hitherto was unimaginable.

35 "God within" would have been a characterization more in keeping with Mairi's

conscious expectation of an "image of God" (like the Hindu *Atman*) according to rudimentary understanding of psyche and Self.

36 Winnicott comments that "it is usual to concentrate on the understanding of the mystic's withdrawal into a personal inner world. . . . Perhaps not enough attention has been paid to the mystic's retreat to a position in which he can communicate secretly with subjective . . . phenomena, the loss of contact with the world of shared reality being counterbalanced by a gain in terms of feeling real" (1963e: 185–6).

Chapter 4

Hadewijch's paradox

What we know of Hadewijch's life and writings indicate that in the thirteenth century, a woman of unusual sensibilities (Hadewijch) underwent what we today think of as an archetypal process of individuation. Her written works out-picture her inner experience of movement from soul to psyche – the reverse direction of Mairi's individuation process which, as we've seen, moved from psyche to soul. In the next chapter we will discuss this contrast.

With a paucity of the kind of personal material we had with Mairi we are not privy to Hadewijch's inner world by way of dreams and therapy notes, but what she did leave us is part of our cultural psyche. We can look at her writings (in which her religious sensibility appears full-blown) and what little we know of her personal life through a psychological lens. As we do so, remember how Mairi's pivotal religious experience rebalanced her life into a self-integrity that was previously unavailable. Just so, centuries earlier but still within the confines of our western European culture, Hadewijch also had a pivotal experience near the end of her collectively contained religious life which must have rebalanced her psyche and soul in a highly individual fashion.[1]

In exploring Hadewijch's material, including her religious visions and ecstasies, we must remember that our contemporary psychology of the individual was still seven centuries in the future. There was no word for "consciousness" when Hadewijch wrote, and the idea of "self-consciousness" is newer still. Even the idea of personality (first used in 1768) was five hundred years away.[2]

In Hadewijch's medieval world, people swam in the Christian religion like fish in the sea, never questioning the supportive medium of faith and biblical truth that sustained their lives in the community of believers. When the Reformation swept through Europe three centuries later it was a crisis not only for the medieval Church, but for the collective consciousness of humanity. Suddenly the unquestioned supremacy of the Church with its dogmatic assumptions about human sin and salvation was challenged by the idea of the individual and his/her private relationship to God and to

God's word. Hadewijch's mystical experience outside the conventional Catholic Rule or Vow constitutes a kind of "personal Reformation" expressed three hundred years ahead of her time, and it resonates with the Reformation's impetus towards personality and self-integrity on an individual level. I think of Hadewijch as a precursor of what in our psychological age Erich Neumann calls the "Great Individual," by which he means a person who out of circumstantial necessity and psychological ability actualizes in his or her inner struggle and psychological awareness what others experience externally and collectively.

Hadewijch's religious experience circles around a central notion of "what the soul is." In a letter addressed to one of her beloved Beguines, Hadewijch says,

> Now understand the deepest essence of your soul, what "soul" is. *Soul is a being that can be beheld by God and by which again, God can be beheld.* Soul is also a being that wishes to content God; it maintains a worthy state of being as long as it has not fallen beneath anything that is alien to it and less than the soul's own dignity. If it maintains this worthy state, *the soul is a bottomless abyss* in which God suffices to himself; and his own self-sufficiency ever finds fruition to the full in this soul, as the soul, for its part, ever does in him. *Soul is a way for the passage of God from his depths into his liberty; and God is a way for the passage of the soul into its liberty, that is, into his inmost depths, which cannot be touched except by the soul's abyss.* (L18: 63, Hadewijch 1980: 86, emphasis mine)

The emphasis here is on the soul as a "way" to God, a "bottomless abyss" and a "state of being" more than the soul as an entity of some kind, and we have already highlighted this distinction and its importance to Mairi. This paragraph brings into focus Hadewijch's notion of what soul is, what soul does, what God does in relation to soul, and her realization that the accomplishment of soul's free being-one-with God takes place in the liberty of what Hadewijch calls the "*soul's abyss.*" Where soul and God are in paradoxical relationship, soul becomes a "way" to God. Hadewijch's stated comprehension of soul anchored her understanding of where she was in her world and where in her world her visions, experience, and poetry took place. Pointing to a paradoxical state similar to that into which Mairi "fell," Hadewijch charts a psychological and religiously imaginative terrain of soul as the site of her struggle with the wondrous yet arbitrary and quixotic presence and/or absence of Lady Love.

Hadewijch's notion of *what soul is* emerges from a large, collectively held idea, but her personally embodied experience and understanding of soul links her religious experience closely to her contemporary "soul-sister," Mairi. Orienting her life, Hadewijch's sense and understanding of soul influenced those around her, whether or not they resonated with her emotionally, just as Mairi's experience of soul, re-orienting her attitude toward her work and life in the world, influences her students in the inner cities, teaching them about silence, an inner world, their bodies, and themselves. As an embodied idea central to her being and life in the world, Hadewijch's definition of soul, deriving as it did from visionary experience, so closely resembles Mairi's experience of soul six centuries later that I think both can be understood as transformative experiences of person-alisation and indwelling. Both notions, for both women, imaginatively affirm a vivid encounter with soul and a corresponding experience of God's presence in feminine form.

In the thirteenth century, what we have tried here to distinguish as psyche and soul were intermingled. A particular notion of soul as well as a peculiar notion of love permeated collective consciousness then, as ubiquitous as air. Religious historian Paul Mommaers (1988: 59–61) marks the beginning of this particular notion of soul in the eleventh century as "an unheard-of *interior* state, in which dream and reality were combined," an understand-ing of soul that began to appear in collective consciousness in the earliest *trouvere* poetry.[3] This new experience of soul (a new *collective experience* of Winnicott's female elements of being) was echoed in the outer world by a new feminine self-consciousness that began to appear in the works of women mystics of the twelfth century and later.

Women who carried this consciousness became known as *mulieres religiosae* (Mommaers 1988: 61). Gathering into a religious movement that premised poverty and recognized a primary role for women, they recruited most of their members from the highest classes of society. These women were not social outcasts, says Mommaers (59); they were capable of taking on conflicts, and as marital or sexual "possessions," they were worth a good fight. They had not learned about love from books or sermons. In this group of religious women, who only in 1216 received permission from the Pope to live together without having to join an already existing order, we find the historical beginnings of the Beguine movement.

Hadewijch and the Beguines

Somewhere during the third decade of the thirteenth century, Hadewijch either founded or joined a Beguine group. Becoming the group's mistress, she had under her authority a number of young Beguines whom she believed to be especially called to the mystical state. Her familiarity with chivalry and courtly love and her knowledge of Scripture and the fathers of the Church, as well as her obvious education in Latin, rhetoric, numero-logy, astronomy, music, verse, and French, suggest that Hadewijch was an educated member of the upper class (Hadewijch 1980; Dreyer 1989; Mommaers 1988). Clearly she was an independent woman and a "feminist before her time" (Mommaers 1988: 58) who had little use for theological systems and could not be fitted neatly into the existing structures of church or society. Perhaps Hadewijch was herself a troubadour or a harpist, which would also explain her considerable knowledge of the poetics of *trouvere* poetry.

With mystical experience as her starting point, Hadewijch was a clear advocate of alternative ways of living one's faith outside any religious order. Says she, "In keeping with a rule of life, people encumber themselves with many things from which they could be free . . . A spirit of good will assures greater interior beauty than any rule of life could devise" (L4: 64, 54). Her attitude exemplifies the religious freedom and affiliation for which the Beguine movement originally stood. Hadewijch's sense of God was full of passionate balance and justice; like Job, says Van Baest (1998: 30), Hadewijch speaks of God as "the thing which is right" (Job 42: 8).

In contrast to those for whom faith was a matter of formal adherence or intellectual assent, the Beguines simply expressed an individual, personal desire for an effective, experimental faith. They insisted that they were not hostile to the church or religious orders, but that they wished to go their own way, to live as simply in the world as the earliest Christians had, and "to live without a why" (McGinn 1994: 6). To me this phrase – living without a why   implies the ability for a spontaneous, individual, personal expression of religious life in the world without worldly ambition or goal. It implies living for its own sake, rather than as a means to an end (salvation).

The main theme of a Beguine's life was dedication to God. Many writers describe what Hadewijch's life might have been like (Southern 1970; Mommaers 1980, 1988; Hadewijch 1980; McGinn 1994; Murk-Jansen 1998). Early in the movement, a woman who became a Beguine might have lived alone or in her original family or family of marriage, or among a small group of like-minded women. She might have been married and divorced. She might have had grown children. To live a life of apostolic poverty and chastity doing works of charity meant that in varying proportions her activities might have included working in a (leper) hospital, feeding the poor, teaching in schools, and earning her way by weaving, embroidery and lace-making. All this took place within the context of an unpretentious spiritual life, which consisted of simple prayer and meditation. Although a Beguine might have been educated and from a wealthy family, she did not live on her inheritance, nor did she rely upon charity. Developing a spirituality that was both in and of the world rather than separated from it, the early Beguines lived from the work of their hands. Two or three of the founders of this movement left considerable records of their prayers and visions, and Hadewijch of Brabant was among them.

In our highly individualized culture it is hard to appreciate what a radical departure the Beguines were from conventional religious life. In 1243, surveying the European scene from his English monastery, a man named Matthew Paris made an entry in his *Chronicle* to which he attached great importance:

> At this time and especially in Germany, certain people – men and women, but especially women – have adopted a religious profession, though it is a light one. They call themselves "religious," and they take a private vow of continence and simplicity of life, though they do not follow the Rule of any saint, nor are they as yet confined within a cloister. They have so multiplied within a short time that two thousand have been reported in Cologne and the neighboring cities.[4]

In 1250, in a second entry which places the new movement alongside the friars as a notable development in religious life, Paris comments that they "live a frugal life on the labor of their own hands . . . no one knows why they are called Beguines, nor how they began" (v. 194).

Sketching the earliest beginnings of Beguine activity, Mommaers (1988: 62) tells us that in Brabant, in approximately 1190, gatherings among women began to seethe with evangelical life. Women who found no place within monastic structures for their ideals and sense of independence began to do without them. As lay women these women were not unchurched, but they participated in a rising apostolic fervor that harkened back to early Christian house churches (if to church at all), in which the good news was preached by each person and Christianity was understood as a way of life more than an indicator of social or political identity.

The Beguine movement differed substantially from all earlier important movements within the western church in two ways: it was a *lay movement*, meaning that it was carried by secular members of the body of Christ rather than by clergy, monastics or scholars, and it was a *women's movement*, not simply a feminine appendix to a movement that owed its impetus, direction and main support to men. The movement came into being toward the end of the twelfth century, originating largely among women of noble and patrician families who apparently rejected not only the narrow life of the lady in the castle but the strict obligations of the nun in the cloister. They sought a new way of life to be arranged by themselves, in which to the recitation of the Hours they could add manual work, study, or teaching, according to their desires (Hadewijch 1980: 3).

Much research has been done in an attempt to clarify the appeal of this "order" that was not an Order. What function did this movement serve, what contribution did it make to medieval religion? New in the Beguine movement was an embodiment of religious feeling and *life in the world*, of which Hadewijch was a prime mover and example. The large numbers of women who flocked to this way of life at this period gave rise to what German medievalists know as the *Frauenfrage*, the "woman-question"

(McGinn 1994: 3): Who were these women and why did so many of them prefer this new way of life?

By linking the *Frauenfrage* with the monastic tradition, which also prefers affective experience (knowledge gained by devotion and loving) to reason or intellect, the *Frauenbewegung* has often been treated only as a movement of the heart, that is, as an outpouring of religious fervor and dedication (McGinn 1994: 3). But this kind of brief characterization of any movement – "of the heart," or "of the head" – leaves out of account the *embodied nature* of all such experience. In Hadewijch's notion of what soul is, the "woman question" is embodied in a movement of the mind as well as the heart, and a great deal of her passion was directed toward *Minne*, or Lady Love; hence the close association of the feminine element with Hadewijch's mystical communion.

Clearly the movement gave many women an alternative to the storms and frustrations of secular life. As a whole, it seemed to point toward what Murk-Jansen describes as "a new conception of Christianity as *a way of life* rather than a collection of dogmas . . . (an) understanding that the gospel's demands were relevant not only to those ordained by the Church but *to everyone, including women*" (1998: 23, emphasis mine), as they had been at the time of Jesus. At the root of all this there was a persistent, individual desire for experiment, a desire to discover for oneself a way of life suited to one's own religious experience and to live it freely in the world.

The popular ferment in which the early Beguines participated had taken many other forms that usually spilled over into heresy. Over time, the Beguines may have become no exception. Indeed, some thought it was from the hated name *Albigensian* that the name "Beguine" derived – a label of contempt given to women who claimed to be holier than others as they resisted the advances of lascivious priests and rejected the inducements of lawful matrimony.[5] As a result of a suspicion of heresy, many Beguines suffered and some died.[6] But if the name was intended as a smear, it was difficult to make a charge of heresy stick. The Beguines were remarkably innocent. They had no quarrel with orthodoxy and no distinctive theological ideas to promulgate. Neither perfectionists nor Manicheans, they claimed no new revelation, only a desire to live freely in the world, "religiously." And so, although they met with dislike, the Beguines also found protectors and made their way forward.

Many people disapproved of the new liberty these women enjoyed. Parish priests who lost parishioners, fathers who lost daughters, and men who resented the women who got away, all became enemies of the Beguines (Southern 1970: 328–9), not to mention other men and women who, even while admiring, were also envious and afraid. The equation of poverty and true freedom roused suspicion that too much freedom – as mystics claimed it – could give birth to something like the Free Spirit, attacked by the Church as the *secta libertatis* and branded heresy (McGinn 1994: 13). And the movement itself did not remain immune from contradiction, corruption and absurdity. By the middle of the century some Beguines had begun to beg, rather than earn their way. Others became increasingly (and vocally) critical of the clergy. As the condemnation of Marguerite Porete in 1310 shows, they also began to preach outside their own communities (Murk-Jansen 1998: 29).

Somewhere during this time of controversy, Hadewijch's authority among the Beguines in her group apparently met with opposition. Hart speculates that perhaps some found her unremittingly high standards a grievance, or that her ascendancy to leadership may have aroused jealousy. Ill-feeling toward the Beguines on the part of outsiders no doubt played a part too, and a few Beguines themselves secretly engaged in undermining Hadewijch's position. Means were devised to send her companions away from her and she was threatened with an accusation of teaching quietism, a charge that carried with it the possibility of being turned out of her community to wander the countryside, or even imprisonment, were she denounced to the Inquisition.[7] In her writings, Hadewijch clearly laments the pain of separation from those dear to her and speaks of being one day reunited with them.

The general opinion of contemporary scholars seems to be that Hadewijch was made the talk of the town and thrown out because of her doctrine that one must "live Love." Unprotected by a rule of enclosure or the strong organization of any order, Hadewijch was evicted from her Beguine community and exiled. Hart poignantly speculates that when Hadewijch finally became homeless, she might have offered her services to a leprosarium or a hospital for the poor. There, nursing those who suffered, she continued to "live Love" and also sleep at least part of the night in some corner with access to the church or chapel that was always attached to such establishments in her time.

Over time, the Church became increasingly uneasy with the Beguines' intellectual and theological activity. According to Mommaers, "Hadewijch and her female friends thus gradually had unpleasant confrontations with those who took religion quite seriously. These women were a *fascinosum* – didn't they make God seen and heard?" (1988: 77). As early as 1272 Gilbert van Doornik reported to the Council of Lyons the *scandalum* that ignorant Beguines were reading and explaining Bible texts (Murk-Jansen 1998: 30): the description of the Beguines as ignorant referred to their lack of clerical education; the scandal was that as women they should dare to read and teach, not that they had not been properly trained.[8] Eventually, the Beguines were felt to stand for an unknown form of religious life that began to threaten basic principles of traditional order. Obedience became an issue. The Beguines were suspected of substituting *individual*, changeable will and *personal experience* for definite and authoritative law. A substitution of individual authority for collective law and custom could make it impossible to be certain of a person's social status, whether ecclesiastical or secular. As the Beguine movement consolidated and voices critical of the clergy began to emerge, charges arose that "these women" were using their liberty as a "veil of wickedness in order to escape the yoke of obedience to their priests and the coercion of marital bonds"; Bruno, bishop of Olmütz in Eastern Germany, wrote to the pope in 1273 to complain about young women who "assumed the status of widowhood against the authority of the Apostle who approved no widows under the age of sixty" and included his remedy for such evils: "I would have them married or thrust into an approved Order" (Southern 1970: 329).

At the end of the great legislative period of the medieval Church, tension between the forces of authority and liberty had only increased. In 1381 the archbishop of Cologne required the dissolution of all Beguine associations and their integration into Orders approved by the pope. Small communities were subjected to strict discipline through the Church. The women were housed in closed complexes with a chapel or church which were later made into parishes and finally into Beguinages. This resulted in the rapid decline of the movement and the transfer of many Beguines to the Franciscan or Dominican tertiaries. In Germany, other frightened Beguines formalized their association with mendicant orders. The condemnatory process went so far that by 1421 Pope Martin V ordered the archbishop of Cologne to search out and destroy any small convents of persons living under the cloak of religion without a definite Rule (Southern 1970: 331). With allegiance to the Church, those who conformed to this discipline escaped condemnation, but similar communities who had failed to align themselves with the Church were affected by punitive decrees and disappeared.

By then the flowering of the Beguines came to an end, their spirit suppressed. Many of their writings were lost: Hadewijch's work, for example, "disappeared" for six centuries. By the middle of the fourteenth century the movement was exhausted and the initial impulse that had so greatly impressed contemporary observers was gone. Southern (1970: 325) tells us that by the end of the fourteenth century there were 169 Beguine convents, providing a home for about 1,500 Beguines. Gradually, as a result of ecclesiastical pressure and for simple convenience, these convents drew in the whole Beguine population. By 1400 all Beguines lived in convents, and the initial phenomenon that had astonished observers in the mid-thirteenth century died away.

As the women gave up their freedom and moved into the confines of convents and approved orders and Rules, they left behind as a memorial to their movement a large number of empty buildings and empty grounds. Hospitals and old people's homes took over these buildings, the shells of which can still be seen today. Although some Beguinages have been restored, they were restored to the time of the convents, not to the time of the original thirteenth century Beguine movement when they were simply "dwellings."[9]

Literary contributions

Hadewijch's writings continue to have an impact today.[10] More than one contemporary scholar lovingly translated her entire work (Jozef Van Mierlo, 1924–52; Mother Columba Hart, 1980); others have written about her extensively. Paul Mommaers (1980: xiii), a foremost contemporary scholar of Hadewijch, calls her "the most important exponent of love mysticism and one of the loftiest figures in the Western mystical tradition," as well as a "feminist in conflict with the social mores of her time" (1988). Theologian Elizabeth Dreyer (1989) focuses upon Hadewijch's passionate love mysticism as it is laid bare in her poetry. Professor of Christian Mysticism Bernard McGinn (1994) traces the influence of Hadewijch's religious perceptions with reference to the work of Meister Eckhart. Professor of Religious History Caroline Walker Bynum addresses Hadewijch's way of life and thought in her essays on the religious significance of food to medieval women (Bynum 1987) and ideas of gender and the human body in medieval religion (1992). Theologian Murk-Jansen relies upon Hadewijch in her study of Beguine spirituality (1998). In a contribution to a series of books on the Body in Culture, History and Religion,[11] Professor John Giles Milhaven writes about Hadewijch as he explores what he calls "other ways of knowing and loving." Religious scholar Paul Verdeyen (1994: 159), tracing Hadewijch's influence on Jan Ruusbroec (John of Ruusbroec, 1293–1381) simply refers to her as "the great Beguine." Mother Placid Dempsey, the illustrator of Hart's translation of Hadewijch's writings, expresses her growing appreciation for Hadewijch as she came to know her by describing her as a "woman of substance, who has – in addition – an extraordinary black humor."[12]

Like other texts left behind by Beguine writers, Hadewijch's written material is essentially mystical. Most of her writings, composed between 1220 and 1244, consist of *Visions, Letters, Poems in Stanzas,* and *Poems in Couplets.* The latter were known as *Mengeldichten,* which means "looking within to the soul as a mirror of God in order to gain knowledge." According to these texts, love for God is increased by a constantly unfulfilled and unfulfillable *longing* for God, and this longing desire is the locus of union with the love that *is* God.

That Hadewijch expressed her love mysticism in the vernacular (common Middle Dutch, or *Diets*), rather than in the learned Latin[13] sanctioned by the scholastic and monastic theology of her time, was unique.[14] By writing in the vernacular, Hadewijch directed her teachings toward a new and potentially wider audience than could be addressed by traditional monastic and scholastic theology. Vernacular writings by lay people made mystical teachings accessible to a lay audience, and no Beguine author stressed the importance of belonging to a religious order in the institutional sense (McGinn 1994; Southern 1970).[15] In this way the Beguines are understood to have been responsible for a transformation of the notion of what it meant to be "literate," or lettered (Mommaers (1988: 73). Their unprecedented vernacular writings became a new branch of literature, the so-called and paradoxical "Illiterate-Literature." Some writers apologized for their lack of Latin, the sanctioned language. But there is no trace of apology in Hadewijch:

> Words enough and Dutch enough can be found for all things on earth, but I do not know any Dutch or any words that answer my purpose. Although I can express everything insofar as this is possible for a human being, no Dutch can be found for all I have said to you, since none exists to express these things, so far as I know. (L17: 112. 84)

Inasmuch as they tend to take personal, poetic and spontaneous form in a familiar language, vernacular writings themselves may be understood as feminine modes of expression of individual personal religious experience. The early Beguines lived what they wrote, embodying their theological beliefs and understandings in their daily lives.

Beguine spirituality

Murk-Jansen suggests that the *mysterium tremendum*[16] aspect of deity and the mysterious otherness of God are central to a Beguine understanding, quoting a biblical text to express the complexities of Beguine spirituality (Psalm 22: 14): "I am poured out like water, and all my bones are out of joint; my heart is like wax." I appreciate Murk-Jansen's choice, particularly her perception of dislocation, for the terms used by Hadewijch for the suffering she experiences in her love and desire for the presence of God are similar. Precisely at an agonized moment of longing love for what is absent, Hadewijch finds that she is closest to God. This is expressive of a major dislocation, a paradox. Somehow the Beguines, Hadewijch among them, were able to articulate what many of us feel but find it hard to speak: wonder at the love that is God while simultaneously trembling in fear and awe at the gulf that separates the creature from the Creator (Murk-Jansen 1998: 13).

The Beguines wrote about the numinous aspect of God, non-rational to the extent that it is far beyond the capacities of a human mind to grasp and comprehend. Rooted neither in theory nor in speculation, Beguine texts contain no constructed philosophical theories or doctrine. Faced with the numinous, says Murk-Jansen (1998: 34),

> they sought to awaken the sense of the numinous in others. This sense cannot be taught . . . it can only be evoked by awakening the latent consciousness in (wo)man. One of the important features of Beguine

writing is therefore their use of paradox, metaphor and image language, all of which are affective, unlike the discursive language of systematic theology which relies on rational explanation.

Hadewijch's experience of the numinous offers us important new "ways of imagining God" (Murk-Jansen 1998: 13). Her visionary imagery (e.g., the whirlpool, the abyss, the wilderness, the theme of longing that is never appeased) expresses her experience of the *awefulness* of God, as well as the immensity of love and the offer of an extraordinary grace of union. Such imagery balances our contemporary tendency toward making the immanence of God paramount and letting the remembrance of God's transcendence fall away. Some examples: "O beloved, why has not Love sufficiently overwhelmed you and engulfed you in her *abyss*? Alas, when Love is so sweet, why do you not fall deep into her? And why do you not touch God deeply enough in the *abyss of his Nature, which is so unfathomable*?" (L5: 28. 56); "In ease, in harshness / In pleasure, in pain: / That *wilderness* / He dares / In Love" (P36: 2. 230); and in a wild description of unappeasable longing, ". . . Love makes the heart taste a violent death and causes it to die without being able to die" (L20: 26. 91).

Hadewijch's language embraces the paradox of pain and suffering as part of her experience of a God that is both Love and infinitely Other. Indeed, for Hadewijch, suffering *is* union, in which both the soul and God remain forever distinct (Murk-Jansen 1998: 71). Yet for Hadewijch suffering is never a good in itself. It is not a means to obtain favor, nor is it primarily a way of paying for sin. We suffer in order to "grow up" ("and all things considered, you have suffered too little to grow up" L2: 39. 49). We suffer with good will and for God, which is pleasing to God. Hadewijch declares that only in the suffering caused by *the absence of love* can desire become so great as to become one with that love, recognizing that God is most intimately present when God seems most absent.

In terms of ordinary everyday living, spiritual union with God consists not in ecstasies, visions and supernatural sweetness, which she, like other Beguines, dismissed as juvenile, but in serving one's fellow human beings while being painfully rejected and despised. Eventually, Hadewijch understood that her attraction to what she calls experiences of "fruitive being-one" with God – her visions and other ecstatic aspects of her mystical experience – was a sign of "non-full grownness." For Hadewijch, what matters in mysticism is so to grow up that one is enabled to live "wholly other" aspects of being-one with God (Mommaers 1980: xiv). Hadewijch insists that the creature can resemble God only in *human suffering* (emphasis mine). In accepting this, Hadewijch accepts the *tremendum* aspect of God, characterized by Murk-Jansen (1998: 58) as "the horror as well as the love, indeed the horror *of* the love." Recognizing that this aspect of Beguine spirituality is foreign to much contemporary Christianity which emphasizes the accessibility of God, Murk-Jansen (58) feels that this in part is where Hadewijch's value lies for us today; to this I would add Hadewijch's understanding of soul.

Mysticism and the body

Most Beguine texts have become known as examples of love mysticism or *minnemystiek*. Mommaers (1980) characterizes this genre as a preeminently feminine phenomenon whose essential message is that union with God is to be lived here on earth as a love relationship. Hadewijch, for example, does not treat love in a systematic fashion, but the word occurs on almost every page of her writing and is obviously a controlling concept in her spirituality. In Mommaers' understanding of Hadewijch, God lets Himself "be experienced as Love (*Minne*) by the person who goes out to meet him with love (*minne*)" (1980: xiii). A poet of great stature, especially in *Poems in Stanzas*, Hadewijch was able to emphasize four main themes within her overarching concept of Love: the relation of passion to reason, the humanity of Jesus, the pain involved in passionate love, and the effects of passionate love – resulting in *the transformed self* that Hadewijch calls "grown-upness," a state analogous to what I describe as the attainment of "fully human consciousness." From out of the divine order, Hadewijch tells us, God called Hadewijch to fully become herself.

As stated earlier, the central theme of love took possession of Hadewijch's heart and mind very early, with her experience of Divine Love at the age of ten (L11: 10. 69). However, there is an on-going debate about what love means for Hadewijch. She uses several different terms: *karitate* usually refers to love of neighbor, *lief* refers to the beloved who is either Christ or the soul (which Hart translates as "the loved one"), while *minne*, a word of feminine gender which belongs to the language of courtly love, is the word Hadewijch uses most often (Hadewijch 1980: 8).[17] Van Mierlo and Hart explain Hadewijch's use of *minne* as signifying primarily God, or Christ, or Divine Love. Norbert De Paepe, another Hadewijch scholar, along with Dreyer (1989: 45), concludes that Hadewijch understands love (*Minne*) as *the soul's experience of God* (emphasis mine) rather than as a personification of God or Christ.[18] "*Minne* in Hadewijch's Poems . . . is not God, Christ, or Divine Love – except in a very limited number of places . . . *Minne is an experience, the way in which the soul experiences its relation to God, a dynamic experience of relationship*" (emphasis mine).[19]

De Paepe's understanding of what Hadewijch means by Love matches my own, especially since my experience with Mairi. As Mairi embodied her dream-in-the-world, her soul's discovery of a relation to God was both her shock and her salvation: Mairi experienced soul as the site in which direct religious experience occurred, soul as a state of being in which she encountered the Holy Spirit as Feminine Presence, and the soul's "abyss" (into which she "fell") as her body's capacity to personalise indwelling spirit. To abstract all of this into psychological language, in Mairi's experience of soul, soul coalesced and was experienced by Mairi as *a symbol of her ability to symbolize experience*, side by side with and in relation to the Holy Spirit as Feminine Presence.

Just as Mairi's experience of soul was impossible without the body, so in Hadewijch's poems and visions there are frequent references to bodily states. *Poems in Stanzas* abounds with references to touch and taste, which are the oldest of our senses – older than smell or hearing or sight – as if Hadewijch sought reference to the deepest, most inaccessible aspects of her own bodily being by way of Love's Body. She celebrates these senses: "He whom Love *touches* cannot die – / Her name is *a-mor*, 'delivered from death' / . . . Love is that living bread – / And above all sweet in taste" (P2: 5. 132); "For Love gives the new good / That makes the new mind, / that renews itself in all / Wherein Love newly *touched* it" (P7: 2. 145); "What is this light burden of Love / and this *sweet-tasting* yoke? / It is the noble load of the spirit, / With which Love *touches* the loving soul" (P12: 3. 158).

Hadewijch also describes times when Love becomes unreliable, whimsical, and arbitrary: "Love . . . has so stirred with her deep *touch* / That he feels himself wholly in Love, / When she also fills him with the wondrous *taste* of Love . . . / On one she adroitly tries her tricks, / Saying: 'I am all yours, and you are all mine!' / On another she rushes so swiftly / that she *touches* him and breaks his heart" (P38: 6. 239); "How would it help if I longed for her *touch*, / Since our behavior keeps us ever poor?" (P11: 7. 157); "What must I – poor woman – do? / Before it came to this point, / Alas, *utinam* [would that] / Her *touch* had been death to me!" (P15: 3. 166); and, more sadly, "But what is *bitter* to me above all / Is that I cannot *touch* you" (P43: 5. 251).

And she mourns the times when Love's touch and taste become so hard as to hurt: "In those whom *Love blesses with her wounds* / And to whom she shows the vastness knowable in her, / Longing keeps the wounds open and undressed, / Because Love stormily inflames them; / If these souls shudder at remaining unhealed, / That fails to surprise us" (P14: 12. 164); "Before the All unites itself to the all, / *Sour bitterness must be tasted.* / Love comes and consoles us; she goes away and *knocks us down.* / This initiates our adventure" (P17: 13. 175); and "She can according to her pleasure, / Adroitly fence under the shield, / *Inflicting wounds* from which no one can recover" (P39: 6. 241).

The embodied, physical nature of Hadewijch's wounding in love is poignantly illustrated in some of her visions. To live in a body is to suffer with Christ *in his humanity* in order to be one with him in his divinity (L6; see also Bynum 1987). Hadewijch never tires of preaching that *without conformity to Christ's humanity, conformity to divinity is not possible.* Hadewijch sees conformity to Christ's humanity as the motive force behind leading a virtuous life. She exhorts her readers "to live Christ" in the fullest sense, participating with the totality of one's being in the totality of Christ. Each mystery of Christ's life – annunciation, nativity, the flight into Egypt,[20] pain, poverty, ignominy, being forsaken yet remaining compassionate – is an invitation to imitate him, to enter into comparable experiences in our own lives (Dreyer 1989: 51–2). In Vision 1 Christ says to Hadewijch, "If you wish to be like me in my Humanity, . . . you will desire to be poor, miserable, and despised by all men" (288).

Being conformed to Christ's humanity, however, was not all misery. In the prologue to Vision 7, Hadewijch describes having a vision at dawn: "My heart and my veins and all my limbs trembled and quivered with eager desire . . . such madness and fear beset my mind . . . so that dying I must go mad, and going mad I must die" (280).[21] Here Hadewijch conveys beyond doubt that she experienced the human person of Jesus as a man. Her descriptions leave little unsaid about the passionate nature of her love affair with the God-man, but she refuses to let go of either the divine or the human in God. The truth of both is found in one single fruition, a unity evident in many of her descriptions. In Vision 7 she says:

> I desired to have full fruition of my Beloved, and to understand and taste him to the full. I desired that his Humanity should to the fullest extent be one in fruition with my humanity, and mine then should hold its stand and be strong enough to enter into perfection until I content him, who is perfection itself, by purity and unity, and in all things to content him fully in every virtue. To that end I wished he might content me interiorly with his Godhead in one spirit and that for me he should be all that he is, without withholding anything from me.

These are not the words of a disembodied woman. For many medieval women, the occasion for such intimate union with Christ was the reception of communion during the Eucharist. In Vision 7 Hadewijch offers a powerfully erotic description of her experience of this union: "After that he came himself to me, took me entirely in his arms, and pressed me to him; and all my members felt his in full felicity, in accordance with the desire of my heart and my humanity. So I was outwardly satisfied and fully transported." And after a while, losing sight of the outward manly beauty, Hadewijch begins to merge with her Beloved: "Then it was to me as if we were one without difference."

Hadewijch's poetry vividly conveys how her entire being, body and soul alike, ached to please the Beloved. Persons in love understand this desire clearly, says Dreyer (1989: 58). In all forms of intense love, the lover wants nothing more than to have the beloved enjoy whatever gives him/her happiness. In turn, the lover experiences great joy when he/she is able to content the loved one. The human sexual relationship is often taken as a paradigm of passion, because when it is authentic it involves a drive to know the other that can extend and stretch to embrace the whole of living and of God. Because by its very nature the sexual relationship contains conditions for its own development toward wholeness, we often think of sexual (or nuptial) relationships when we think of body in relation to our spiritual lives.

But the experiences of Hadewijch and Mairi point to a second, simultaneous paradigm of marriage and/or mating, which (after Winnicott) I think of as a personalisation of indwelling spirit in body as soul. This deeply inner event takes place in a landscape of interiority – according to Hadewijch, in soul's abyss. The essence of this "incarnation" requires a tension between the Human and Divine, between the longing for God and the total otherness of God, that allows a "third" space to open, and this "third" finds expression in Hadewijch's Trinitarian mysticism.

Trinitarian thought is to theology as symbolic thought is to psychology. In Hadewijch's conception of the doctrine of the Trinity resides, says Hart, a mysterious parallel "between the structure of our spiritual life and the Trinitarian life in the very bosom of the Divine Being" (Hadewijch 1980: 10–11). To Hadewijch the Trinity demonstrates that:

> God gave us his Nature in the soul, with three powers whereby to love his Three Persons: with enlightened reason, the Father; with the memory, the wise Son of God; and with the high flaming will, the Holy Spirit. This was the gift that his Nature gave ours to love him with. (L22: 137. 97)

To me, Hadewijch's insights into these parallels between the structure of spiritual life and the Trinity mark a turning in her unconsciously psycho-spiritual development. Her "turn" toward a feminine inclusivity points to a transformation in the quality of her consciousness, just as it did for Mairi. Hadewijch's capacity for insight can be imagined as an event, a "turn" from either/or (either God or the world, either joy or pain, either presence or absence) to both/and – *both* opposites, yes, and something more. From a religious point of view, "something more" happens when Hadewijch discovers in her "being-one" with Love *an unacceptable contradiction which nevertheless she must embrace*: Love is unpredictable and cruel: there are, in experience of the fruitive being-one, dark and empty places. For Mairi, there was fear and terror. How to come to terms with this?

Hadewijch's poetry offers successful attempts to clarify this contradiction (is it only in poetry that such an attempt can be made?) As Mommaers characterizes Hadewijch's experience, no matter how dark the territory wherein she loses her way in her adventure with Love, she (relying on her experience) wishes "to place a few beacons" (her poems?) to let it be seen that in the "strange tricks" of Love, meaning is hidden, and that *there exists a form of experience that is capable of integrating the being-absent of the Beloved* (1980: xix, emphasis mine). Hadewijch comes to embrace both the presence and absence of Love with gratitude by detaching herself from her desire for either one. "Since I gave myself to Love's service, / Whether I lose or win, / I am resolved: / I will always give her thanks, / Whether I lose or win; / I will stand in her power" (P30: 3. 212–13). Placing herself beyond her attachment to Love in a prescribed form (i.e., as absent or present, as loving or cruel), Hadewijch willingly chooses to remain in Love's power.

That the basic problem in Hadewijch's poems is not the absence of God but the alternation of the presence and absence of the Beloved is arresting: "That she who knows herself to be experientially united in Love must live in taking and giving, that is the riddle," says Mommaers (1980: xvii). Hadewijch herself says (P5: 7. 141), "Sometimes indulgent and sometimes harsh, / Sometimes dark and sometimes bright: / In liberating consolation, in coercive fear, / In accepting and in giving, / Must they who are / Knight-errants in Love / Always live here below."

The important point here is that the taste of the Other, earlier limited to moments of consolation (experiences of fruitive "being-one"), now also includes misery. Yet this very painful experience is the point and will bring her through. In Hadewijch's words, "I must then live out what I am" (P22: 1. 186). Here Hadewijch demonstrates the feminine mode's ability to integrate opposites, whether presence or absence, or – in psychological terms – the "dark side" of the Self. Says Hadewijch of her arrival in this new place, "The madness of love / Is a rich fief; / Anyone who recognized this / Would not ask Love for anything else; / It can unite opposites / And reverse the paradox. / I am declaring the truth about this: / The madness of love makes bitter what was sweet, / It makes the stranger a kinsman, / And it makes the smallest the proudest" (P28: 4. 206).[22]

Often Hadewijch expresses her remarkable embrace of paradox in words where the landscape of the soul (interiority) turns itself inside out, just as Mairi experienced the outer and the inner becoming one. In a kind of reverse gestalt, and in order to appease a longing which can never be appeased, height becomes depth and mountains become valleys.[23] This also bring to mind Bly's (1996) comments on "vertical thinking," with its implied capacity for soaring and tumbling both. "Alas, if your mountains were valleys / And we could then see / Our journey toward you pressed to the end, / All would be well with us" (P21: 2. 183); or "We find valleys in Love's heights; / Whoever finds heights in these valleys / Is of rich insight" (P23: 7. 191; or "Now we forsake Love's high mansion for the valley . . . the deeper sunk in Love, the higher ascended . . . the deeper wounded, the easier cured" (P27: 6. 7. 204–5).

The demand for full-grownness, which I read as the capacity to integrate such opposites, resounds in many places throughout Hadewijch's work, but it never means that she forgoes her longing for fruitive being-one or that she would prefer to lead an ordinary Christian life without mystical experience. It means that she understands that her conception of the being-one and her manner of experience must be *enlarged* (Mommaers 1980: xxi). In her *living* of oneness, Hadewijch must stretch to integrate elements that at first sight would seem to vanish in the "being-one." Here again is paradox: Hadewijch's enlightenment consists of insight into her relation to God, which falls to her lot only in fruitive experiences of being-one, which she herself must dismiss as only "*aids* to becoming fully-grown." Hadewijch learns that she must learn to do without experiences of "being-one," while realizing that she never could have come to this very realization without them. Here Hadewijch stretches to integrate positive attitudes and understanding toward her misery; to willingly embrace her suffering, caused by Love's absence, right alongside her joy in Love's presence.

In some passages, fruitive "being-one" with God is associated with a total absence of will, indeed with an absence even of a self to have a will.[24] Such an absence of personal will and a self which could have individual desires can advocate apparent impassivity and an unusual indifference to personal fate. Yet Hadewijch insists that the mystic continue to do good, simply relinquishing any sense of personal involvement in the outcome – an existential example of "living without a why." "Do good in all things. But do not care about success, neither about blessing nor about cursing, nor about salvation, nor about torment, but do and leave undone all things for the sake of love's honor" (L2: 14. 49).

Such detachment is intended to lead to an aspect of union which Hadewijch considers potentially and ideally a permanent state of being rather than a fleeting experience. Eventually, she suggests, the mystic is to lose even awareness of God, for being so closely united involves the loss of consciousness of the other and even of the sweetness of union. When this happens, paradox looms. Moments of fruitive "being-one" come to an end and the mystic (Hadewijch) moves into the world to "live Love" in a different fashion, no longer relying on unitive experience. Now the mystic experiences a fuller union in Love's absence. A "great Voice" tells Hadewijch, "Your great privation of Love has given you the highest way in fruition of me" (V8: 33. 283).

From a psychological point of view, the *enlarged form of experience* into which Hadewijch's consciousness expands can be seen as entrance into a state (painful *and* joyful) in which she recognizes the Other not only as object (not-me) but as Subject, implying a capacity for a dimension of consciousness similar to the psychological inter-subjectivity described by Benjamin (1988). This is not to say that soul is a capacity for inter-subjectivity, but to say that soul defines a state of being in which the reality of the Other as subject may be fully received, right alongside an experience of self as subject. Our capacity for inter-subjectivity opens into the depths of human interiority as if it were a country to be shared with others *and* the

Other, both without and within. Inter-subjective theory postulates that the other (or the Other) must be recognized as another subject (as Subject, rather than Object) in order for the self to fully experience his or her own subjectivity *in the other's presence* (Benjamin 1992: 45).

While the psyche tends toward subject–object awareness and differentiation, we cannot begin to relate to the subjectivity of another from a point of self–other differentiation, for within self–other differentiation the reference is always back to either/or, "me" or "not-me." Psyche, too, speaks a language of mirroring and reflection, identification and personification. But the reality of the Other as Subject (rather than object) is not something we can reflect upon or even perceive. It is something that we affectively sense, touch, and experience, as Hadewijch did, from the depths of inspired flesh, and within the depths of soul. In the state of soul, inter-subjectivity happens. Soul receives the secret, the hidden knowledge, of the subjectivity of the object. Soul experiences the other as wholly Other, sufficient unto itself. In its knowledge of the "otherness" of the Other, and of the unfathomability of the Subject, as well as one's subjectivity, soul deepens even into an abyss of "unfaith," says Hadewijch, "which greatly enlarges consciousness" (L8: 27. 65). A state of soul – a state of being wherein this enlargement of consciousness happens – makes Hadewijch's imagery for the ineffable character of such union without difference strikingly appropriate.

Union without difference happens in barren wilderness (as in Mairi's angel dream), in the desert, in the ocean or the abyss – in a space potently symbolic of indistinguishable merger, especially the mutual abyss of soul, through which God and the soul realize their final mutual lack of distinction and mutual liberty to Be. Then, as now, the ineffable character of union without difference made it profitable to suggest aspects of its mysterious reality in symbolic form, rather than trying to fix it in concepts or essentialist language, which ultimately tend to betray the very thing they attempt to serve: thus the relevance of spontaneously inclusive, poetic, personal, particular and familiar (vernacular) forms of the feminine mode of expression.

With Hadewijch's "turn" into a quality of consciousness that can participate in both the presence and absence of the Other, as well as in joy and suffering, a potential capacity for fully human consciousness comes into being. I am supposing that Hadewijch would have called this the "full-grownness"[25] toward which she lived. Integrating what Jung later points to as the light and dark sides of the Other as God, Hadewijch's stand is amazingly mature. Jung would have us recognize that on an experiential level, soul always needs an "I" and a "you" in order to be whole, while on a collective level, the presence, or the experience of soul, describes a dimension of being which enables a "spirit of the age" to make way for a "spirit of the depths." Hadewijch would have us shape our lives on the rhythm of the Trinitarian parallels she sees, turning outward in the activity of the virtues and inward again into union with God. Hadewijch points to a parallel between the Trinity and our spiritual life. She points to both the *contrast and the union* between the ways in which we strive to serve God in the Divine Persons as we strive for the different virtues, and the times when – established by Love in simplicity – we only love, and the virtues flow from the fullness and unity of life of themselves.

> This is how we court the Beloved. As long as we do not possess him we must serve him with all the virtues. But when we are admitted to intimacy with the Beloved himself, all the things by which service was previously carried on must be excluded and banished from remembrance . . . As long as we serve in order to attain Love, we must attend to this service. But when we love the Beloved with love, we must exclude all the rest and have fruition of Love with all the promptings of our heart and all the surrender of our being, and stand ready to receive the exceptional wisdom the loving soul can win in love. For this the powers of our soul and all the veins of our mind must always stand ready, and toward it our eyes must always gaze; and all the floods of the sweet flood shall all flow through and into one another. So must love live in Love. (L21: 35–40. 94)

The difference between serving in order to attain Love and Hadewijch's definition of Loving the Beloved points to what I have called a hinge in our experience, or what Hadewijch calls the "glue": "If two things are to become one, nothing may be between them except the glue wherewith they are united together. That bond of glue is Love, whereby God and the blessed soul are united in oneness" (L16: 28. 80). Analogously, I have pointed to a parallel between Trinity and our psychological life: to both the *contrast* (when we are separating self from other into self–other awareness and differentiation) and *the union* (when we become able to regard the object as Subject and begin to love reality outside ourselves), and between an enabling therapeutic situation in which physical, psychological and emotional scope are engendered by the emergence of embodied personhood and fully human consciousness.[26]

With the soul's abyss as the site of suffering affection for both the presence and absence of Love, Hadewijch found the paradoxical "third" place where both "being one" with God and "being herself" were joined like the figure eight on its side, symbolizing infinity and, for the mystic, the infinite dimensions of selfhood (see Mairi's dream, "Ordeal by Spiders"). Says Hadewijch, "the Truth of both the Humanity and the Divinity is in one single fruition" (L6: 117. 59). Here the mysteries of body and mind, psyche and soul are conjoined in quantum fashion, forever separate yet conjoined. Times of merger and "being one" are not ends in themselves but only a means to "full-grownupness". There is no winning through to experience of "being-one" in the soul's abyss without participation of the *whole* person – of all that one is, affect and intellect, body and soul, in an all-out, no-holds-barred capacity for an experience of Love "with all thy might, with all thy heart, with all thy soul," and with all thy body, too.

The apex of mystical experience, of "being-one," consisted not at all in Hadewijch's disappearance in God, still less in ecstatic or fruitive experience. Hadewijch insisted that *being-one with God demanded of her that she be herself.* For Hadewijch, experience must not, exclusively or by preference, aim at the Godhead. She must also – and at the same time – be able to taste everything that belongs to her concrete humanity. "I have integrated all my diversity," says Hadewijch, "and I have *individualized* all my wholeness" (L28: 242, Hadewijch 1980: 113, emphasis mine).

Hadewijch and the feminine

Let us review what "the feminine" encompasses from a psychological point of view. In my commentary on the image of the Lunar Tree (Mairi's Dream #20), I characterized the feminine according to Winnicott's (1971) ideas of female elements of being and A. Ulanov's (1971, 1981) feminine modes of being. I suggested that the feminine has to do with being-at-the-core-of-oneself (Ulanov 1981: 77) as opposed to a more instinct-backed, masculine mode of doing. Whereas the feminine always refers to the relation of men to women (Jung's understanding of the *function* of the anima), it also refers to the relation of women to women, and the relation of women to aspects of themselves *as* women. In A. Ulanov's words, (Ulanov & Ulanov 1989: 134) the feminine refers especially to what seems to be a pattern of relationship that answers the question, how is being received through "Eros life?" Its hallmark is a capacity and a willingness to receive being, to be-with-being (135). The feminine refers to

> a style of openness, a dimension of being that involves the flesh of life – the spirit unmistakably caught up in the flesh, not the spirit abstracted into thought-forms. The flesh of life means the body and the imagination, means an emphasis upon elements of play, of delight and simple *openness to what is there* [i.e., *presence, especially presence of the other*] in contrast to what we feel should be or think we need or wish to be. The feminine symbolizes a style of being and doing, of thinking and relating, both actively and passively, that takes the downward-going road into the dark origins of things, into the felt impact of thought and of images out of which we abstract conceptions. Here our knowing acts by being one with and our doing is anchored in and arises out of antecedent being . . . Such knowing and doing strongly accent *immediate participation* . . . an experience in which a sense of nearness may overcome reflection . . as one gets all mixed up in things . . . The sense of self here arises from

> identity with others . . . the feminine can be called *an animating con-*
> *nection, a link that conveys, confers, and connects to being, making us feel*
> *alive and real*, and for the sake of which we can betray, bear guilt, even
> die. (Ulanov & Ulanov 1989: 135, emphases mine)

I quote Ulanov at length because she is articulate about an aspect of human
existence which in essence resists and withdraws from most efforts to
conceptualize it. The feminine resists whatever seeks to abstract and define
its essential characteristics and then generalize, or apply generalizations to
"all women or to narrowing specific acts and thoughts of the 'feminine'"
(Ulanov & Ulanov 1989: 143). The feminine has to do with the psyche, and
with images and imagination as Jung understands images – as "life," in
contrast to the coined and negotiable values of concepts. The feminine has
to do with body and body awareness, with soul and with a capacity to dive
deep enough to find soul. The feminine has to do with self-transformation
when self-transformation includes receptivity to religious experience and a
capacity to participate in a relation to God.

In Hadewijch's time, concepts of masculine and feminine were more
interchangeable than they are in our world and gender roles shifted fluidly.
Hadewijch easily refers to herself as a woman but she also knows herself as
a knight, a lover, and a fighter. In Vision 1: 172, for example, a voice
addresses her, saying, "O strongest of warrioresses, you have conquered
everything and opened the closed totality, which was never opened by
creatures who did not know, with painfully won and distressed love, how I
am God and Man!" In addition to *Minne*, or Lady Love – the major image
of the feminine in Hadewijch's work (especially in her poetry) – Hadewijch
had other thoughts about being a woman and she expressed these thoughts
imagistically.

The image of warrioress suggests that Hadewijch thought of the feminine
principle as anything but passive: receptive, yes, enduring, yes, persevering,
yes, but passive? No. Focusing on Hadewijch's notion of Love from the
point of view of the strength and intensity of passion, Dreyer (1989: 81 n.
45) muses upon how the mystical experience is always spoken of as passive,
as something that *happens* to us; in this sense, mystical experience *is* passive,
and relates female elements of being to receptivity, openness to what is, and
enfleshed spirituality. However, the passive nature of mystical experience is
anything but lifeless or apathetic. Hadewijch's writings convey unstinting
emotional ("fiery fierceness") and physical activity in cooperating with the
gift of union with God. The relation of a warrioress to God requires
courage, dedication and endurance, no matter the gender of the person who
wins through.

Other feminine figures imply similar courage and perseverance. After the
importance of the Trinity Hadewijch honors Mary for her causal role in the
Incarnation: "The Father in the beginning / Kept his Son, Love, / Hidden

in his bosom, / Until Mary, / With deep humility indeed, / In a mysterious way disclosed him to us. / Then the mountain flowed down into the deep valley / And that valley flowed aloft to the height of the palace, / Then was the castle conquered / Over which long combat had taken place" (P29: 5. 209). "Mountain" here means God, and valley means Mary, while palace, I think, refers to the divinity.[26]

Poem 2 of the *Mengeldichten* states simply that the most powerful of all things is woman. There, to symbolize the power of woman, Hadewijch substitutes for an heroic woman of familiar legend the Virgin Mary and the strength of her humility. In Poem 3 Mary appears under the title, "Mother of Love," and Poem 14 develops the theme that the devout soul must become the mother of Christ.[27] In Hadewijch's thought, we are instructed to carry God's Son "maternally" (L30: 200). Hadewijch also has a unique perspective on Reason, whom she depicts as feminine and addresses as "Queen" (V9: 285). She does not disdain Reason but describes it as noble, as that part of a person that is renewed and enlightened as a result of ecstatic, affective mystical experience. In the image of Queen Reason a feminine image stands for wholeness and completion. For Hadewijch, reason is one of soul's faculties (just as for Mairi, psyche is one of the soul's faculties). Like a stern but loving mother, Queen Reason oversees both Hadewijch's wholeness as a person and an illumination of the soul's abyss. Reason has the all-important function of keeping one's eyes on the truth:

> Lightning is the light of Love, which shows her in one flash and confers grace in many things, in order to show who Love is and how she can receive and give . . . Thunder is the fearful voice of threat and it is retraction; and *it is enlightened reason which holds before us the truth, and our debt, and our failure to grow up to conformity with Love, and our smallness compared to Love's greatness.* (L30: 155–62)

(When I read this passage I thought of Mairi's dream of lightning tearing apart the tent on the mountaintop at night, #7.)

Hadewijch is not naive about the possible risk to Love that Reason brings, but she knows that Love without Reason is incomplete (Dreyer 1989). Reason is like a mirror reflecting truly, even if we are pained by what we see. Reason reminds Hadewijch that she is human and therefore not capable of experiencing the fullness of Love for which she hungers. Reason teaches Hadewijch to live the truth and has a key role in the process of discernment, so important to the spiritual life (L24: 1). Playing a part in the highest mystical experience, Queen Reason throws light on the transcendence of God, and thereby she herself becomes enlightened.

Because Reason illuminates the entire abyss of Love (P19: 4. 177), it is through Reason's intervention that Hadewijch learns to love God in God's independence and wholly being-Other (Mommaers 1980: xvii). Placing her experience of mystical love within the context of truth and the totality of the human person, Hadewijch knows that it is the whole person who lives, loves, thinks, and makes decisions. If love is cordoned off from other aspects of existence, love cannot be authentic. Here Hadewijch's attitude reflects the feminine element of being as regal as a queen who seeks to reign completely over all parts, not just a chosen few. Nevertheless, Hadewijch does not covet Reason and what Reason brings her for herself. She knows that Reason is a gift, and prays that all those who love may win Reason's favor. Hadewijch writes, "In winning the favor of Reason / Lies for us the whole perfection of Love" (P30: 15. 215). Although the pearl of great price is Love, Love without Reason is ripe for deception. "She [Reason] herself is Love's surgeonness: / She can best heal all faults against her" (P25: 9. 199). I understand Hadewijch's respect for Reason as another example of her capacity for fully human consciousness, her balanced ability for both/and thinking. She presents Love as the best and highest way to approach God, but not without Reason.

In discarding what psychology might call rationalizations for living in a certain fashion,[29] Hadewijch's Beguine notion of "living without a why" never dismisses Reason itself. Queen Reason even makes it clear why "living without a why" is so important. Reason brings understanding to Hadewijch's experience of passion and leads Hadewijch to see the point, the goal of Love. Reason also makes it possible to receive the completion or fruition of Love, and – because Reason reflects the Son – to know (to become conscious of) how this is so, even when the counsel of Reason seems confusing or cruel.

Soul and self-transformation

To envision what Hadewijch tells us soul is like (rather than "what soul is") is to enter another country. Her descriptions of soul's terrain are astonishing. Murk-Jansen (1998) characterizes the Beguines as "brides of the desert," and Hadewijch paints for us a glimpse of a desert beyond imagination in which wilderness is both a metaphor for soul's essential nature and the locus of meeting between God and the soul. We glimpse how pure love might exist: in a wild "overcoming" or "crossing over" which becomes an example of *mors mystica* or mystical death. Nudity, purity, simplicity and unity are synonyms, which indicate the *telos* of soul's process of self-annihilation (Dietrich 1994). In the country of soul, the poor in spirit live in unity and emptiness in a vast, wild, simplicity without beginning or end, beyond form, modality, reason and sense, beyond the mental operations of imagination, thought and contemplation, beyond all knowledge, in a boundless desert, an abyss of soul. Stripped of all images, Hadewijch's soul recovers simple unity.

With the fierce intensity of her language Hadewijch pours herself and her readers into this country as if we, too, were to be melted like the wax of Psalm 22. She *shows* us how this vast wilderness is simultaneously the soul's own recovered primal nature and how "living Love" means living a manifest/unmanifest openness and emptiness beyond space and time, "without a why." She demonstrates how soul is the locus of unmediated union with the abyss, the desert, and the ocean of the Godhead in its primal nature. Her descriptions are chilling and awesome: "I was in a very depressed frame of mind one Christmas night, when I was taken up in the spirit. There I saw a very deep whirlpool, wide and exceedingly dark; in this abyss all beings were included, crowded together and compressed. The darkness illuminated and penetrated everything" (V11: 1. 289).

In union, Hadewijch tells us, the soul swallowed up in God returns to her origins, to where and how she was *before she was created* – without distinction in God, the source of all creation: *become nothing*. Good becomes goodness, the will becomes willingness, into forgetful annihilation. In becoming nothing, the soul goes beyond the feminine modality, too. The soul is conscious of nothing except God whose will is her life. Thus it is that being *without* God is also directly associated with union. Hadewijch speaks of the need to be free of love (God), and of Love's satisfaction when this is achieved. She acknowledges the loss involved in giving up the sweet consciousness of close association. Yet the need to do without a sense of the presence of God is associated with the most intense union, with being drawn utterly into Love. Precisely those who are received by Love, drawn into her utterly, are those who owe it to Love wholly to fulfill her by doing without the fulfillment of union. For Hadewijch, the union which she is dedicated to achieving and towards which she urges her audience is a terrifying paradox of *experiencing fulfillment only when embracing and welcoming the reality of an eternal lack of fulfillment*. Descriptions like this enable us to peer with Hadewijch over the edge of the abyss and feel something of the awe she describes as she looks into the dark, swirling vortex which is the reality of her experience of union with God: "And in the middle under the disc (the seat of God), a whirlpool revolved in such a frightful manner, and was so terrible to see that heaven and earth might have been astonished and made fearful by it" (VI: 214, 267).

The only reason Hadewijch can "speak" these descriptions is because in becoming fully herself she has been carried far beyond her "original measure" and stretched to conceive of that which is inconceivable. I am using "conceive" here in the sense of giving birth to, rather than conceptualize. Soul is a gift, says Hadewijch, given to us by God, with which we are to love God. And in loving God, soul undoes itself. Soul becomes a country, a wilderness of flesh. Soul becomes a way, a solitude, and an abyss. Soul consists of detachment and bare being, an initiation into liberty and nothingness. The only way this happens is that God "gave us His Nature in the soul" (L22: 137).

Hadewijch is clear that the greatness of the soul is beyond opposites (like Love and Reason, L18: 1. 85). She also tells us that coming to full growth happens by way of wisdom, but that wisdom is only a way, and not "it," i.e., Love (L18: 154. 87–8). In self-transformation, Hadewijch discovers, affection comes into power, and this is what hinders us from knowing the other as Other. She has discovered that in our "tasting" of the other there always hides an insidious tasting of ourselves. In other words, Hadewijch discovers what Mairi came to know as psychological projection. But in full-grownupness (in becoming transformed), Hadewijch finds a form of experience that is no longer determined by self-feeling, and her experience oddly parallels Mairi's differentiation of psyche from soul. For Hadewijch, her discovery did not mean that the inexplicable alternation of Love's giving and taking (presence and absence) was removed. Nor did misery, as if by magic, no longer cause pain. What *did* happen, thanks to a process of cruel alternation,[30] was that there regularly came to Hadewijch a free ability to look at the Other, as if this ability to see the other *as* Other were being honed, or forged, out of the fires of passion itself.

There came a point when Hadewijch discovered that Love *is*, apart from what she felt of Love; a point when she tasted Love without there being a taste left over; when she gazed upon Love without feeling herself see. There came a point when projection, withdrawn, enabled her eager interest in the Other, who had summoned forth the projection in the first place. When this state was reached, the simple alternation of joy and pain in "loving" Love became insufficient. Hadewijch describes an experience of recognition so complete and profound that it is impossible to say what is recognized. That is why it is experienced as a "gap," an abyss, so content-less that the person recoils. Passion is the thrust that leaps that void in a leap of faith without guarantee or even knowledge. The leap is not primarily emotional, although powerful emotion is released by it. The breakthrough of passion is a self-giving toward wholeness that is intensely desired, but across a gap of unknowing. This is what makes it passionate. This is what makes it difficult. This is what brings pain. Outgrowing her "original measure," Hadewijch stretched beyond affective caring one way or the other, into the farthest reaches of the country of soul.

Some writers suggest that Hadewijch's endurance of this paradoxical state of being refers us to a mystical gift which enabled her to abstract herself from the concrete situation in which she moved, raising herself interiorly above what touched her sensibilities. Paul Mommaers suggests that this gift speaks to a "higher" fruition, which in a "spiritual" manner compensated Hadewijch for pain in body and feeling. But I do not think so. I do not think that Hadewijch for a single moment supposed that Christ on earth escapes from the full desolation of the human condition. Nor would she. Soul bore the pain in body and in feeling, enabling Hadewijch to bear what was unbearable. She did not use her spiritual wisdom to compensate this deprivation. This deprivation was her spiritual wisdom, because it represented the quintessential reality of the human condition.

Hadewijch's address to a paradoxical site of soul, a transformation from one state into another (from soul into soul's abyss?), parallels, I believe, Mairi's emphatic differentiation of psyche from soul. Hadewijch moved from an initial state of "fruitive" consolation into a state which – for the sake of the Other – encompassed the possibility of presence and absence both. From there, Hadewijch progressed into a third state of being, a paradoxical embrace of body and soul that enabled her to taste embodiment to the full, experiencing her incarnate physical body as a container of life *and* an abyss of soul, in touch with the body of Christ.

A human body, a human person, is in creation, enmeshed with it totally – as, from the moment of his conception, Jesus was in creation. Likewise, it is *in* creation that the extraordinary leap that Hadewijch describes happens, just as it is *in the world* that extraordinary transformation occurs. "O wonderful exchange," writes the twelfth-century Cistercian Guerric of Igny in his *Christmas Sermons*: ". . . you take flesh and give divinity, a commerce in charity . . . emptying yourself, you have filled us. You have poured into men all the plenitude of your divinity. You have transformed but not confounded" (quoted in Haughton 1981). This genuine Christian insight brings human beings into union with God not by dissolving in Him or dissolving Him in them, but by bringing human persons to a glory of distinctness through an exchange of Love with the "one adored substitution." Hadewijch's insight was similar. As she struggled with soul's capacity to receive that plenitude of being for which she longed, a plenitude of Being which was far beyond the bounds of any human imagination, Hadewijch found that soul itself becomes a country of no return.

Endurance of such a paradoxical state is the wedding of soul to body, of personalisation embodied and engraved with indwelling spirit. Endurance (and understanding) of this paradoxical self-state transformed Hadewijch's self-feeling – which heretofore had hindered her from knowing the other as Other – and enabled her to exercise her full capacity for love in a context of inter-subjectivity. Hadewijch uses a Dutch word, *ongherijnlec* (unmoved, unmovable, unaffected, untouched, or impassive, i.e., detached), to describe how soul *is*, once the hidden, insidious tasting of self has gone (L19: 4. 6. 89–90): "The soul which is most untouched is the most like God. Keep yourself untouched by all men in heaven and on earth until the day when God is lifted up above the earth and draws you and all things to himself (John 12: 32)."

In order to be like God, the soul becomes impassive and without desire. For Hadewijch, this state was a means to union with God. Yet such impassivity to earthly events and personal fate also simply describes "living without a why." It does not contradict the emphasis laid elsewhere in Hadewijch's writings on the need for passionate desire for God. Rather, it suggests that only one who is as though "dead to the world" is able to concentrate her love and desire sufficiently on God to see Him (Murk-Jansen 1998: 27). Like Mairi, Hadewijch discovered that soul is a state of being, a location of being which is deeper than (and prior to?) psyche, self-feeling and projection. In becoming fully-grown, Hadewijch's "original measure" was transformed into an extension of experience and a capacity for love that cannot be embraced by human understanding.

Notes

1 When I read of Hadewijch's life, I wondered whether her end-of-life experience was comparable to that of Thomas Aquinas. Near the end of his life, Thomas said to a friend, "I have seen things that make all my writings seem like straw." Certainly Mairi's visionary experience rearranged the priorities of her inner world. We have no evidence of later visions for Hadewijch, but I suspect that for both her and Thomas, religion as ethics, ritual, dogma, scripture, institution and social action were understood to be secondary, and in the long run counted for less, relative to visionary experience.

2 Barfield 1953: 170.

3 The Troubadours fundamentally changed the western conception of love between men and women, says Mommaers (1988: 59). Contemporary with this social revolution was a religious upheaval, a "return to the apostles," a movement in which poverty and the announcement of glad tidings were taken upon oneself in which women played a major role. The troubadours referred to an unheard-of form of love that laid the ground for *trouvere* poetry and the ideals of courtly love. Mommaers' description of an "unheard-of interior state in which dream and reality are combined" resembles what I describe as a dream-in-the-world. Having emerged more fully into collective consciousness over the centuries, this state of combined dream-and-reality is no longer "unheard-of," but it is still elusive.

4 Paris, *Chronica Majora*, iv. 278, quoted in Southern 1970: 319–22.

5 The precise origins of the name are obscure. Some, like Paris, assumed that the origins were unknown. Others, including the authors of rules for Beguinage, claimed that it was derived from the name of a supposed founder of the movement. Still others, more sympathetic, suggest that the word comes from the Latin *benignus* (the kind, liberal, or bounteous), or – because the women burned with pious zeal – "quasi bono igne ignitate." At any rate, by the time the Beguines used the word of themselves (around the middle of the thirteenth century), any pejorative meaning it had, including its Albigensian implications, must have faded.

6 In June 1310 the Beguine Marguerite Porete was burned at the stake for disseminating her work *Le Mirouer des Simples Ames* (*The Mirror of Simple Souls*). Two years later the Church at the Council of Vienne used the same articles that had been used to prove her guilty of heresy to condemn the whole Beguine movement as heretical. The posthumous condemnation of Meister Eckhart followed (1329).

7 While Hadewijch did not in fact advocate a deviant teaching (Mommaers 1988), we cannot be sure whether she was arrested or not, or persecuted as a heretic.

Her allusions – "whether I am wandering in the country or put in prison" (L29: 1) – are hypothetical. But she complains repeatedly that she was forced to wander and be separated from her own kind.

8 The heresy trials of Porete and Eckhart focused especially on the fact that they had spoken in the vernacular of matters too profound for the laity to comprehend (Murk-Jansen 1998: 30).

9 While researching the life of Hadewijch I roamed through some of these places in Europe, journeying up to the coast of the North Sea to get a sense of the land through which Hadewijch most probably made her way so many centuries earlier. There at the coast, my husband and I took shelter in a restaurant during an extraordinary thunderstorm, flashing and roaring over the North Sea. I looked through my postcard pictures of women making lace, purchased at one of those Beguinages, and pondered Hadewijch's life.

10 Hadewijch has been variously situated in Brussels, Antwerp, Bruges and Nivelles. The dialect in which she wrote was Brabant, named for a district in Flanders now central to Belgium. The main source for all Hadewijch scholarship is Jozef van Mierlo, who edited her entire corpus, and Mother Columba Hart, my major resource for Hadewijch's works in English. All page numbers referring to quotations from Hadewijch's works in this Chapter refer to Hart's *Hadewijch: The Complete Works*, 1980.

11 SUNY Series, State University of New York Press, Howard Eilberg-Schwartz, Editor.

12 Personal conversation. The fact that Hadewijch gladly declared that Love is fulfilled in unfulfillment, or that those who are loved with an eternal love "are never seized by the ground of Love, just as they can never seize what they love" (L12: 40. 70–1), or "Consolation and ill-treatment both at once / This is the essence of the taste of Love" (P31: 4. 217), is almost unimaginable without attributing the paradoxical dissonance of these words to Hadewijch's ability to see (as did Dante) beyond tragedy to a black yet divine comedy inherent in the entire situation.

13 Vernacular theology's distinguishing mark was linguistic expression in medieval vernacular tongues. Latin, the learned second language (in addition to a "mother" tongue, e.g., French, German, etc.) of the clerical and educated male hierarchy of Hadewijch's time was not totally closed to women, but difficult for all but a few to gain access to it in a substantial fashion. With vernacular language, men and women began on the same footing, as they do today with dreams and the grammar of the psyche.

14 Modern hermeneutics teaches us how great a role language plays in all thinking. The language through which any form of experience is born into expression, particularly psychological or theological reflection, is an essential part of what gets expressed.

15 The mystical message of Hadewijch appears potentially universal, accessible to any Christian who truly seeks to love God. For Hadewijch, a new awareness of God was not restricted to the clerical elite of the schools but available to women and men of every walk of life. For a Beguine, finding one's ground in the depths of the godhead did not require adopting a traditional religious way of life, especially not one that involved fleeing from the world.

16 See Otto, *The Idea of the Holy*, 1958; Otto's ideas and these terms are discussed earlier.

17 All forty-five of Hadewijch's *Poems in Stanzas* are in the tradition of courtly love. The imagery of courtly love – the unattainable lover, the submissive service to love, the complaints, hope and despair, the all-pervading power of love –

provides the poems with a strong thematic link which takes on a new, existential spiritual significance in Hadewijch. The "lady" in the courtly love tradition becomes God or Love to whom the soul offers the service of love. At times Hadewijch becomes the knight-errant, courting dangers and adventures for Love's sake (Dreyer 1989: 46).

18 De Paepe even distinguishes three basic moments in Hadewijch's experience of *minne*: the awareness of a distance between *minne* and herself, the complete surrender to *minne*, and restored balance (Dreyer 1989: 45).

19 From De Paepe 1967: 331.

20 In Vision 13, Hadewijch wants the soul to join Christ in the flight into Egypt. Here, she insists, we must *grow up* [emphasis mine] with him, fleeing danger, in a place of exile and homelessness; the soul must live as man with his Humanity, living "together with him in all like pains" with compassion for those with whom justice was angry, and – like him – never receiving consolation from other than Love itself (L6: 249).

21 Perhaps more than a few churchgoers saw how all the limbs of Hadewijch "trembled and quivered with eager desire" during prayer. Apparently Hadewijch was not always in a position to foresee the intensity of her bodily reactions as she had before her first vision, and wisely remain at home (Mommaers 1988: 64; see also the beginnings of Visions 1, 14).

22 Says Mommaers (1980: xviii), "That she who knows herself to be experientially united with Love must live in taking and giving, that is the riddle; . . . and [that] this instability of her experience is not the result of any moral shortcoming. Love's incomprehensible – if you wish, immoral – way of acting is the cause of it."

23 In the 6th century BC Isiah characterizes coming back into the world out of exile in similar terms: "every valley shall be lifted up, and every mountain shall be laid low. / The uneven ground shall become level, and the rough places a plain" (Ias. 40: 4).

24 Although Hadewijch can be radical about self-effacement, she was clear about her choice to surrender to Love's demands (Dreyer 1989: 64–6). Hadewijch was involved in having a life and being free before she began to talk about surrendering it. She is honest and speaks with abandon about her experience of loss of self that accompanies her involvement with God, for there is terror in passionate love. But she reminds us that we are free to respond to the call of passion or reject it. The possibility of renewal through passion is not automatic or magical but depends on choice to abandon oneself to its power. The risk of loss of self is real, and one would be foolish to ignore the seriousness of the stakes involved. Yet loss of the old self is a *sine qua non* of the emergence of the new. In this way Hadewijch is both forced and chooses to leave her former life and friends behind in her desire to "live Love" freely.

25 According to Hadewijch, a *full-grown* mystical experience (emphasis mine) means that "all griefs will taste sweeter to you than all earthly pleasures" (Vl: l). Yet Hadewijch does not consider herself fortunate to suffer. Only because human suffering is the only place where the human creature begins to approximate God (as in the passion of Christ) does Hadewijch admit to the virtue of letting suffering into her life.

26 Reflecting upon how Winnicott's work has influenced her own, Benjamin tells that in his differentiation of identification with the object and use of the object Winnicott offers a notion of *reality that can be loved*, something beyond the integration of good and bad. "While the intrapsychic ego has reality imposed from the outside, the intersubjective ego *discovers reality*," writes Benjamin;

"This reality principle does not represent a detour to wish fulfillment, a modification of the pleasure principle. Nor is it the acceptance of a false life of adaptation. Rather it is a continuation under more complex conditions of the infant's *original fascination with a love of what is outside, his appreciation of difference and novelty* . . . [this leads to] *love of the world*" (1992: 53, emphases mine). This is how separation truly becomes the other side of connection to the other.

27 Hadewijch 1980: 377, n. 57. Note that in the imagery of this poem, mountain *flows* into valley and valley *flows* into the height of the palace, rather than referring to an abrupt transformative reversal or change (see above). I take this change in the *quality* of moving transformation to indicate the presence of the feminine in Hadewijch herself, as Good becomes goodness, and Will becomes willingness. Other poems portray times when Hadewijch had less access within herself to feminine modes of being and experience.

28 Hart (Hadewijch 1980: 33) reminds us that this theme is much older than Hadewijch, being found in Origen, Augustine, Bede, and Guerric of Igny.

29 "Defensively," in Jungian terms, or "reactively," according to Winnicott, or (in archetypal terms) in unconscious identification with collective roles or institutions like family, tribe, religious denomination, professional or political allegiance, or nationality.

30 The "backing and forthing" of this cruel alternation brings to my mind the Hindu image of the Churning of the Sea of Milk, described with reference to Mairi's Dream #18.

Chapter 5

Summary and conclusions

In the previous pages I have suggested that in some cases of depth psychotherapy, religious experience may take priority over psychological experience, and I have tried to differentiate between the two. When religious experience predominates, religious language may be more appropriate than psychological language for describing what happens within the therapeutic situation. I have suggested that by implication the possibility for a fully human consciousness occurs when religious experience is engaged, and that the religious aspect of that experience may bring physiological change along with it. This is to say that, at times, the psychological "wholeness," of which fully human consciousness gives an indication, may include physiological/religious experience and not depend upon psychological experience alone.

By distinguishing religious and psychological experience, I have framed my approach somewhat differently from C. G. Jung, who proposed that everything we experience *is in the psyche* and can be described in psychological language. Although Mairi's transformative experience took place within psychotherapy, and could be formulated (in Jung's language) as an ego–Self encounter, her instinctive way of describing her experience called up religious language and a religious referent: i.e., the soul in relation to God. When psychological realization is explicitly concerned with soul, religious experience takes pride of place. Mairi taught me that the ultimate concerns to which religious experience points and to which tradition tries to bear witness may become for some of us more primordial and more fundamental than the psychological world through which these concerns are realized.

Like psychological experience, religious experience seems to consist of the simultaneous existence of different dimensions of consciousness. Whether we reach religious experience through "psycho-spiritual senses" (Corbin) or differing "reality planes" (Neumann) or the "quantum mind" (Zohar) or my "participating consciousness" as a prerequisite for fully human consciousness, the underlying idea seems to be that consciousness evolves through a "trinitarian" sequence from one-ness to two-ness to three-ness. This final synthesis is known in various traditions as the place where psychological experience and religious life intersect. Neumann calls it the reality plane on which "mystical man apprehends the Unus Mundus; Thomas Berry describes it as a glimpse of what Plato called the World Soul or *anima mundi*. Sometimes a fourth dimension is included: Masters and Houston (1966) describe a fourth level of consciousness known as the *mysterium*, a level of deep mystical awareness. And Jung, towards the end of his life, describes simply a "feeling of kinship with all things." Through a description of Mairi's experience of soul *in the body*, in which she became conscious of the underlying archetypal ignition of self–other differentiation and inter-subjectivity, I have tried to demonstrate how fully human consciousness implicates awareness of a *sacred* or *numinous* dimension of Being that we cannot account for in purely rational or verbal terms, or describe, except in poetry or metaphor.

Educator and mathematician Michael Schneider (1995) makes a similar point. Emphasizing the profound mystery of awareness, not just the aware-ness of mystery, Schneider says that there is a *sacred dimension of conscious-ness* that points toward a more subtle center, touching upon the power that motivates actions and emotions, thoughts and desires. The witness of this center of gravity is not in space, he suggests, but in pure, imageless awareness, the place in the reader that is now aware of these words. "This is the motivating power-with-which-we-are-conscious, identical to the heart of every natural form and symbolized by the center of the circle. It is the seed of our mysterious ability to be aware" (9). To bring consciousness to this seed of our mysterious ability to be aware is to penetrate to the sacred dimension of Being, imageless, and seek the center's correspondence with oneself:

> Sacred space is within us, not in body or brain, but in the volume of our consciousness. Wherever we go, we bring the sacred within us to the sacred around us. We consecrate locations and studies by the presence of this awareness, not just the other way around . . . Aware-ness is the ultimate sacred wonder though we tend to endow objects outside ourselves as sacred while ignoring the same source within us. The timeless, symbolic patterns of the world's religions, art and architecture remain symbolic of our own sacred inner realm. To find this space within us, *we pay attention to paying attention*, in imageless awareness, directing sustained attention to that which the symbols and images refer within us. (Schneider 1995: xxii–xxiiii, italics mine)

In this view, consciousness itself is the ultimate sacred mystery. When Mairi fell through her known ego-world, she glimpsed what Schneider describes as that "imageless, sacred dimension of Being." She came out of this experience with a transformed consciousness and a transformed sense of her "place" in the cosmos. She felt the profound truth that *we are not separate from the universe but braided into it, complete wholes, living in a greater whole*. This restored her sense of "place" in the world – hence my formulation of her experience as her "dream-in-the-world."

In such a transformed consciousness, while nothing may change, everything is different. The dream-in-the-world has happened. Enlightenment or awakening becomes understood not as the creation of a new state of affairs but as *the recognition and acceptance of what already is*. The underlying, more subtle consciousness that surfaces is, I suggest, more powerful than the kinds of thought and sensory consciousness that usually dominate our awareness not because it has been, or can be, measured, but because it has been, and can be, *felt*. Mairi's recognition and acceptance encompassed soul-birth.[1]

A psychological approach to what I have called Mairi's fully human consciousness visualizes a development within object relations through a similar trinitarian pattern leading to *symbolic consciousness*, a prerequisite for fully human consciousness. The first level of consciousness is described as a dual unity within infant-experience giving way to a second capacity for self–other differentiation, object constancy and what Melanie Klein calls the "depressive position." (Our Judaeo-Christian culture is based on a similar, but religious, differentiation of creature from Creator.) Further development, *including direct religious experience*, extends this capacity for psychological differentiation to include a third, simultaneously active dimension of consciousness characterized by "inter-subjectivists" as an ability to recognize the other (object or Object) *as another Subject* with an existence and a core of mystery similar to but different from one's own. Where an individual capacity for inter-subjectivity predominates (or where it develops, as it did in the case of Mairi), we find the fierce, passionate engagement of a Hadewijch, loyal to her experience of Love despite Love's whims and blows. We find a capacity for union of creature and Creator despite, and even because of, the Other's radical separation.

Both women of this narrative – Mairi and Hadewijch – describe the paradoxical, mysterious "space" within human interiority that can know God this way, as soul. Not only does Hadewijch know (despite moments of "being-one") that she is not God and that God is not herself, but over time she becomes able to accept the on-going, astounding reality of the Other from the bottom of what she calls soul's abyss. God gives us soul so that we may love God, says Hadewijch. She recognizes not only the impossibility of relating to God (or Love) without soul, but without soul's *abyss*, which resides in the innermost recesses of incarnate being. For Mairi and Hadewijch both, bodily life ensouled in this world offers the only place or state of being that is spacious enough to house deep, dark, suffering aspects of human existence right alongside joy, magnificence and the paradoxical wonder of God's suffering love for his creatures.

Different dimensions of consciousness fed into what Mairi experienced as a "second chance" in life, new life as a *person*. The process of growing into full personhood and what contributes to this process marks an important area of debate between psychology and religion. Winnicott calls this process personalisation and he relates it to the mysterious descent of a true-self spirit into the body as the mother continually introduces and re-introduces her infant's mind and body to each other. But I do not think that personalisation is only a process in infancy, nor do I believe that Mairi's "second chance" depended upon a corrective emotional experience alone. As Mairi's innate nature expanded in a process of individuation (reaching what Hadewijch might have called "grownup-ness," or expanding one's original measure), her inherent personality evidenced an abrupt, experiential transformation of consciousness. The depersonalisation evident in her self–object relations gave way to personalisation (ensoulment) of psychological and physiological awareness which was healing and restorative, balancing ego and body, and psyche and soul.

As Mairi discovered for herself (as a woman), a sense of personhood is inherently related to the concrete, particular realities of embodied existence. The historical, physiological "once-only" quality of embodied personhood validates personal identity in the unique definition of an individual thumb-print, a voice-print, or the iris of the eye. Each of us, male or female, is born of one particular woman and not another. The discrete, singular, unique nature of personhood thus partakes of feminine elements of being that transcend the personal mother. When we are born, the physiological and genetic imprint of our personal identity already exists, but our personhood exists only potentially. Unfolding personhood must be claimed consciously and experientially over a lifetime. A transformative experience which bap-tizes[2] us with personhood enables us to leave behind old, "stuck" identi-fications within us – of the person we think we are, of the archetypal roles with which we believe ourselves to be identical.[3] We assume instead what Jung (CW14: 13–14) calls a symbolic "orphan" or "widow" nature, beyond the influence of family and history. Individual consciousness of personhood may come about slowly, over time, or it may come about in an almost miraculous manner, as it did with Mairi. Beginning with an experience of "one part of my mind meeting another" in an experiential understanding of "virgin birth," the gift of personhood resulted in Mairi's sense of new Being. Only because of personhood does "who" one is come to matter *within one's person*. Our traditional Western collective insight into the sacred nature of this reality is embodied in the partly historical, partly mythic story of the incarnation of the Godhead in one limited, particular person, Jesus of Nazareth.

Analytical psychologist Toni Wolff emphasizes the specifically feminine nature of how personhood can come about through the concrete and the particular. In Wolff's understanding, the Logos principle (the Second Person of the Trinity) becomes flesh and is incarnate through woman like the Chinese Yin, where the woman power or the feminine principle is the *concrete principle* which makes the ideas visible, when the masculine principle is hidden in the sky, so to speak, not yet formed. [The masculine principle] needs the Yin principle to bring . . . [ideas] *down to earth*, to give birth to them in the *concrete world*. (emphases mine)[4]

Wolff imagines the Yin as the essence of the concrete (feminine) principle of "being," rising into Yang and finding its meaning there. This process brings to birth an experience of personhood *from the side of Yin by way of the masculine* (by way of consciousness), rather than personhood from a masculine point of view, or Yang Spirit. Wolff's perspective on the kind of transformative experience which brought Mairi into personhood emphasizes the struggle to give particular form and expression to this experience. It underscores Mairi's efforts to speak, to express her experience in language, to become articulate, part and parcel of the self-definition requisite to personhood. Hadewijch, too, struggled to carry her experiences in full awareness and communicate them to others. The transformative experience itself, however – the "soul" level of Mairi's experience, or the wordless depths of Hadewijch's experience of soul – emerges not so much from a particular kind of relationship between Yang and Yin, as it does from transformation within the feminine or the Yin principle itself.[5]

Experience of soul, which I call Mairi's dream-in-the-world, gave Mairi a sense of incarnate being. It gave her a sense of embodied personhood, filling a missing place in her life and her sense of herself to such a degree that she felt herself rearranged not only in relation to herself and others, but to God. Areas of her personality that had not reached definition as "personal" and were still unconscious would continue to exert their influence in real but unconscious ways. Nevertheless, although she was still a "fledgling" when she left therapy (relative to Hadewijch's psychological and religious stature, let us say), it was clear to me that Mairi's newly restored capacity for inter-subjectivity would continue to expand, and she would deepen her relationship to the divine. It seems important to realize that when a personality has been transformed, it stays transformed. Whatever happens, the definition of personality thus achieved continues. It can be refused, but it is still there. The effects of transformation are once and for all. They cannot be undone.

Individuation and the religious instinct

Jung's notion of individuation, described in Chapter 1, provides a useful lens through which to compare the experience of Mairi and Hadewijch. Jung was an evolutionary thinker and his theoretical account of individuation articulates a revolutionary process of consciously bringing the archetypal psyche to unique realization and expression in a personal life.

Jung felt that this could happen gradually as the ego developed, and found a way to relate to the unconscious contents that came up in the process of therapy. During this process as Jung experienced it with his patients, archetypal images of a center of wholeness began to emerge (artichokes and roses for Mairi, the Tree of the Knowledge of God for Hadewijch), and this imaged center (Self) appeared more and more in the personality as opposites were integrated by a growing and healthy ego. As a *mysterium* and a *coniunctio oppositorum*, the Self, in Jung's conception, had its roots in the numinous dimension of Being, and therefore it constituted an inner image commonly projected outward as the Godhead. During individuation, the Self appeared to have a special relationship to the ego, as a father might to a son, or a mother to a daughter, unfolding its implicate order within the personality as a guiding function towards wholeness. Another way to say this is to say that to be aware of the Self as an inner reality is to become conscious of a religious instinct in the psyche, and hence, of a larger meaning to life than was heretofore imagined – a meaning that is intensely personal and utterly impersonal at the same time.

Strictly speaking, individuation is a modern conception, relevant to the transformation of secular consciousness through a depth psychotherapeutic process. It would have been impossible for Hadewijch to "become aware of her religious instinct." Hadewijch simply had her relationship to God or *Minne*, and the "soul's abyss" was not equivalent to what we mean today by the "reality of the psyche."[6] This illustrates what Jung meant when he suggested that religion is where the psyche was, before modern psychology made it the object of investigation.

Nonetheless, Jung believed that as a natural psychic process, individuation can occur without the participation of consciousness.[7] However, the difference between the natural individuation process which runs its course unconsciously and one which is consciously realized is enormous. "In the first case consciousness nowhere intervenes; the end remains as dark as the beginning," says Jung (CW11: 756); "in the second case so much darkness comes to light that *the personality is permeated with light, and consciousness necessarily gains in scope and insight*" (emphasis mine). Whence comes all this light, we may ask? Mairi would reply that it rose from the depths of the body, matter enfleshed. Jung might suggest that it comes from the psychoid world. In this flowing, flowering light, the Good becomes goodness, the Will becomes willingness, illuminating the darkness of the interior, the darkness of the body, and reveals soul. Once the light is within, it lights the interiority of the spirit – God as the structure of invisible interiority that is called, in Kierkegaard's sense, true Subjectivity. On the archaic level, Jung tells us (CW11: 448),

> the numinous experience of individuation is the prerogative of shamans and medicine men; later, of the physician, prophet and priest; and

finally, at the civilized stage, of philosophy and religion. The shaman's experience of sickness, torture, death and regeneration implies, at a higher level, the idea of being made whole through sacrifice, of being changed by transubstantiation and exalted to the pneumatic man – in a word, of apotheosis.

So we have to imagine that individuation was different for Mairi and her thirteenth-century medieval counterpart. Nevertheless, Mairi's "beguine-like" attitude, couched in the psychological language of individuation, resonates with the formative attitudes expressed by Hadewijch and her Beguines toward the desire for an effective, personal and experimental faith, and an experience of "living without a why" (Hadewijch's phrase) (McGinn 1994: 13). Marie Louise von Franz tells us that the creative aspect of individuation also only develops when the ego frees itself from thoughts of gain and achievement in order to get nearer to true and deeper being by giving itself over, "free of all purpose," to an "inner need to grow" (von Franz 1994: 296).

While both women experienced spiritual "breakthroughs," for Hadewijch the reality that "broke through" already had a name. Her life of prayer and self-sacrifice was already dedicated to serving and worshipping her Lord, and God was not a total surprise. The great symbol system in which Hadewijch was embedded carried the Self in projection. Her religious instinct had an appropriate "object" and her life made sense *sub specie aeternitatis*. We have to assume that the reality of the psyche played handmaid to the Divine in Hadewijch's circumstantially enforced unconscious individuation, upholding her body and soul during the latter part of her life. Her individuation was no less than Mairi's, but one in which self-consciousness and the religious instinct *per se* remained unconscious. Hadewijch's allegiance to *Minne*, and her embodied love for Jesus and the story of his life, death and suffering enabled her to live out her years, despite feeling betrayed by those she loved and trusted, and thrust as she was into the heightened subjectivity of lonely individuality. Similar examples of unconscious individuation can be glimpsed in the autobiographies of many mystics: John of the Cross, bereft, sang of the soul's Dark Night; Teresa of Avila outlined stages of growth in prayer that proceeded to union with His Majesty; Rumi of Konya tells us how the Beloved comes and goes, and how soul soaks into existence everywhere "except my rough, contemptuous personality" (Barks and Green 1997: 53).

In spite of Hadewijch's understanding that she had to change – to willingly undergo misery, for example – the emergence of Hadewijch's notion of "what soul is" suggests that Hadewijch's "broadening" or expansion of consciousness meant suffering new depths of the soul's abyss (perhaps the change of reality planes to a more vertical measure). We know little of Hadewijch's personal life, but I suggest that her attitude toward her mystical experience, and her struggle to understand and cope with all that she felt was demanded of her indicates a remarkable psychological sophistication and subtlety of mind. Clearly Hadewijch chose an individual path, even a path of personal initiation, rather than falling into collectively sanctioned roles. That she may have been thrust even more deeply into her individuality through unexpected life circumstances (being cast out) simply underscores our understanding of individuation as a process that wrenches us free of all our collective fusions and identifications, conscious and unconscious both. To my knowledge, Hadewijch neither married nor had children, but even if she had, her spirit sounds too big to have settled easily into a circumscribed life. And although she felt marked from an early age by a relationship with God, even so, she attached herself to no social or religious order, no institution or Rule.

Yet individuation has never meant individualism, and despite her remarkable individuality Hadewijch was not unrelated to the collective. She had her small circle of close relationships and she mourned their loss. If indeed Hadewijch ended up in exile, bereft of those she loved, surely she continued to embody her chosen way of life in the vicinity of some nearby chapel or church, in worship (solitary, if necessary), and in serving others – the poor, the sick, and the old – until she died as one of them. I wonder if she continued to write. I suspect that she did not. From finding and experiencing herself as a woman and a warrioress, as knight and lover, a courtier and a poet, and passionately embodying these identities, Hadewijch underwent an embodied negation of all that she knew as she courageously endured the length and breadth and depths of what she knew from the inside out as the "soul's abyss" – the awesome divide between Creator and creature (herself) – to the end of her life. Individuation can become a crushing experience of individuality, too – as on a collision course with Love's insistence that the truth of Being lies within the heart of another. After an individuating crash, Hadewijch emerged hurt, dazed, alone, hollowed out by loss, but triumphant, possessed by the broken heart of Being enthroned within her own, glimpsed through fragments which more resembled wreckage of her life than anything else. Like Mairi, it appears that Hadewijch *personalised* her indwelling experience of soul.

Images typical of the individuation process, such as a numinous "center" (or Self in Jung's language) were not unknown to Hadewijch, even though they were not part of an unfolding process like my dialogue with Mairi. The most noteworthy among Hadewijch's images of a center (Jung's Self) is her vision of the great upside-down[8] Tree of the Knowledge of God, which appears near the beginning of Vision 1 (Hadewijch 1980: 263–6). After an experience of "being-one" with the Lord, Hadewijch tells us that she was led by an angel (charged with discernment) into a meadow-like expanse called "the space of perfect virtue," full of trees. There she was shown a Tree of Knowledge of Ourselves, a Tree of Humility, a Tree of Perfect Will, a Tree of Discernment, and a Tree of Wisdom. Then, after drinking a chalice of blood (reminiscent of Mairi's immersion in a pool of blood), Hadewijch's attention was drawn to the very center of the meadow, where she saw a tree

> with its roots upward and its summit downward . . . The angel said to me ". . . O Mistress, you climb this tree from beginning to end, all the way to the profound roots of the incomprehensible God! Understand that this is the way of beginners and of those who persevere to perfection." And I understood that it was the Tree of the Knowledge of God, which one begins with faith and ends with love.

In this remarkable image of reversal, Hadewijch is given to understand that the roots of the Tree of the Knowledge of God are in the heavens (spirit). Since knowledge of God happens in soul, this is to say that the tree of soul is rooted in God, and God's "gift." But the Tree's crown is its manifestation on earth (its summit points downward) and human embodiment. In order that we may experience soul at all, we must be the earth and the matter that we are. Even though spirit gives us soul, we climb the Tree of the Knowledge of God from the bottom up, beginning in faith and ending in love. The world, matter, the body, underlie any capacity for faith, which, in turn, ignites the presence of soul and the soul's capacity for love and Knowledge of God.[9]

We are accustomed to thinking about right-side-up trees. The Tree of Life and the Tree of the Knowledge of Good and Evil with their awesome implications stand upright in the Garden of Eden. If we experience what these trees symbolize, we will do so in a manner we somehow expect – right-side-up, so to speak, the way that trees grow in the world around us. We will experience what these trees symbolize in forms for which our culture prepares us: within the language and imagery inherent in myths and education of all kinds of social and cultural experiences that we hold in common (e.g., biblical text). This same upright, daylit point of view, I suggest, leads us to believe that the psyche may be all that we can know, and that self–object differentiation precedes the development of what psychologists call a capacity for inter-subjectivity and mature human development.

But *experience* of The Tree of the Knowledge of God (the "soul" tree), says Hadewijch, turns these conscious expectations upside-down. Seen through the lens of direct religious experience, soul is revealed as *fundamental* and, as Mairi, too, discovered, the psyche is revealed as soul's handmaiden. Seen through the lens of direct religious experience, the ego-mind must reverse its hegemony in order to recognize an *a priori* regnancy of body and soul, and flesh and blood – and a feminine mode of being.[10] It must accept that the seeds of inter-subjectivity (of a capacity to recognize the Other as Subject) may lie within the womb of body and earth itself, accompanied by, but not dependent upon, our necessary capacities for self–object differentiation. A capacity to recognize the subjectivity of the Other (the object) may accompany life from life's inception. To put this in the symbolic language of Mairi's dreams, "twoness has existed from the very beginning" (Dream #5). Thus Hadewijch's spiritual development can suggest an accompanying process of psychological individuation, albeit unconsciously (by way of Mercurius, meaning life's unexpected twists and turns, according to Jung CW13: 277).

For Mairi, living in a psychological culture, the situation was entirely different. Mairi's religious instinct had had nowhere to go, so to speak, and imagery of the Self had been projected into her secular world (e.g., adolescent heroes, passionate causes, etc.) and into the issue of relationship itself (her several "failed" marriages). During psychotherapy, slow, pains-taking work on un-owned aspects of her personal life (the "shadow") gradually released blocked instinctive energy so that her religious sensibility could begin to emerge. For Mairi, experiences of the center emerged as Self-directive dreams, and in Chapters 2 and 3 I explored why that might be so. The appearance of Self-directive dreams supported my growing impression that a centering or guiding presence had established itself in Mairi's inner world and that in our psychotherapeutic struggles we were, in effect, not alone. Mairi's growing awareness that a centering and guiding function came to presence in the unfolding of her analytic process constituted the earliest glimmers of her awareness of a religious instinct *in the psyche* that was being withdrawn from various outer carriers with which it was con-taminated. Hence her experience was intensely inward. While her process included all of the emotions of a religious experience or enlightenment, the result felt like an intensely psychological transformation *of* consciousness, *in* consciousness. Von Franz (1997: 296) says that with such personal con-sciousness of individuation, we have the feeling that something is watching us, something that we do not see – perhaps the "great man" in one's heart. Patočka tells us that a person can become what a person is only in being held, in its very singularity, by the gaze of God (cited in Derrida 1992: 6). In any case, says von Franz, "this creative aspect (of individuation) can only develop if the ego frees itself from all thoughts of gain and achievement in order to get nearer to this true and deeper being; it must give itself over, free of all purpose, to this inner need to grow" (von Franz 1997: 296).

And here we are back again to "living without a why." In individuation, that which is let go of, given over, sacrificed – libido? life? – is in that instant given back to the one who sacrifices precisely because she renounces calculation, as in "He who loses his life shall gain it." The great demand is that one live without knowing, without calculating, reckoning, or hoping, that one give without counting, i.e., without a "why." The annihilation of the created will which appears in Hadewijch's writings implies a similar freedom, along with a return to primordial existence and metaphysical poverty (McGinn 1994: 13).

Realizing that Lady Love watched her whether or not she could feel Her gaze, and knowing that feeling Her gaze had never been the point of loving Love to begin with, Hadewijch felt that God's reality, whether present or absent, offered no need for a further "why" for simply being alive. Letter 20 (90–3) gives us Hadewijch's description of soul's mystical ascent as a progressive experience of a series of twelve "nameless" hours (I assume that she means "nameless" dimensions of experience) that she nevertheless divides into three groups of four each, corresponding respectively to experience by way of "the seeking mind," "the desiring heart," and "the loving soul." As experienced by the soul that has progressed through these "nameless hours," Hadewijch describes God's transcendence as obscure, nameless, unknown, unawares, unbidden, and unheard-of. This kind of transcendent obscurity led Mairi to describe her experience as experience of soul, rather than dwelling upon descriptions of what she could barely describe – at best – as "the Holy Spirit as Feminine Presence." The similarity of Mairi and Hadewijch's experience of the transcendent – its obscurity and unnameableness – leads me to think that Hadewijch's three groups of "nameless" hours point to a development of consciousness exceeding that which was common in Hadewijch's time that parallels an evolution of fully human consciousness not common enough, but appropriate for our time, and corresponds with the transformation of consciousness experienced by Hadewijch during her initiation into relatively unconscious individuation.

Jung is specific about the ethical claim made upon the individuating person, i.e., the necessity for a contribution of new value to replace one's presence and loyalty to collective containers that one has abandoned in search of true individuality. Hadewijch "lived Love," which is to say that she lived her contribution – leading, writing, teaching – into the society of her time. Her contribution lies, I think, in the area of the feeling value of passionate individuality and a stubborn subjectivity that from our perspective seems far ahead of her time. Mairi's contribution came, I think, in the area of bringing back into collective consciousness the importance and feeling value of soul and a sense of soul, offering by example an individual way in which the religious instinct comes to expression outside the collective containers of our day and age. She brought into consciousness her dream-in-the-world from the depths of her embodied self, shedding light on the "hidden sparks," the seeds of light, that Jung tells us are a mystery, hidden in the depths of the unconscious and the darkness of matter and all that we do not know. She contributed to a growing recognition of the value of body awareness in psychotherapy and in all disciplines that study the phenomenon of human consciousness. Her yoga studies played a part in this, along with her faithful practice of a physical discipline. She brought her experience of soul out into the world as she expanded her individual yogic discipline into inner-city teaching. And her desire to live religiously in the world resonated not only with the Beguines but with the great current collective expansion of yogic and other spiritual disciplines into our common language and our collective experience of a secular world, in business, in "New Age" efforts to combine Eastern and Western modes of spiritual expression, in a growing synthesis of Eastern and Western cultures, and into changing definitions of community and church.

Just as Mairi was pushed down to her roots, so, it seems to me, the contemporary Christian Church is being pushed back to its roots: to the Bible, to forms of early Christian community, and to the writings of the early mystics as well as the early Church Fathers. Like Mairi, the Church (the tradition) is being pushed to articulate the nature of the Christian experience, which first came into being nearly two thousand years ago and has been sustained. Hadewijch and her sister Beguines played a role in that sustaining. So does Mairi. People today want to know not just how to think, but how to feel, how to listen, how to see. They want to know how to experience themselves, the material world, the reality of other people, and the culture which surrounds them. People today want to reach bedrock, and personal experience provides tools with which to dig. As the values of subjectivity and individual experience become more and more central to our concept of a contemporary life, it is not a cultural accident that questions concerning the nature of the Christian experience should emerge. By way of this kind of synthesizing movement in the collective unconscious, culture is renewed from within.

And the germs of such a renewal manifest themselves in breakthrough experiences of the divine such as those of Mairi and Hadewijch. These individual moments accrue, becoming the "movements" in which a kind of collective dream-in-the-world seems to emerge. Founded in individual, personal, religious experience, including the relatively new languages and expressions of depth psychotherapy, this collective movement may be as different from the old and traditional as the religious and secular shift heralded by the vernacular writings of the Beguines was to the secular and ecclesiastical authorities of society in the thirteenth and fourteenth centuries.

Centrality of the soul in religious experience

A concern in the foregoing pages has been to reveal some of the ways in which a psychological process uncovers or makes way for something *beyond* the psyche. What I describe as fully human consciousness is first and foremost an openness to penetration by the Otherness of this "something beyond the psyche," whether it comes from within as soul (Mairi) or from the cosmic surround as the God who gives us soul in order to know Him (Hadewijch). By comparing the religious experience of these two women, separated by seven centuries, I have tried to suggest (following Mairi's example) that today, transformative religious experience comes up from below, emerging through the feminine principle as experience in the body, not (as is frequently described) from above, as a kind of celestial enlightenment of the mind, although the mind is always immediately engaged, trying to make sense of the soul's experience.

The idea that another dimension of reality traditionally expressed as "religious" experience might need to be given ontological status equivalent to psychological experience was a surprise to me and something I learned from Mairi. As a psychotherapist, I did not start out this way. I thought that psychology – especially "depth" or Jungian psychology – encompassed pretty much every aspect of religious experience within its meta-theoretical understanding.[11] In the course of writing this book, it came to my attention that Jung himself had undergone an "awakening" similar to my own. For most of his life, Jung focused on the image of the Self in the psyche, seeing it as the super-ordinate archetype of centrality and wholeness, the *Imago Dei* in the deep unconscious and as close as we will ever get to God, because everything we experience is psychic. We cannot escape the psyche, said Jung, even though affects and archaic images of the collective unconscious or "objective psyche" *feel* as if they come from another dimension of being.

No concept in analytical psychology was as central to Jung's ideas as his notion of the Self. Sometimes Jung used the concept of the Self to denote the presence of a kind of entity, the center and circumference of the whole personality, out-pictured in the image of the "two-million-year-old man" in the psyche. Sometimes he used it to refer to a process. Sometimes he described the Self's function as denoting a "bunch of opposites" which makes up the archetypal field. Often Jung wrote about the Self as if it were a mighty content hidden in the midst of the unconscious, the true "atomic nucleus" of the psyche. Later, in his alchemical writings, Jung found the Self revealed in the alchemists' search for that incorruptible essence, the "pearl of great price," found in the dross "prima materia" with which the alchemical process began. In a 1929 letter to Walter Robert Corti, Jung describes a "classical" version of his idea of the Self by referring to his "inner principle" and the Self's appearance in what he calls Self-images:

> My inner principle is: *Deus et homo*. God needs man in order to become conscious, just as he needs limitation in time and space. Let us therefore be for him limitation in time and space, an earthly tabernacle . . . Jesus–Mani–Buddha–Lao-tse are for me the four pillars of the temple of the spirit. I could give none preference over the other. (1929: 64)

By 1955 Jung has seen beyond image – beyond the psyche's spontaneous personification, of the Self-as-image – and into a process, an approach to something numinous, something "Other." The classic form of his notion of the Self undergoes change. One way to mark this change would be to say that Jung's consciousness begins to display a greater capacity for inter-subjectivity. In his letter to Bernet (1955b: 258) Jung now characterizes the Self as a series of "endless approximations" (Self-images), all of which point to an "empty center" which designates not absence or vacancy but the presence of "something unknowable endowed with the highest intensity." By this time Jung is referring to the Self as a "borderline concept," by which he means a concept which is not filled out with known psychic processes (1955b: 258). Here I imagine that Jung is beginning to peer over the edge of what Hadewijch described as soul's abyss, but Jung, because of his nature, does this from the side of the mind, rather than the body.

At one point, Jung tells us that at times *the Self undoes its own symbolism* (1932–1934: 473). We saw how this idea was relevant to Mairi's process as all her dreams stopped and she fell through into her experience of soul. It was as if the Self, deconstructing its own symbolic structure, stopped sending imagery of any kind, preparatory to descent.

Finally, in a late interview, in 1957, with Miguel Serrano, the Chilean ambassador in New Delhi, Jung no longer posits the Self in the same empirical fashion. He writes, "So far I have found no stable or definite center in the unconscious, and I don't believe such a center exists. *I believe that the thing I call the Self is a dream of totality*" (Serrano 1966: 50, emphasis mine). In this letter, written near the end of his life, Jung openly equates his notion of the Self as the "atomic center" of the personality with a "dream of totality." With this suggestion, I think, Jung tells us that his *idea* of the Self, that had served him all his life, was no longer necessary. His religious sensibility had deepened into experience of soul. What formerly Jung thought of as "a powerful center in the unconscious" was replaced by a new perspective on soul itself.

Jung does not mention the "thinning" of psyche with respect to a return of soul, or even experience of soul. Usually his concept of the psyche, the anima, and the Self, and his way of thinking about the Self covers over the possibility of imagining the kind of experience Mairi could call "experience of soul." Yet that Jung experienced something similar is briefly revealed on a page in the second chapter of his *Red Book*, above which he wrote "The Rediscovery of the Soul." In the first chapter, counterposing a "spirit of the times" and a spirit who "rules over the depths of everything in the present," Jung critiques his previous attitude, or his unconscious identification with the "spirit of the times" which he now sees was in conflict with what he called the "spirit of the depths":

> Filled with human pride and blinded by the presumptuous spirit of the time, I long sought to hold that other spirit away from me. But I did not pause to consider that the spirit of the depths from time

immemorial and for all time to come possessed a greater power than the spirit of the times, who changes with the generations . . . I felt the spirit of the depths, but I did not understand him. (Jaffé 1984: 155)

This critique leads into the second chapter, where Jung writes,

I thought and spoke much about the soul; I knew many learned words about the soul; I judged it and made a scientific object of it. *I did not consider that the soul cannot be the object of my judgment and knowledge*. Much more are my judgment and knowledge the object of my soul . . . Therefore the spirit of the depths pressed me to speak to my soul, to call upon it as a living and independent being whose rediscovery means good fortune for me. I had to become aware that I had lost my soul, or rather that I had lost myself from my soul, for many years. (Jaffé 1984: 155, emphasis mine)

These are important words from a man who has done so much for depth psychology. In this quote, Jung does not obfuscate soul with psyche, anima, or Self. Instead he recognizes that what earlier enabled him to assert that any knowledge of God can be only knowledge of a God-image in the human psyche, telling us nothing about the existence and being of God, proceeded from his own removal from soul, his own loss of soul in psyche. Like Mairi, Jung came to realize that experience of God proceeds from soul, and that his separation from soul had resulted in his unconscious possession by a "spirit of the times," i.e., his identification with a dispassionate, scientific attitude at the expense of soul's reality. Jung continues,

The spirit of the depths sees the soul as an independent, living being, and therewith contradicts the spirit of the times for whom the soul is something dependent on the person, which lets itself be ordered and judged, that is, a thing whose range we can grasp. Before the spirit of the depths this thought is presumption and arrogance. Therefore the joy of my re-discovery was a humble one . . . Without the soul there is no way out of this time. (Jaffé 1984: 156)

For me, Jung's progressive understanding of his notion of the Self in relation to his "experience" of soul is moving. It suggests that, after all, Jung experienced all that he might have meant by the Self, by losing it. In the closing sentences of *Memories, Dreams, Reflections*, "clouded with old age" but speaking from a daylit sense of the Unus Mundus, the earth around him feeling as intimate as his inner life, Jung (1963: 359) muses,

The difference between most people and myself is that for me the "dividing walls" are transparent . . . the unexpected and the incredible belong in *this* world. Only then is life whole . . . the more uncertain I have felt about myself, the more there has grown up in me *a feeling of kinship with all things.* (emphases mine)

Jung's intimate, personal surrender to a reality of soul turned his sense of indebtedness to mind and intellectual capacities inside-out (Jaffé 1984: 156) – or upside-down, if we remember Hadewijch's upside-down Tree of the Knowledge of God. Like Mairi, Jung felt blessed by *this* life, here and now. Under the new aegis of a "spirit of the depths," Jung discovered that his earlier theorizing with regard to psyche and psychological reality (under the aegis of a "spirit of the times") was indebted to a profundity of soul, rather than a profound theory (Jaffé 1984: 155). By implication, if not by outright statement, Jung came to acknowledge soul as a fundamental state of being greater than his psychological theories and, simultaneously, the source of them all. I suppose that by definition, a state of being must be more encompassing than the principles or theories to which it gives rise. But only Jung's change of perception (and change of heart) with regard to the priority of soul over psyche enabled him to recognize his notion of the Self as a "dream of totality."

Mairi's dream-in-the-world, her experience of soul, gives us an example of a contemporary woman who suffered her way through to a sensed, felt, embodied indwelling. She "moved" with Hadewijch's dearly won wisdom that to be fully alive is to find the "way" to Love (L18: 87–8), but never Love itself. With Mairi, we journeyed out of psyche and into soul, into an embodied realization of an entirely other realm of being. Experience of soul was a state of being in which Mairi felt "beheld by God and [in] which . . . God [could] be beheld" (L18: 63).

As I companioned Mairi, my own quantum stance emerged. An indeterminacy of psyche and soul allowed me to stay open to the mystery unfolding in her process and not prejudge its meaning in either religious or psychological language. I opened to the possibility of an embodied experience of either psyche or soul, and was encouraged to a larger inclusiveness which allows for the simultaneous presence of psyche *and* soul, both. It became clear to me that whichever of these elements was about to differentiate itself, one from the other, or whatever undifferentiated combination of psyche and soul might have been pressing to occur, could not have been predicted from knowledge of Mairi's past, nor predicted for her future, in the moment. Particle or wave, we cannot know in which form a realization of consciousness will occur.

I came to realize that over against the world of becoming, of process, of generation and decay, is a world of being which is not in the least like the caricature offered by so many metaphysical and theoretical systems. The fullness of being is more concrete than the most concrete human experience and more personal than the human person. The fullness of being is, and proceeds from, the God who revealed Himself out of the Burning Bush: I am who I am: Self-existent Being. Being and personality are communicated to the created order from a divine source. When belief in this divine source grows weak and formal, or the existence of God is denied or ignored, then the presence of being and personality in the created order will also be denied or ignored. By means of abstraction, people and things are eviscerated, made porous and transparent, and they reveal a cavity of unreal space in which one thing can be swallowed up in the void of another.

My quantum stance is aimed at getting beyond the forms of alienation which plague life in this era. It addresses itself to the growing collective sense that we human beings are strangers in this universe, accidental by-products of blind evolutionary forces; that we have no particular role to play in the scheme of things and no meaningful relationship with the inexorable forces that drive on a larger world of insensate matter. To this sense my quantum stance protests. It would remind us that the participatory universe described by quantum physics describes an *interdependency* between the being of a person (or animal or thing) and its overall environment as a contextual condition. The implications of perceiving environmental context are vast, both for our collective conceptions of reality and for understanding ourselves as partners and participants in the unfolding reality in which we find ourselves.

In a time like ours, when both theological and psychological discourse grow threadbare, suspect, and irrelevant, emptied (as all language can be) of much former significance, there can be joy and challenge in the reconstruction and recognition of the dimensionality of Being, and language itself. Perhaps a collective experience of soul needs building anew. As before, the goal seems to be to find words adequate to the mystery; to find language that takes into account a world we did not make but which we have been given, in all fullness, which includes the sacred. Mairi's language of the body, Hadewijch's language of the soul, Jung's language of the Self, and the psyche's language of dreams, help us here.

Mairi's experience of soul offers a counterpoint in a secular society – even a psychological society – wherein soul (let alone God) is seldom referred to because *images* of God, conceived in the mind, take up all the space. In a culture which encourages increasing disembodiment,[12] the dimension of soul becomes less and less likely to enter our awareness. Here Hadewijch's image of the soul stands before us, turning like a faceted jewel, conundrum, cast of destiny, and irresolvable paradox, as true today as it was in the thirteenth century: "Soul is a way for the passage of God from his depths into his liberty; and God is a way for the passage of the soul into its liberty, that is, into his inmost depths, which cannot be touched except by the soul's abyss" (L18: 63, in Hadewijch 1980: 86).

Anima mundi

In our review of Mairi's dreams and Hadewijch's visions I have said that in an essentially feminine mode of being, the body responds freely to "what is," i.e., to Being itself. Soul deepens the body's response to "what is" into experience. We have reason to think that this new awareness heralds the emergence of a "feminine aspect of being" in men and in women in our culture and time. This feminine principle or mode of Being was known to our ancestors variously as the "soul of the world" or the *anima mundi*. In mythic language, von Franz appoints this mode of Being the "feminine aspect of the Anthropos" that is often lost in matter. On lower levels, "lost" elements of feminine being form the basis for mass suggestion and psychic infection. On higher levels, elements of feminine being form the basis for love and compassion. Just as the feminine aspect of the Anthropos can be lost in matter, so we can find it there – in nature and in ourselves, embodied aspects of the feminine that we hold most intimate.

To encounter the presence of the "soul of the world" in other than mythic language is difficult. We need a quantum consciousness, or what I call fully human consciousness, to approach it. Such an awareness can stretch to glimpse the soul of the world as well as the earth's reality. Fully human consciousness can welcome the movement and reality of the Holy Spirit, as well as the solid, yet precarious remains of history, tradition and culture, tentatively balanced within our technological age. Fully human consciousness touches upon both faith and belief, as well as uncertainty and doubt. It has allegiance to both psyche and soul, and to mind as well as heart. It bows to consciousness and the unconscious matrix. It honors spirit and flesh. It stretches to reflect upon the feminine aspect of the archetypal figure of humanity, still so entangled in matter and darkness, and in our unavoidable suffering, as well as the shining forms that express where we all came from to begin with, and what we might (still) become. All quantum systems are a little like poems, pregnant with as-yet-unrealized meaning, always begging evocation and interpretation. As persons, we ourselves are quantum systems.

In our struggle towards a genuine encounter with the "soul of the world," I have tried to show that the secret hinge may be the body – body as it is expressed in the individual person, physical, concrete, ensouled. As we reach for a mode of expression that links our scientific world view and the social and cultural contexts in which we live and out of which a world view continues to emerge, the human body is an experiential reality shared by all as the residence of soul: body as manger, body as manor, soul as resident welcome to indwelling spirit.

The ways and means of the universal soul or the *anima mundi* lie far beyond our human understanding. But by way of personally embodied participation in the "soul of the world," the psychological reality of Her

Presence in-forms us that *She is present*, that She "works" through each of us for a world-communal re-balancing of our contemporary experience of the archetype of the Anthropos, what von Franz calls the "masculine and feminine aspects of the hermaphroditic nature of the Whole Human Being." The Anthropos is simply a symbol for what it means to be fully human. As an archetypal figure, the Anthropos is androgynous. As individual persons, we are not. The symbol of the Anthropos unites the "higher" and "lower," and civilized and uncivilized human being in one image. Jung suggests that the inner dynamic of a progressive development of consciousness indicates *evolution* in the image of the Anthropos. Although the development of consciousness has not been the main point of this book, a similar evolutionary thrust underlies my definition of a quantum stance or fully human consciousness. What is more central to this work is the following: in light of the psyche's image of human wholeness (the Anthropos), and at the soul's behest, we may assume that the "whole" human being consists of feminine and masculine elements of being, of soul as well as psyche, of body as well as mind, and of matter as well as spirit.

The figure of the Anthropos has been with us since the beginnings of time and will probably remain with us as long as our species exists. We cannot see beyond it, except into mystery. That we *do* see beyond it – into mystery, into what we cannot solve, let alone comprehend – seems enormously important. Else, with the cessation of time and the collapse of space, we simply die. Not that we do not die anyway. But soul – which is home to mystery of this kind – implies a state of being that, if it does not survive death, is not fazed by it. Somehow soul continues, perhaps not in personal form, but as the "interconnectedness of all things," as a darkness and an indeterminacy which recognizes both empty tomb and luminous womb and is inexplicably the source of all life.

We need the dimension of soul. Soul's dimension seems absolutely necessary in order to give a full account of a sense of the mystery and multidimensionality of experience. We do without it to our peril. If the body's response to "what is" is lost or uncontained, suppressed or split away, a piece of soul will be lost, as well. Like flesh, like feminine being itself, soul is substantive and "weighty," and inclusive of all that is. Only a "person" experiences soul, and when we are deprived of soul, a return to God is not easy.

Loss and recovery of a world view

Describing how her insights into modern physics helped her better understand her relationship to herself, to others, and to the world at large, physicist Dana Zohar (1990: 232) describes the alienation that happens when we lose a sense of the "whole," whether we experience that sense of "wholeness" through the *anima mundi* (its feminine aspect) or as the *Unus*

Mundus, under the aegis of Yang. Jung also understood the importance of this sense of irrational "wholeness" and its religious basis, as did Thomas Berry and Huston Smith. To most of us, a world view is a lived truth, something we take for granted and seldom try to describe. On a personal level, it is a theme which runs through our lives, drawing the disparate pieces together into a coherent whole. If at this level we fail to sense some coherent world view, life itself fragments. "She has lost her sense of direction," we say; or, "he doesn't know who he is." Alienation suffered at this level is alienation from the self. At a social level, a world view draws together the many elements of our relationships with others both intimate and general – to our family, to a circle of friends, to our neighbors, our country, and our culture. If at this social level we fail to sense some coherent world view, the sense of self-and-others breaks down. We suffer alienation from society and we feel like loners, outsiders, and misfits. At a more general level still, a world view is the theme that integrates a sense of self, a sense of self and others, and a sense of how we relate to the larger world – to Nature, to other creatures, to the planet, the universe, and God. It provides an overall purpose and sense of direction. Without a world view here, our sense of self and world disintegrates. We feel as if we do not have a world. We feel that we are empty, pointless, and absurd. All is for nothing. At this level, alienation consists of a general, spiritual alienation (Zohar 1990: 233).

At one time, the Judaeo-Christian world view seemed to draw together every aspect of the individual and every level of life into one coherent whole. At one time, the Judaeo-Christian world view told us that we were all interdependent, and that our human lives were inseparably intertwined with Nature. What happened? Jung would say that we moved away from this understanding. He would tell us that we have to learn to understand the Judaeo-Christian world view again in a way that makes sense to us today, that we have forgotten how to find meaning in what still meaningfully enfolds us, even within our technological and multi-cultural world. I suggest that being in touch with the feminine principle of being, whether as feminine elements of being or as feminine modes of being, as body or as soul itself, helps us regain this understanding because it draws us back to particularized, personally embodied experience. Perhaps a dream-in-the-world is a kind of offering an individual person can make toward the renewal of some kind of universally meaningful world view. A dream-in-the-world is something someone brings back from his or her experience of deep inner space, a "treasure" gained during his or her experience of human interiority and individuation.

In the recent discoveries of quantum physics, in the story of the universe as told by Brian Swimme and Thomas Berry and in the exciting discoveries of the Hubble Telescope looking back to the very edge of the original darkness that followed the Big Bang, there is emerging a new story that once again restores mystery to our place in the cosmos. At least this is my hope, and the reason for my interest in quantum mechanics and in a "quantum stance." The seething equivalence of matter and energy, the flux suggested by particle and wave duality, and the tantalizing unfixedness of reality suggested by Heisenberg's uncertainty principle excite my imagination and verify my sense that the universe is alive. If we grant that quantum theory is both a state of mind and a state of being (which it manifestly is), what we find staring through our self-reflection is the face of divinity itself. This is not a dead world. Such an "alive world" resonates with my admittedly somewhat mystical sense that the dynamics between psyche and soul are also alive and in flux, moment by indeterminate moment. My quantum stance combines both these sensibilities, partaking of feminine elements of being in its very inclusivity, its insistence upon particularity, its recognition of changeability and flux and flow, its use of analogical thinking. In a self-reflective manner, my quantum stance is directed toward the vicissitudes of human consciousness and the inter-relatedness of all things, issues of personal identity (how much of "me" is really "me"), the mind–body problem (how does my conscious mind, or soul, relate to my material body or other matter?), interest in feelings of empathy or even telepathy between self and others, and the way the material world impinges upon consciousness, and the freedom and spontaneity of primordial experience, along with determinism and imposition, intentionality and meaning.

I am no physicist, so I have scant knowledge of actual quantum physics. At times my imaginative elaboration of what little I know serves me as a useful metaphor, drawing my reflections into new and sharper focus. At other times it offers evidence and explanations for how consciousness and hence daily experience actually work. I know that we must be cautious in extrapolating any theory beyond its logical bounds; yet quantum theory questions the theory of logical bounds, and metaphor and analogy are invaluable in dealing with the mysteries of the mind. Words feel poor when dealing with the significance of emotionally laden communication (as is all communication, to some degree), and metaphor and analogy are necessary to describe not only what happens within us (between mind and body), but to describe what happens between us, person to person. In its ability to symbolize experience – to symbolize even the capacity for symbolization – perhaps what I herein point to as "soul" embodies the deep inter-space or ligature from whence analogy and metaphor spring.

The divisions in our fractured contemporary religious mentality are not as simple as a division into intellectual or affective understanding, science or religion, mind or body, Christian or Jew, East or West, rich or poor, masculine or feminine, or even First, Second and Third World economies. The density and complexity of our times carry fracturing to an extreme. Only from way down deep in the unfathomable depths of life itself does there seep slowly to the surface of our collective consciousness some felt sense of the essential coherence of everything, of all that we live and all that is around us. This felt sense heralds the arrival of the presence of soul, perhaps the presence of the world soul, her hands holding our world in being like the hands of the woman who cradled the earth in Mairi's dream (#22). Certainly in our time the World Soul is hurt, is maimed and suffers, and expresses herself through the soulful suffering of us all; but also, literally and figuratively, she holds body and soul together, Holy Spirit, Water over the Deep.

Notes

1 Indian sage Sri Aurobindo comments gently that for the seeker the psychic realization or discovery of soul is not an end in itself but only the small beginning of another voyage which (will be made) in consciousness, now, rather than ignorance. Quoted in Judith 1996: 445–6.

2 Baptism has always been recognized as a ritual of death and rebirth or a dangerous crossing from one mode of consciousness to another. Thus we are ritually recognized and often renamed as a child of God in a ceremony that acknowledges a "second birth," a "rebirth," or the spiritual birth of the individual person.

3 These roles are like the endless forms depicted by Mairi's Self-directive dreams of role-engraved artichoke leaves (Dream #6) and rose petals (Dream #16).

4 Quoted in Champernowne 1980: 9 from *The Kundalini Yoga: Notes on the Seminar given by Professor Dr. J. W. Hauer with Commentary by Dr. C. G. Jung*, Zurich, privately printed, 1932, 82.

5 In inter-subjective terms, differentiation that takes place within the maternal dyad (Benjamin 1992: 56) allows for self and object separation and the establishment of the distinction between the symbol and the symbolized. The subject who begins to make this distinction now has access to a triangular field – symbol, symbolized, and interpreting subject – a triangle created without a literal third person, which constellates transformation within the structure of the feminine or Yin principle.

6 It is important to differentiate what we mean by psychic reality and what a religious person might describe in language that sounds like depth psychology. We can be psychologically astute and without a soul; we can be soulful and psychologically naive; we can have a conscious grasp of psychological reality and an unawakened religious sensibility, and we can have no sense of the reality of the psyche and consider ourselves mystics and religious persons.

7 Jung (CW16: 444ff.) tells us that there is a chance of individuating at the cost of a loss of soul: "If the inner consolidation of the individual is not a conscious achievement, it will occur spontaneously and will then take the well-known form of that incredible hard-heartedness which collective man displays towards his fellow men . . . His soul, which can live only in and from human relationships, is irretrievably lost." Von Franz (1997: 153) comments that this shows itself today in the increasing tendency towards acts of violence which can be seen everywhere. See also Zaehner 1974a, 1974b.

8 See also the image of the upside-down cosmic tree of the Sefirot, in Jewish Kabballah. Imaging God in terms of a male-female polarity and participation (by way of ritual obedience) in the strength of the Creator, the Kabballah

pictures the Sefirot either as an upside-down cosmic tree of primary ciphers or as primordial man (*The Harper Collins Dictionary of Religion*, 585–87).

9 Jung tells us that the inverted tree plays a role among East Siberian shamans, representing the shaman herself or her greater personality. The shaman climbs the tree to find her true self in the upper world (CW13: 462). "Stations" of the journey are positioned like the chakras along the human spine. Eliade says that the shaman needs these ecstatic journeys because during trance she becomes truly herself. *The mystical experience is necessary as a constituent of her true personality* (1964: 293, emphasis mine).

10 "The old ego dies hard," observed the playwright Samuel Beckett, "such as it was, a minister of dullness, it was also an agent of security" (quoted in Foster 1989: 93).

11 This issue was at the center of the debate between Martin Buber and C. G. Jung.

12 I am thinking here of "virtual reality" in our lives, or models of human intelligence put forth by early research in Artificial Intelligence which declare rule-based, conscious thinking the essence of intelligence, devoid of presence and awareness; or the "couch-potato syndrome," in front of the TV, or the hours of "living being" poured into computer screens while the body in which being dwells barely breathes. Linguists G. Lakoff and M. Johnson claim that the body is even the source of abstract reason, usually thought of as the opposite of flesh: "This is not just the innocuous and obvious claim that we need a body to reason," they tell us, "rather it is the striking claim that the very structure of reason itself comes from the details of our embodiment" (quoted in Ullman 2002: 67).

Select bibliography

Abram, D. (1996) *The Spell of the Sensuous: Perception and Language in a More-than-Human World*, New York: Pantheon Books.

Ackerman, D. (1991) *A Natural History of the Senses*, New York: Vintage Books.

Adler, G. (1961) *The Living Symbol: A Case Study in the Process of Individuation*, Bollingen Series LXIII, New York: Pantheon Books.

Alvarez, A. (1992) "Annals of Science: Sleep," *The New Yorker*, February 10, 85–94.

Amis, R. (1995) *A Different Christianity: Early Christian Esotericism and Modern Thought*, Albany, N.Y.: State University of New York Press.

Apocryphal New Testament (1924) M. R. James (trans.), Oxford: Clarendon Press.

Arraj, J. (1986) *St. John of the Cross and Dr. C. G. Jung: Christian Mysticism in the Light of Jungian Psychology*, Chiloquin, Ore.: Tools for Inner Growth.

Atkinson, C. W. (1991) *The Oldest Vocation: Christian Motherhood in the Middle Ages*, Ithaca, N.Y.: Cornell University Press.

Atwood, G. and Stolorow, R. (1984) *Structures of Subjectivity*, Hillsdale, N.J.: Analytic Press.

Augustine (1991a) *Confessions*, H. Chadwick (trans.), Oxford: Oxford University Press.

—— (1991b) *The Trinity*, E. Hill (trans.), New York: New City Press.

Ayliffe, R., Dubin, M. and Gawthrop, J. (1992) *Turkey: The Rough Guide*, London: Rough Guides Ltd.

Aziz, R. (1990) *C. G. Jung's Psychology of Religion and Synchronicity*, Albany, N.Y.: State University of New York Press.

Bachelard, G. (1971) *The Poetics of Reverie*, Boston: Beacon Press.

Bakhtiar, L. (1976) *Sufi: Expressions of the Mystic Quest*, London: Thames & Hudson.

Balint, M. (1969) *The Basic Fault: Therapeutic Aspects of Regression*, New York: Brunner/Mazel.

Barfield, O. (1953) *History in English Words*, rev. edn, Gt. Barrington, Mass.: Lindisfarne Books, 1967.

—— (1965) *Saving the Appearances: A Study in Idolatry*, New York: Harcourt, Brace and World, Inc.

Barks, C. and Green, M. (1997) *The Illuminated Rumi*, New York: Broadway Books.

Barks, C. and Moyne, J. (1995) *The Essential Rumi*, San Francisco: HarperSanFrancisco.

Bass, A. (2001) "It Takes One to Know One; Or, Whose Unconscious Is It Anyway?" *Psychoanalytic Dialogues: A Journal of Relational Perspectives* 11. 5: 683–701.

Bataille, G. (1955) "Prehistoric Painting: Lascauz or the Birth of Art," in A. Skira (ed.), *The Great Centuries of Painting*, Cleveland: The World Publishing Company.

Bateson, G. (1972) *Steps to an Ecology of Mind*, New York: Ballantine.

Benjamin, J. (1988) *The Bonds of Love*, New York: Pantheon.

—— (1992) "Recognition and Destruction: An Outline of Intersubjectivity," in N. J. Solnick and S. C. Warshaw (eds), *Relational Perspectives in Psychoanalysis*, New York: Analytic Press, 43–60.

—— (1995) *Like Subjects, Love Objects: Essays on Recognition and Sexual Difference*, New Haven: Yale University Press.

Bentov, I. (1988) *Stalking the Wild Pendulum: On The Mechanics of Consciousness*, Rochester, Vt.: Destiny Books.

Berman, M. (1989) *The Reenchantment of the World*, New York: Bantam New Age.

—— (1990) *Coming To Our Senses: Body and Spirit in the Hidden History of the West*, New York: Bantam Books.

Berry, T. (1988) *The Dream of the Earth*, San Francisco: Sierra Club Books.

Bettelheim, B. (1983) *Freud and Man's Soul*, New York: Alfred A. Knopf.

Bion, W. R. (1970) *Attention and Interpretation*, London: Tavistock.

Bishop, P. (1990) *The Greening of Psychology: The Vegetable World in Myth, Dream, and Healing*, Dallas: Spring Publications.

Bloom, H. (1996) *Omens of Millennium: The Gnosis of Angels, Dreams and Resurrection*, New York: Riverhead Books.

Bly, R. (1996) *The Sibling Society: An Impassioned Call for the Rediscovery of Adulthood*, New York: Vintage Books.

Bollas, C. (1987) *The Shadow of the Object*, New York: Columbia University Press.

Borchert, B. (1994) *Mysticism: Its History and Challenge*, York Beach, Me.: Samuel Weiser.

Bouyer, L. (1989) *Figures Mystiques Féminines: Hadewijch D'anvers, Thérèse d'Avila, Thérèse de Lisieux, Elisabeth de la Trinité, Edith Stein*, Paris: Editions du Cerf.

Buechner, F. (1988) *Whistling in the Dark: An ABC Theologized*, San Francisco: Harper & Row.

Bührmann, M. V. (1984) *Living in Two Worlds: Communication between a White Healer and Her Black Counterparts*, Cape Town: Human & Rousseau.

Burckhardt, T. (1995) *Introduction to Sufism*, D. M. Matheson (trans.), San Francisco: HarperCollins.

Burnside, J. (2000) "The Unprovable Fact: A Tayside Inventory: III The Mediciners," in *The Asylum Dance*, London: Jonathan Cape, 70.

Bynum, C. W. (1987) *Holy Feast and Holy Fast: The Religious Significance of Food to Medieval Women*, Berkeley: University of California Press.

—— (1992) *Fragmentation and Redemption: Essays on Gender and the Human Body in Medieval Religion*, New York: Zone Books.

Ceronetti, G. (1993) *The Silence of the Body: Materials for the Study of Medicine*, M. Moore (trans.), New York: Farrar, Straus & Giroux.

Champernowne, I. (1980) *A Memoir of Toni Wolff*, San Francisco: C. G. Jung Institute of San Francisco.

Chaudhuri, H. (1965) *Integral Yoga: The Concept of Harmonious and Creative Living*, London: George Allen & Unwin.

Chittick, W. C. (1989) *The Sufi Path of Knowledge: Ibn Al-Arabi's Metaphysics of Imagination*, Albany, N.Y.: State University of New York Press.

—— (1994) *Imaginal Worlds: Ibn al-'Arabi and the Problem of Religious Diversity*, Albany, N.Y.: State University of New York Press.

Chodron, P. (1997) *When Things Fall Apart*. Boston & London: Shambhala.

Christou, E. (1963) *The Logos of the Soul*, Vienna: Dunquin Press.

Cirlot, J. E. (1962) *A Dictionary of Symbols*, J. Sage (trans.), New York: Philosophical Library.

Clift, W. B. (1983) *Jung and Christianity: The Challenge of Reconciliation*, New York: Crossroad.

Corbin, H. (1953) *Spiritual Body and Celestial Earth: From Mazdean Iran to Shi'ite Iran*, N. Pearson (trans.), Bollingen Series XCI:2, Princeton, N.J.: Princeton University Press, 1977.

—— (1954) *Avicenna and the Visionary Recital*, W. R. Trask (trans.), Irving, Tex.: Spring Publications, 1980.

—— (1955) *Creative Imagination in the Sufism of Ibn Arabi*, R. Manheim (trans.), Bollingen Series XCI, Princeton, N.J.: Princeton University Press, 1969.

—— (1971) *The Man of Light In Iranian Sufism*, N. Pearson (trans.), Boulder & London: Shambhala, 1978.

—— (1972) *Mundis Imaginalis or the Imaginal and the Imaginary*, Ipswich, England: Golgonooza Press, 1976 (originally published in *Spring*, 1972).

Corrigan, E. G. and Gordon, P. (eds) (1995) *The Mind Object: Precocity and Pathology of Self-Sufficiency*, Northvale, N.J.: Jason Aronson.

Cousins, E. (1992) *Christ of the Twenty-First Century*, Rockport, Mass.: Element Books.

Craine, R. (1997) *Hildegard: Prophet of the Cosmic Christ*, New York: Crossroad.

—— (1998) "Hildegard of Bingen, a Spiritual Guide for the 21st Century," unpublished paper.

Crews, F. (ed.) (1998) *Unauthorized Freud: Doubters Confront a Legend*, New York: Viking Penguin.

Crownfield, D. (ed.) (1992) *Body/Text in Julia Kristeva: Religion, Women, and Psychoanalysis*, Albany, N.Y.: State University of New York Press.

Dalrymple, W. (1990) *Xanadu: A Quest*, London: Flamingo.

Damasio, A. (1990) *The Feeling of What Happens: Body and Emotion in the Making of Consciousness*, San Diego: Harcourt.

Danto, A. C. (1999) *The Body/Body Problem: Selected Essays*, Berkeley, Calif.: University of California Press.

Davies, O. (ed., trans.) (1990) *The Rhineland Mystics: Writings of Meister Eckhart, Johannes Tauler, and Jan van Ruusbroec and Selections from the "Theologia Germanica" and the "Book of Spiritual Poverty"*, New York: Crossroad.

Dawood, N. J. (1961) *Tales from the Thousand and One Nights*, N. J. Dawood (trans.), Penguin Books.

De Paepe, N. (1967) *Hadewijch, Poems in Stanzas: A Study of Love (*minne*) in connection with 12th and 13th Century Mysticism and Profane Love-Lyric*, in *Hadewijch: The Complete Works*, Hart (trans.), New York: Paulist Press, 1980, 331.

de Vitray-Meyerovitch, E. (1987) *Rumi and Sufism*, S. Fattal (trans.), Sausalito, Calif.: Post-Apollo Press.

de Waal, F. (2001) *The Ape and the Sushi Master: Cultural Reflections of a Primatologist*, New York: Basic Books.

Derrida, J. (1992) *The Gift of Death*, D. Wills (trans.), Chicago and London: University of Chicago Press (1995).

Dietrich, P. A. (1994) "The Wilderness of God in Hadewijch II and Meister Eckhart and His Circle," in B. McGinn (ed.), *Meister Eckhart and the Beguine Mystics: Hadewijch of Brabant, Mechthild of Magdeburg, and Marguerite Porete*, New York: Continuum, 31–43.

Dossey, L. (1999) "Dreams and Healing: Reclaiming a Lost Tradition," *Alternative Therapies in Health and Medicine*, 5.6: 12–18.

—— (2001) *Healing Beyond the Body: Medicine and the Infinite Reach of the Mind*, Boston: Shambhala.

Dreyer, E. (1989) *Passionate Women: Two Medieval Mystics: 1989 Madeleva Lecture in Spirituality*, New York: Paulist Press.

Eco, U. (1980) *The Name of the Rose*, W. Weaver (trans.), New York: Harcourt Brace Jovanovich.

Edelman, S. (1998) *Turning the Gorgon: A Meditation on Shame*, Woodstock, Conn.: Spring Publications.

Edinger, E. F. (1972) *Ego and Archetype: Individuation and the Religious Function of the Psyche*, New York: G. P. Putnam's Sons.

—— (1991) "Transforming the God-Image," *Psychological Perspectives: Psyche and Spirit*, 25 (Fall–Winter).

—— (1994) *The Mystery of the Coniunctio: Alchemical Image of Individuation*, Toronto: Inner City Books.

—— (1995) *The Mysterium Lectures: A Journey Through C. G. Jung's Mysterium Coniunctionis*, Toronto: Inner City Books.

—— (1996) *The New God-Image: A Study of Jung's Key Letters Concerning the Evolution of the Western God-Image*, D. D. Cordic and C. Yates (eds), Wilmette, Ill.: Chiron.

Eigen, M. (1992) *Coming Through the Whirlwind: Case Studies in Psychotherapy*, Wilmette, Ill.: Chiron.

—— (1993a) "The Area of Faith in Winnicott, Lacan, and Bion," in A. Phillips (ed.), *The Electrified Tightrope*, Northvale, N.J.: Jason Aronson, 109–38.

—— (1993b) "Breathing and Identity," in A. Phillips (ed.), *The Electrified Tightrope*, Northvale, N.J.: Jason Aronson, 43–7.

—— (1998) *The Psychoanalytic Mystic*, London: Free Association Books.

Eliade, M. (1958a) *Yoga: Immortality and Freedom*, W. R. Trask (trans.), Bollingen Series LVI, New York: Pantheon Books.

—— (1958b) *Rites and Symbols of Initiation: The Mysteries of Birth and Rebirth*, W. Trask (trans.), Woodstock, Conn.: Spring Publications.

—— (1960) *Myths, Dreams, and Mysteries: The Encounter Between Contemporary Faiths and Archaic Realities*, P. Mairet (trans.), New York: Harper & Row.

Eliade, M. (1964) *Shamanism: Archaic Techniques of Ecstasy*, W. R. Trask (trans.), Bollingen Series LXXVI, Princeton, N.J.: Princeton University Press.

Ellenberger, H. F. (1970) *The Discovery of the Unconscious: The History and Evolution of Dynamic Psychiatry*, New York: Basic Books.

Emre, Y. (1989) *The Drop That Became the Sea: Lyric Poems of Yunus Emre*, K. Helminski and R. Algan (trans.), Putney, Vt.: Threshold Books.

Epiney-Burgard, G. and Brunn, E. Zum (1988) *Femmes Troubadours de Dieu*, Turnhout: Brepols.

Epstein, M. (1995) *Thoughts Without a Thinker: Psychotherapy from a Buddhist Perspective*, New York: Basic Books.

—— (1998) *Going to Pieces Without Falling Apart: A Buddhist Perspective on Wholeness: Lessons from Meditation and Psychotherapy*, New York: Broadway Books.

Ernst, C. W. (1997) *The Shambhala Guide to Sufism: An Essential Introduction to the Philosophy and Practice of the Mystical Tradition of Islam*, Boston: Shambhala.

Ferenczi, S. (1988) *The Clinical Diary of Sandor Ferenczi*, J. Dupont (ed.), Cambridge, Mass.: Harvard University Press.

Fierz-David, L. (1988) *Women's Dionysian Initiation: The Villa of the Mysteries in Pompeii: A Guide to the Depths of the Female Psyche*, Dallas, Tex.: Spring Publications.

Finke, L. A. (1993) "Mystical Bodies and the Dialogues of Vision," in U. Wiethaus (ed.), *Maps of Flesh and Light: The Religious Experience of Medieval Women Mystics*, Syracuse, N.Y.: Syracuse University Press, 28–44.

Fogel, G. I. (ed.) (1991) *The Work of Hans Loewald: An Introduction and Commentary*, Northvale, N.J.: Jason Aronson.

Fosdick, H. E. (1956) *The Living of These Days: An Autobiography*, New York: Harper & Brothers.

Fosshage, J. L. and Loew, C. A. (eds) (1987) *Dream Interpretation: A Comparative Study*, rev. edn, New York: PMA Publishing.

Foster, P. (1989) *Beckett and Zen: A Study of Dilemma in the Novels of Samuel Beckett*, London: Wisdom Publications.

Fox, M. (1999) *Sins of the Spirit, Blessings of the Flesh: Lessons for Transforming Evil in Soul and Society*, New York: Harmony Books.

Freud, S. (1900) *The Interpretation of Dreams, First Part. The Standard Edition of the Complete Psychological Works of Sigmund Freud*, J. Strachey (trans.), vol. 4, London: Hogarth Press and the Institute of Psychoanalysis, 1986, 1–626.

—— (1918) "From the History of an Infantile Neurosis," *The Standard Edition of the Complete Psychological Works of Sigmund Freud*, J. Strachey (trans.), vol. 17, London: Hogarth Press and the Institute of Psychoanalysis, 1960, 7–122.

—— (1927) *The Future of an Illusion*, New York: Doubleday, 1967.

Garfield, D. A. S. (1995) *Unbearable Affect: A Guide to the Psychotherapy of Psychosis*, New York: John Wiley & Sons.

Gellert, M. (1994) *Modern Mysticism: Jung, Zen and the Still Good Hand of God*, York Beach, Me.: Nicolas-Hays.

Godwin, R. W. (1991) "Wilfred Bion and David Bohm: Toward a Quantum Metapsychology," *Psychoanalysis and Contemporary Thought* 14.4: 625–54.

Goldman, D. (1993) *In Search of the Real: The Origins and Originality of D. W. Winnicott*, Northvale, N.J.: Jason Aronson.

Gozier, Dom A. (1994) *Beguine, Ecrivain et Mystique: Portrait et Textes de Hadewijch d'Anvers (XIII siècle)*, Montrouge: Nouvelle Cité.

Greene, B. (1999) *The Elegant Universe: Superstrings, Hidden Dimensions, and the Quest for the Ultimate Theory*, New York: Vintage Books.

Griffiths, J. (ed.) (1981) *A Letter of Private Direction*, New York: Crossroad.

Grinnell, R. (1970) "Reflections on the Archetype of Consciousness: Personality and Psychological Faith," *Spring*.

—— (1973) *Alchemy in a Modern Woman*, Zurich: Spring Publications.

Grof, S. (1985) *Beyond the Brain: Birth, Death and Transcendence in Psychotherapy*, Albany, N.Y.: State University of New York Press.

—— (1988) *The Adventure of Self-Discovery: Dimensions of Consciousness and New Perspectives in Psychotherapy and Inner Exploration*, Albany, N.Y.: State University of New York Press.

Grof, S. and Grof, C. (eds) (1989) *Spiritual Emergency: When Personal Transformation Becomes a Crisis*, Los Angeles: Jeremy Tarcher.

Grotstein, J. S. (1997) "'Internal Objects' or 'Chimerical Monsters'?: The Demonic 'Third Forms' of the Internal World," *Journal of Analytical Psychology* 42: 47–80.

—— (2000) *Who Is the Dreamer Who Dreams the Dream?* Hillsdale, N.J.: Analytic Press.

Hadewijch (1980) *Hadewijch: The Complete Works*, Mother Columba Hart (trans.), Classics of Western Spirituality, New York: Paulist Press.

Hanh, T. N. (1995) *Zen Keys: A Guide to Zen Practice*, New York: Doubleday.

Harding, E. U. (1993) *Kali: The Black Goddess of Dakshineswar*, York Beach, Me.: Nicolas-Hays.

Harris, J. (2001) *Jung and Yoga: The Psyche–Body Connection*, Toronto: Inner City Books.

Harvey, A. (ed.) (1998) *Teachings of the Christian Mystics*, Boston: Shambhala.

—— (2000) *The Direct Path: Creating a Personal Journey to the Divine Using the World's Spiritual Traditions*, New York: Broadway Books.

Haughton, R. (1981) *The Passionate God*. New York: Paulist Press.

Henderson, J. L. (1967) *Thresholds of Initiation*, Middletown, Conn.: Wesleyan University.

—— (1990) *Shadow and Self: Selected Papers in Analytical Psychology*, Wilmette, Ill.: Chiron.

Hick, J. (1993) *The Metaphor of God Incarnate: Christology in a Pluralistic Age*, Louisville, Ky.: Westminster/John Knox Press.

Hillman, J. (1960) *Emotion: A Comprehensive Phenomenology of Theories and Their Meanings for Therapy*, Evanston, Ill.: Northwestern University Press.

—— (1975) *Re-visioning Psychology*, New York: Harper & Row.

—— (1979) *The Dream and the Underworld*, New York: Harper & Row.

—— (1981) "The Thought of the Heart," *Eranos Yearbook 48–1979*, Frankfurt a.M.: Inset Verlag.

—— (1989) *Blue Fire*, T. Moore (ed.), New York: Harper & Row.

Hobson, J. A. (1988) *The Dreaming Brain: How the Brain Creates both the Sense and the Nonsense of Dreams*, New York: Basic Books.

Hoffer, E. (1951) *The True Believer*, New York: Harper & Row.

Hogan, L. (1994) "Department of the Interior," in P. Foster (ed.), *Minding the Body: Women Writers on Body and Soul*, New York: Bantam Doubleday Dell.

Homans, P. (1979) *Jung in Context: Modernity and the Making of a Psychology*, Chicago: University of Chicago Press.

Jackson, M. (1998) *Minima Ethnographica: Intersubjectivity and the Anthropological Project*, Chicago: University of Chicago Press.

Jaffé, A. (1984) *Jung's Last Years and Other Essays*, Dallas, Tex.: Spring Publications.

James, M. R. (trans.) (1924) *The "Oxyrhynchus" Sayings, in The Apocryphal New Testament*, Oxford: Clarendon Press.

James, W. (1902) *The Varieties of Religious Experience: A Study in Human Nature*, New York: Collier Books, 1961.

Jaynes, J. (1976) *The Origin of Consciousness in the Breakdown of the Bicameral Mind*, Boston: Houghton Mifflin.

Johari, H. (1987) *Chakras: Energy Centers of Transformation*, Rochester, Vt.: Destiny Books.

Johnson, F. (1998) "Beyond Belief: A Skeptic Searches for an American Faith," *Harper's Magazine* 297.1780 (September): 39–54.

Johnston, S. I. (1990) *Hekate Soteira: A Study of Hekate's Roles in the Chaldean Oracles and Related Literature*, Atlanta, Ga.: Scholars Press.

Johnston, W. (1973) *The Cloud of Unknowing and the Book of Privy Counseling*, New York: Doubleday.

Judith, A. (1996) *Eastern Body, Western Mind: Psychology and the Chakra System as a Path to the Self*, Berkeley, Calif.: Celestial Arts.

Julian of Norwich (1978) *Showings*, E. Colledge and J. Walsh (eds), New York: Paulist Press.

Jung, C. G. (1907) "The Psychology of Dementia Praecox," in *The Psychogenesis of Mental Disease*, Collected Works, vol. 3, R. F. C. Hull (trans.), Bollingen Series XX, New York: Pantheon Books, 1960, 1–152.

—— (1915) "Letter to Hans Schmid," *Letters*, vol. 1: *1906–1950*, R. F. C. Hull (trans.), G. Adler (ed.), London: Routledge & Kegan Paul, 1973, 30–2.

—— (1916) "Adaptation, Individuation, Collectivity," from *Two Essays on Analytical Psychology*, in *The Symbolic Life: Miscellaneous Writings*, Collected Works, vol. 18, R. F. C. Hull (trans.), Bollingen Series XX, Princeton, N.J.: Princeton University Press, 1976.

—— (1920a) "Definitions," in *Psychological Types*, Collected Works, vol. 6, H. G. Baynes (trans.), rev. R. F. C. Hull, Princeton, N.J.: Princeton University Press, 1971, 408–86.

—— (1920b) "The Type Problem in Poetry," in *Psychological Types*, Collected Works, vol. 6, H. G. Baynes (trans.), rev. R. F. C. Hull, Princeton, N.J.: Princeton University Press, 1971, 166–272.

—— (1923) "Human Relationships in Relation to the Process of Individuation," in *The Cornwall Lectures*, M. E. Harding and K. Mann (notes), Polzeath, Cornwall, July (unpublished).

—— (1925) *Analytical Psychology: Notes of a Seminar Given in 1925*, W. McGuire (ed.), Bollingen Series XCIX, Princeton, N.J.: Princeton University Press, 1989.

—— (1926) "Spirit and Life," *The Structure and Dynamics of the Psyche*, Collected Works, vol. 8, R. F. C. Hull (trans.), New York: Pantheon Books, 319–37.

Jung, C. G. (1929) "Letter to Walter Robert Corti," *C. G. Jung Letters*, vol. 1: *1906–1950*, G. Adler (ed.), R. F. C. Hull (trans.), Bollingen Series XCV: 1, Princeton, N.J.: Princeton University Press, 1973, 64.

——(1930–1932) *The Visions Seminar*. From the Complete Notes of Mary Foote. Book One, Parts One to Seven. Zurich: Spring Publications, 1976, 113–49.

—— (1931) "Mind and Earth," *Civilization in Transition*, Collected Works, vol. 10, R. F. C. Hull (trans.), Bollingen Series XX: New York: Pantheon Books, 1964, 29–49.

—— (1932–1934) *The Visions Seminar*. From the Complete Notes of Mary Foote. Book Two, Parts Eight to Thirteen. Zurich: Spring Publications, 1976, 437–516.

—— (1933) *Modern Man in Search of a Soul*, W. S. Dell, C. F. Baynes (trans.), New York: Harcourt Brace & World.

—— (1934a) "Letter to James Kirsch," *C. G. Jung Letters*, vol. 10: *1906–1950*, G. Adler (ed.), R. F. C. Hull (trans.), Bollingen Series XVC:1, Princeton, N.J.: Princeton University Press, 1973, 172.

—— (1934b) "The Development of Personality," in *The Development of Personality*, Collected Works, vol. 17, R. F. C. Hull (trans.), Bollingen Series XX, New York: Pantheon Books, 1954, 165–86.

—— (1937) "Psychology and Religion," in *Psychology and Religion: West and East*, Collected Works, vol. 11, 2nd edn, R. F. C. Hull (trans.), Bollingen Series XX, Princeton, N.J.: Princeton University Press, 1969, 3–106.

—— (1940) "On the Psychology of the Concept of the Trinity," G. V. Hartman (trans.), *Quadrant*, 27.1 (Winter 1998), New York: C. G. Jung Foundation for Analytical Psychology.

—— (1942) "Paracelsus as a Spiritual Phenomenon," in *Alchemical Studies*, Collected Works, vol. 13, R. F. C. Hull (trans.), Bollingen Series XX, Princeton, N.J.: Princeton University Press, 1969, 109–90.

—— (1943) "The Relations Between the Ego and the Unconscious," in *Two Essays on Analytical Psychology*, Collected Works, vol. 7, R. F. C. Hull (trans.), Bollingen Series XX, Princeton, N.J.: Princeton University Press, 1953, 121–294.

—— (1944a) "Individual Dream Symbolism in Relation to Alchemy," in *Psychology and Alchemy*, Collected Works, vol. 12, R. F. C. Hull (trans.), Bollingen Series XX, Princeton, N.J.: Princeton University Press, 1953, 39–213.

—— (1944b) "The Psychic Nature of the Alchemical Work," in *Psychology and Alchemy*, Collected Works, vol. 12, R. F. C. Hull (trans.), Bollingen Series XX, Princeton, N.J.: Princeton University Press, 1953, 231–75.

—— (1945) "Letter to P. W. Martin," *C. G. Jung Letters* vol. 1: *1906–1950*, G. Adler (ed.), R. F. C. Hull (trans.), Bollingen Series XCV:1, Princeton, N.J.: Princeton University Press, 1973, 376.

—— (1946a) "The Spirit of Psychology," in *Spirit and Nature: Papers from the Eranos Yearbooks*, Bollingen Series XXX:1, New York: Pantheon Books, 1954, 371–444.

—— (1946b) "The Psychology of the Transference," in *The Practice of Psychotherapy*, Collected Works, vol. 16, R. F. C. Hull (trans.), Bollingen Series XX, Princeton, New York: Pantheon Books, 1954, 163–321.

—— (1948a) "On the Nature of Dreams," in *The Structure and Dynamics of the Psyche*, Collected Works, vol. 8, R. F. C. Hull (trans.), Bollingen Series XX, New York: Pantheon Books, 1960, 281–97.

Jung, C. G. (1948b) "The Psychological Foundations of Belief in Spirits," in *The Structure and Dynamics of the Psyche*, Collected Works, vol. 8, H. G. Baynes and C. G. Baynes (trans.), Bollingen Series XX, New York: Pantheon Books, 1960, 301–18.

—— (1948c) "Instinct and the Unconscious," in *The Structure and Dynamics of the Psyche*, Collected Works, vol. 8, R. F. C. Hull (trans.), Bollingen Series XX, New York: Pantheon Books, 1960, 129–38.

—— (1948d) "A Psychological Approach to the Dogma of the Trinity," in *Psychology and Religion: West and East*, Collected Works, vol. 11, 2nd edn, R. F. C. Hull (trans.), Bollingen Series XX, Princeton, N.J.: Princeton University Press, 1969, 107–200.

—— (1948e) "The Phenomenology of the Spirit in Fairytales," in *The Archetypes and the Collective Unconscious*, Collected Works, vol. 9i, 2nd edn, R. F. C. Hull (trans.), Bollingen Series XX, Princeton, N.J.: Princeton University Press, 1969, 207–54.

—— (1948f) "The Spirit Mercurius," in *Alchemical Studies*, Collected Works, vol. 13, R. F. C. Hull (trans.), Bollingen Series XX, Princeton, N.J.: Princeton University Press, 1967.

—— (1950a) *Symbols of Transformation: An Analysis of the Prelude to a Case of Schizophrenia*, Collected Works, vol. 5, R. F. C. Hull (trans.), Bollingen Series XX, New York: Pantheon Books, 1956.

—— (1950b) "The Structure and Dynamics of the Self," in *Aion*, Collected Works, vol. 9ii, R. F. C. Hull (trans.), 2nd edn, Bollingen Series XX, Princeton, N.J.: Princeton University Press, 1959, 222–65.

—— (1951a) "The Psychology of the Child Archetype," in *The Archetypes and the Collective Unconscious*, Collected Works, vol. 9i, R. F. C. Hull (trans.), Bollingen Series XX, Princeton, N.J.: Princeton University Press, 1959, 151–81.

—— (1951b) "Letter to Heinrich Boltze," *C. G. Jung Letters*, vol. 2: *1951–1961*, R. F. C. Hull (ed.), A. Jaffé (trans.), Bollingen Series XCV:2, Princeton, N.J.: Princeton University Press, 1975, 4–5.

—— (1951c) "Fundamental Questions of Psychotherapy," in *The Practice of Psychotherapy*, Collected Works, vol. 16, R. F. C. Hull (trans.), Bollingen Series XX, New York: Pantheon Books, 1954, 111–25.

—— (1951d) "The Syzygy: Anima and Animus," in *Aion: Researches into the Phenomenology of the Self*, Collected Works, vol. 9ii, R. F. C. Hull (trans.), Bollingen Series XX, 2nd edn, Princeton, N.J.: Princeton University Press, 1968.

—— (1952a) "Answer to Job," in *Psychology and Religion: West and East*, Collected Works, vol. 11, 2nd edn, R. F. C. Hull (trans.), Bollingen Series XX, Princeton, N.J.: Princeton University Press, 1969, 355–470.

—— (1952b) "Synchronicity: An Acausal Connecting Principle," in *The Structure and Dynamics of the Psyche*, Collected Works, vol. 8, R. F. C. Hull (trans.), Bollingen Series XX, Princeton, N.J.: Princeton University Press, 1969, 417–519.

—— (1952c) "Appendix on Synchronicity," in *The Structure and Dynamics of the Psyche*, Collected Works, vol. 8, R. F. C. Hull (trans.), Bollingen Series XX, Princeton, N.J.: Princeton University Press, 1969, 520–31.

—— (1953) "Introduction to the Religions and Psychological Problems of Alchemy," in *Psychology and Alchemy*, Collected Works, vol. 12, R. F. C. Hull (trans.), Bollingen Series XX, New York: Pantheon Books, 1–37.

Jung, C. G. (1954a) "On the Nature of the Psyche," in *The Structure and Dynamics of the Psyche*, Collected Works, vol. 8, R. F. C. Hull (trans.), Bollingen Series XX, Princeton, N.J.: Princeton University Press, 1969, 159–234.

—— (1954b) "Letter to Père Lachat," in *The Symbolic Life*, Collected Works, vol. 18, R. F. C. Hull (trans.), Bollingen Series XX, Princeton, N.J.: Princeton University Press, 1976, 679.

—— (1954c) *Mysterium Coniunctionis: An Inquiry into the Separation and Synthesis of Psychic Opposites in Alchemy*, Collected Works, vol. 14, Bollingen Series XX, New York: Pantheon Books, 1963.

—— (1954d) "The Philosophical Tree," in *Alchemical Studies*, Collected Works, vol. 13, R. F. C. Hull (trans.), Bollingen Series XX, Princeton, N.J.: Princeton University Press, 1967, 251–350.

—— (1954e) "Transformation Symbolism in the Mass," in *Psychology and Religion: West and East*, Collected Works, vol. 11, 2nd edn, R. F. C. Hull (trans.), Bollingen Series XX, Princeton, N.J.: Princeton University Press, 1969.

—— (1955a) "Letter to Michael Fordham," in *The Symbolic Life*, Collected Works, vol. 18, R. F. C. Hull (trans.), Bollingen Series XX, Princeton, N.J.: Princeton University Press, 1976, 508.

—— (1955b) "Letter to Pastor Walter Bernet," in *C. G. Jung Letters*, vol. 2: *1951– 61*, G. Adler (ed.), Bollingen Series XCV:2, Princeton, N.J.: Princeton University Press, 257–64.

—— (1960) "A Letter on Parapsychology and Synchronicity: Dr. Jung's Response to an Inquiry," H. Nagel (trans.), *Spring* (1961): 50–7.

—— (1963) *Memories, Dreams, Reflections*, A. Jaffé (ed.), R. and C. Winston (trans.), New York: Pantheon Books.

—— (1974) "Individual Dream Symbolism in Relation to Alchemy," in *C. G. Jung: Dreams*, R. F. C. Hull (trans.), Princeton, N.J.: Princeton University Press, Collected Works, vol. 12, *Psychology and Alchemy*, 2nd edn, R. F. C. Hull (rev.), H. C. Baynes (trans.), Bollingen Series XX, Princeton, N.J.: Princeton University Press, 1968.

—— (1975) "Letter to Robert C. Smith," in *C. G. Jung Letters*, vol. 2: *1951–61*, G. Adler (ed.), Bollingen Series XCV:2, Princeton, N.J.: Princeton University Press, 583.

Jung, C. G. and Kerenyi, C. (1949) *Essays on a Science of Mythology*, Bollingen Series XXII, New York: Pantheon Books.

Jung, C. G. and Pauli, W. (1955) *The Interpretation of Nature and the Psyche*, Bollingen Series LI, New York: Pantheon Books.

Kainer, R. G. K. (1999) *The Collapse of the Self and Its Therapeutic Restoration*, Hillsdale, N.J.: Analytic Press.

Kalsched, D. E. (1996) *The Inner World of Trauma*, London: Routledge.

—— (2002) "Trauma and Daimonic Reality in Ferenczi's Later Work," unpublished manuscript, Ferenczi Panel, San Francisco History Symposium, Tiburon, California, April 6.

Kapleau, P. (1995) "Introduction," in Thich Nhat Hanh, *Zen Keys: A Guide to Zen Practice*, New York: Doubleday, 1–19.

Keleman, S. (1981) *Your Body Speaks Its Mind*, Berkeley, Calif.: Center Press.

Khan, M. M. R. (1963) "The Concept of Cumulative Trauma," in *The Privacy of the Self*, New York: International Universities Press, 42–58.

Khan, M. M. R. (1972) "The Use and Abuse of Dream in Psychic Experience," in *The Privacy of the Self*, New York: International Universities Press, 306–15.

—— (1983) "Beyond the Dreaming Experience," in *Hidden Selves: Between Theory and Practice in Psychoanalysis*, New York: International Universities Press, 42–50.

Kirschner, S. R. (1996) *The Religious and Romantic Origins of Psychoanalysis: Individuation and Integration in Post-Freudian Theory*, Cambridge: Cambridge University Press.

Koestenbaum, P. (1974) *Managing Anxiety*, Englewood Cliffs: Prentice-Hall.

Kohut, H. (1971) *The Analysis of the Self: A Systematic Approach to the Psychoanalytic Treatment of Narcissistic Personality Disorders*, New York: International Universities Press.

Krystal, H. (1988) *Integration and Self-Healing: Affect, Trauma, Alexithymia*, Hillsdale, N.J.: Analytic Press.

Kühlewind, G. (1984) *Stages of Consciousness: Meditations on the Boundaries of the Soul*, M. St. Goar (trans.), West Stockbridge, Mass.: Lindisfarne Press.

Labouvie-Vief, G. (1994) *Psyche and Eros: Mind and Gender in the Life Course*, New York: Cambridge University Press.

Lacan, J. (1949) "The Mirror Stage as Formative of the Function of the I as Revealed in Psychoanalytic Experience," in *Ecrits: A Selection*, A. Sheridan (trans.), New York: Norton, 1977, 1–7.

Lambert, K. (1987) "Some Religious Implications of the Work of Freud, Jung, and Winnicott," *Winnicott Studies: The Journal of the Squiggle Foundation* 2: 49–70.

Lear, J. (1990) *Love and Its Place in Nature: A Philosophical Interpretation of Freudian Psychoanalysis*, New York: Farrar, Straus & Giroux.

Libit, B. (1981) "The Experimental Evidence for Subjective Referral of a Sensory Experience Backwards in Time: Reply to P. S. Churchland," *Philosophy of Science* 48: 182–97.

—— (1989) "The Timing of Subjective Experience," *Behavioral and Brain Science* 12.1: 183–5.

Loewald, H. W. (1978) *Psychoanalysis and the History of the Individual*, New Haven: Yale University Press.

—— (1988) *Sublimation*, New Haven: Yale University Press.

—— (2000) *The Essential Loewald: Collected Papers and Monographs*, Hagerstown, Md.: University Publishing Group.

Lovejoy, A. O. (1964) *The Great Chain of Being: A Study of the History of an Idea*. Cambridge, Mass.: Harvard University Press.

MacDermot, V. (trans.) (2001) *The Fall of Sophia: A Gnostic Text on the Redemption of Universal Consciousness*, Great Barrington, Mass.: Lindisfarne Books.

McFague, S. (1993) *The Body of God: An Ecological Theology*, Minneapolis: Fortress Press.

McGinn, B. (ed.) (1994) *Meister Eckhart and the Beguine Mystics: Hadewijch of Brabant, Mechthild of Magdeburg, and Marguerite Porete*, New York: Continuum.

McGinn, C. (1999) *The Mysterious Flame: Conscious Minds in a Material World*, New York: Basic Books.

McGrath, A. E. (1994) *Christian Theology: An Introduction*, Oxford: Blackwell.

McGuire, W. and R. F. C. Hull (eds) (1977) *C. G. Jung Speaking: Interviews and Encounters*, Bollingen Series XCVII, Princeton, N.J.: Princeton University Press.

MacInnes, E. (1996) *Light Sitting in Light: A Christian's Experience in Zen*, London: HarperCollins.

McIntosh, M. A. (1998) *Mystical Theology: The Integrity of Spirituality and Theology*, London: Blackwell.

MacKenzie, N. (1965) *Dreams and Dreaming*, New York: Vanguard Press.

Mansfield, V. and J. M. Spiegelman (1989) "Quantum Mechanics and Jungian Psychology," *The Journal of Analytical Psychology* 34.1: 3–31.

Marais, E. N. (1937) *The Soul of the White Ant*, New York: Dodd, Mead & Company.

Masters, R. E. L. and Houston, J. (1966) *Varieties of Psychadelic Experience*. A Delta book. New York: Dell Publishing Company.

Matthews, B. (1998) "Book Review: The Archetypal Dimensions of the Soul: Archetypische Dimensionen der Seele (by M. L. von Franz)," *Journal of Analytical Psychology* 43.1: 184–5.

Matthews, C. (1991) *Sophia: Goddess of Wisdom*, London: Mandala.

Meissner, W. W. (1984) *Psychoanalysis and Religious Experience*, New Haven: Yale University Press.

Merkur, D. (1993) *Gnosis: An Esoteric Tradition of Mystical Visions and Unions*, SUNY Series in Western Esoteric Traditions, D. Appelbaum (ed.), Albany, N.Y.: State University of New York Press.

—— (1999) *Mystical Moments and Unitive Thinking*, Albany, N.Y.: State University of New York Press.

Milhaven, J. G. (1993) *Hadewijch and Her Sisters: Other Ways of Loving and Knowing*, SUNY Series, The Body in Culture, History and Religion, H. Eilberg-Schwarz (ed.), Albany, N.Y.: State University of New York Press.

Miller, P. C. (1994) *Dreams in Late Antiquity: Studies in the Imagination of a Culture*, Princeton, N.J.: Princeton University Press.

Milner, M. (1979) *On Not Being Able to Paint*, 2nd edn, New York: International Universities Press.

Mindell, A. (2000) *The Quantum Mind: The Edge Between Physics and Psychology*, Portland, Ore.: Lao Tse Press.

Mitchell, S. (1988) *Relational Concepts in Psychoanalysis: From Attachment to Intersubjectivity*, Cambridge, Mass.: Harvard University Press.

Model, A. H. (1984) *Psychoanalysis in a New Context*, New York: International Universities Press.

Mommaers, P. (1980) Preface, in *Hadewijch. The Complete Works*, C. Hart (trans.), Classics of Western Spirituality, New York: Paulist Press, xiii–xxiv.

—— (1988) "Hadewijch: A Feminist in Conflict," *Louvain Studies* 13: 58–81.

—— (1989) *Schrijfster Begijn Mystica: Hadewijch*, Antwerp: Averbode.

—— (1990) *De Brieven van Hadewijch*, Antwerp: Averbode.

—— (1994) *Hadewijch D'Anvers*, Paris: Editions du Cerf.

Moore, T. (1992) *Care of the Soul*, New York: HarperCollins.

Murk-Jansen, S. (1994) "Hadewijch and Eckhart," *Meister Eckhart and the Beguine Mystics: Hadewijch of Brabant, Mechthild of Magdeburg, and Marguerite Porete*, B. McGinn (ed.), New York: Continuum, 17–30.

Murk-Jansen, S. (1998) *Brides in the Desert: The Spirituality of the Beguines*, Maryknoll, N.Y.: Orbis Books.

Nachmanovitch, S. (1990) *Free Play: Improvisation in Life and Art*, Los Angeles: Tarcher.

Natterson, J. M. and Friedman, R. J. (1995) *A Primer of Clinical Intersubjectivity*, Northvale, N.J.: Jason Aronson.

Neihardt, J. G. (Flaming Rainbow) (1961) *Black Elk Speaks: Being the Life Story of a Holy Man of the Oglala Sioux*, Lincoln: University of Nebraska Press.

Neumann, E. (1948) "Mystical Man," in *The Mystic Vision: Papers From the Eranos Yearbooks*, R. Manheim (trans.), Bollingen Series XXX, vol. 6, Princeton, N.J.: Princeton University Press, 375–415.

—— (1953) "The Psyche and the Transformation of the Reality Planes: A Metaphysical Attempt," H. Nagel (trans.), *Spring* (1956): 81–111, published also in *Eranos-Jarbuch XXI*, Zurich: Rhein-Verlag, 1953.

—— (1954) *The Origins and History of Consciousness: The Psychological Stages and the Evolution of Consciousness*, vols. 1, 2, New York: Harper Torchbooks.

—— (1955a) "Narcissism, Normal Self-formation and the Primary Relation to the Mother," *Spring* (1966): 81–106.

—— (1955b) *The Great Mother: An Analysis of the Archetype*, R. Manheim (trans.), Bollingen Series XLVII, New York: Pantheon Books.

—— (1959) "The Significance of the Genetic Aspect for Analytical Psychology," R. F. C. Hull (trans.), *Current Trends in Analytical Psychology: Proceedings of the First International Congress for Analytical Psychology*, G. Adler (ed.), London: Tavistock Publications, 1961, 37–53.

—— (1969) *Depth Psychology and a New Ethic*, E. Rolfe (trans.), New York: Harper & Row.

—— (1973) *The Child*, R. Manheim (trans.), New York: G. P. Putnam's Sons.

—— (1994) "The Meaning of the Earth Archetype for Modern Times," in *The Fear of the Feminine and Other Essays on Feminine Psychology*, Bollingen Series LXI, Princeton, N.J.: Princeton University Press.

Newman, B. (1987) *Sister of Wisdom: St. Hildegard's Theology of the Feminine*, Berkeley: University of California Press.

Ogden, T. H. (1986) *The Matrix of the Mind: Object Relations and the Psychoanalytic Dialogue*, Northvale, N.J.: Jason Aronson.

Oliver, M. (1992) *New and Selected Poems*, Boston: Beacon Press.

Olney, J. (1972) *Metaphors of Self: The Meaning of Autobiography*, Princeton: Princeton University Press.

Orange, D. M., Atwood, G. E. and Stolorow, R. D. (1997) *Working Intersubjectively: Contextualism in Psychoanalytic Practice*, Hillsdale, N.J.: Analytic Press.

Otto, R. (1958) *The Idea of the Holy: An Inquiry into the Non-rational Factor in the Idea of the Divine and its Relation to the Rational*, J. W. Harvey (trans.), New York: Oxford University Press.

Oxford English Dictionary (1971) *The Compact Edition*, Oxford: Oxford University Press.

Oxford English Dictionary (1993) *The New Shorter, Fourth Edition*, Oxford: Clarendon Press.

Pagels, E. H. (1976) "What Became of God the Mother? Conflicting Images of God in Early Christianity," *Signs: Journal of Women in Culture and Society* 2: 302.

Pannikar, R. (1981) *The Unknown Christ of Hinduism: Towards an Ecumenical Christophany*, rev. edn, Maryknoll, N.Y.: Orbis Books.

—— (1989) *The Silence of God: The Answer of the Buddha*, R. R. Barr (trans.), Maryknoll, N.Y.: Orbis Books.

Pascal, B. (1966) *Pensées*, A. J. Krailsheimer (trans.), London: Penguin Books.

Perry, J. W. (1999) *Trials of the Visionary Mind: Spiritual Emergency and the Renewal Process*, Albany, N.Y.: State University of New York Press.

Petroff, E. A. (ed.) (1986) *Medieval Women's Visionary Literature*, New York: Oxford University Press.

—— (1994) *Body and Soul: Essays on Medieval Women and Mysticism*, New York: Oxford University Press.

The Philokalia, the Complete Text (1981) Compiled by St. Nikodimos of the Holy Mountain and St. Makarios of Corinth, G. E. H. Palmer, P. Sherrard and K. Ware (trans.), vols. 1, 2, 3, London: Faber.

Picard, M. (1951) *The Flight from God*, M. Kuschnitsky and J. M. Cameron (trans.), Washington D.C.: Regnergy Gateway.

Polkinghorne, J. (1995) *Serious Talk: Science and Religion in Dialogue*, Harrisburg, Pa.: Trinity Press International.

—— (1996) *Beyond Science: The Wider Human Context*, Cambridge: Cambridge University Press.

Polyani, M. (1962) *Personal Knowledge*, Chicago: University of Chicago Press.

Powell, R. A. (2000) *The Most Holy Trinosophia and the New Revelations of the Divine Feminine*, Great Barrington, Mass.: Anthroposophic Press.

Prigogine, I. (1997) *The End of Certainty: Time, Chaos, and the New Laws of Nature*, New York: Free Press.

Quispel, G. (1979) *The Secret Book of Revelation: The Last Book of the Bible*, New York: McGraw-Hill.

—— (1986) "The Birth of the Child: Some Gnostic and Jewish Aspects," *Jewish and Gnostic Man*, Dallas: Spring Publications.

Ranft, P. (2000) *Women and Spiritual Equality in Christian Tradition*, New York: St. Martin's Press.

Reed, E. S. (1996) *The Necessity of Experience*, New Haven: Yale University Press.

—— (1997) *From Soul To Mind: The Emergence of Psychology from Erasmus Darwin to William James*, New Haven and London: Yale University Press.

Reymond, L. (1995) *To Live Within: A Woman's Spiritual Pilgrimage in a Himalayan Hermitage*, N. Pearson and S. Spiegelberg (trans.), Portland, Ore.: Rudra Press.

Richard of St. Victor, *Treatise on Trinity, Book III*, Classics of Western Spirituality, New York: Paulist Press, 1979.

Ricoeur, P. (1977) *Freud and Philosophy: An Essay on Interpretation*, D. Savage (trans.), New Haven: Yale University Press.

Rizzuto, A. M. (1979) *The Birth of the Living God*, Chicago: University of Chicago Press.

Rossi, E. L. (1985) *Dreams and the Growth of Personality: Expanding Awareness in Psychotherapy*, 2nd edn, New York: Bruner/Mazel.

—— (1994) "A Quantum Psychology for the Future?" *Psychological Perspectives* 30 (Fall–Winter): 6–11.

Roszak, T. (1992) *The Voice of the Earth*, New York: Simon & Schuster.

Sagan, C. (1996) *The Demon-Haunted World: Science as a Candle in the Dark*, New York: Ballantine Books.

—— (1997) *Billions and Billions: Thoughts on Life and Death at the Brink of the Millennium*, New York: Ballantine Books.

Sardello, R. (1992) *Facing the World With Soul: The Reimagination of Modern Life*, Hudson, N.Y.: Lindisfarne Press.

—— (ed.) (1995) *The Angels*, New York: Continuum.

—— (1997) "Introduction," in *The Visions of Joa Bolendas*, 11–29, Hudson, N.Y.: Lindisfarne Books.

—— (2001) *Love and the World: A Guide to Conscious Soul Practice*, Great Barrington, Mass.: Lindisfarne Books.

Schaup, S. (1997) *Sophia: Aspects of the Divine Feminine, Past and Present*, York Beach, Me.: Nicolas-Hays.

Schneider, M. S. (1995) *A Beginner's Guide to Constructing the Universe: The Mathematical Archetypes of Nature, Art, and Science: A Voyage from 1 to 10*, New York: Harper Perennial.

Searles, H. F. (1960) *The Nonhuman Environment: In Normal Development and in Schizophrenia*, New York: International Universities Press.

—— (1972) "The Patient As Therapist to His Analyst," *Countertransference and Related Subjects: Selected Papers*, New York: International Universities Press, 1979, 380–459.

Sells, M. (1994) "The Pseudo-Woman and the Meister: 'Unsaying' and Essentialism," in B. McGinn (ed.), *Meister Eckhart and the Beguine Mystics: Hadewijch of Brabant, Mechthild of Magdeburg, and Marguerite Porete*, New York: Continuum, 114–46.

Serrano, M. (1966) *C. G. Jung and Herman Hesse: A Record of Two Friendships*, New York: Schocken Books.

Sheldrake, R. (1985) *A New Science of Life: The Hypothesis of Formative Causation*, London: Blond & Biggs.

—— (1988) *The Presence of the Past: Morphic Resonance and the Habits of Nature*, London: Collins.

—— (1991) *The Rebirth of Nature: The Greening of Science and God*, New York: Bantam Books.

Smith, H. (2001) *Why Religion Matters: The Fate of the Human Spirit in an Age of Disbelief*, San Francisco: HarperSanFrancisco.

Smith, J. Z. (1995) *The HarperCollins Dictionary of Religion*, New York: HarperCollins.

Southern, R. W. (1970) *The Penguin History of the Church*, vol. 1: *Western Society and the Church in the Middle Ages*, London: Penguin Books.

Steere, D. (1985) *Together in Solitude*, New York: Crossroad.

Stein, M. (1998) *Transformation: Emergence of the Self*, College Station: Texas A & M University Press.

Stern, M. M. (1988) *Repetition and Trauma: Toward a Teleonomic Theory of Psychoanalysis*, L. B. Stern (ed.), Hillsdale, N.J.: Analytic Press.

Stevens, A. (1982) *Archetype: A Natural History of the Self*, London: Routledge & Kegan Paul.

—— (1994) *Jung*, New York: Oxford University Press.

Storr, A. (1996) *Feet of Clay: Saints, Sinners and Madmen: A Study of Gurus*, New York: Simon & Schuster.

Swami Rama, H. H. (1976) *Lectures on Yoga: Practical Lessons on Yoga*, rev. edn, Glenview, Ill.: Himalayan International Institute of Yoga Science & Philosophy of the USA.

Swimme, B. (1984) *The Universe is a Green Dragon: A Cosmic Creation Story*, Santa Fe, N. Mex.: Bear and Co.

Swimme, B. and T. Berry (1992) *The Universe Story: From the Primordial Flaring Forth to the Ecozoic Era – A Celebration of the Unfolding of the Cosmos*, San Francisco: Harper.

Symington, N. (1993) *Narcissism: A New Theory*, London: Karnac.

—— (1994) *Emotion and Spirit: Questioning the Claims of Psychoanalysis and Religion*, New York: St. Martin's Press.

Tamburello, D. (1996) *Ordinary Mysticism*, New York: Paulist Press.

Tarrant, J. (1998) *The Light Inside the Dark: Zen, Soul, and the Spiritual Life*, New York: HarperCollins.

Tart, C. T. (ed.) (1990) *Altered States of Consciousness*, San Francisco: HarperSanFrancisco.

Tillich, P. (1948) *The Shaking of the Foundations*, New York: Charles Scribner's Sons.

—— (1952) *The Courage to Be*, New Haven: Yale University Press.

—— (1963) *Christianity and the Encounter of the World Religions*, New York: Columbia University Press.

—— (1981) "The Relation of Religion and Health," in *The Meaning of Health*, Richmond, Calif.: North Atlantic Books, 13–50.

Tresan, D. (1996) "Jungian Metapsychology and Neurobiological Theory," *Journal of Analytical Psychology: An International Quarterly of Jungian Practice and Theory* 41.3: 399–436.

Ulanov, A. B. (1971) *The Feminine in Jungian Psychology and in Christian Theology*, Evanston, Ill.: Northwestern University Press.

Ulanov, A. (1981) *Receiving Woman: Studies in the Psychology and Theology of the Feminine*, Philadelphia: Westminster Press.

—— (1987) "The God You Touch," in D. S. Lopez, Jr., and S. C. Rockefeller (eds), *Christ and the Bodhisattva*, Stonybrook, N.Y.: State University of New York Press, 117–39.

—— (1988) *The Wisdom of the Psyche*. Cambridge, MA: Cowley Publications.

—— (1994) *The Wizard's Gate: Picturing Consciousness*, Einsiedeln: Daimon Verlag.

Ulanov, A. and B. Ulanov (1975) *Religion and the Unconscious*, Philadelphia: Westminster Press.

—— (1987) *The Witch and the Clown: Two Archetypes of Human Sexuality*, Wilmette, Ill.: Chiron.

—— (1989) "Between Anxiety and Faith: The Role of the Feminine in Tillich's Theological Thought," in J. A. K. Kegley (ed.), *Paul Tillich on Creativity*, California State University, Bakersfield: University Press of America, 131–55.

—— (1991) *The Healing Imagination: The Meeting of Psyche and Soul*, New York: Paulist Press.

Ulanov, A. and B. Ulanov (1997) "Surviving in a Drifting Culture," editorial, *Journal of Religion and Health*, 36.1: 3–4.

Ullman, E. (2002) "Programming the Post-Human: Computer Science Redefines 'Life,'" *Harper's* 305.1829: 60–70.

van Baest, M. (1998) *Poetry of Hadewijch*, Studies in Spirituality Supplement 3, Leuven: Peeters.

Van de Castle, R. L. (1994) "Experimental Studies in Dreaming," in *Our Dreaming Mind: A Sweeping Exploration of the Role that Dreams have Played in Politics, Art, Religion, and Psychology, from Ancient Civilizations to the Present Day*, New York: Ballantine Books, 207–87.

Van Eenwyk, J. R. (1997) *Archetypes and Strange Attractors: The Chaotic World of Symbols*, Toronto: Inner City Books.

van Löben Sels, R. E. (1972) "Moving Patterns of Change in Expressed Religious Attitudes," *Main Currents in Modern Thought* 28.4: 136–41.

—— (1981) "Shaman: A Differentiation of Image from Instinct", unpublished thesis.

Vaughan-Lee, L. (ed.) (1995) *Traveling the Path of Love: Sayings of Sufi Masters*, Inverness, Calif.: Golden Sufi Center.

Vaughn, S. C. (1997) *The Talking Cure: The Science behind Psychotherapy*, New York: G. P. Putnam's Sons.

Verdeyen, P. (1994) *Ruusbroec and His Mysticism*, A. Lefevere (trans.), Collegeville, Minn.: Liturgical Press.

von Franz, M. L. (1974) *Number and Time: Reflections Leading toward a Unification of Depth Psychology and Physics*, Evanston, Ill.: Northwestern University Press.

—— (1975) *C. G. Jung: His Myth in Our Time*, W. H. Kennedy (trans.), London: Hodder & Stoughton.

—— (1980) *Projection and Re-Collection in Jungian Psychology: Reflections of the Soul*, W. H. Kennedy (trans.), La Salle and London: Open Court.

—— (1986) *On Dreams and Death: A Jungian Interpretation*, E. X. Kennedy and V. Brooks (trans.), Boston: Shambhala.

—— (1991) *Dreams*, Boston and London: Shambhala.

—— (1992) *Psyche and Matter*, Boston: Shambhala.

—— (1997) *Archetypal Dimensions of the Psyche*, Boston: Shambhala.

—— (1999) *The Cat: A Tale of Feminine Redemption*, Toronto: Inner City Books.

Walker, B. G. (1983) *The Woman's Encyclopedia of Myths and Secrets*, San Francisco: Harper & Row.

Walker, E. H. (2000) *The Physics of Consciousness: The Quantum Mind and the Meaning of Life*, Cambridge, Mass: Perseus.

Watt, D. (1997) *Medieval Women in their Communities*, Toronto: University of Toronto Press.

Watts, A. W. (1954) *Myth and Ritual in Christianity*, London: Thames & Hudson.

—— (1975) *Tao: The Watercourse Way*, New York: Pantheon Books.

Weil, S. (1963) *Gravity and Grace*, London: Routledge & Kegan Paul.

—— (1974) *Gateway to God*, Glasgow: Collins.

White, V. (1960) *Soul and Psyche: An Enquiry into the Relationship of Psychotherapy and Religion*, London: Collins and Harvill Press.

Whyte, L. L. (1962) *The Unconscious Before Freud*, Garden City, N.Y.: Doubleday.

Wiethaus, U. (ed.) (1993) *Maps of Flesh and Light: The Religious Experience of Medieval Women Mystics*, Syracuse, N.Y.: Syracuse University Press.

Wilber, K. (ed.) (1984) *Quantum Questions: Mystical Writings of the World's Great Physicists*, Boulder: Shambhala.

—— (1995) *Sex, Ecology, Spirituality: The Spirit of Evolution*, Boston: Shambhala.

—— (1999) *One Taste: The Journals of Ken Wilbur*, Boston: Shambhala.

Williams, C. (1939) *Descent of the Dove: A Short History of the Holy Spirit in the Church*, Grand Rapids, Mich.: Eerdmans.

Williams, D. D. (1981) "Love and Self-Sacrifice," in *The Spirit and The Forms of Love*, Lanham, Md.: The University Press of America, 192–213.

Williams, M. (1971) *The Velveteen Rabbit: Or How Toys Become Real*, Garden City, N.Y.: Doubleday.

Wilmer, H. A. (1986) "The Healing Nightmare: A Study of the War Dreams of Vietnam Combat Veterans," *Quadrant: Journal of the C. G. Jung Foundation for Analytical Psychology* (Spring).

Winnicott, D. W. (1935) "The Manic Defense," in *Through Paediatrics to Psycho-Analysis*, New York: Basic Books, 1975, 129–44.

—— (1947) "Hate in the Countertransference," in *Through Paediatrics to Psycho-analysis*, New York: Basic Books, 1975, 194–203.

—— (1949) "Mind and its Relation to the Psyche-Soma," in *Through Paediatrics to Psycho-Analysis*, New York: Basic Books, 1975, 243–54.

—— (1953) "Transitional Objects and Transitional Phenomena," *International Journal of Psycho-Analysis* 34: 89–97.

—— (1958) *Collected Papers: Through Paediatrics to Psycho-Analysis*, London: Tavistock.

—— (1960) "The Theory of the Parent–Infant Relationship," in *The Maturational Processes and the Facilitating Environment: Studies in the Theory of Emotional Development*, New York: International Universities Press, 1965, 37–55.

—— (1961) "Psychoanalysis and Science: Friends or Relations," in C. Winnicott, R. Shepherd and M. Davis (eds), *Home is Where We Start From: Essays by a Psychoanalyst*, New York: Norton, 1986, 13–18.

—— (1962) "Ego Integration in Child Development," in *The Maturational Processes and the Facilitating Environment: Studies in the Theory of Emotional Development*, New York: International Universities Press, 1965, 56–63.

—— (1963a) "The Development of the Capacity for Concern," *Bulletin of the Menninger Clinic* 27: 167–76.

—— (1963b) "The Mentally Ill In Your Caseload," in *The Maturational Processes and the Facilitating Environment: Studies in the Theory of Emotional Development*, New York: International Universities Press, 1965, 217–29.

—— (1963c) "From Dependence towards Independence in the Development of the Individual," in *The Maturational Processes and the Facilitating Environment: Studies in the Theory of Emotional Development*, New York: International Universities Press, 1965, 83–92.

—— (1963d) "Morals and Education," in *The Maturational Processes and the Facilitating Environment: Studies in the Theory of Emotional Development*, New York: International Universities Press, 1965, 93–105.

—— (1963e) "Communicating and Not Communicating Leading to a Study of Certain Opposites," in *The Maturational Processes and the Facilitating*

Environment: Studies in the Theory of Emotional Development, New York: International Universities Press, 1965, 179–92.

Winnicott, D. W. (1964) "Psychosomatic Disorders," in C. Winnicott, R. Shepherd and M. Davis (eds), *Psychoanalytic Explorations*, Cambridge, Mass.: Harvard University Press, 1989, 103–18.

—— (1969) "The Use of the Object and Relating through Identification," *International Journal of Psycho-Analysis* 50: 711–16.

—— (1970) "On the Basis for Self in Body," in C. Winnicott, R. Shepherd and M. Davis (eds), *Psychoanalytic Explorations*, Cambridge, Mass.: Harvard University Press, 1989, 261–83.

—— (1971) *Playing and Reality*, New York: Penguin Books, 1980.

—— (1988) *Human Nature*, London: Free Association Press.

Wolf, F. A. (1981) *Taking the Quantum Leap: The New Physics for Non-Scientists*. New York: Harper & Row.

—— (1994) *The Dreaming Universe: A Mind-Expanding Journey into the Realm where Psyche and Physics Meet*, New York: Simon & Schuster.

Wood, R. L. (ed.) (1947) *The World of Dreams: An Anthology: The Mystery, Grandeur, Terror, Meaning and Psychology of Dreams, as Told by the World's Great Writers, Philosophers, Theologians, Historians, Scholars, Scientists, Psychiatrists and Psychologists, from Ancient Times to Today*, New York: Random House.

Zaehner, R. C. (1974a) *Our Savage God: The Perverse Use of Eastern Thought*, New York: Sheed & Ward.

—— (1974b) *Zen, Drugs and Mysticism*, New York: Vintage.

—— (1981) *The City Within the Heart*, New York: Crossroad.

Zajonc, A. (1993) *Catching the Light: The Entwined History of Light and Mind*, New York: Oxford University Press.

Ziegler, J. E. (1993) "Reality as Imitation: The Role of Religious Imagery Among the Beguines of the Low Countries," in U. Wiethaus (ed.), *Maps of Flesh and Light: The Religious Experience of Medieval Women Mystics*, Syracuse, N.Y.: Syracuse University Press, 112–26.

Zinkin, L. (1987) "The Hologram as a Model for Analytical Psychology," *Journal of Analytical Psychology* 32.1: 1–21.

Zohar, D. (1990) *The Quantum Self: Human Nature and Consciousness Defined by the New Physics*, New York: Quill/William Morrow.

Zohar, D. and I. Marshall (1994) *The Quantum Society: Mind, Physics, and a New Social Vision*, New York: William Morrow.

Index

Index compiled by Frank Pert